Placenames of Russia
and the Former
Soviet Union

Recent Works by Adrian Room
and from McFarland

*Dictionary of Pseudonyms: 13,000 Assumed
Names and Their Origins*, 5th ed. (2010)

Dictionary of Sports and Games Terminology (2010)

Alternate Names of Places: A Worldwide Dictionary (2009)

*African Placenames: Origins and Meanings
of the Names for Natural Features, Towns, Cities,
Provinces and Countries*, 2d ed. (2008)

*The Pronunciation of Placenames:
A Worldwide Dictionary* (2007)

*Nicknames of Places: Origins and Meanings of the
Alternate and Secondary Names, Sobriquets, Titles,
Epithets and Slogans for 4600 Places Worldwide* (2006; paperback 2011)

*Placenames of the World: Origins and Meanings of the Names
for 6,600 Countries, Cities, Territories, Natural Features
and Historic Sites*, 2d ed. (2006; paperback 2013)

*Placenames of France: Over 4,000 Towns, Villages,
Natural Features, Regions and Departments* (2004; paperback 2009)

Encyclopedia of Corporate Names Worldwide (2002; paperback 2008)

*A Dictionary of Art Titles: The Origins of the Names
and Titles of 3,000 Works of Art* (2000; paperback 2008)

*A Dictionary of Music Titles: The Origins of the Names
and Titles of 3,500 Musical Compositions* (2000; paperback 2008)

Placenames of Russia and the Former Soviet Union

Origins and Meanings of the Names for More Than 2000 Natural Features, Towns, Regions and Countries

Adrian Room

McFarland & Company, Inc., Publishers
Jefferson, North Carolina

For Sue,
who loves Russia as much as I do

The present work is a reprint of the library bound edition of Placenames of Russia and the Former Soviet Union: Origins and Meanings of the Names for Over 2,000 Natural Features, Towns, Regions and Countries, *first published in 1996 by McFarland.*

LIBRARY OF CONGRESS CATALOGUING-IN-PUBLICATION DATA

Room, Adrian.
    Placenames of Russia and the former Soviet Union : origins and meanings of the names for more than 2,000 natural features, towns, regions and countries / Adrian Room.
      p.   cm.
    Includes bibliographical references and index.

    ISBN 978-0-7864-9369-2
    softcover : acid free paper ∞

    1. Names, Geographical—Russia (Federation)—Dictionaries. 2. Names, Geographical—Former Soviet republics—Dictionaries. 3. Onomastics—Dictionaries. 4. Russia (Federation)—Gazetteers. 5. Former Soviet republics—Gazetteers. I. Title.
DK15.R66 2014
914.7'003—dc20   96-1916

BRITISH LIBRARY CATALOGUING DATA ARE AVAILABLE

© 1996 Adrian Room. All rights reserved

No part of this book may be reproduced or transmitted in any form or by any means, electronic or mechanical, including photocopying or recording, or by any information storage and retrieval system, without permission in writing from the publisher.

On the cover: *clockwise from top left* monument in Moscow, Russia; scene in Russia; Caucasus Mountain range; Ashtarak town under the Ararat mountains, Armenia; *bottom* world globe (iStock/Thinkstock).

Manufactured in the United States of America

McFarland & Company, Inc., Publishers
  Box 611, Jefferson, North Carolina 28640
    www.mcfarlandpub.com

Contents

Introduction
1

The Placenames
19

Appendix I: Common Placename Elements
243

Appendix II: Regional Names
246

Select Bibliography
251

Cyrillic-to-Roman Index
257

Introduction

This new dictionary presents the origins and meanings of more than 2,000 placenames in Russia and the countries of the former Soviet Union; that is, of Armenia, Azerbaijan, Belarus, Estonia, Georgia, Kazakhstan, Kyrgyzstan, Latvia, Lithuania, Moldova, Russia, Tajikistan, Turkmenistan, Ukraine, and Uzbekistan. Also included are the names of major natural areas with territory formerly also part of the USSR, such as the Baltic Sea, Bering Sea, Black Sea, and Caspian Sea.

The territory covered is extensive, for the Soviet Union was the largest country in the world, over twice the size of Canada, the second largest. Latitudinally it extended from Cape Fligeli on Rudolf Island, Franz Josef Land, in the north, on a level with Canada's Ellesmere Island, to the village of Childukhter, near Kushka, Turkmenistan, in the south, on a par with Charlotte, North Carolina. Longitudinally it extended (as Russia today still extends) from the Baltic Spit in the Gulf of Gdańsk, in the west, on a par with Corfu, Greece, to Ratmanov Island in the Bering Strait, in the east, on a line with southern New Zealand. And although often popularly thought of as European, the old Soviet empire had only a quarter of its territory in that continent, with the remaining 75 percent in Asia.

This means that a wide range of peoples and languages, past and present, are involved in the linguistic history of the component countries, and it would be as well first to consider what they are or were.

I. Languages and nationalities

Today over 80 percent of the 15 countries' peoples speak some Indo-European language. The main language family, spoken by three-quarters of the population, is Slavic, and of that, Russian itself comprises just over half, followed at some remove (around 16 percent) by Ukrainian. Belorussian also belongs here.

The majority of the placenames in this book are thus actually Russian, at least in present terms.

The next largest linguistic presence is that of the Turkic peoples of Central Asia, those (in decreasing order of population strength) of Uzbekistan, Kazakhstan, Azerbaijan, Turkmenistan, and Kyrgyzstan. They are augmented by Tatars, Chuvash, Bashkirs, and Yakuts within the territory of Russia itself.

Next come the Armenians, speaking a distinctive language, and the

Caucasian people of Georgia. The latter are joined by the Abkhazians, Chechen, Ingush, and Kabardians (Circassians), mostly in southern Russia.

Following numerically are the Moldovans, in the extreme southwest of the territory, speaking a Romance language (a dialect of Romanian). After them come the Baltic languages, spoken by the peoples of Lithuania and Latvia. They in turn are followed by the Tajiks of Central Asia, whose language is of Iranian origin, as is that of the Ossetians, in the Caucasus Mountains.

Speakers of Finno-Ugrian languages come next. Of these, only the Estonians have a separate independent state, but the group is also represented, chiefly in western Russia, by the Mordovians, Udmurts, Mari, Komi, and Komi-Permyak. The people of Karelia also belong here, speaking their own language, a dialect of Finnish.

As far east as these are west are the Buryats, speaking a Mongolian language and inhabiting a region around Lake Baykal, north of Mongolia. Further east still, and also furthest north, are the minor peoples indigenous to Siberia, such as the Evenki, Chukchi, and Koryaks.

Of this diversity of languages, only the Slavic, Romance, Baltic, Armenian, and Iranian are Indo-European. The rest are non-Indo-European. (The Finno-Ugrian languages are not Indo-European despite being spoken in Europe.)

II. Names old and new

As elsewhere in the world, the placenames of this extensive territory are a mixture of old — sometimes very old — and relatively new. In fact, the contrast between old and new is perhaps nowhere greater than in the former Soviet Union, since several of the historic names, especially of towns, villages, and administrative divisions, were replaced by modern ideological ones after the coming of Communism in the first quarter of the 20th century. Thus 13th-century *Nizhny Novgorod* was renamed *Gorky* in 1932, and even older *Samara* became *Kuybyshev* in 1935. On the breakup of the Soviet Union in 1991, they reverted to their original names.

As in most lands, it is the river names that are the oldest, and for this reason they are often the hardest to interpret meaningfully. Russia's capital, *Moscow*, takes its name from the *Moskva* River on which it arose in the 12th century. But the meaning of the river name itself is still uncertain, and even its language of origin is problematical. When considering river names, it is often reasonable to assume that the original meaning was in some sense a "watery" one, since that is in the nature of rivers.

Similarly, hill and mountain names often relate to an appropriate characteristic: the color of the soil, the type of terrain (rocky or smooth), the degree of loftiness, the contour or shape, the seasonal appearance (with or without snow cover), and so on. These are the features that distinguish one hill or mountain from another. But where the language is obscure, or the original river or hill name has become distorted over the years, one can only surmise what the true meaning once was.

Introduction

Again as elsewhere in the world, many of the names in this particular territory are ethnic in origin, from the people who originally inhabited a certain region, and may still do so. Broadly speaking, and "broadly" is in many ways the right word, the larger the territory, the more likely it is to be of ethnic origin. Thus *Russia* is named for the Russians, *Latvia* for the Latvians, and *Tajikistan* for the Tajiks. But where did *their* names come from? This is a prime question that is also the responsibility of the toponymist.

Sometimes, of course, the indigenous inhabitants of a country or region take their name from their land, not the other way round. Thus the Ukrainians are so called because they inhabit *Ukraine*, and the Georgians because their homeland is *Georgia*. Here one must deal with the name directly, rather than through an ethnic medium.

As the oldest river names often mean "water," so many ethnic names originally meant "person," or something similar, the implication being that "we are the people, and this is our land." Where one's world is made up of one's immediate group and environment, and one's nearest boundary (and source of water for cultivation and drinking) is a river, the most obvious designations in each case are simply "the folk" and "the water." For this reason, many river and territorial names in this dictionary will be found to go back respectively to such prime senses.

In some cases, however, names cannot finally be traced back to any precise meaning, and one must regretfully say as much. Toponymics is a relatively young science, and cannot furnish all the answers. The reader must therefore appreciate that to be told that such-and-such a name is "of uncertain origin" or "of unknown meaning" does not mean that no attempt has been made to discover its source. It usually means that no satisfactory etymology can be provided, and that it is better to say so rather than offer a tentative explanation or, even worse, a mere conjecture.

The history of a place is often present in its name, even where the language is now itself in a historic form. The more recent the place, the easier it is to interpret the name and read the history. *St. Petersburg*, for example, has been in existence only since 1703, and enshrines the name of its founder, Peter the Great. In the Soviet period, as *Leningrad*, it similarly paid homage to the founder of Communism. It will be found generally, both in the territory under consideration and outside it, that the naming of a place for a particular person is a fairly common characteristic of the naming process. This applies as much to modern times as to historic. England, for example, has many placenames derived from Anglo-Saxons or Vikings, even if little or (in many cases) nothing is known about them apart from their name. So it is in the former Soviet Union. The reason for this is purely territorial. A particular place is the home or possession of a particular person, and is named for that person. A development of this prime circumstance is the place that has been *deliberately* named for a person, especially commemoratively, to mark a special association. *Gorky*, now once again *Nizhny Novgorod*, as mentioned, was the birthplace of the writer Maxim Gorky, for example, and the much more modest *Semyonovka*, in Ukraine, is named for its 17th-century founder, one Semyon Samoylovich.

III. Patterns of naming

Examination of a map or atlas of the former USSR will reveal both similarities of name elements and the grouping of certain types of names in particular territorial regions.

Even the non-Russian speaker will observe a high proportion of common name suffixes, such as *-o*, *-ka*, *-sk*, and *-sky*. These have a particular linguistic significance.

Names ending in *-ka* or *-aya* are respectively noun and adjectival suffixes of names relating to the feminine word *derevnya*, "village." This is one of the smallest settlements there are. Examples are *Dubrovka* and *Leninskaya*.

Names ending in *-o* or *-oye* are respectively noun and adjectival suffixes of names relating to the neuter word *selo*, "rural center," "township." (The word is translated "village" in many dictionaries. But a *selo* is bigger than a *derevnya*. A rule-of-thumb distinction, at least in prerevolutionary Russia, is that a *derevnya* has no church, being too small for one, whereas a *selo* always has a church.) Examples are *Yelizovo* and *Dobroye*.

Names ending in *-sky* (in this book, and frequently elsewhere) are adjectival and relate to the masculine noun *posyolok*, "settlement," the next step up from a *selo*. An example is *Oktyabrsky*.

However, such principles are not rigidly adhered to, and the suffixes may have been retained (misleadingly) for the next major stage up, which is a town proper (Russian *gorod*). In fact the actual next stage up, from the 1930s, has usually been a "settlement of town type" (Russian *posyolok gorodskogo tipa*). But as these are still settlements, the suffixal form still applies.

One of the most common suffixes of all, it will be seen, is *-sk*. This is essentially a noun form of adjectival *-sky*, and denotes a particular type of possession or location, as designated by the first and main part of the name. Familiar examples are major towns or cities named for the rivers on which they are located, such as *Omsk* on the Om, *Tomsk* on the Tom, *Irkutsk* on the Irkut, *Lugansk* on the Lugan, and *Minsk* on the Mina. However, the relation may not be with a river, but with a particular individual. The Siberian city of *Khabarovsk*, for example, takes its name from the Russian explorer Khabarov, while there were a number of places named *Leninsk* and *Stalinsk*, more for reasons of veneration than actual personal association. It should be noted in this respect that if the person's name ends in *-sky*, as frequently happens, the final *-y* is dropped to give the *-sk*. *Dzerzhinsk* was thus named for Dzerzhinsky, and the former *Zagorsk*, now once again Sergiyev Posad, for Zagorsky. This can also happen with standard adjectives ending in *-sky*, so that *primorsky*, "maritime," gives *Primorsk*, and *sovetsky*, "Soviet," gave *Sovetsk*.

One of the best known final elements (as distinct from suffix) of a Soviet placename is *-grad*. This can also appear in the form *-gorod*, but either way the meaning is "town," "city." (There are no separate Russian words to distinguish the two.) Familiar examples, past and present, are *Leningrad*, *Stalingrad*, *Belgorod*, and *Novgorod*. Another fairly common final element is *-gorsk*. This is not quite so straightforward. It may mean "town," from *gorod*, or "mountain," from *gora*, or "mine," from *gorny*, the adjectival form of *gora*.

(Mining was first carried out in a hill before shafts were sunk underground, as for coal.) One thus needs to know something of a place's history or topography, or both, before deciding which sense is appropriate. *Belogorsk*, for example, is named for its mountains, *Uglegorsk* for its coalmining, and *Zelenogorsk* for its "garden city" plan.

When it comes to the first element of a name, either *Krasno-* or *Nov-* will be frequently found.

The first of these can vary its meaning. Its earliest and most basic sense is "beautiful" (now Russian *krasivy*). However, it can also mean "red" (modern *krasny*), either literally, or in an ideological revolutionary sense. Here, too, caution is needed when interpreting such names. Even if they predate the 1917 Revolution, they could still have either meaning. *Krasnoyarsk* is probably "beautiful" rather than "red," for instance, but *Krasnovodsk* is likely to be for the reddish hue of the water here (by the Caspian Sea) rather than its attractiveness. By contrast, *Krasnodar*, *Krasnograd*, and *Krasnoznamyonsk* are all "red" in its socialist shade. Their names are modern, and replaced earlier names (respectively *Yekaterinodar*, *Konstantinograd*, and *Lasdehnen*). (The *Official Standard Names Gazetteer* of the USSR, published in 1970 by the United States Department of the Interior's Board on Geographic Names, has approximately 1,920 *krasny*-based names, making this word the commonest in Soviet placenames.)

The second element, *nov-*, means "new" and is more straightforward. It usually denotes a new settlement, frequently an industrial one, and is frequently named for an older place, whether this is nearby or more remote. Examples are *Novokuznetsk* (for Kuznetsk), *Novomoskovsk* (for Moscow), and *Novosibirsk* (for Siberia). Of course, "new" here is or was not without its overtones of "progressive," and therefore could well have a socialist or Communist implication. ("Old," by contrast, implies prerevolutionary or czarist, and therefore backward and undesirable.)

"New" is not of course confined to the Soviet period. *Novgorod*, "new town," is one of the oldest Russian cities, first mentioned in the 9th century. Its name implies that it arose at or near the site of an even more ancient place.

Other first and last elements found frequently in Soviet placenames are listed in Appendix I, page 243.

Aside from the general frequency of the above and other elements, a map of the former Soviet Union will also reveal particular types of names in particular geographical regions. One such is the Finno-Russian names of Karelia (northwestern Russia), a land of many lakes, where several towns and villages have names combining a Finnish (or Karelian) word with Russian *ozero*, "lake." Examples are *Alozero*, *Bedlozero*, *Keskozero*, *Porosozero*, *Rugozero*, *Segozero*, and *Virandozero*. The names are primarily those of the lakes, but have been transferred to settlements of various types.

A more striking group comprises the Greek-style names that are found chiefly in Ukraine and Moldova (and notably the Crimea) but that also exist, if rather more sparsely, in other parts of the former Soviet Union.

The Crimea was settled in the 6th century B.C. by Greek traders and subsequently became a seat of the Greek kingdom of the Cimmerian Bosporus.

Greek towns on the Black Sea coast here were commercially active in the Byzantine Empire until the early 11th century A.D. However, most of the present names here date only from the 18th century. They are either entirely Greek, such as *Sevastopol* and *Kherson*, or partly Greek, such as *Yelizavetpol* and *Olgopol*. The *-pol* suffix represents Greek *polis*, "town." It should not be assumed, however, that all Russian names in *-pol* are Greek or Greek-style in origin! In a few instances the *-pol* represents Russian *pole*, "field." One town with a name of this kind (not in the Crimea) is *Chistopol*. Its name means "clear field."

The first Russian town to have a Greek name surviving to modern times is *Stavropol*, on the Volga. (It was renamed *Tolyatti* in 1964.) The name means "town of the cross," and dates from 1739. (See the entry *Tolyattigrad* for a more detailed background.)

Most of the 18th-century Greek names, however, followed later, and were the result of the "Greek plan" of Catherine the Great, which aimed to divide Turkey between Russia and Austria and re-establish the Greek empire as Russian trust territory. Accordingly, new towns were given names that in many cases were revivals of ancient Greek placenames.

The first name resurrected thus on the "road to Constantinople" was that of *Kherson*, a town founded in 1778, but with a name recorded three years earlier. It was adopted from that of the Dorian city which existed in the 7th century B.C. in the extreme southwestern peninsula of the Crimea, close to modern Sevastopol. Its full official Greek name was Χερσόνασος α ποτι τα Ταθρικα, "peninsula on the side of Tauris," or more colloquially *Khersonēsos* (English *Chersonesus*). This was subsequently shortened in about the 3rd century B.C. to *Khersōn*, a form used for the Russian name.

The second city with a name of this type was *Mariupol*, founded in 1780 to accommodate Greeks driven to the Crimea as a result of the war with Turkey. The name, meaning "Mary's town," is one of a type that became familiar in the formula "personal name + *-pol*." Others are *Yekaterinopol*, "Catherine's town" and *Olgopol*, "Olga's town." (See their entries for the identities of the women concerned.)

A (hypothetical) romanized form of Russian names of this type in present-day Ukraine and Moldova gives them an even more distinctive Greek flavor, and in many instances a fairly transparent meaning:

Russian name	*Romanized form*	*Meaning*
Feodosiya	Theodosia	God-given (town)
Grigoriopol'	Grigoriopolis	Gregory's town
Melitopol'	Melitopolis	honey town
Nikopol'	Nicopolis	Nike's town
Ovidiopol'	Ovidiopolis	Ovid's town
Sevastopol'	Sebastopolis	royal town
Simferopol'	Sympheropolis	useful town
Tiraspol'	Tyrasopolis	Tyras (River) town
Yevpatoriya	Eupatoria	(town) of noble origin

Introduction 7

In Russian literary works one occasionally finds similar names devised for towns and cities that actually have non-Greek names. A famous example is Alexander Pushkin's *Petropol'* (as if Petropolis) for St. Petersburg.

Such Greek-style names are not unknown elsewhere in the world, and there is a close parallel in the United States, where one has the cities of *Annapolis* (founded 1694), *Indianapolis* (1821), *Minneapolis* (1856), *Philadelphia* (1682), and *Syracuse* (1825), among others.

In southwestern Russia, around the Southern Urals, lie grouped a number of places named for (mainly) European battles in which the Russians were victorious. Their concentration here is explained by the fact that Cossacks from this region took part in many Russian campaigns, and in particular the Napoleonic Wars. In the mid-19th century it was thus decided to commemorate these campaigns and battles by bestowing their names on Cossack settlements. They include *Balkany* (named for victory in the Balkans), *Berlin* (Berlin), *Cheshme* (Çeşme, Turkey), and *Leyptsig* (Leipzig), among others. (A fuller list is given at the entry for *Varna*.) Sometimes the Russian form of the name disguises the original, such as *Fershampenuaz*, which commemorates the French village of Fère-Champenoise. (See its entry for battle details.)

Although every country of the former Soviet Union has always had its own indigenous names for populated places among the specifically Soviet names, there is one part of Russia that remains unique in having *all* such places with Soviet names. This is the Kaliningrad Region, on the Baltic between Lithuania and Poland, where all the former German names were replaced by Russian ones, many of them ideological. This took place following the 1945 Potsdam Conference, when the area concerned was annexed by the Soviet Union from East Prussia. A listing of the best known names in this region is provided on pages 9-10. They are typical of their kind, and for 45 years served as a socialist showcase in the westernmost outpost of the former Soviet empire.

IV. Regular names of recent times

As mentioned, the oldest names in the constituent republics of the former Soviet Union, as in most countries elsewhere, are those of natural objects, especially rivers, and of ethnic groups. In more recent times particular types of names have emerged.

From medieval times to the 19th century, and notably in European countries, the names have often been those of the founder of a particular place or of an original landowner. This means that many placenames derive from personal names, whether first name, nickname, or surname. Some 65 to 70 percent of placenames in the Moscow region, for example, are of this type, and include such villages as *Pleshcheyevo*, *Varvarino*, *Vlasyevo*, *Yakovlevo*, and *Zakharino*.

The use of personal names to provide placenames was also highly favored after the 1917 Revolution, especially where the person concerned was "politically correct." Names were thus given for both living individuals and, commemoratively, for those no longer alive, with the surname usually selected rather than any other name. Hence the many places named for political leaders, such as *Dzerzhinsky, Leninsky, Stalinsky, Sverdlovsky* and the rest. (It might be mentioned in passing that many political leaders adopted party pseudonyms, and it was these, rather than the actual surnames, that were normally used for placename purposes. The exception was Lenin, whose family name, Ulyanov, was also drawn on for placenames, as was his patronymic, Ilich. Hence such placenames as *Ulyanovsk* and *Ilichyovsk*.)

The establishment of the Soviet Union in 1922 brought with it a vast renaming program, and something like half the total 700,000 or so populated places in the USSR had their names officially changed. The changes, whether alterations, replacements, coinages, or abolitions, were made entirely for ideological purposes, with the aim of lauding all that was new in the sense of being revolutionary and socialist.

Distinct categories of Soviet placenames may be discerned.

The first, as stated, is the cult of the personal. Predictably, Lenin had the greatest number and greatest variety of names. In their heyday they included *Lenin, Lenino, imeni Lenina* (the first word means "named for"), *Leninka, Leninovka, Leninovo, Leninsky, Leninskoye, Leninskaya, Leninsk, Leningrad, Leningradsky, Leningradskoye, Leninabad* and *Leninakan*. Except for major cities, the names were often repeated many times, with *Leninsky* particularly prolific.

Names of political leaders remaining on the map in some form even after the demise of the Soviet Union in 1991 include Dzerzhinsky, Frunze, Kalinin, Kirov, Kuybyshev, Ordzhonikidze, Sverdlov, and Zhdanov. Here and there a place named for Stalin still survives, although almost all of the many places that bore his name in the 1950s were renamed for Lenin in 1961 following condemnation of his "personality cult." Earlier, an official decree of 1957 banned the naming of settlements for living people, thus conveniently expunging all placenames honoring such undesirables as Voroshilov, Molotov, Malenkov, and Kaganovich. (Voroshilov was later rehabilitated and his name restored. Such rehabilitations, where they occurred, only added to the fluidity of the renaming process. Thus *Lugansk*, in Ukraine, was renamed *Voroshilovgrad* in 1935, reverted to *Lugansk* in 1958, became *Voroshilovgrad* again in 1970, and reverted once more to *Lugansk* in 1990 when the republic gained its independence.)

Places named for personalities were not restricted to political figures and revolutionary heroes. Also honored were military leaders such as Budyonny and Zhukov, and scientists such as Chaplygin and Michurin. The cosmonaut Yury Gagarin was similarly saluted when Gzhatsk was renamed for him in 1968. Nor were the arts neglected, and the names of writers such as Tolstoy, Chekhov, Lermontov, and Pushkin are still firmly on the map, as is that of the composer Tchaikovsky.

The second major category of Soviet placename was the descriptive, especially where it related to an industrial activity regarded as favorable both to the Soviet economy and to the cause of Communism. They include such names as *Elektrostal* ("electric steel"), *Zugres* (from the acronym for "Zuyevsky

Introduction

state regional electric power station"), and *Shakhty* ("mines"). A high percentage of such names relate directly to a valuable local mineral deposit, such as *Antratsit* (anthracite), *Boksitogorsk* (bauxite), *Magnitogorsk* (magnetic iron ore), and *Nektekamsk* (oil). This last name illustrates another distinctive feature of Soviet renaming: the blending of one word or name with another. In this instance *neft'*, in its combining form, blends with the name of the *Kama* River. But as also shown in the examples here, a common element with which mineral words combine is *-gorsk*, "mountain." Others include *Mednogorsk* (copper), *Soligorsk* (salt), and *Uglegorsk* (coal).

Some descriptive names are not industrial or economic but generally pleasant or propitious. Names of this type are useful when replacing an ugly or undesirable name. Thus *Svetlovodsk* ("bright water") replaced *Kremges* ("Kremenchug hydroelectric power station"), which itself replaced *Khrushchyov* in 1961. Names of this type are not new, however, and an interesting pre-Soviet group of generally propitious names can be found in southwestern Russia, northwest of Krasnodar. See *Tikhoretsk* for examples. (This place has a name meaning "quiet river," even though it has no actual river.)

Typical examples of Soviet names can be seen in those substituted for German names in the Kaliningrad (formerly Königsberg) Region when this was annexed by the USSR following the 1945 Potsdam Conference. All of the original inhabitants of this region of East Prussia were relocated, and a Russian population was imported to take their places. Over 1,500 names were changed, of which the following are among the most important:

New Russian name	*Old German name*
Bagrationovsk	Preussisch-Eylau
Baltiysk	Pillau
Chernyakhovsk	Insterburg
Dobrovolsk	Schlossberg
Druzhba	Allenburg
Geroyskoye	Gertlauken
Guryevsk	Neuhausen
Gusev	Gumbinnen
Gvardeysk	Tapiau
Kaliningrad	Königsberg
Komsomolsk	Löwenhagen
Krasnolesye	Hardteck
Krasnoznamensk	Haselberg
Ladushkin	Ludwigsort
Mamonovo	Heiligenbeil
Matrosovo	Uggehnen
Mayskoye	Mallwen
Neman	Ragnit
Nesterov	Ebenrode
Nivenskoye	Wittenberg
Novostroyevo	Trempen
Ozyorki	Gross-Lindenau

New Russian name	Old German name
Ozyorsk	Angerapp
Polessk	Labiau
Pravdinsk	Friedland
Primorsk	Fischhausen
Pushkino	Posmahlen
Rybachy	Rossitten
Slavsk	Heinrichswalde
Sovetsk	Tilsit
Svetlogorsk	Rauschen
Svoboda	Janichen
Ulyanovo	Breitenstein
Vesnovo	Kussen
Yantarny	Palmnicken
Zelenogradsk	Kranz
Zheleznodorozhny	Gerdauen
Znamensk	Wehlau

Many of these names are those of World War II Red Army heroes who lost their lives in the battle for Königsberg in the opening months of 1945. (Entries for most of them will be found in the main text.) Others are descriptive, such as *Geroyskoye* ("heroic"), *Krasnolesye* ("beautiful wood"), *Novostroyevo* ("new building"), *Ozyorki* ("lakes"), *Polessk* ("forestland"), *Primorsk* ("maritime"), *Rybachy* ("fishing place"), *Svetlogorsk* ("bright mountain"), *Svoboda* ("freedom"), *Yantarny* ("amber"), *Zelenogradsk* ("green town"), and *Zheleznodorozhny* ("railroad").

In most cases, it will be noticed, the new names bear no resemblance, either in form or meaning, to the German originals. There is sometimes a slight similarity in pronunciation or spelling, however, as for Geroyskoye and Gertlauken, Kaliningrad and Königsberg, Ladushkin and Ludwigsort, Mayskoye and Mallwen, although Rybachy (from Russian *ryba*, "fish") would have been a closer equivalent to Fischhausen than to Rossitten.

Similar renamings took place in other parts of the USSR, and many of the names now in southern Sakhalin island and throughout the Kuril Islands, in the Far East, have replaced earlier Japanese names. In the Crimea, apart from the Greek-style names already considered, a number of Tatar names were altered to unrelated Russian ones in 1945 when Stalin banished the Crimean Tatars to Central Asia and Siberia. Only *Bakhchisaray* survived as a major Tatar name, together with those of a few Black Sea resorts in the region of Yalta.

In the region northwest of St. Petersburg, many formerly Finnish names were converted to Russian ones when the Karelian Isthmus and other border districts were ceded to the USSR after Finland lost the 1939-40 war. (The lost territory was temporarily regained in 1941-44 but then again reverted to the USSR with slight boundary adjustments.) Russian names in this region are thus very recent, and include *Kamennogorsk* ("rock mountain," formerly Antrea), *Primorsk* ("seaside," formerly Koivisto), *Priozyorsk* ("lakeside," formerly

Introduction

Käkisalmi), *Sovetsky* ("Soviet," formerly Johannes), *Svetogorsk* ("bright mountain," formerly Enso), and *Zelenogorsk* ("green town," formerly Terijoki).

In the sparsely inhabited Arctic island territories of northern Russia, such as Franz Josef Land, Novaya Zemlya, North Land (Severnaya Zemlya), and the New Siberian (Novosibirskiye) Islands, the names are mainly those of 19th century travelers, traders, and explorers, not all of them Russian. There are a few exceptions, however, notably that of *Franz Josef Land* itself, named for the emperor of Austria. Some of its islands have retained equally royal names, such as *Alexandra Land, George Land,* and *Rudolf Island.*

Although generally outside the scope of the present book, the names of former kolkhozes (collective farms) and sovkhozes (state farms) illustrate best of all the blatantly propagandist nature of Soviet names. Some were also given as village, settlement, and even town names. The following selection is taken from Charles B. Peterson's "The Nature of Soviet Place-Names" in *Names*, March 1977 (see Select Bibliography, page 251):

Aktivist (Activist)
Avangard (Vanguard, i.e. of Communism in the forefront of history)
Avrora (Aurora, the cruiser that fired on the Winter Palace in 1917)
Bol'shevik (Bolshevik)
Borets (Fighter)
Burevestnik (Stormy Petrel, i.e. a revolutionary)
Druzhba (Friendship)
Gigant (Giant, used of a large farm)
imeni XVIII parts"ezda (named for the 18th Party Congress, held 1939)
imeni XXI s"ezda KPSS (named for the 21st CPSU Congress, held 1959)
imeni Lenina (named for Lenin)
Iskra (Spark, the title of the first Bolshevik newspaper)
Komintern (Comintern, i.e. Communist International)
Kommunist (Communist)
Kommunizm (Communism)
Komsomolets (Komsomol member, i.e. of the Communist Youth League)
Krasnaya zvezda (Red Star)
Krasnoye znamya (Red Banner)
Krasny mayak (Red Lighthouse, i.e. the guiding light of Communism)
Krasny Oktyabr' (Red October, i.e. the Revolution)
Leninsky luch (Lenin's Ray, i.e. the guiding light of Leninism)
Leninsky put' (Lenin's Way, i.e. history as interpreted by Leninism)
Novaya zhizn' (New Life, i.e. Communism)
Novoye vremya (New Time, i.e. Communism as a new era)
Novy byt (New Way of Life)
Novy mir (New World, i.e. the one that Communism will bring)
Pamyat' Il'icha (In Memory of Ilich, i.e. Lenin, named by his patronym)
Pamyat' Lenina (In Memory of Lenin)
Partizan (Partisan)
Pervoye Maya (First of May, May Day, the workers' official holiday)

Pioner (Pioneer, both generally and as a young Communist member)
Pobeda Oktyabrya (Victory of October, i.e. of the Revolution)
Pravda (Truth, the name of the official Communist Party newspaper)
Progress (Progress, i.e. as moving forward and being progressive)
Put' Il'icha (Way of Ilich, i.e. of Lenin; cf. *Leninsky put*)
Put k kommunizmu (Way to Communism)
50 let Oktyabrya (50 Years of October, i.e. 50th anniversary of the Revolution, celebrated in 1967)
Pyatiletka (Five-Year Plan)
Rassvet (Dawn, i.e. Communism as the dawning of a new era and order)
Rodina (Motherland)
Serp i Molot (Hammer and Sickle, symbolizing industrial and rural workers)
Sotsializm (Socialism, regarded as a stage on the road to Communism)
Triumf (Triumph, i.e. of Communism)
Trud (Labor)
Udarnik (Shock-Worker)
Verny put' (True Way, i.e. socialism, then Communism)
Volna revolyutsii (Wave of Revolutionary, i.e. spread worldwide of Communism)
Voskhod (Rise, i.e. of Communism)
Vostok (East)
Vperyod (Forwards, i.e. to Communism)
Zavety Lenina (Lenin's Legacy)
Zarya (Dawn, cf. *Rassvet*)

Soviet street names, on the other hand, were generally more pragmatic, largely commemorating laudable people and events. One need only mention Moscow's *Gorky Street*, honoring the writer Maxim Gorky, and *Revolution Square*. *Red Square*, however, has a prerevolutionary name.

Such names set the tone for many, but by no means all, of the entries in this book.

Amongst all this godless innovation, it is perhaps surprising that any religious names should survive, especially since religion was formally disavowed by the Soviets. In fact more such names remained than might be supposed. Two well known examples are *Arkhangelsk*, often known as *Archangel*, in the northwest of Russia, and *Blagoveshchensk* ("Annunciation"), in the southeast. These both represent church dedications. Other places of similar origin include *Bogorodsk* ("Our Lady"), *Borisoglebsk* ("St. Boris and St. Gleb"), *Pokrovsk* ("Protection of the Virgin"), *Preobrazhenskoye* ("Transfiguration"), *Spassk* ("Savior"), *Sretensk* ("Purification"), *Troitsk* ("Trinity"), *Voskresensk* ("Resurrection"), *Vozdvizhenskoye* ("Exaltation of the Cross"), *Vsekhsvyatskoye* ("All Saints"), and the latter half of *Zavodouspenskoye* ("Assumption" or "Dormition").

A few major places named for medieval princes also stayed the course, such as *Mstislavl*, *Vladimir* and *Yaroslavl*.

Even so, and despite their positive presence, such names were the exception rather than the rule in the Soviet era.

V. Compound names

Many names in the former Soviet Union consist of blended or connected words. Blended names are those such as *Dnepropetrovsk* where two distinct words or names have combined. In this case they are *Dnieper* (the river) and the surname *Petrovsky*. In early Soviet times, many compound names arose with a form of *krasny*, "red," as the first word, either in combining form (*krasno-*) or as a separate word. Hence such names as *Krasnokamsk* ("red Kama"), *Krasnoturinsk* ("red Tura"), and *Krasnooktyabrsky* ("red October"), on the one hand, and *Krasny Luch* ("red ray"), *Krasny Mayak* ("red lighthouse"), and *Krasny Oktyabr'* ("red October"), on the other.

In some cases an existing name is followed by the adjectival form of another name for distinguishing purposes. When this happens, it is always joined by a hyphen. An example is *Aleksandrovsk-Sakhalinsky*, "Sakhalin Aleksandrovsk," so named to denote its location on Sakhalin island, as distinct from any other Aleksandrovsk. Further instances are *Belgorod-Dnestrovsky*, "Dniester Belgorod," in Ukraine, distinguished from *Belgorod* in Russia, and *Vladimir-Volynsky*, "Volynia Vladimir," also in Ukraine, distinguished from *Vladimir* in Russia.

The added adjective may also be geographically descriptive. Examples are *Pereslavl-Zalessky*, "Pereslavl beyond the forest," and *Petrovsk-Zabaykalsky*, "Petrovsk beyond (Lake) Baykal." As always, there are exceptions, and the added adjective may not be to distinguish from another place of the same name but simply to serve as a commemoration. Thus *Korsun-Shevchenkovsky*, in Ukraine, was originally *Korsun* (a form of the Greek name *Kherson* referred to earlier). In 1944, however, the second part was added as the adjectival form of the name of the Ukrainian poet Taras *Shevchenko*, who was born near here. Similar to this is the Lithuanian town of *Kudirkos-Naumiestis*, although here the addition comes as the first part. The name commemorates the Lithuanian patriot Vincas Kudirka, who died in *Naumiestis*.

The Russian town of *Vladimir*, mentioned above, is sometimes itself distinguished as *Vladimir-na-Klyazme*, "Vladimir on the Klyazma," for its location on this river. This type of compound name is found in the former USSR as it is elsewhere in Europe (Germany's Frankfurt-am-Main, France's Châlons-sur-Marne, England's Stratford-upon-Avon). One of the best known names of this "town-on-river" type is the southwestern Russian city of *Rostov-na-Donu*, usually known in English as Rostov-on-Don.

The distinction here is from the ancient town of *Rostov*, from which it actually took its name. (As in English, other languages also commonly translate the "on," so that the French know this city as *Rostov-sur-le-Don*, the Germans as *Rostow am Don*, and the Italians as *Rostov sul Don*.) Further examples of such names are *Kalach-na-Donu* (Kalach-on-Don), *Kamen-na-Obi* (Kamen-on-Ob), and *Komsomolsk-na-Amure* (Komsomolsk-on-Amur).

In a few cases a compound placename is based on a person's first name and surname. In such instances the first name usually has a combining form (often in -*o*) and is joined to the surname with a hyphen. An example is the Ukrainian city of *Ivano-Frankovsk*, named for the writer Ivan Franko. Similar is the

Ukrainian village of *Karlo-Libknekhtovsk*, named for the German socialist leader Karl Liebknecht. But a combination of first name and surname is also sometimes used "neat," with no combining form. In such cases there is usually no hyphen. One example is the settlement *Lev Tolstoy*. The writer Leo Tolstoy died at the railroad station here, then known as *Astapovo*. Another is the Azerbaijani town of *Stepan Razin*, named for the 17th-century Cossack rebel.

It can also happen that a hyphenated name simply means that two places have combined to form a new town. This is the case with *Orekhovo-Zuyevo*, a town formed from these two villages (and others) in 1917. Such names exist in other countries, so that the North Carolina city of *Winston-Salem* was created in 1913 from the two separate towns of Winston and Salem, while France's *Clermont-Ferrand* arose in 1630 as a merger of Clermont and Montferrand.

VI. Postcommunist names

Following the dissolution of the Soviet Union in 1991 and the concomitant collapse of Communism, many places reverted to their prerevolutionary names, sometimes in corrected form. Thus *Frunze*, capital of Kyrgyzstan, did not revert to its pre-1926 name of *Pishpek* but assumed the more accurate form *Bishkek*.

In fact names had gradually been reverting or altering to indigenous forms for some time before this, especially in non-Russian republics. Thus *Dushanbe*, capital of Tajikistan, reverted to its native name in 1961 following 32 years as *Stalinabad*, while even earlier, the Turkmen capital, *Ashkhabad*, bore the Russian name of *Poltoratsk* for only eight years before resuming its indigenous name in 1927. However, some abandonments of Russian names were nevertheless for ideological reasons. The Buryat capital, *Ulan-Ude*, has an indigenous name, but it means "red Uda," the latter being the river name that also lay behind the pre-1934 Russian name of *Verkhneudinsk*. Such apparent "reversions" to native names may actually be modern Soviet-style creations, albeit in an indigenous form.

True postcommunist reversions to prerevolutionary names at first involved only major cities, such as *Leningrad* to *St. Petersburg*, *Kuybyshev* to *Samara*, *Sverdlovsk* to *Yekaterinburg*, and *Gorky* to *Nizhny Novogorod*. These are all in the Russian Federation. In the other republics, the reversion was less marked, even where a Russian name had an earlier indigenous form to revert to, such as *Leninsk* in Uzbekistan (originally *Assake*). However, the further south one goes in the former republics, the less frequently one now finds Russian placenames. The chief exceptions are those places that have no earlier indigenous name to revert to, such as *Pavlodar*, Kazakhstan, or *Krasnovodsk*, Turkmenistan. These in due time will almost certainly undergo a further renaming operation, so that eventually all major places in a non-Russian country will have indigenous names.

If there is no earlier name to readopt, there are still several options available for a new name. Where a place grew up around a railroad station,

Introduction 15

for example, its own name can be called on. Thus *Stuchka*, Latvia, arose in 1961 near the station of *Aizkraukle*, and this is an obvious choice to replace the revolutionary name. If the place is on a river, the river name can serve similarly. *Ordzhonikidzeabad*, Tajikistan, lies on the *Kafirningan*, and its own name, or an indigenous form of it (*Kofarnikhon*), is a suitable candidate. The same would apply to *Azizbekov*, Armenia, on the *Arpa*. Such choices assume, of course, that the proposed new name is not already in use or earmarked for adoption by another town or village.

Names in this book have generally been based on those in the 1993 revised reprint of the 9th (1992) edition of *The Times Atlas of the World* (see Select Bibliography, page 251). Since renaming is an ongoing process, some places will have inevitably assumed new names in the interval between writing and publication. They will be reentered under these names in any future updated edition.

VII. Arrangement of entries

Apart from the cross-references, each entry contains four "strands" or items of information: (1) the name itself, as the headword; (2) its Cyrillic equivalent, in parentheses; (3) a brief description of the named place, with its country and its approximate geographical location in that country; (4) the meaning of the name. To particularize:

(1) The headword is in the standard English spelling of the name, which takes no account of Russian hard or soft signs and which represents the masculine adjectival ending -ый or -ий as -y. It is thus *Tver*, not *Tver'*, and *Grozny*, not *Groznyj*. Equally, the Russian letter ё is regularly rendered *yo*, giving *Budyonnovsk*, not *Budënnovsk* (or *Budenovsk*), and *Oryol*, not *Orël* (or *Orel*). Although names in non–Russian countries such as Belarus and Ukraine now appear on maps in their Belorussian or Ukrainian form, it is the traditional Russian form of the name that is entered here. The reader will thus find *Grodno*, not *Hrodna*, and *Krivoy Rog*, not *Kryvyy Rih*. This is of course strictly speaking inaccurate, and to a country's native people possibly even politically offensive. But it is for the benefit of the reader, who may find even the Russian versions of the names difficult enough, let alone the unfamiliar indigenous forms. In any future edition of the dictionary, this policy will be reviewed.

The standard English form of the name usually corresponds to the indigenous form, where the Roman alphabet is used, or to a more or less exact transliteration of the Cyrillic in countries where this alphabet applies (Russia, Belarus, Ukraine). Certain conventions have been observed, however, as follows:

(i) The use of the English (Latin) suffixal form *-ia* for the Russian territorial suffix -ия. Examples are *Karelia* (not *Kareliya*) and *Mordovia* (not *Mordoviya*).

(ii) The use of translated English names for the major island groups of *Franz Josef Land* (Russian *Zemlya Frantsa Iosifa*), *North Land* (Russian

Severnaya Zemlya), and *New Siberian Islands* (Russian *Novosibirskiye ostrova*). *Novaya Zemlya* retains its Russian name, however, as English *New Land* is rarely if ever used for this group. (Even on old English maps it appeared as *Nova Zembla*.)

(iii) The use of English *on* to translate Russian на for towns and cities whose name refers to the river on which they stand. This is partly to avoid a presentation of the river name in an oblique form (the locative case), as would then be required. Examples are *Rostov-on-Don*, not *Rostov-na-Donu*, and *Komsomolsk-on-Amur*, not *Komsomolsk-na-Amure*.

(iv) Major territorial units and cities have their conventional English names, so that it is *Lithuania*, not *Lietuva* (or Russian *Litva*), *Siberia*, not *Sibir*, and *St. Petersburg*, not *Sankt-Peterburg*. Such conventions, however, do not extend to traditional forms such as *Archangel* for *Arkhangelsk*, although names of this type, where they still exist, appear in the text as cross-references. Former forms such as *Bashkiria*, *Belorussia*, *Kirghizia*, and *Moldavia* are also cross-referred to their present official names, respectively *Bashkortostan*, *Belarus*, *Kyrgyzstan*, and *Moldova*.

Aside from the conventions mentioned above, the following transliterations have generally been used in the entries for the Roman (English) equivalents of the Cyrillic (Russian) letters:

а	a	р	r
б	b	с	s
в	v	т	t
г	g	у	u
д	d	ф	f
е	e*	х	kh
ё	yo	ц	ts
ж	zh	ч	ch
з	z	ш	sh
и	i	щ	shch
й	j	ъ	"
к	k	ы	y
л	l	ь	'
м	m	э	e
н	n	ю	yu
о	o	я	ya
п	p		

Ye to start a word or after a vowel.

(2) The Cyrillic equivalent is also given in its standard form, with stress marks as appropriate. Equivalents are given for *all* names, even where the places concerned are not now actually in Russia.

(3) The geographical location is approximate, by "compass" (western,

Introduction 17

southeastern, east central, etc.) within the stated country (and also within the Crimea, as a distinct geographical entity). Since Russia is a very large country, a more precise location is given, usually by relation to a particular town, as the opening words of the explanatory part of the entry. It should be noted that, with regard to Russia, "western" means west of the Urals, "southwestern" generally means south of Volgograd (i.e. in the region bordered by Ukraine to the west, Kazakhstan to the east, and the Caucasus to the south), "northwestern" means generally north of a line from St. Petersburg to the Gulf of Ob (i.e., mostly in Karelia), "southern" means approximately in the extensive region between the Transsiberian Railway and the northern borders of Kazakhstan and Mongolia, "southeastern" means generally south and east of the Sea of Okhotsk, including the Kuril Islands and the region bordering northeastern China. Major Arctic island groups follow the general rule, so that Novaya Zemlya and Franz Josef Land are in "northwestern" Russia, North Land (Severnaya Zemlya) is in "northern" Russia, and the New Siberian Islands are in "northeastern" Russia.

(4) As stated, the explanatory text of the entry, its main part, opens with a locational description, e.g. "The town, northwest of Odessa...." If the named object is a river, its course is briefly outlined. An account of the name origin and meaning then follows. There may be cross-references to other names within the text or at its conclusion. Cyrillic equivalents of well known former names are usually supplied in parentheses, but the less familiar names are not normally so treated. In one or two cases a popular or "folk" etymology is quoted, purely for interest and *not* for serious academic consideration! There are still those who like to derive the name of the *Vorskla* River from Peter the Great's lost monocle and to see *Odessa* as commemorating the famous but fabular Odysseus.

Where places have changed their name, sometimes more than once, the meaning of any earlier name is also usually given, although not always those of places in non-Russian or non-Soviet territory. Thus, the German names of places formerly in East Prussia, now renamed with Russian names in the Kaliningrad province of the Russian Federation, are stated but not always etymologized. However, the year of renaming is usually provided.

The dictionary concludes with two appendices. The first lists common placename elements and the second considers regional names. They are followed by a select bibliography and a Cyrillic-to-Roman index to all entered names, including most cross-references and previous names. All of these additional items have their own brief introduction.

Adrian Room
March 1996
Stamford, England

The Placenames

Abakan (Абакáн) *Town, southern Russia*. The town, west of Minusinsk, is named for the river on which it stands, at the point where it flows into the Yenisey. Hence its name until 1931, *Ust-Abakanskoye* (Усть-Абакáнское), "[place at the] mouth of the Abakan." The river's own name is of uncertain origin. It is not "bear's blood," as sometimes popularly explained, from the chance resemblance of the name to Khakass *aba*, "bear," and *kan* "blood."

Abastumani (Абастумáни) *Village, southwestern Georgia*. The village, south of Kutaisi, has a name deriving from Georgian *khabaz*, "baker," and *ubani*, "district." Its ancient name was *Otskhe*, from Georgian *olkhis*, "bear's den," and *khevi*, "ravine."

Abay (Абáй) *Town, east central Kazakhstan*. The town, southwest of Karaganda, was originally known as *Churubay-Nura* (Чурубáй-Нурá). It was renamed as now in 1961 for the Kazakh poet *Abay* Kunanbayev (1845–1904).

Abaza (Абазá) *Town, southern Russia*. The town, southwest of Abakan, arose in 1867 as a settlement for workers at the Abakan iron and steel works, and this gave the name, an abbreviation of *Abakanskij zavod*, "Abakan works."

Abdulino (Абдýлино) *Town, western Russia*. The town, northeast of Samara, takes its name from Tatar settler *Abdulla* here some time before the original village arose in the late 18th century. The town has had urban status since 1923.

Abez (Áбезь) *Town, northwestern Russia*. The town, southwest of Vorkuta, has a Komi name meaning "slovenly." This was the nickname of an early settler here, *Abez* Mish, "Slovenly Mike."

Abkhazia (Абхáзия) *Republic, northwestern Georgia*. The republic is named for its indigenous inhabitants, whose own name is based on Georgian *ans*, "soul," i.e. "those who have a soul," "those speaking their own tongue," as distinct from neighboring peoples who did not speak the same language.

Abovyan (Абовя́н) *Town, central Armenia*. The town, northeast of Yerevan, was founded in 1963 on the site of the former village of *Elar*. It was named for the Armenian writer Khachatur *Abovyan* (1805–1848), who was born near here.

Abramtsevo (Абрáмцево) *Village, western Russia*. The village, north of Moscow, and famous for its museum and its literary and artistic connections, appears at first sight to have a name based on one or other of the personal names *Abram* or *Abramov*. However, neither the forename nor the surname occurs in any document relating to Abramtsevo, so some other origin must be sought. Local historians propose it in the standard word *obramok*, a term for a marshy meadow surrounded by woodland, itself related to Russian *obramit'*, "to frame." The initial *o*- of this would have become *a*- under the influence of Moscow pronunciation and the linguistic process known as *akanie* (the pronunciation of an unstressed *o* as *a*). The description suits the topography, and this etymology thus seems likely.

Abrau-Dyurso (Абра́у-Дюрсо́) *Town, southwestern Russia*. The town, near the Black Sea coast west of Novorossiysk, takes its name from Abkhaz *abrau*, "gap," and *dyursu*, "four springs."

Academy Bay (Акаде́мии зали́в) *Bay, Sea of Okhotsk, eastern Russia*. The bay, on the southwestern coast of the Sea of Okhotsk, was named in honor of the St. Petersburg *Academy of Sciences* by the Russian traveler A. F. Middendorf during his exploration of 1844–45.

Academy of Sciences Range (Акаде́мии Нау́к хребе́т) *Mountain range, northern Tajikistan*. The range, in the western Pamirs, was named in 1927 for the *Academy of Sciences* of the USSR following its discovery by N. L. Korzhenevsky. It contains **Communism Peak**, Russia's loftiest mountain.

Achinsk (Ачи́нск) *Town, southern Russia*. The town, west of Krasnoyarsk, arose around the fortress built here on the Chulym River in 1641 and itself named for the *Achyg*, the Tatar people who inhabited the region. The place was raised to town status in 1782.

Achit (Ачи́т) *Town, southwestern Russia*. The town, west of Pervouralsk, arose around a fortress built here in 1735, itself named for the river on which it stood. The name has been traditionally interpreted from Tatar words meaning "hungry dog," although this is clearly a folk etymology. The origin may lie in a Turkic word of Mongol origin meaning "generous," "bountiful," referring to its waters or its fish.

Adai Khokh (Адайхо́х) *Mountain, southwestern Russia*. The mountain, in the central Caucasus, has an Ossetic name meaning "grandfather mountain," from *adai*, "grandfather," and *khokh*, "mountain."

Adler (А́длер) *Town, southwestern Russia*. The town, on the Black Sea coast northwest of Gagra, takes its name from a nearby cape. Its own name is said to come from a local people, the *Arto*, whose name in turn has been associated with Turkish *ada*, "island."

Adygeia (Адыге́я) *Republic, southwestern Russia*. The republic takes its name from the indigenous Adygey people, whose own name may derive from Abkhazian *adzy*, "water," so that they are the "waterside dwellers." The "water" would be that of the marshy flood plain of the Kuban River, which forms the northern border of the region. See also **Kabardino-Balkaria**.

Adzharia (Аджа́рия) *Republic, southwestern Georgia*. The republic is named for its indigenous population, who themselves take their name from the river here, the *Adzharis Tskali*. Its own name is of uncertain origin.

Adzva (А́дзьва) *River, northwestern Russia*. The river, a tributary of the Usa, has a Komi name representing *adz*, "floodland," "river valley," "water meadow," and *va*, "water."

Agapovka (Ага́повка) *Town, southwestern Russia*. The town, just south of Magnitogorsk, was founded in 1902 and given the surname, *Agapov*, of the land tenure manager here who leased land to settlers.

Aginskoye (Агинское) *Town, southern Russia*. The town, southeast of Krasnoyarsk, takes its name from the *Aga* River on which it lies. The river name is said to derive from Evenki *aga*, "plain," "steppe," descriptive of the terrain here. The town is the capital of the Agin-Buryat Autonomous District.

Agnessa See **Shokalsky Island**.

Agro-Pustyn (Агро-Пустынь) *Village, western Russia*. The village, north of Ryazan, appears at first sight to have a name beginning with an element related to the international *agro-* found in English *agronomist*, meaning "field," "farm." However, local records, dating from 1506, show that the name as a whole is a shortened form of *Agrafenina Pustyn'*, where the first word represents the female forename *Agrafena* and the second, related to Russian *pustynya*, "desert," is a term for a small isolated monastery or nunnery. The forename was the religious name adopted by Princess Agrippinina, who founded the nunnery here on an isolated site at the edge of the Meshchera lowland. She lived and died within its walls. The present village grew up round the buildings, and the full name was shortened as now by the Soviet authorities in the 1930s or 1940s in order to avoid any religious association (and presumably to suggest an agricultural one).

Akademgorodok (Академгородок) *Science city, southern Russia*. The city, southeast of Novosibirsk, was laid out over the period 1957–66 as a scientific research settlement. Its name is an abbreviation of the words *akademicheskiy gorodok*, "academic campus."

Akademiya Bay See **Academy Bay**.

Akademiya Nauk Range See **Academy of Sciences Range**.

Akbulak (Акбулак) *Town, southwestern Russia*. The town, east of Sol-Iletsk near the border with Kazakhstan, has a Kazakh name meaning "white spring," from *ak*, "white," and *bulak*, "spring," "source." This could denote a freely flowing spring, with good, clear water, as distinct from *Karabulak*, "black spring," meaning one that is stagnant, and fed by underground water.

Akdarya See **Zeravshan**.

Ak Dovurak (Ак-Довурак) *Town, southern Russia*. The town, west of Kyzyl near the Mongolian border, has a Tuvan name meaning "white earth." It arose in 1964 when an asbestos plant was opened here on the site of chrysolite mineral deposits.

Akhalkalaki (Ахалкалаки) *Town, southern Georgia*. The town, southeast of Akhaltsikhe, has a name representing medieval Georgian *akhal*, "new," and *kalaki*, "fortress." It dates from the 11th century, and implies that there must have been an even older fortification on the site.

Akhaltsikhe (Ахалцихе) *Town, southwestern Georgia*. The town, northwest of Akhalkalaki, was founded in the 10th or 11th century and takes its name from medieval Georgian *akhal*, "new," and *tsikhe*, "town."

Akhmatov Bay (Ахматова залив) *Bay, North Land, northern Russia*. The bay, on the north coast of Bolshevik island, was discovered by a Russian Arctic expedition in 1913 and named for the Russian hydrographer and geodesist Viktor Viktorovich *Akhmatov* (1875–1934), who recorded soundings off Spitsbergen in 1899–1901.

Akhtuba (Ахтуба) *River, western Russia*. The river, a northern tributary of the lower Volga, is said to take its name from Turkic words related to modern Turkish *ak*, "white," and *tuba*, "whirlpool." However, the name is almost certainly pre-Turkic in origin.

Akhtyrka (Ахтырка) *Town, northern Ukraine*. The town, northwest of Kharkov, has a name traditionally derived from Turkic words corresponding to modern Turkish *ak*, "white," and *tura*, "town." However, the region here was under Lithuanian domain until at least the 15th century, and the name may thus be of Lithuanian origin. If so, its meaning is obscure.

Akhunbabayev (Ахунбабáев) *Town, eastern Uzbekistan*. The town, southeast of Andizhan, was originally the village of *Sufikishlak* (Суфикишлáк). In 1975 it was raised to town status and renamed as now for the Uzbek Soviet politician Yuldash *Akhunbabayev* (1885–1943), who was born near here.

Akkerman See **Belgorod-Dnestrovsky.**

Ak-Mechet See (1) **Chernomorskoye,** (2) **Kzyl-Orda,** (3) **Simferopol.**

Akmola (Акмолá) *City, north central Kazakhstan*. The city, northwest of Karaganda, was founded in 1830 as the fortified post of *Akmoly* (Акмолы́), from Kazakh *ak*, "white," and *mola*, "grave." In 1832 the settlement was raised to town status as *Akmolinsk* (Акмо́линск). In 1961 the growing town was renamed *Tselinograd* (Целиногрáд), meaning "town of the virgin land," from Russian *tselina*, "virgin land," and *grad*, "town." The new name referred to the extensive program of land reclamation then under way in this part of Kazakhstan. In 1994, when the Kazakh parliament voted to move the capital here from Alma-Ata, the city reverted to its original name (in its indigenous form).

Akmolinsk See **Akmola.**

Akmoly See **Akmola.**

Aksakovo (Аксáково) *Town, western Russia*. The town, in Bashkortostan southwest of Ufa, takes its name from the Russian writer Sergey Timofeyevich *Aksakov* (1791–1859), who was born in Ufa and whose family estate of Kuroyedovo was here.

Aksay (Аксáй) *River, southwestern Russia*. The river, a tributary of the Don, has a Turkic name meaning "white channel." There are several rivers of the name, not only in this part of Russia but also in Kazakhstan and Kyrgyzstan. See also **Aksu.**

Aksu (Аксý) *River, southeastern Kazakhstan*. The river, flowing north into Lake Balkhash, has a Turkic name meaning "white water," from words corresponding to modern Turkish *ak*, "white," and *su*, "water." The reference is not so much to the color of the water as to the melting snows that feed its source, in this case a western range of the Ala Tau. The name also implies a contrast with **Karasu,** "black water." There are other rivers of the name in Central Asia.

Aktau See **Shevchenko.**

Aktyubinsk (Актю́бинск) *Town, west central Kazakhstan*. The town, southwest of Orsk, arose around the fortress of *Ak-Tyube* built here in 1869. Its own name is Kazakh in origin, from *ak*, "white," and *tube*, "hilltop."

Akyar (Акъя́р) *Village, southwestern Russia*. The village, northwest of Orsk, has a Bashkir name meaning "white bank," from *ak*, "white," and *yar*, "bank."

Alagir (Алагир) *Town, southern Russia*. The town, in the foothills of the central Caucasus west of Vladikavkaz, has a name deriving from Ossetic *ualag*, "upper," and *Ir*, "Ossetia," in other words "upper Ossetia," or politically North Ossetia.

Alakol (Алако́ль) *Lake, eastern Kazakhstan*. The lake, east of Lake

Balkhash, has a name deriving from Kazakh *ala*, "variegated," and *kol*, "lake," referring to the changing colors of the waters.

Alapayevsk (Алапа́евск) *Town, west central Russia*. The town, northeast of Yekaterinburg, takes its name from the *Alapaikhi* River here. The river's own name comes from the local word *alapa*, "floodlands." The town arose around the ironworks built here in the opening years of the 18th century, and gained urban status in 1781.

Ala Tau (Алата́у) *Mountain ranges, Kazakhstan/Kyrgyzstan*. The ranges, around and northeast of Issyk-Kul, have a name from Turkic words that gave modern Turkish *ala*, "speckled," and *dağ*, "mountain." The reference is to snowy peaks contrasting with darker vegetation lower down the slopes. Cf. **Altay**, and see also **Dzungarian Ala Tau**.

Alatyr (Ала́тырь) *Town, west central Russia*. The town, southwest of Kazan, has a name that is popularly derived from Turkish *ala*, "speckled," and a local word, *tura*, meaning "dwelling-place," "town." The name is actually that of the river here, and is of uncertain origin.

Alaverdi (Алаверди́) *Town, northern Armenia*. The town, northeast of Stepanavan, probably takes its name from the *Alan* people who lived here and Georgian *gverdi*, "valley." A folk etymology derives the name from the exclamation of a Turkish army officer on capturing the fortified cathedral here: "*Allah verdi!*" "God has given!"

Alazani (Алаза́ни) *River, northeastern Georgia*. The river, flowing south and east from the Caucasus, has a name representing Georgian *ala*, "damp," "moist," and *zani*, "place."

Alchevsk See **Kommunarsk**.

Aldan (Алда́н) *Town, eastern Russia*. The town, southwest of Irkutsk, takes its name from the river on which it lies. The river's own name may derive from a word related to modern Turkish *altın* "gold," referring to the gold deposits in its waters. The town arose in the 1920s when gold was first discovered, and the settlement that arose was originally named *Nezametnyj* (Незаме́тный), "imperceptible," presumably referring to the hidden riches. In 1939 the present name was adopted.

Aleksandriya (Александри́я) *Town, central Ukraine*. The original settlement here, northeast of Kirovograd, was founded in 1754 as *Usovka*. In 1784 it was raised to the status of a town and was renamed in honor of the future emperor of Russia, *Alexander* I (1777–1825), grandson of Catherine the Great.

Aleksandropol See **Kumayri**.

Aleksandrov (Алекса́ндров) *Town, western Russia*. The town, northeast of Moscow, gained urban status in 1778. Its name is clearly based on either the forename *Aleksandr* (Alexander) or the surname *Aleksandrov*. The reference must be to an early settler or landowner.

Aleksandrovsk (Алекса́ндровск) *Town, western Russia*. The town, to the west of the Central Urals southeast of Berezniki, arose from the ironworks built on the Lytva River here. The settlement was at first named *Lytvinsky*, or simply *Lytva*, but in 1808 it was renamed by the ironworks owner, V. A. Vsevolzhsky (see **Vsevolodo-Blagodatsky**), for his successor, *Aleksandrovsky*. The present form of the name was adopted in 1951 when the settlement attained town status.

Aleksandrovsk See (1) **Belogorsk**, (2) **Zaporozhye**.

Aleksandrovsk-Grushevsky See **Shakhty**.

Aleksandrovsk-Sakhalinsky (Александровск-Сахалинский) *Town, Sakhalin, eastern Russia.* The town and port, on the west coast of Sakhalin island, was founded in 1881 as *Aleksandrovsky post* (Александровский пост), so named for emperor *Alexander* II (1818–1881). In 1926 it was renamed as now, with *Sakhalinsky*, "of Sakhalin," distinguishing it from other places so called.

Aleksandrovsky post See **Aleksandrovsk-Sakhalinsky**.

Alekseyevka (Алексеевка) *Town, southwestern Russia.* The town, southwest of Ostrogozhsk, gained urban status in 1954 and has a name based on the male forename *Aleksey* (Alexis). The name is found for many other places and must relate to an early settler or landowner.

Alekseyevsk See **Svobodny**.

Aleksin (Алексин) *Town, western Russia.* The town, south of Moscow, is said to have been founded in the 13th century by Prince Daniil, son of Alexander Nevsky, who was here when he learned that his son *Aleksey* had been born and who named the place for him. However, history does not record that Daniil had a son of this name, and the name is likely to be that of Metropolitan *Aleksey*, the town's administrator at that time. The original name of the place is unknown.

Alexandra Land (Александры Земля) *Island, Franz Josef Land, northwestern Russia.* The westernmost island of the group was visited by the British Arctic explorer Leigh Smith during his expedition of 1880-81 and named for Princess *Alexandra* (1844–1925), wife of the Prince of Wales, the future King Edward VII.

Ali Bayramly (Али-Байрамлы) *Town, eastern Azerbaijan.* The town, southwest of Baku, is named for the Azerbaijani revolutionary *Ali* Bayram ogly *Bayramov* (1889–1920), killed in the Civil War by members of the Muslim counterrevolutionary Musavat faction, founded in Baku in 1911.

Alma (Альма) *River, southwestern Crimea, southern Ukraine.* The river, flowing west to the Black Sea, has a name made famous by a battle (1854) in the Crimean War. It derives from a Turkic word meaning "apple" (modern Turkish *elma*). The river runs through orchards.

Alma Ata (Алма-Ата) *Capital of Kazakhstan.* The city, in the southeast of the republic, was founded in 1896 on the site of the fortified settlement of *Almaty*, "apple tree," "orchard," from Kazakh *alma*, "apple," and takes its name from it. (The present form of the name has been popularly but erroneously interpreted as "father of apples," as if the second part were Kazakh *ata*, "father.") Until 1921 the town was known as *Verny* (Верный), "true," "faithful," implying that the fortified site was a reliable one.

Almazny (Алмазный) *Town, central Russia.* The Siberian town, southeast of Mirny, is so named for its diamond mine, from Russian *almaz*, "diamond."

Altay (Алтай) *Mountain system, Central Asia.* The western end of the system lies in southern Russia and eastern Kazakhstan. The name is a Turkic one probably meaning "speckled mountains," from words related to modern Turkish *ala*, "speckled," and *dağ*, "mountain" (cf. **Ala Tau**). The reference would be to the mountains' white snow-patched peaks, black scattered boulders, green vegetation, and gray granite rocks.

Altynay (Алтынай) *Town, southwestern Russia.* The town, northeast of Asbest, was originally the village of *Irbitskiye Vershiny*, "Irbit heights," from the river here. Its present name is Tatar in origin, and literally translates as "golden moon," from *altyn*, "gold," and *ay*, "moon." This must have originally been a personal name.

Alupka (Алу́пка) *Town and resort, southern Crimea, southern Ukraine*. The Black Sea resort, southwest of Yalta, has a name which evolved from that of *Alopekia*, the original Greek settlement here. This comes from Greek *alōpēx*, "fox." Foxes were common here at one time.

Alyoshki See **Tsyurupinsk**.

Amangeldy (Амангельды́) *Village, north central Kazakhstan*. The village, west of Arkalyk, was originally known as *Batnakkara*. It was renamed in 1936 for *Amangeldy Imanov* (1873–1919), a local Communist hero who led a revolution here in 1916.

Ambarchik (Амба́рчик) *Port, northeastern Russia*. The port is located near the mouth of the Kolyma River on the East Siberian Sea, and arose on the site where the Arctic explorer Dmitry Laptev (see **Laptev Sea**) wintered in 1740-41. He built a small storehouse (Russian *ambarchik*) here for his supplies, and this gave the name.

Amderma (А́мдерма) *Town, northwestern Russia*. The town, on the Kara Sea west of the Yamal Peninsula, has a name deriving from the Nenets verb *ngamdaras'*, "to seat firmly," "to settle for good," referring either to a site where a nomadic tribe had made their home or, according to some authorities, to a breeding ground of walruses.

Aminyevo (Ами́ньево) *District, Moscow, western Russia*. The western district of Moscow takes its name from the former village here. This itself was so called for the original landowner, Ivan *Amin'*, a comrade-in-arms of Dmitry Donskoy, prince of Moscow in the 14th century.

Amudarya (Амударья́) *River, central Asia*. The river flows generally northwest from the Pamirs to the Aral Sea, forming the border between Turkmenistan and Uzbekistan for much of its course. It takes its name from *Amu*, said to be that of a now-vanished city on its banks, and an Iranian word meaning "big river" (modern Turkish *derya*, "sea"). However, the first element may be simply Uzbek *amu*, "long." In classical times the river was known as the *Oxus*, perhaps deriving from a Turkic word meaning "flowing." Cf. **Syrdarya**.

Amur (Аму́р) *River, northeastern Asia*. The river rises in northern Mongolia as the Argun and flows southeast then northeast to the Sea of Okhotsk, forming the border between Manchuria and Russia as far as Khabarovsk. The name probably represents a Tungusic word meaning simply "river," although some authorities derive it from Mongolian *amar*, "calm," "peaceful." The Chinese know it as *hēilóngjiāng*, "river of the black dragon," no doubt with reference to the color of its waters.

Anabar (Анаба́р) *River, northern Russia*. The river, flowing into the Laptev Sea, has a name that is probably related to the Koryak word *vanav*, "pitch," presumably with reference to the dark color of its waters.

Anadyr (Ана́дырь) *Town, eastern Russia*. The town, capital of the Chukot Autonomous Region, lies at the mouth of the *Anadyr* River, and takes its name from it. It was founded as a frontier post in 1889 and was originally named *Anadyrsky ostrog*, "Anadyr stockade." It was then renamed *Novo-Mariinsk* (Но́во-Марии́нск), "new Mary's (settlement)," for the empress *Maria Fyodorovna*, consort of Czar Alexander III. It received its present name in 1923. The river name itself represents Yukaghir *onun*, "river," and *dyr*, "source." Its Chukot name is *Yaayvaam*, "tea river."

Anapa (Анáпа) *Town and port, southern Russia*. The town, on the northern Black Sea coast west of Krasnodar, is said to derive its name from the Cherkess words *ane*, "table," and *ppe*, "nose," "point," describing the level promontory on which it is situated. However, it is possible the source is in Adygey *ape*, "river mouth," and the conjectural name *Khan* of a river here, with the initial *Kh*- of this lost.

Andreapol (Андреáполь) *Town, northwestern Russia*. The town, northeast of Velikiye Luki, arose from the merging of three settlements: the *pogost* (church and clergy house with adjacent buildings) Dubka, the village Machikhino, and the estate Gorki. The original form of the name (in 1783), *Andreyano Pole*, "Andrey's field," was given to Machikhino, and much later (in 1905) to the railroad station that was built here. The settlement that grew up around the station gained the shorter name of *Andreapol'*, as now, and in 1967 became a town. The personal name *Andrey* (Andrew) is that of *Andrey* Kushelev, who first owned land here, then the village.

Andropov See **Rybinsk**.

Andzhiyevsky (Анджиéвский) *Town, southwestern Russia*. The town, northwest of Mineralnyye Vody, takes its name from the Russian Communist activist Grigory Grigoryevich *Andzhiyevsky* (1897–1919), captured by the British in the Civil War and executed in Pyatigorsk.

Angara (Ангарá) *River, southern Russia*. The Siberian river, flowing north and west from Lake Baykal to the Yenisey, derives its name from a Tungusic word *anga*, meaning "yawning," "gaping." The reference is to the deep gorge through which the river first passes, which appears to "swallow" it as it exits from Lake Baykal. It was earlier known as the *Upper Tunguska* (Вéрхняя Тунгýска). See **Tunguska**.

Angarsk (Ангáрск) *Town, southern Russia*. The industrial city, northwest of Irkutsk, takes its name from the **Angara** River by which it arose in 1946 during construction of a major hydroelectric dam here.

Anipemza (Анипéмза) *Town, western Armenia*. The town, southwest of Kumayri, has a name combining ancient and modern. *Ani* is the name of a historic settlement here that was a medieval capital of Armenia; *pemza* is Russian for "pumice," which is manufactured here.

Antratsit (Антрацúт) *Town, eastern Ukraine*. The town, southeast of Krasny Luch, is a noted coal mining center formed from a number of mining settlements in 1938. Its name designates its main product, from Russian *antratsit*, "anthracite." Until 1962 it was known as *Bokovo-Antratsit* (Бóково-Антрацúт), the first part of this being the name of one of the settlements.

Anuchin Island (Анýчина óстров) *Island, Kuril Islands, southeastern Russia*. The small island, near the southern end of the chain, was so named in 1946 for the Russian anthropologist and geographer, Dmitry Nikolayevich *Anuchin* (1843–1923).

Anzhu Islands (Анжý островá) *Island group, northeastern Russia*. The islands, in the Arctic Ocean, form a group in the New Siberian Islands. They are named for the Russian polar explorer Pyotr Fyodorovich *Anzhu* (1796–1869), who charted the north Siberian coast in the early 1820s.

Apatity (Апатúты) *Town, northwestern Russia*. The town, south of Murmansk, arose in 1935 when apatite and nepheline deposits were first mined here. Hence its name, from Russian *apatit*, "apatite" (a mineral consisting of calcium phosphate and fluoride).

Aprelevka (Апрéлевка) *Town, western Russia*. The town, northwest of Moscow, takes its name from the river on which it stands. The river name appears to derive from Russian *prel'*, "mold," or *prelyj*, "moldy," referring to a damp and musty place. The name is not related to Russian *aprel'*, "April," despite appearances.

Apsheron (Апшерóнский полуóстров) *Peninsula, eastern Azerbaijan*. The peninsula, with Baku on its southwestern coast, projects into the western Caspian Sea. Its name is said to derive from Persian *ab*, "water," and *shirin*, "salt," but may in fact represent the ethnic name of a local people here at one time. Their own name is of uncertain origin.

Arabat, Tongue of (Арабáтская Стрéлка) *Peninsula, northeastern Crimea, southern Ukraine*. The peninsula is a narrow sandy projection on the western side of the Sea of Azov. It takes its name from the fortress of *Arabat* located here until 1771. Its own name means "outskirts," from a Turkic word *arabat* borrowed from Arabic *ribāṭ*, "frontier fort" (which also gave the name of the Moroccan capital *Rabat*). The peninsula has also been known by the Russian name of *Ton'kaya*, "slender."

Aragats (Арагáц) *Mountain, northwestern Armenia*. The extinct volcano, northwest of Yerevan, has a name that has been variously explained. Proposed origins include: (1) Turkish *ala*, "speckled," and *güz*, "eye" (referring to the lake at its summit); (2) Turkish *allagiyaz*, a plant of the sorrel family; (3) Sumer *Hur-agies*, "mountain of wine." However, these were probably all devised to account for a name that is actually Armenian or pre-Armenian in origin.

Aragvi (Арáгви) *River, central Georgia*. The name of the river, a northern tributary of the Kura, is of doubtful origin. It may not even be Georgian. Some authorities have linked it with that of the *Aragon* River in Spain, and it could well share the initial Indo-European *ar-* of this, meaning simply "water."

Araks (Арáкс) *River, eastern Azerbaijan*. The river rises in eastern Turkey and flows east to form the border between Armenia and Azerbaijan to the north and Turkey and Iran to the south before joining the Kura west of Baku. Its name may mean "rushing one," from a word related to Greek *arassō*, "I dash," or Arabic *rakaḍ*, "to run." But more likely it evolved from a word basically meaning "river," with the initial *ar-* the Indo-European root word for "water" seen in many other names. Cf. **Aragvi**.

Aral Sea (Арáльское мóре) *Sea, southern Kazakhstan/northern Uzbekistan*. The inland sea probably derives its name from a word meaning "island," as in the related Kazakh and Kyrgyz *aral*, Uzbek *orol*, and Mongolian *aral*. This would refer to the many former islands and peninsulas in the southern part of the lake, where the Amudarya had its broad, marshy delta. These have now largely disappeared, since from 1960 to 1990 the area of the sea was reduced by 40 percent owing to the diversion of water from the Syrdarya and Amudarya rivers for irrigation purposes. A Russian name for the lake was *Sineye more*, "Blue Sea."

Aralsk (Арáльск) *Town, central Kazakhstan*. The town originally lay at the northeastern extremity of the **Aral Sea** and was named for it. It arose in 1905 when a railroad was built from Orenburg to Tashkent. Owing to the shrinkage of the area of the sea since 1960, however, Aralsk is now many miles from the shore.

Aralsulfat (Аралсульфа́т) *Town, central Kazakhstan*. The town, east of **Aralsk**, takes the first part of its name from the latter town (or from the *Aral Sea* to the west of it), and the second part from its former main commercial product, sodium sulfate, from Russian *sul'fat*, "sulfate." Since 1963 it has specialized in the manufacture of table salt (sodium chloride).

Aramil (Арами́ль) *Town, west central Russia*. The town, southeast of Yekaterinburg, arose in 1675 on the small *Aramilka* River here and takes its name from it. The river name itself derives from the dialect word *urema*, "riverside scrubland." (It is possible, however, that the habitation name derives directly from this.) The settlement gained town status in 1966.

Ararat (Арара́т) *Town, western Armenia*. The town, southeast of Yerevan, arose in 1929 as a settlement for constructors of a new cement plant here. It takes its name from the famous biblical Mt. *Ararat*, which lies 30 miles (48 km) to the west across the Turkish border. The mountain's own name is ancient, and is probably based on a pre-Indo-European root element, *ar*, meaning simply "mountain." The Armenian settlement was raised to urban status in 1962.

Archangel See **Arkhangelsk**.

Arctic Institute Islands (Аркти́ческого Институ́та острова́) *Island group, Kara Sea, northern Russia*. The four islands, south of the Izvestia Islands, were discovered by a Soviet expedition of 1932-33 on board the icebreaker *Sibiryakov* (see **Sibiryakov Island**) and named for the Arctic Scientific Research Institute.

Arctic Ocean (Се́верный Ледови́тый океа́н) *Ocean, northern Russia*. The ocean surrounds the North Pole north of the Arctic Circle and extends along the whole northern coast of Russia. The Russians have known it by various names, including *Arkticheskoye more*, "Arctic Sea," but since 1935 have standardized their name for it as *Severny Ledovity okean*, "Northern Ice Ocean," a translation of the German name *Nördisches Eismeer*. The ocean was first given a distinctive name in 1650 by the German geographer Varenius (Bernhard Varen), when in his *Geographia Generalis* he referred to it as the Hyperborean Ocean.

Ardatov (Арда́тов) *Town, western Russia*. The town, northeast of Saransk, has a name that probably represents the Moldovan forename *Ardat* with the Russian possessive suffix *-ov*, so that it is "Ardat's town."

Ardon (Ардо́н) *Village, southwestern Russia*. The village, northwest of Vladikavkaz to the north of the Caucasus, takes its name from the river on which it lies. The river name represents Ossetic *arra*, "furious," and *don*, "river," alluding to its fast-flowing and turbulent current.

Arensburg See **Kuressaare**.

Argayash (Аргая́ш) *Town, west central Russia*. The town, northwest of Chelyabinsk, takes its name from the lake on which it lies. According to some authorities, the lake's own name is of Bashkir origin and means literally "sun bank," from *yar*, "bank," and *koyash*, "sun." This could be understood literally, as "sunny bank," or metaphorically, as "beautiful bank." But this looks rather like a folk etymology, and an attempt to explain a name of uncertain meaning.

Argun (Аргу́нь) *River, southeastern Russia*. The river rises in Inner Mongolia, China, and flows generally north along the border between China and Russia to unite with the Shilka and form the Amur. Its name has been explained as deriving from Buryat *ergun*, "wide."

Arkhangelsk (Арха́нгельск) *City and port, northwestern Russia*. The city, long familiar in the West as *Archangel*, was founded by Ivan the Terrible in 1584 on the Northern Dvina at the head of the Dvina Gulf around the 12th-century monastery of St. Michael the *Archangel*. It was originally known as *Novyye Kholmogory*, "New Kholmogory," since it was intended to supersede the existing port of *Kholmogory* on this same river (but upstream, to the south). In 1613 it was given its present name, which despite its obvious religious provenance remained unchanged throughout the Soviet period.

Arkhangelskoye (Арха́нгельское) *Estate, western Russia*. The estate, west of Moscow, takes its name from the church of *Mikhail Arkhangel*, "St. Michael the Archangel," built here in the 1660s. The estate, with classical-style buildings and park, arose in the late 18th century as the work of Russian and European architects and was the property of various aristocratic owners, including the princely Golytsin family from 1703 to 1810 and the Yusupovs from 1810 to 1917. The estate is now a museum. The same name occurs for a number of places elsewhere in western Russia and usually has an identical origin.

Arkhipo-Osipovka (Архи́по-Оси́повка) *Town and resort, southwestern Russia*. The Black Sea resort, southwest of Krasnodar, is named for *Arkhip Osipov*, hero of the Russian conquest of the Caucasus (1817–64).

Armavir (Армави́р) *City, southwestern Russia*. The city, north of the Caucasus, was founded in 1839 when an Armenian colony was set up here. It was named for *Armavir*, the pre-second century B.C. capital and religious center of Urartu, the ancient kingdom north of Assyria that later became Armenia. The meaning of the historic name itself is uncertain.

Armenia (Арме́ния) *Republic, southeastern Europe*. The present republic evolved from the ancient kingdom between the Caspian Sea and the Black Sea that was known to exist in the 9th century B.C. The name *Armenia* is first recorded in a rock inscription of 521 B.C. near what is now the Iranian city of Kermanshah. It is that of the indigenous people, who themselves traditionally derive it from their legendary ancestor *Armenak*. Their own name for themselves, however, is *Hay*, which they similarly trace back to an ancient hero called *Hayg* or *Hayk*. (According to one account, Armenak was Hayg's son.) Neither of these names has yet been satisfactorily explained. The Armenian name for Armenia is thus *Hayastan*, "land of the Hay."

Armyansk (Армя́нск) *Village, northern Crimea, southern Ukraine*. The settlement, south of Perekop, arose in 1783 when Armenians and Greeks escaped here from the battle-wrecked Turkish fortress of Orkapi some 4 miles (7 km) away. It was at first known as *Armyanskiy bazar*, "Armenian market," but in the early 20th century this was shortened as now.

Arpa (Арпа́) *River, central Armenia*. The river, a tributary of the Araks, which here forms the border with Turkey, has a Turkic name meaning "barley." The river flows west through barley fields.

Arsenyev (Арсе́ньев) *Town, southeastern Russia*. The town, northeast of Vladivostok, was formed in 1953 from the village of *Semyonovka* and named in honor of the Russian explorer and writer Vladimir Klavdiyevich *Arsenyev* (1872–1930), who undertook many expeditions in this part of Russia, between

Manchuria and the Sea of Japan. (He was described by the Russian writer Maxim Gorky as "a cross between Brehm [the German zoologist] and Fenimore Cooper.")

Arsk (Арск) *Town, western Russia.* The town, in Tatarstan northeast of Kazan, takes its name from *Ur*, the indigenous Udmurt people's name for themselves. In their own language this means simply "people."

Artashat (Арташа́т) *Village, western Armenia.* The village, southeast of Yerevan, was formerly known as *Kamarlyu*. It adopted its present name in the 1950s from that of the ancient capital of Armenia that was located in this region. It was itself founded in 176 B.C. by the Armenian ruler *Artashes* (*Artaxas*) and named for him. It was subsequently destroyed by the Romans in A.D. 58.

Artek (Арте́к) *Resort, southern Crimea, southern Ukraine.* The Black Sea resort, northeast of Yalta and famous as a pioneer camp, arose on the site of the ancient Greek settlement of *Kardiatrikon*. Its present name is said to have evolved as a much distorted and truncated form of this. The meaning of the Greek name is uncertain. However, some authorities propose another origin: either in *Ortygia*, one of the bynames of the Greek goddess Artemis (from the island where she was born) or in Greek *ortux*, "quail," for the presence of these birds here.

Arti (Арти́) *Town, west central Russia.* The town, southwest of Nizhniye Sergi, takes its name from the river on which it lies, the *Artya*. The derivation of the river name is uncertain, but it is almost certainly of Turkic origin and could mean "pass." Arti itself is in a deep hollow surrounded by mountains.

Artsiz (Арци́з) *Town, southern Ukraine.* The town, northeast of Izmail, was founded in 1816 and named for the 1814 victory of Russia and her allies over the French forces of Napoleon near *Arcis*-sur-Aube, northeast of Troyes, France.

Artyom (Артём) *Town, southeastern Russia.* The town, northeast of Vladivostok, was founded in 1924 as a mining settlement and named for *Artyom*, the party nickname of F. A. Sergeyev (see **Artyomovsk**).

Artyom Island (Артёма о́стров) *Island, Caspian Sea, Russia.* The island, near the Apsheron peninsula, was originally known as *Svyatoy ostrov*, "Holy Island." It was renamed for *Artyom*, the party nickname of F. A. Sergeyev (see **Artyomovsk**).

Artyomovsk (Артёмовск) *City, eastern Ukraine.* The city, in the Donbass north of Donetsk, was originally known as *Bakhmut* (Бахму́т), for the river on which it stands. In 1924 it was renamed for *Artyom*, the party nickname adopted by the Communist leader and Donbass miners' union president Fyodor Andreyevich Sergeyev (1883-1921), who headed the local defense headquarters here in 1919 during the Civil War. (He was killed testing a new type of passenger plane and as a vintage Bolshevik was buried in Moscow's Red Square.)

Artyomovsky (Артёмовский) *Town, west central Russia.* The town, northeast of Yekaterinburg, arose in 1938 and took its name from the mining settlement of *Artyom*, itself named in 1921 for the party pseudonym of the Bolshevik leader Fyodor Andreyevich Sergeyev (1883-1921), who was politically active in the Urals in 1906. See also **Artyomovsk**.

Arzamas (Арзама́с) *Town, western Russia.* The town, south of Nizhny Novgorod and dating from 1578, has a name that is probably ethnic in origin, although some authorities link its last element with Hungarian *mező*, "field." Until 1991 a town code-named *Arzamas*-16, a nuclear research center, existed on the site of the earlier (and present) **Sarov**, a Moldovan town some 40 miles (64 km) southwest of Arzamas.

Asbest (Асбе́ст) *Town, west central Russia.* The town, east of Yekaterinburg, arose around a rich source of asbestos deposits, discovered in 1885. It was at first named *Kudelka* (Куде́лька), from a local term for asbestos that translates literally as "rock tow," but on gaining urban status in 1933 was renamed for the mineral that had caused its original emergence.

Asha (Аша́) *Town, southwestern Russia.* The town, northeast of Chernikovsk, takes its name from the river here. Its own name has been derived from Turkic *asha*, "through," "across," said to refer to its course through the mountains. But this may well be an attempt to explain a name of uncertain origin.

Ashkhabad (Ашхаба́д) *Capital of Turkmenistan.* The city, in the south of the republic, has a name representing Turkmen *uskh*, "dear" (related to Arabic *'ishk*, "love"), and *abad*, "inhabited place" (a word of Iranian origin, as for *Abadan*, *Islamabad*, *Hyderabad*, and other Asian cities.) The sense can thus be interpreted as "place of delight," "abode of love." The present town arose in 1881 as a military post on the site of the ancient settlement of *Askhabad* and adopted its name. In 1919 the city was renamed *Poltoratsk* (Полтора́цк) in honor of Pavel Gerasimovich *Poltoratsky* (1888–1918), a revolutionary active in Turkestan killed by counterrevolutionary forces during the Civil War. It became the capital in 1924, and in 1927 reverted to its original name.

Askaniya-Nova (Аска́ния-Но́ва) *Village and nature reserve, southern Ukraine.* The nature reserve, southeast of Kakhovka, was founded in 1875 as a sheep farm and wildlife sanctuary by F. E. Falts-Feyn, a German-born Russian landowner, who gave it the Roman name, *Ascania*, of his native state of Anhalt, then in Prussia, now in eastern Germany. The name is thus Latin, meaning "New Ascania." The name passed from the reserve to the village. The local name of the reserve is *Chapli*, from its location on the slopes of the Bolshoy *Chapelsky* Foothills.

Askarovo (Аска́рово) *Town, southwestern Russia.* The town, west of Magnitogorsk, derives its name from the Turkic male name *Askar*, itself apparently from Arabic *asrar*, "younger," or *asker*, "warrior."

Askhabad See **Ashkhabad**.

Askino (А́скино) *Village, southwestern Russia.* The village, north of Chernikovsk, takes its name from the small *Askyn* River here. The river name is said to represent Bashkir *ak*, "white," and *syn*, "statue," although there is no good authority for this.

Assake See **Leninsk**.

Astapovo See **Lev Tolstoy**.

Astrakhan (А́страхань) *City, southwestern Russia.* The city, on the Volga delta at the northern end of the Caspian Sea, dates from at least the 13th century. Despite copious documentation of the name, such as *Agitarcam* on a map of 1375, its origin and meaning remain obscure. The 14th-century Arab traveler ibn-Batuta derived it from Turkic words corresponding to modern Turkish *hacı*, "pilgrim," and *tarhan*, "free of taxes," meaning that a Muslim pilgrim had settled here and that the town had arisen subsequently. The evolution of *Astrakhan* from these words need not necessarily be ruled out. The traditional origin is in Persian words meaning "star city."

Astrakhan-Bazar See **Dzhalilabad**.

Atbasar (Атбасáр) *Town, north central Kazakhstan*. The town, southwest of Kokchetav, takes its name from Kazakh *at*, "horse," and *basar*, the participial form of *basmak*, "to trample." The place arose in the steppes on the site of a corral and was well known for its horse markets.

Atkarsk (Аткáрск) *Town, western Russia*. The town, northwest of Saratov, was originally known as *Yetkara*, and was recorded as such in the 14th century. The name is that of the *Itkara* River here, itself traditionally associated with that of *Itkar*, a commander of the Golden Horde. The town gained its present name in 1780.

Auezov (Ауэ́зов) *Town, eastern Kazakhstan*. The town, southwest of Ust-Kamenogorsk, arose as a gold-mining settlement called *Bakyrchik* (Бакырчи́к). In 1967 it was renamed as now for the Kazakh writer Mukhtar Omarkhanovich *Auezov* (1897–1961).

Aulie-Ata See **Dzhambul**.

Ay (Ай) *River, west central Russia*. The river, a tributary of the Ufa to the west of the Southern Urals, derives its name from Bashkir *ay*, "moon." In Turkic languages this has the metaphorical sense "beautiful," which here could mean either a river flowing through a picturesque landscape, or one with shining waters, as if reflecting the moon. However, an origin has also been proposed in the name of the *Ay*, a Bashkir people, whose symbol, coincidentally, is a crescent.

Ayan (Аян) *Port, eastern Russia*. The port, southwest of Okhotsk on the Sea of Okhotsk, has a name representing Evenki *ayan*, "bay."

Ay Petri (Ай-Пе́три) *Mountain, southern Crimea, southern Ukraine*. The mountain, southwest of Yalta, has a name deriving from a Turkic form (modern Turkish *aziz*) of Greek *hagios*, "saint," and *Petri*, "Peter," so that the meaning is "[mountain of] St. Peter." Cf. **Ay Todor**.

Ay Todor (Ай-Тодо́р) *Mountain, southern Crimea, southern Ukraine*. The mountain, southwest of Yalta, derives its name from a Turkic form (modern Turkish *aziz*) of Greek *hagios*, "saint," and *Todor*, "Theodore." The meaning is thus "[mountain of] St. Theodore." Cf. **Ay Petri**.

Ayu Dag (Аюда́г) *Mountain, southern Crimea, southern Ukraine*. The mountain, southwest of Yalta, has a Tatar name meaning "bear mountain," from *ayu*, "bear" (modern Turkish *ayı*), and *dag*, "mountain" (Turkish *dağ*). The mountain's outline suggests a bear stooping to drink from the Black Sea. Cf. **Medvezhyegorsk**.

Azanka (Аза́нка) *Village, west central Russia*. The village, northwest of Tyumen, takes its name from the small river here, a tributary of the Tavda. The river name appears to represent the Tatar male name *Azan*, a form of the Arabic name *Hasan*.

Azerbaijan (Азербайджа́н) *Republic, central Asia*. The republic, bounded by Georgia to the north, the Caspian Sea to the east, Iran to the south, and Armenia to the west, is an ancient one, and is mentioned by classical writers as *Antropatana* or *Atropatena*. A Persian manuscript of the 3rd century A.D. has the name as *Aturpatakan*. This is said to derive from the personal name *Atropates*, that of a general who proclaimed the independence of this land in the time of Alexander the Great. The origin may more realistically be in local words *azar*, "fire," and *baydjan*, the latter from Persian *baykān*, "guardian." This would give a meaning "guardian of the fire," referring to an ancient cult of fire worship here. Finally, the name has been traced back to an ancestral eponym *Azerbad*, said to be the son of Ebran, son of Aswad, son of the biblical Shem (the son of Noah).

Azizbekov (Азизбéков) *Town, south central Armenia*. The town, southeast of Yerevan, was founded in 1956 and named for the Azerbaijani revolutionary Meshad Azim-bek-ogly *Azizbekov* (1876-1918), one of the so called "26 Baku commissars" executed during the Civil War.

Azov (Азóв) *Town, southwestern Russia*. The town, near the mouth of the Don River on the Sea of **Azov**, has a name traditionally explained as commemorating the Polovtsian prince *Azum* or *Azuf*, slain when the Polovtsian armies captured the town in 1067. However, it almost certainly predates this, and may derive from a word related to modern Turkish *aşağı*, "lower," referring to the location of the town on the lower reaches of the Don.

Azov, Sea of (Азóвское мóре) *Sea, southeastern Ukraine/southwestern Russia*. The sea, a shallow northern arm of the Black Sea, takes its present name from the town of **Azov**, on its northeastern shore. The Roman name for it was *Maeotis Palus*, "Maeotian Marsh," for the *Maeotae*, the people who lived on its southern and eastern shores. The Arabic name was *Baḥr al-Azow*, from *baḥr*, "sea," and a word that became associated with Arabic *al-lāzaward*, "the blue," which itself gave English *azure*. This produced an alternate Russian name for the sea as *Sineye more*, "Blue Sea."

Babadag (Бабадáг) *Mountain, northeastern Azerbaijan*. The mountain, at the eastern end of the Caucasus, has a name of Turkic origin meaning "father mountain," from words related to modern Turkish *baba*, "father," and *dağ*, "mountain."

Babushkin[1] (Бáбушкин) *Town, southern Russia*. The present town, on the northern shore of Lake Baykal, was originally a station on the Siberian railroad. The station was named *Mysovaya*, from Russian *mys*, "promontory." The settlement that arose was named *Mysovsk* (Мы́совск), and in 1941 this was renamed as now to commemorate the Bolshevik revolutionary Ivan Vasilyevich *Babushkin* (1873-1906), who after leading an armed uprising in Chita was captured and executed at the station here by czarist forces when railroading arms and ammunition ahead to Irkutsk.

Babushkin[2] (Бáбушкин) *District, Moscow, western Russia*. The northeastern district of Moscow, from 1925 to 1960 an independent town, was given its present name in 1939 for the Soviet polar air pilot Mikhail Sergeyevich *Babushkin* (1893-1938), who was born in the locality and who was killed in an air crash. The original name of the village here was *Losinoostrovsky*, so called from the nature reserve founded here in the 16th century and long known as *Losiny Ostrov*, "Elk Island." (Elk are still preserved in the wildlife park here.) On gaining town status in 1925 the village name was modified slightly to *Losinoostrovsk* (Лосиноострóвск).

Badakhshan (Бадахшáн) *Autonomous republic, southern Tajikistan*. The republic has the same name as the province of *Badakhshan* in northeastern Afghanistan, across the frontier to the south. Its meaning is traditionally explained as "ruby mountains," from the similarity of the first part of the name to Persian *badash*, "ruby." This interpretation has been questioned by some authorities, but appears to be supported by the ruby deposits found in the Afghan region.

Badkhyz (Бадхы́з) *Plateau, southern Turkmenistan*. The semi-desert region of low mountains, by the border with Afghanistan, has a name of Tajik or Persian origin meaning "bad hills," alluding to its barrenness. The province of *Badghiz*, northern Afghanistan, has a name of identical origin.

Bagdadi (Багда́ди) *Town, west central Georgia*. The town, southeast of Kutaisi, has an Iranian name meaning "gift of God" (as for the Iraqi capital, *Bagdad*). In 1940 it was renamed *Mayakovsky* (Маяко́вский), for the Soviet poet Vladimir Vladimirovich *Mayakovsky* (1893–1930), who was born here. It reverted to its original name in 1991.

Bagrationovsk (Багратио́новск) *Town, western Russia*. The town, southeast of Kaliningrad on the border with Poland, was founded in 1336 and was formerly in East Prussia, when it was known as *Preussisch Eylau*, "Prussian Eylau." The latter word is of Slavic origin and means "mud," "silt" (Russian *il*). In 1946 the town was renamed as now in honor of the Russian general Pyotr Ivanovich *Bagration* (1765–1812), who led the Russian army here in the 1807 Battle of Eylau against the forces of Napoleon.

Baikal, Lake See **Baykal, Lake**.

Bakal (Бака́л) *Town, west central Russia*. The town, west of Chelyabinsk, is in the southern foothills of the Central Urals. Its name alludes to its location, from a Turkic word meaning "high."

Bakhchisaray (Бахчисара́й) *Town, southern Crimea, southern Ukraine*. The town, southwest of Simferopol, has a name of Turkic origin meaning "garden palace," i.e. a palace among gardens, from words related to modern Turkish *bahçe*, "garden," and *saray*, "palace" (as in English *caravanserai*). The name arose in the late 15th century when Bakhchisaray became the capital of the Tatar khanate (to 1783).

Bakhmut See **Artyomovsk**.

Baksan (Бакса́н) *River, southwestern Russia*. The river, rising in the central Caucasus, has a name that has inspired much colorful speculation, such as an origin in Cherkess *bakhe*, "steam," and *sana*, "wine," or a Turkic word meaning "just look," related to modern Turkish *bakım*, "glance," or *bakmak*, "to look at." The true origin of the name is uncertain.

Baku (Баку́) *Capital of Azerbaijan*. The city and oil port, in the east of the republic on the Caspian Sea, has an ancient name that remains of disputed origin and meaning. Two possible versions are currently under consideration. One is a source in a Turkic word meaning "hill." The other is a derivation in the name of the *Bakan* people who inhabited the Apsheron peninsula in historic times and who were known to be fire worshippers.

Bakyrchik See **Auezov**.

Balabanovo (Балаба́ново) *Town, western Russia*. The town, southwest of Moscow, derives its name from a personal name or nickname, itself coming from Russian *balaban*, meaning either "large falcon," "stallion," or "booby," "blockhead." The surname *Balabanov* is recorded in 1585 for an inhabitant of Arzamas.

Balakhna (Балахна́) *Town, western Russia*. The town, on the Volga northwest of Nizhny Novgorod, has a name of uncertain origin. It may derive from Russian *balakhon*, a term for a loose overall or baggy clothing generally, given as a nickname to a person who was an early settler here. The town has existed since 1536.

Balaklava (Балаклáва) *Town and port, southern Crimea, southern Ukraine*. The town, a Black Sea port southeast of Sevastopol, was known to Greek writers such as Strabo and Ptolemy as *Symbolon*, apparently representing Greek *sumbolon*, "sign," "mark" (literally "a coming together"). This developed into the 14th-century Genoese colony of *Cembalo*. The present name has been explained as deriving from Turkic words meaning "fish nest" (modern Turkish *balık*, "fish," and *yuva*, "nest"). This would refer to the rich fishing grounds that indeed exist off the coast here. But the forms of the words do not square with the present name, and some other origin should probably be sought.

Balashikha (Балашúха) *Town, western Russia*. The town, on the eastern outskirts of Moscow, has a name that appears to be based on Russian dialect *balakh*, "kingcup," "marsh marigold" (*Caltha palustris*). This flower either grew abundantly here or perhaps had its name given as a nickname to a local healer, who would have used the plant in her herbal remedies.

Balashov (Балашóв) *Town, southwestern Russia*. The town, west of Saratov, arose from the village of *Balashovo* that belonged to the medieval prince Ivan *Balashov*, who owned land and settlements on the Khoper River here. The village was raised to town status in 1780 and took the present form of its name then.

Balkaria See **Kabardino-Balkaria**.

Balkhash, Lake (Балхáш) *Lake, southeastern Kazakhstan*. The name represents a Kazakh or ultimately Tatar word meaning "marshy place." The town of *Balkhash* on the lake's northern shore arose in 1937 from a copper smelting works and is named for it.

Balta (Бáлта) *Town, southwestern Ukraine*. The town, northwest of Odessa, is not far from the Moldovan frontier and has a Moldovan name, from *balte*, "marsh." Balta lies on low ground on a tributary of the Bug River. In 1795 the town was renamed *Yelensk* (Елéнск), for Princess *Yelena* Pavlovna, a granddaughter of Catherine the Great, but reverted to its old name in Soviet times. Cf. **Olgopol**, **Yekaterinopol**.

Baltic Sea (Балтúйское мóре) *Sea, northern Europe*. On its southern and eastern sides, the sea extends along the coasts of Lithuania, Latvia, Estonia, and northwestern Russia. Its name remains of disputed origin, but could relate to Lithuanian *baltas* or Latvian *balts*, "white," referring to the pale sands of its coasts. Its Old Russian name was *Varyazhskoye more*, "Varangian Sea," for the *Varangians*, the Scandinavian people who invaded and settled parts of Russia from the 8th century. It was also at one time known as the *Sveyskoye more*, "Suevian Sea," for the *Suevi*, the Germanic peoples who gave the name of *Sweden*, which lies on its northern side. The Swedish name for it is *Östersjön*, "Eastern Sea," while the Estonian name, conversely, is *Läänemeri*, "Western Sea."

Baltiysk (Балтúйск) *Town, western Russia*. The town, west of Kaliningrad, was founded in 1686 and takes its present name from the **Baltic Sea** on which it is located. Before 1946, when in East Prussia, it was known as *Pillau*, a name of uncertain origin. Cf. **Paldiski**, the town's northern counterpart.

Baltiysky Port See **Paldiski**.

Baltser See **Krasnoarmeysk**.

Bam (Бам) *Village, southeastern Russia*. The village, northwest of Skovorodino, grew around the railroad station constructed in 1933 at the junction of the Transsiberian Railway and the new Baykal-Amur Magistral (Russian *Bajkalo-Amurskaya magistral'*), taking its name from *BAM*, the common acronym for the latter. The railroad itself was so designated at the planning stage in 1930. Since it was not then certain precisely from where or to where it would eventually run, it was named generally for Lake *Baykal*, at the western end, and the *Amur* River, in the east. The acronym *BAM* is first recorded in 1932, and the railroad station *Bam* was the first on the new line. (English *magistral* here renders Russian *magistral'*, "main road," "main line," itself ultimately from Latin *magistralis*, "main.")

Baranovichi (Барáновичи) *Town, west central Belarus*. The town, southwest of Minsk, arose as a village in the 1870s and is presumably named for the original landowner, with family name *Baranovich*.

Barents Sea (Бáренцево мóре) *Sea, Arctic Ocean*. The sea, between Svalbard, Norway, and Novaya Zemlya, Russia, is named commemoratively for the Dutch explorer Willem *Barents* (c. 1550–1597), who commanded the expedition that in 1594 reached Novaya Zemlya in the search for a northeast passage to Asia. Barents perished in the Arctic when his ship became trapped in ice after rounding Novaya Zemlya on a third voyage in 1596. The name is first recorded on a chart published in 1853.

Barnaul (Барнаýл) *Town, southern Russia*. The town, south of Novosibirsk, arose in 1738 around a silver-smelting works. It takes its name from the river here, itself said to be of Ket origin and meaning "wolf river," from *boruan*, "wolves," and *ul*, "river."

Baronsk See **Marks**.

Barsa-Kelmes (Барсакельмéс) *Island, Aral Sea, southwestern Kazakhstan*. The island lies in the north central part of the lake and has a Turkic name said to mean "if you go you will not come back," referring to its relative inaccessibility. There is a saltmarsh of the same name southwest of the Aral Sea in western Uzbekistan.

Bashanta See **Gorodovikovsk**.

Bashkiria See **Bashkortostan**.

Bashkortostan (Башкортостáн) *Republic, western Russia*. The republic, to the west of the Southern Urals, and familiar to the early 1990s as *Bashkiria* (Башкúрия), has a Turkic name meaning "land of the *Bashkorts*." The origin of the people's own name is uncertain. It may derive from Turkic words that gave modern Turkish *baş*, "head," "chief," and *kurt*, "wolf," referring to an ancient cult of the wolf as a totemic animal. A wolf's head is known to have been the emblem of local Bashkir leaders until as recently as the 19th century.

Batalpashinsk See **Cherkessk**.

Batumi (Батýми) *City and port, southwestern Georgia*. The city, on the Black Sea near the Turkish border, is the capital of Adzharia and is of ancient origin. The Roman writer Pliny the Elder mentions a port here named *Batis*, as if from Greek *bathus*, "deep," but this is an attempt to explain the name, which is probably from a word related to modern Svan *bat*, "rock." In medieval times, the name was recorded in the form *Batomi*. This became *Batum* in 1878 and *Batumi* in 1939.

Baturin (Батýрин) *Town, northern Ukraine*. The town, northwest of

Konotop, was founded as a Polish defensive post in 1625 and named for the Hungarian-born king of Poland Stephen *Báthory* (1533-1586).

Baumanabad See **Pyandzh**.

Baydarsky Pass (Байда́рские воро́та) *Mountain pass, southern Crimea, southern Ukraine.* The pass, on the Sevastopol to Yalta road, is named for the nearby village of *Baydary*. The second part of the name is of Turkic origin and means "ravine" (cf. modern Turkish *dere*, "stream"). The first part (*Bay-*) is of uncertain meaning.

Baykal, Lake (Байка́л) *Lake, southern Russia.* The large lake, north of Mongolia, has a name traditionally derived from Turkic words meaning "rich lake" (modern Turkish *bol*, "abundant," and *göl*, "lake"), referring to its rich stocks of fish. However, the name is very likely Yakut in origin, representing *baykhal* or *baygal*, literally "big water," in other words "sea." Large inland lakes in Russia are often known as sea, even to non-Russians, e.g. Aral Sea, Caspian Sea.

Bayram-Ali (Байра́м-Али́) *Town, eastern Turkmenistan.* The town, east of Mary, was founded in 1935 and given a religious name meaning "festival of Ali," deriving from a Turkic word meaning "holiday" (modern Turkish *bayram*) and the name of *Ali*, son-in-law of Muhammad, founder of Islam, and revered by the Shi'ite branch of Islam as his true successor.

Bear Islands (Медве́жьи острова́) *Island group, East Siberian Sea, northeastern Russia.* The group of six small islands, north of the mouth of the Kolyma River, is named for the polar bears seen here by early explorers.

Bednodemyanovsk (Беднодемья́новск) *Town, western Russia.* The town, northeast of Tambov, arose on the site of the village of *Bogdanovo*, known since 1647. It was subsequently renamed *Spasskoe* for the local church, dedicated to St. Savior (Russian *Spas*, "Savior"), and in 1779 was raised to town status as *Spassk* (Спасск). In 1925 it was given its present name, commemorating the Soviet poet *Demyan Bedny* (1883-1945) (real name Yefim Alekseyevich Pridvorov), although he was not born here. The poet's pseudonym translates literally as "Demyan the Poor," and despite the literary tribute it is strange that a placename with the negative element *Bedno-* should have been chosen for a Soviet renaming.

Begoml (Бего́мль) *Town, north central Belarus.* The town, north of Borisov, is in a somewhat isolated location, which gives grounds for deriving its name from the Russian root *beg-*, meaning "run," "escape." If so, the settlement could have arisen as a place of refuge for fugitives.

Begovat See **Bekabad**.

Bekabad (Бекаба́д) *Town, eastern Uzbekistan.* The town, northeast of Kokand, has a Turkic name meaning "town of the beg," the latter being a form of *bey*, the title of a Turkish governor. The town arose in 1945 on the site of the small Uzbek village of *Begovat* (Белова́т) and until 1964 was known under this form of the name.

Belarus (Белару́сь) *Republic, eastern Europe.* Until gaining independence in 1991 under its present indigenous name, the country was familiar as the former Soviet republic of *Byelorussia* (or *Belorussia* (Белору́ссия), formed in 1919, and also generally under its English name of *White Russia*. This certainly translates the present name, but the exact sense of "white" remains disputed. The name was recorded as long ago as the 12th century, but the location of the region so designated varied, and is first recorded for the present territory in a 14th-century Polish document. As *Belaya Rus'*, the name seems to have arisen by contrast with that of a neighboring territory called *Chyornaya Rus'*, "Black Russia." This has not been precisely located, however. Possibly the White Russians simply distinguished themselves on social, linguistic or religious grounds from their "Black" neighbors, so that they were the "pure" people while the others were "tainted."

Belaya (Бе́лая) *River, southwestern Russia*. The river rises in the Southern Urals and flows generally west and northwest to enter the Kama south of Sarapul. Its name is the Russian word for "white," as a translation of its Turkic name *Ak-Itil*, from *ak*, "white," and *Itil*, an alternate name of the Volga, as opposed to some other river (or to an upper stretch of the Volga) named *Kara-Itil*, "black Itil." There are other rivers named *Belaya* elsewhere in Russia.

Belaya Tserkov (Бе́лая Це́рковь) *Town, northern Ukraine*. The town, south of Kiev, has a Russian name meaning "white church." It is first mentioned in 1155 and to the end of the 14th century was known as *Yuryev*. The local bishop had his seat here, and the ruins of his whitewalled church served as a landmark for travelers headed north from the Black Sea to Kiev.

Belgorod (Бе́лгород) *City, southwestern Russia*. The city, north of Kharkov, was founded as a fortified settlement in 1593 and given a name found commonly elsewhere meaning "white settlement" (modern Russian *belyj*, "white," and *gorod*, "town"). There have been various interpretations of "white." One theory claims that the reference is to water, since all towns named Belgorod (including Belgrade, capital of Serbia) are by water. Another holds that the adjective is intended figuratively to mean "beautiful." A third theory gives "white" the sense of "western." However, the true origin for this particular place is probably more prosaic. There are chalkpits in the vicinity, and the town's original fortifications were built with stone hewn from cretaceous rocks.

Belgorod-Dnestrovsky (Бе́лгород-Днестро́вский) *City, southwestern Ukraine*. The city, southwest of Odessa, is an ancient one with a basic Slavic name meaning "white city" (cf. **Belgorod**). The Greek settlement of *Tyras* existed on the site of the present town in the 6th century B.C. In the 13th century it was captured by the Tatars, who called it *Ak-Libo*, "white fort." On 14th-century Genoese maps, however, it appears under the Greek name of *Maurocastron*, "black fortress." In 1484 it was captured by the Turks who renamed it *Akkerman* (Аккерма́н), "white fort" (Turkish *ak*, "white," and *kerman*, "fort"). This name generally remained until 1944 when it was renamed as now, with the second part of the name meaning "of the Dniester," referring to its location on the estuary of this river and distinguishing it from other places named *Belgorod*. Under Romanian occupation from 1918 to 1940 the town was known by the equivalent name of *Cetatea Albă*, from Romanian *cetate*, "city," and the feminine form of *alb*, "white."

Belinsky (Бели́нский) *Town, southwestern Russia*. The town, west of Penza and south of Moscow, was earlier known as *Chembar* (Чемба́р). This comes from the *Malyj Chembar* River on which the village was built. There is a Russian dialect word, *chembary*, used for a type of baggy leather trousers, and it may be that the union of the Chembar and Malyj ("Little") Chembar here suggested the legs of a pair of trousers. In 1948 the town was renamed as now to mark the centenary of the death of the Russian literary critic Vissarion Grigoryevich *Belinsky* (1811–1848), whose family moved here in 1816 from Sveaborg in what was then Russia but is now (as Suomenlinna) Finland.

Belkovsky Island (Бельковский остров) *Island, New Siberian Islands, northeastern Russia*. The island, the westernmost in the group, was discovered in 1808 by a Yakut trader, Nikolay Semyonovich *Belkov* (?–?), and is named for him.

Belogorsk[1] (Белогорск) *Town, eastern Russia*. The town, northeast of Blagoveshchensk, has a name found elsewhere in the former Soviet Union meaning "white mountain" (Russian *belyj*, "white," and *gora*, "mountain"). The town was founded in 1860 and until 1935 was known as *Aleksandrovsk* (Александровск). From 1935 until 1957, when it received its present name, it was known as *Kuybyshevka-Vostochnaya* (Куйбышевка-Восточная), "Eastern Kuybyshevka," the latter name commemorating the Communist leader V. V. *Kuybyshev* (see **Kuybyshev**).

Belogorsk[2] (Белогорск) *Town, southern Crimea, southern Ukraine*. The town, southeast of Simferopol, has a name meaning "white mountain" (Russian *belyj*, "white," and *gora*, "mountain). Until 1944 it was known as *Karasubazar* (Карасубазар), meaning "Karasu market," from the name of the *Karasu* River on which it is located (itself of Turkic origin and meaning "black water") and a Persian word that gave the English *bazaar*.

Belomorsk (Беломорск) *Town and port, northwestern Russia*. The town, west of Arkhangelsk, is a port on the **White Sea** (Russian *Beloye more*) and takes its name from it. It arose in 1938 on the site of the coastal settlement of *Soroka* (Сорока), so named from the river on which it lies. The river name has been influenced by Russian *soroka*, "magpie," but actually represents Karelian *sarajoki* or *saari-joki*, "river of sedge" or "river of islands."

Beloozyorsk (Белоозёрск) *Town, southwestern Belarus*. The town, northeast of Brest, takes its name from the lake by which it lies. This is named *Beloye ozero*, "white lake," presumably for the purity or clarity of its water.

Belorechensk (Белореченск) *Town, southwestern Russia*. The town, southeast of Krasnodar, takes its name from the **Belaya** River (Russian *Belaya reka*) on which it is located. Cf. **Beloretsk**. It arose from the Cossack fortress of *Belorechenskaya* that was set up here in 1862 and that was itself named for the river. The resulting settlement was raised to town status in 1958 and the present form of the name was taken then.

Beloretsk (Белорецк) *Town, west central Russia*. The town, northwest of Magnitogorsk in the Southern Urals, lies on the upper reaches of the **Belaya** River (Russian *Belaya reka*) and is named for it. It arose from the iron works set up here in 1762 and in turn named for the river as the *Beloretsky zavod*, "Belaya works." The present form of the name was given in 1923 when the settlement was raised to town status. Cf. **Belorechensk**.

Belorussia See **Belarus**.

Beloshchelye See **Naryan-Mar**.

Belotsarsk See **Kyzyl**.

Beloye Ozero (Белое озеро) *Lake, northwestern Russia*. The lake, east of St. Petersburg, has a name meaning simply "white lake" (Russian *belyj*, "white," and *ozero*, "lake").

The name is an old one and is probably a translation of a Finno-Ugrian name. There are several lakes in the former Soviet Union named "white," often for the color of the water but in some cases possibly in a sense "holy." This particular lake is also not all that far south of the **White Sea**.

Belozyorsk (Белозёрск) *Town, northwestern Russia*. The town, east of St. Petersburg, takes its name from the **Beloye Ozero** lake on which it is located.

Beltsy (Бе́льцы) *Town, north central Moldova*. The town, northwest of Kishinyov, arose in the 15th century and has a name meaning "swamp," "marsh," from a Moldovan word related to Russian *boloto* in this sense.

Belukha (Белу́ха) *Mountain, southern Russia*. The mountain lies in the Altay mountain system near the border with Kazakhstan. Its name is based on Russian *belyj*, "white," and refers to its white peaks, with their many glaciers and snow-clad slopes. The Kazakh name for it is similar: *Mus-du-tau*, "ice mountain."

Bely (Бе́лый) *Town, western Russia*. The town, west of Moscow, has a name that means "white." This does not necessarily refer to the color of the soil or of its buildings, but could also denote a town that was exempt from particular tolls or taxes. It is not clear what the sense is in this particular case. The town is known to have existed in 1359.

Belyov (Белёв) *Town, western Russia*. The town, south of Kaluga, was raised to urban status in 1777. The origin of its name is uncertain. It may derive from the dialect term *belyovaya zemlya*, "white earth," referring to the sterile gray-white soil or podzol here. It could not come from *belyj*, "white," since this would have given a name identical to that of **Bely** (above).

Bendery (Бенде́ры) *Town, southeastern Moldova*. The town, southwest of Tiraspol, lies on the Dniester River and has a Turkic name meaning "harbor," from a word *bender* that was itself borrowed from Iranian. The town was a Genoese trading center in the 12th century and when part of Bessarabia, Romania, from 1918 to 1940, was known as *Tighina*. The meaning of this is not known.

Bennett Island (Бе́ннетта о́стров) *Island, De Long Islands, northeastern Russia*. The westernmost island in the group was discovered in 1881 by De Long's expedition (see **De Long Islands**) and named for the expedition's sponsor, the American editor and philanthropist James Gordon *Bennett* (1841-1918). See also **Henrietta Island, Jeannette Island**.

Berdichev (Берди́чев) *Town, west central Ukraine*. The town, south of Zhitomir, is said to take its name either from a Slavic word *berda* meaning "hill" (modern Serbo-Croat *brdo*) or "steep slope," "precipice." But the fact that the name ends in the possessive suffix *-ev* may indicate an origin in the personal name *Berdich*.

Berdyansk (Бердя́нск) *Town, southeastern Ukraine*. The town, a port and resort on the Sea of Azov southwest of Mariupol, was founded in 1827 and presumably named for a landowner here. In 1939 it was renamed *Osipenko* (Осипе́нко), commemorating the Soviet airwoman Polina Denisovna *Osipenko* (1907-1939), who was born in the village of Novospasovka (now also *Osipenko*), some 11 miles (17 km) north of Berdyansk, and who lost her life in a flying accident. The town reverted to its earlier name in 1958.

Berezan (Березáнь) *Island, Black Sea, southern Ukraine.* The island is a small one near the northern Black Sea coast east of Odessa. Its name may derive from an Iranian (perhaps Scythian) word *brezant*, "high," referring to its steep cliffs. But it could equally have evolved from the Greek name of the Dnieper River that enters the sea here. This was *Boristhenes*, which could also have given the name of the **Berezina** River.

Berezina (Березинá) *River, central Belarus.* The river, a tributary of the Dnieper, has a name that suggests a Slavic word meaning "birch" (Russian *beryoza*). But it is possible the name actually evolved from an earlier name of the **Dnieper**, which was known to the Greeks as *Boristhenes*, as if meaning "from the north," from Greek *boreas*, "north," and the suffix *-then*, denoting motion from a place. However, this was probably an attempt to explain an earlier name. See also **Berezan**.

Berezniki (Березникú) *Town, western Russia.* The town, just west of the Middle Urals, takes its name from the Slavic word for "birch" (Russian *beryoza*). Cf. **Beryozovo**, also **Vyazniki**.

Beringovsky (Бéринговский) *Town, eastern Russia.* The town and port, southeast of Anadyr on Anadyr Bay, an inlet of the Bering Sea, arose in 1941 as a coal-mining settlement. Hence its original name of *Ugolny* (Ýгольный), the adjectival form of *ugol'*, "coal." In 1957 it was renamed as now for its proximity to the **Bering Sea**.

Bering Sea (Бéрингово мóре) *Sea, northern North Atlantic.* The sea, between Russia and Alaska, is named for the Danish navigator Vitus Bering (1681–1741), who was employed by the Russian czar Peter the Great to establish whether Russia and North America were geographically connected. He discovered that they were not when he sailed through the *Bering Strait*, also named for him, in 1728. Bering died on one of the **Commander Islands** (which see). The sea name was proposed in 1778 by the German traveler and writer Georg Forster, who had accompanied Captain Cook on his voyage round the world a few years previously. The name did not become generally current until the 19th century, however. The earlier name of the sea was the Kamchatka Sea (see **Kamchatka**).

Bering Strait See **Bering Sea**.

Beryozovo (Берёзово) *Town, west central Russia.* The town, east of the Northern Urals, arose as a Cossack fortress in the late 16th century. Its present name, meaning "birch" (Russian *beryoza*) is a translation of its Mansi name *Khal-ush* or Khanti name *Sumgut-vazh*, from *khal* or *sumgut*, both meaning "birch."

Beshtau (Бештáу) *Mountain, southwestern Russia.* The mountain, in the northern Caucasus near Pyatigorsk, has a Turkic name meaning "five mountains" (modern Turkish *beş*, "five," and *dağ*, "mountain"), referring to its five peaks. It was this mountain that gave the name of **Pyatigorsk** itself.

Bessarabia (Бессарáбия) *Historic region, Moldova/Ukraine.* The region that now corresponds to Moldova and part of Ukraine was originally a much larger territory extending north from the Black Sea to Poland. In Roman times it was part of the province of Dacia. At the end of the 14th century its southern part became part of Walachia. Hence its name, from the *Basarab* dynasty of Walachian princes. Their own name comes from Turkish *basar*, related to *baskı*, "oppression" (appropriately enough, considering the region's subsequent turbulent history).

Betpak-Dala (Бет-Пак-Далá) *Steppe region, southeastern Kazakhstan*. The region, between the Aral Sea and Lake Balkhash, has a name said to mean either "marshy plain" or "plain of danger," from Turkic *batpak*, "marshy," or Persian *bet-pak*, "evil," "danger," and Turkic *dala*, "plain." The Russian name of the region is *Golodnaya step'* (Голóдная степь), "Hunger Steppe." The plain has many salty lakes and is virtually uninhabited.

Bezhetsk (Бéжецк) *Town, western Russia*. The town, north of Moscow, was originally known as *Gorodetsko*, "township," a name recorded in a Novgorod manuscript of about 1138. From the 14th century it adopted various forms of a name that settled to the present *Bezhetsk*, said to relate to its founding by settlers who had fled (Russian *beglets*, "fugitive") here from Novgorod.

Bezhitsa (Бéжица) *Town, southwestern Russia*. The town lies immediately northwest of Bryansk, and officially became part of that city in 1956. The origin of the name is uncertain. From 1935 to 1943 the town was renamed *Ordzhonikidzegrad* (Орджоникидзегрáд), for the Georgian Communist politician Grigory Konstantinovich *Ordzhonikidze* (1886–1937), a leading supporter of Stalin. Cf. **Ordzhonikidzeabad**.

Bilibino (Билúбино) *Town, northeastern Russia*. The Siberian town, east of Anyuysk, arose in 1958 as a gold-mining settlement and was named for the Soviet geologist Yury Aleksandrovich *Bilibin* (1901–1952), who specialized in the study of gold deposits in this region.

Birobidzhan (Биробиджáн) *Town, eastern Russia*. The town, west of Khabarovsk, arose in 1928 on the site of a railroad station named *Tikhonkaya*. It gained urban status in 1937 and takes its present name from two local rivers: the *Bira*, on which it stands, and the *Bidzhan*, to the west, both as northern tributaries of the Amur. The rivers' own names are Evenki in origin and respectively mean "river" and "camp." The town is capital of the autonomous Jewish Region, and its name is sometimes used for this region.

Biruintsa See **Suvorovo**.

Biruni (Бирунú) *Town, western Uzbekistan*. The town was known as *Shabbaz* (Шаббáз) until 1957, when it was renamed as now in honor of the Arab scholar Al-*Biruni* (973–1048), who was born in the Khorezm region here.

Birzhi See **Madona**.

Birzula See **Kotovsk**.

Bishkek (Бишкéк) *Capital of Kyrgyzstan*. The city, in the north of the republic, was founded in 1878 on the site of a fortress in the Kokand khanate known as *Pishpek*, a name of uncertain origin and meaning. In 1926 the town was renamed *Frunze* (Фрýнзе), in honor of the Soviet military leader Mikhail Vasilyevich *Frunze* (1885–1925), who was born here. In 1991 the city reverted to its original name, but in the more correct form of *Bishkek*.

Bityug (Битю́г) *River, western Russia*. The name of the river, a tributary of the Don, has been explained as of Turkic origin to mean "camel." This is highly unlikely, however. A recent theory has linked the name with a phonetic variant of a Turkic word meaning "high," referring to the steep right bank of the river on its course from the village of Mechetka to its confluence with the Don.

Biysk (Бийск) *Town, southern Russia*. The town, southeast of Barnaul, was founded in 1707 and takes its name from the *Biya* River on which it lies. The origin of the river name is uncertain, but it probably comes from a local word meaning simply "river."

Black Sea (Чёрное мо́ре) *Sea, southwestern Russia*. The sea is bounded by six countries: Ukraine and Russia to the north, Georgia to the east, Turkey to the south, and Bulgaria and Romania to the west. Its name probably describes its appearance during stormy weather. In bright sunny weather it is as blue as any other sea. The sea is noted for its storms, and the Old Persian word used to describe it was *akhshaēna*, "dark." This word was adopted without being translated by the Greeks, who called it the *Pontos Axeinos*, *pontos* meaning "sea." But *Axeinos* came to be understood as *Axenos*, "inhospitable," so that it was the "Inhospitable Sea." Later, perhaps out of superstition, the Greeks altered this ill-omened name to *Pontos Euxenos*, "Hospitable Sea," and this name was traditionally rendered in English, without being translated, as *Euxine Sea*. Another theory claims that the Black Sea is so named because some Asiatic languages use color words for the four points of the compass. The Black Sea would thus be the "North Sea," just as the Red Sea, according to this concept, would be the "South Sea" and the White Sea the "West Sea." Support for this is lent by the fact that the modern Turkish name for the Mediterranean is *Akdeniz*, "White Sea" (although this may be an attempt to give a meaning for *Ege denizi*, the Turkish name for the Aegean, as an arm of the Mediterranean). Russian documents of the 15th and 16th centuries often refer to the Black Sea as the *Russkoye more*, "Russian Sea."

Blagodat (Благода́ть) *Mountain, western Russia*. The mountain, in the Middle Urals, is a rich source of iron ore. Its name means "abundance" (Russian, *blagodat'*), and was given in 1735 by the Russian historian Vassily Tatishchev. The reference would seem to be to the ore, but the intention may have been to translate the name of the Russian empress Anna Ivanovna (reigned 1730-40), since *Anna* was popularly understood to mean "grace" (from the Hebrew), the religious sense of Russian *blagodat'*.

Blagoveshchensk (Благове́щенск) *City, eastern Russia*. The city, southwest of Belogorsk near the Chinese border, was founded in 1856 as a military station named *Ust-Zeysky post*, from its location on the Amur at the mouth (Russian *ust'ye*) of the *Zeya* River. It was renamed as now in 1858 following the building of the Church of the Annunciation (Russian *Blagoveshcheniye*, literally "good news"). According to some accounts the "good news" in question, which was first made known here, was that this Far Eastern region had become part of Russia. The name is found elsewhere in Russia, for example in the southwest for a town north of Ufa. The church dedication will have given the name similarly in most such cases.

Bobriki See **Novomoskovsk**.

Bobrov (Бобро́в) *Town, southwestern Russia*. The town, southeast of Voronezh, was founded in 1711 at a time when this region was noted for its beavers (Russian *bobr*), and was named for this animal.

Bobruysk (Бобру́йск) *Town, east central Belarus*. The town, northwest of Gomel, dates back to the first half of the 14th century, and from 1649 to 1793 was part of Poland, after which it passed to Russia. It takes its name from the small river now known as the *Bobruyka*, this being based on Russian *bobr*, "beaver."

Bogdanovich (Богдано́вич) *Town, west central Russia*. The town, east of Yekaterinburg, was originally a railroad station built in the mid-1880s, with the settlement that developed raised to urban status in 1947. It takes its name from the Russian general and diplomat Yevgeny Vasilyevich *Bogdanovich*, a keen promoter of the scheme to construct the Transsiberian railway (which now passes through the town).

Bogolyubovo (Боголю́бово) *Town, western Russia*. The town, northeast of Vladimir, arose as the princely fortress of *Bogolyubov* in 1158, and probably derives its name from the icon of the Virgin Mary here known as the *Bogolyubivyj obraz*, "God-loving image." The name has popularly been connected with Prince Andrey *Bogolyubsky*, murdered here by jealous boyars in 1174. But his byname derives from the castle that was his fortified residence.

Bogoroditsk (Богоро́дицк) *Town, western Russia*. The town, southeast of Tula, was raised from a village to urban status in 1777. It is named for the dedication of its church to the Virgin Mary (Russian *Bogoroditsa*, literally "God-bearer"). According to local legend, the church was built specially to house an icon found here, that of the Most Holy Virgin Mary "the Passion Sufferer" (Russian *Strastoterpitsa*).

Bogorodsk (Богоро́дск) *Town, western Russia*. The town, southwest of Nizhny Novgorod, was raised from a village to a town in 1923 and takes its name from its church, dedicated to the Virgin Mary (Russian *Bogoroditsa*, literally "God-bearer").

Bogorodsk See **Noginsk**.

Bogorodskoye See **Kamskoye Ustye**.

Bogoslovsk See **Karpinsk**.

Boguchar (Богуча́р) *Town, western Russia*. The town, southeast of Voronezh, takes its name from the river on which it lies. The river's own name is of uncertain origin. It may have arisen from two Turkic words: *bag*, "rope," and *uchar*, "market," referring to a market or trading ground that was roped off.

Boguslav (Богусла́в) *Town, central Ukraine*. The town, west of Cherkassy, dates from at least 1195 and derives its name from the Old Russian personal name *Boguslav* ("glory of God").

Bokovo-Antratsit See **Antratsit**.

Boksitogorsk (Бокситого́рск) *Town, western Russia*. The town, southeast of St. Petersburg, arose in 1932 around a bauxite processing plant and is named for it, from Russian *boksit*, "bauxite," and *gorod*, "town." Bauxite is the principal ore of aluminum, which was first produced in the Soviet Union here.

Bolgrad (Бо́лград) *Town, southwestern Ukraine*. The town, near the Moldovan border northwest of Izmail, was founded in 1821 by Bulgarians seeking refuge here from Turkish oppression in their own country. The name means "big town," from the Bulgarian dialect word *bol*, "big," and the common Slavic *grad*, "town." The name also happens to reflect that of the Bulgarians (Russian *bolgary*) themselves.

Bolkhov (Бо́лхов) *Town, western Russia*. The town, north of Oryol, takes its name from the male personal name (or nickname) *Bolkh* or *Bolokh*, from Russian dialect *bolokh*, "ranter," "babbler." The person so named must have owned land here before the settlement became a town in 1556. Cf. **Bolokhovo**.

Bologoye (Боло́гое) *Town, western Russia*. The town, almost midway between St. Petersburg and Moscow, appears to have a name meaning "damp," from a general Slavic word related to Russian *vlaga*, "moisture." On the other hand, the origin may lie in a Slavic source represented by Russian *blagoy*, "good," referring to some physical aspect of the site. The town is on level terrain by the lake of the same name.

Bolokhovo (Бо́лохово) *Town, western Russia*. The town, southeast of Tula, was raised to urban status in 1943 and probably takes its name from the male personal name (or nickname) *Bolkh* or *Bolokh*, from Russian dialect *bolokh*, "ranter," "babbler." Cf. **Bolkhov**.

Bolshevik (Большеви́к) *Island, North Land, northern Russia*. The southernmost and second largest of the four main islands in the group is named for a member of the *Bolsheviks*, or Russian Communist party. ("Bolshevik" was part of the official party title until 1952.)

Bolshiye Soli See **Nekrasovskoye**.

Bolshoy Begichev (Большо́й Бе́гичев, о́стров) *Island, northern Russia*. The island, north of Nordvik Bay at the mouth of the Khatanga River, was so named in 1908 for the Russian polar explorer Nikifor Alekseyevich *Begichev* (1874–1927), who that year rounded the supposed peninsula here and established that it was an island. He perished while wintering near the mouth of the Pyasina River, west of the Taimyr Peninsula. The first word of the name means "big." There is a *Maly Begichev*, "Little Begichev," to the west, but it is very small and does not even appear on some maps. It was first discovered in 1739, then again by Begichev in 1908, who named it *Nikolay* (Nicholas), for his fellow explorer *Nikolay* Semyonov. It was renamed as now in 1933.

Bolshoye Boldino (Большо́е Бо́лдино) *Town, western Russia*. The town, southeast of Arzamas, was originally simply *Boldino*, a name that may derive from *Balda*, as the name of the original landowner here. This would have been a nickname, meaning either literally "sledgehammer" or figuratively "blockhead." If the first of these, the person so nicknamed may have resembled a hammer in appearance, rather than actually using one. *Bolshoye* ("Big") distinguishes this town from a smaller settlement of the same name.

Bolshoy Iremel (Большо́й Иреме́ль) *Mountain, southwestern Russia*. The mountain, in the Southern Urals, with a name meaning "Great Iremel'," is paired by a second, smaller peak named *Maly Iremel'*, "Little Iremel." *Iremel'* itself is a word of Turkic origin meaning "sacred," "holy."

Bolvansky Nos (Болва́нский Нос) *Peninsula, northern Russia*. The peninsula, at the northern end of Vaygach island, opposite Novaya Zemlya, takes its name from Old Russian *bolvan*, "idol," and modern Russian *nos*, "cape" (literally "nose"). A wooden idol stood on this peninsula at one time.

Bondyuzhsky See **Mendeleyevsk**.

Bor (Бор) *Town, western Russia*. The town, just north of Nizhny Novgorod, takes its name from Russian *bor*, "pine forest." The town was founded in 1938 in such a forest, small areas of which remain today on its outskirts.

Borisoglebsk (Борисогле́бск) *Town, western Russia*. The town, southeast of Tambov, was founded in 1646 as the military post of *Pavlovskaya krepost'*, "Paul's fortress." Its present name derives from the church built here in 1704 and dedicated to the 10th-century Russian saints *Boris* and *Gleb*. They were the youngest sons of the Kievan prince Vladimir

Svyatoslavich, but were both killed in 1015 by their elder brother Svyatopolk in an internecine wrangle.

Borisov (Борúсов) *Town, north central Belarus.* The town, northeast of Minsk, is said to have been founded in 1032 and to take its name from its founder, *Boris*, son of Prince Vseslav of Polotsk.

Borisovo (Борúсово) *District, Moscow, western Russia.* The southeastern district of Moscow takes its name from the Russian czar *Boris Godunov* (c. 1551–1605), who owned lands here.

Borispol (Борúсполь) *Town, north central Ukraine.* The town, east of Kiev, is first recorded in 1590. Its Greek-style name means "Boris's town," and judging by the date, this must refer to the Russian czar *Boris Godunov* (c. 1551–1605), although he did not succeed to the throne until 1598. He was, however, the chief member of the regency during the reign (1584–98) of Fyodor I, his brother-in-law.

Borodino[1] (Бородинó) *Village, western Russia.* The village, west of Mozhaysk, and the site of the Battle of Borodino (1812) in the Napoleonic Wars, probably takes its name from the personal nickname *Boroda*, "bearded," referring to the original owner of land here. The placename is first recorded in the 17th century. The battlesite is now a historical museum and park.

Borodino[2] (Бородинó) *Town, southwestern Ukraine.* The town, west of Ovidiopol, arose in the 19th century and was named for the Battle of *Borodino* (see **Borodino**[1]).

Borovichi (Боровичú) *Town, western Russia.* The town, southeast of St. Petersburg, derives its name from a root Slavic word *bor*, "pine forest." The ending *-ichi* indicates that the name originated not from the forest itself but from the people here, so that the overall sense is "pine forest dwellers." Cf. **Bor, Borovoye, Borovsk.**

Borovoye (Боровóе) *Town and resort, northern Kazakhstan.* The resort, southeast of Kokchetav, takes its name from the lake on which it is located. The lake's own name is based on a root Slavic word *bor* meaning "pine forest." The name emphasizes the fact that the lake is not in a valley, as many are, but in a forest. Cf. **Bor, Borovichi, Borovsk.**

Borovsk (Бóровск) *Town, western Russia.* The town, southwest of Moscow, takes its name from the Slavic root word *bor*, "pine forest." There was a settlement here as early as 1356. Cf. **Bor, Borovichi, Borovoye.**

Borshchyov (Борщёв) *Town, southwestern Ukraine.* The town, north of Chernovtsy, is said to take its name from an East Slavic word *borshch*, the name of a medicinal plant related to the hogweed (*Heracleum sphondylium*). This presumably grew here, as well as elsewhere in Ukraine at places similarly named.

Borzna (Борзнá) *Town, northern Ukraine.* The town, west of Konotop, takes its name from the river on which it stands. The river name is said to be based on a Slavic word meaning "fast," "speedy" (Russian *borzyj*). Hence *borzoi* dogs, a Russian hunting breed.

Boshnyakovo (Бошнякóво) *Town, Sakahlin, eastern Russia.* The town and port, on the west coast of Sakhalin island north of Lesogorsk, is named for the Russian naval officer Nikolay Konstantinovich *Boshnyak* (1830–1899), who explored this region of Sakhalin in 1852.

Bozdag (Боздáг) *Hill chain, north central Azerbaijan.* The chain of hills, to the south of the Mingechaur Reservoir, has a name found for individual mountains and for hill and mountain chains in many parts of Turkey and Iran. It means "gray mountain," from Turkic words corresponding to modern Turkish *boz*, "gray," and *dağ*, "mountain."

Bozhedarovka See **Shchorsk**.

Bragin (Брáгин) *Town, southeastern Belarus*. The town, southwest of Gomel, is mentioned in documents dated 1147. The name is based on a personal name, itself from Russian *braga*, a type of home-brewed beer. (The word may itself be related to English *brew*.) As a nickname, *Braga* would thus have been used for a drunkard or "tippler."

Braslav (Брáслав) *Town, northwestern Belarus*. The town, west of Polotsk, probably derives its name from Baltic *brastà*, "ford," alluding to its location on one of the streams of Lake Drivyati here. Less likely is a derivation from the name of the 11th-century Polovtsian prince *Bryachislav*, if only because archaeological evidence points to the place's earlier existence.

Bratsk (Брáтск) *City, southern Russia*. The Siberian city, east of Krasnoyarsk, takes its name from the indigenous Mongoloid *Buryat* people of this region. The present form of the name has been influenced by Russian *brat*, "brother." This association was put to positive ideological use from 1964, when the Bratsk hydroelectric station, one of the world's largest, was built on the Angara River here.

Bredy (Брéды) *Town, southwestern Russia*. The town, northeast of Orsk, was founded in 1843 and named for *Breda* in the Netherlands, where the Russians defeated the French in 1813. Cf. **Varna**.

Brest (Брест) *City, southwestern Belarus*. The city, on the Polish border, here formed by the Western Bug, takes its name from the Slavic word *berest*, "birch" (Russian *beryoza*). Until 1921 the town was known as *Brest-Litovsk* (Брест-Литóвск), "Lithuanian Brest," indicating its possession by Lithuania from 1319. It was part of Poland from 1569 to 1795 and again from 1919 to 1939, and has the current Polish name of *Brześć nad Bugiem*, "Brest on the Bug."

Brest-Litovsk See **Brest**.

Brezhnev See **Naberezhnyye Chelny**.

Brodokalmak (Бродокалмáк) *Village, southwestern Russia*. The village, northeast of Chelyabinsk, arose in the early 18th century on the site of a crossing of the Techa River called *Kalmytsky Brod*, and takes its name from this. The original name means "ford of the Kalmyks," referring to the people who regularly attacked the Bashkirs and Russians in this region and who crossed the Techa here to do so. There are other crossings over other rivers with the same name.

Brody (Брóды) *Town, western Ukraine*. The town, northeast of Lvov, is mentioned in a document of 1096 and has a name meaning "ford," "way," "route," from Old Russian *brod* (related to Latin *vadum* and English *ford*).

Bronnitsy (Брóнницы) *Town, western Russia*. The town, southeast of Moscow, has a name apparently associated with Old Russian *bronnik*, "armorer" (modern Russian *bronya*, "armor"). Support for such an origin is lent by the fact that from the 15th through 17th centuries the nearby village of Sinkovo was noted for its manufacture of shirts of mail, as well as for gold, silver, and copper chains. Such chains are still made as jewelry in the workshops here. The town of Bronnitsy dates from 1781.

Brovary (Бровáры) *Town, northern Ukraine.* The town, just northeast of Kiev, has a name referring to its brewery, from Ukrainian *brovar*, "brewer" (the English word is related). Other places of similar names will have the same meaning.

Bryansk (Брянск) *City, western Russia.* The city, southwest of Moscow, was recorded in the 12th century with the name of *Debryansk*, apparently from Old Russian *debr'* (modern Russian *debri*), "thicket." This seems a likely origin for a place that arose on a site that was formerly overgrown with trees. However, in the 11th century the name was recorded in the form *Bryn'*, so that the later name may have arisen in an attempt to explain the meaning.

Buda-Koshelyovo (Бýда-Кошелёво) *Town, southwestern Belarus.* The town, northwest of Gomel, derives its name from the two villages of *Buda* and *Koshelyovo*, out of which it was formed in the late 19th century. *Buda* derives from the obsolete Russian word *buda*, "booth," "temporary shelter." *Koshelyovo* represents the family name *Koshelyov*.

Budyonnovsk (Будённовск) *Town, southwestern Russia.* The town, northeast of Pyatigorsk, was founded in 1799 and was originally known as *Svyatoy Krest*, "Holy Cross." In 1920 it was renamed *Prikumsk* (Прикýмск), "[place] by the Kuma," from the prefix *pri-*, "near," "by," and *Kuma*, the name of the river on which it lies. It was first given its present name in 1935, in honor of Marshal Semyon Mikhaylovich *Budyonny* (1883-1973), a hero of the Civil War. The town's name reverted to *Prikumsk* in 1957, however, following Budyonny's fall from favor after his disastrous career in World War II, but his name was restored to the town in 1973 on the occasion of his death, by which time he had been more or less rehabilitated.

Bug (Буг) *River, southwestern Ukraine.* The river, also known as the Southern Bug to distinguish it from its namesake (the Western Bug) in east central Poland, has a name that has been the subject of much speculation. It probably means simply "river," and as such may be related to German *Bach* and English *beck*, "stream."

Bugulma (Бугульмá) *Town, western Russia.* The town, in Tatarstan southeast of Kazan, was founded in 1736. Its name may relate in some way to Turkish *boğa*, "bull." Cf. **Buguruslan**.

Buguruslan (Бугуруслáн) *Town, western Russia.* The town, southeast of Samara, has a name that may be related to Turkish *boğa*, "bull." Buguruslan is only about 70 miles (112 km) from **Bugulma**, but any link between the names remains uncertain. The name of Buguruslan may actually be related to that of the **Eruslan** River.

Buinsk (Буи́нск) *Town, western Russia.* The town, in Tatarstan south of Kazan, has a name that has been popularly explained as deriving from Russian *buynyj*, "violent," "turbulent," as if notorious for its brigands. But the name is almost certainly of Turkic origin, and doubtless comes from a word *bua* meaning "dam," "weir." Buinsk stands on the Karly River.

Bukachacha (Букачáча) *Town, southeastern Russia.* The town, northeast of Chita, has a name deriving from Evenki *bukachan*, "island," "hill."

Bukhara (Бухарá) *City, western Uzbekistan.* The ancient city, long a holy place of Islam, gave the name of the former khanate here. The name has been linked with Sanskrit *vihāra*,

"Buddhist monastery," a word brought to this part of Central Asia with the spread of Buddhism and acquiring its present form (with *b* for *v*) under Mongol influence.

Bukovina (Буковйна) *Historic region, east central Europe.* The territory has changed hands several times, but following its seizure by the Soviet Union in 1940, with subsequent incorporation into Bessarabia, now has its northern half in Ukraine and its southern in Romania. The name derives from the Slavic root word *buk*, "beech," referring to the abundance of these trees in this part of Europe.

Bulun (Булўн) *Village, northern Russia.* The village lies on the lower reaches of the Lena River in Yakutia. Its name represents the Turkic word *bulung*, used of a broad river pool.

Bunge Land (Бўнге Земля́) *Plainland, Anzhu Islands, Arctic Ocean, northeastern Russia.* The name is that of a low-lying semidesert region between Kotelny and Faddeevsky islands. It is named for the Russian zoologist Aleksandr Aleksandrovich *Bunge* (1851–1930), leader of an expedition to the New Siberian Islands in 1885-86.

Burmantovo (Бўрмантово) *Village, west central Russia.* The village, north of Ivdel, was founded in the late 19th century by Nikita *Burmantov*, a Komi settler, and is named for him.

Bursol (Бурсо́ль) *Town, southern Russia.* The town, near the border with Kazakhstan southeast of Karasuk, takes the first part of its name from Lake *Burlinskoye*, on which it lies. The second part represents Russian *sol'*, "salt," indicating its main industry, the manufacture of table salt.

Buryaad (Буря́ад) *Republic, southeastern Russia.* The republic, east of Lake Baykal on the border with Mongolia, was formerly familiar as *Buryatiya*. It is named for its indigenous inhabitants, the *Buryat* people, whose own name was given them by their southern Mongol neighbors and means "forest dwellers."

Buryatiya See **Buryaad**.

Bussol Strait (Буссо́ль проли́в) *Strait, Kuril Islands, southeastern Russia.* The strait, midway in the chain south of Simushir island, was so named in 1787 by the French navigator La Pérouse (see **La Pérouse Strait**) for his ship, the frigate *Boussole* ("Compass"). (The name is meaningful in Russian since *bussol'* is the standard term for a surveying compass.)

Buturlinovka (Бутурли́новка) *Town, southwestern Russia.* The town, southeast of Voronezh, takes its name from the *Buturlin* family who owned estates here in the 18th century. The specific reference is to the estate granted by Empress Yelizaveta Petrovna to Field Marshal-General Aleksandr Borisovich *Buturlin* (1694–1767) in the 1740s.

Buy[1] (Буй) *Town, western Russia.* The town, northeast of Yaroslavl, takes its name from Old Russian *buy*, a word that has survived in dialect use to denote an area of rising ground with a flat top, typically one on which a church stands. Russian churches were deliberately built on such sites so that they served as a visible focal point for the locality, both as a religious symbol and as an attractive architectural ensemble.

Buy[2] (Буй) *River, western Russia.* The river, a tributary of the Vyatka, rises in the Central Urals and has a name representing Bashkir or Tatar *buy*, "long."

Buynaksk (Буйна́кск) *Town, southwestern Russia.* The town, in north central Dagestan, derives its current name from Ulluby Daniyalovich *Buynaksky* (1890–1919), a Communist activist in Dagestan who was executed by counterrevolutionaries in the Civil War, allegedly at the instigation of the British. Before 1922 the town was known as *Temir-Khan-Shura* (Темир-Хан-Шура́), a name traditionally associated with that of the 14th-century Mongol conqueror *Timur* (Tamerlane), said to have rested from his campaigns by the lake here (dialect *shura*, "lake").

Buzuluk (Бузулу́к) *City, western Russia.* The city, southeast of Samara, takes its name from the river on which it lies, at its confluence with the Samara. The river name is probably of Turkic origin, and may mean "steppe," although according to some authorities it is based on Bashkir *byzau* or **bozau**, "calf," with *-lyk*, a Turkic plural suffix. If so, the name means "(river of) calves."

Byelorussia See **Belarus**.

Byrranga (Бырра́нга) *Mountain range, northern Russia.* The mountains, in the north of the Taymyr Peninsula, have a name derived from Yakut *byran*, "hill," "rocky range," with the Evenki plural suffix *-nga*, commonly found in the placenames of eastern Siberia.

Bystritsa (Бы́стрица) *River, western Ukraine.* The river rises in the Carpathians and is a tributary of the Dniester. Its name represents the Slavic root word *bystr* (Russian *bystryj*), "rapid," referring to its current. The name is found elsewhere in eastern Europe for various smallish, fast-flowing rivers, for example the *Bistriça* in northern Romania, also rising in the Carpathians.

Carpathians (Карпа́ты) *Mountain system, western Ukraine.* The mountains form the border between Poland and the Czech Republic to extend southward through western Ukraine into Romania. The name has been traced back to a Thracian word, *karpe*, meaning simply "cliff," or to an even earlier pre–Indo-European element *kar*, meaning "stone" (as possibly also for the ancient settlement of *Karnak* in Egypt, or the equally historic site of *Carnac* in Brittany, northwestern France, famous for its historic stone monuments).

Caspian Sea (Каспи́йское мо́ре) *Sea, southwestern Russia.* The sea is bounded by five countries: Kazakhstan to the north and northeast, Turkmenistan to the southeast, Iran to the south and southwest, Azerbaijan to the west, and Russia to the northwest. Its name derives from the ancient *Kaspi* people, who at one time inhabited its southwestern coast and who are mentioned (as the *Caspii*) by classical writers such as Herodotus. Their own name is of uncertain origin but may perhaps be related to that of the *Cushitic* peoples of North Africa. The Old Russian name of the Caspian was *Khvalynskoye* or *Khvalisskoye*, perhaps from the *Khvalis*, the Old Russian name of the inhabitants of **Khwarism**. See also **Khorezm, Khvalynsk**. The Romans knew the sea as the *mare Hyrcanum*, and the Greeks as *to Hurkanion pelagos*, this itself from the personal name *Hurkanos*.

Catherine Strait (Екатери́ны проли́в) *Strait, Kuril Islands, southeastern Russia.* The strait, at the southern end of the chain, between Iturup and Kunashir islands, was so named in 1811 in memory of the *Catherine* (Russian *Yekaterina*), the ship on which the Russian naval commander Grigory Lovtsov sailed through it in 1792 en route to Japan. The ship itself was presumably named for *Catherine* the Great, Empress of Russia at the time.

Caucasus (Кавка́з) *Mountain range, southwestern Russia.* The mountains, between the Black Sea and Caspian Sea, form the border between Russia (and Europe) to the north and Georgia and Azerbaijan (and Asia) to the south. The name has been traced back through Greek to a Pelasgian word *kauk* meaning simply "mountain," although Pliny derived it from a Scythian source meaning "snow-white." It may be linked with Hittite *Kaz-Kaz*, the name of a people living on the southern Black Sea coast. The name in its present form is first found in Aeschylus's tragedy *Prometheus Bound* (5th century B.C.). Whatever the case, the original name probably referred only to **Elbrus**, the highest peak in the range.

Cernăuţi See **Chernovtsy**.

Cetatea Albă See **Belgorod-Dnestrovsky**.

Chadyr Lunga (Чадьıр-Лу́нга) *Town, southern Moldova*. The town, northeast of Kagul, arose in the first half of the 19th century. The first half of its name represents the Tatar word for "tent" (Russian *shatyor*), referring to a tented settlement. The second word is the name of the river here, itself meaning "long."

Chamzinka (Чáмзинка) *Town, western Russia*. The town, in Mordovia northeast of Saransk, takes its name from the Mordovian first name *Chamz*.

Chapayev (Чапáев) *Town, north central Kazakhstan*. The town, on the Ural River northwest of Goryachensky, was originally known as *Lbishchensk* (Лбищенск), from the local word *lbishche* denoting a steep, rocky headland on a river (Russian *lob*, "brow"). In 1939 it was renamed *Chapayevo*, for the Russian Civil War commander Vasily Ivanovich *Chapayev* (1887-1919), who was killed in action here on the night of September 5, 1919, when attempting to cross the Ural. In 1971 the name was modified to its present form. Cf. **Chapayevsk**.

Chapayevka (Чапáевка) *River, western Russia*. The river, a tributary of the Volga, takes its present name from **Chapayevsk**, which lies on it. Until the 1930s it was known as the *Mocha*, a name that misleadingly suggests Russian *mocha*, "urine."

Chapayevsk (Чапáевск) *Town, western Russia*. The town, southwest of Samara, was originally known as *Ivashchenkovo* (Иващéнково). In 1919 it was renamed *Trotsk* (Троцк), for the revolutionary leader Leon *Trotsky* (1879-1914). Following his expulsion from the party in 1927, it was renamed as now, for the Civil War hero Vasily Ivanovich *Chapayev* (see **Chapayev**), who had been active in this region.

Chaplygin (Чаплы́гин) *Town, western Russia*. The town, northwest of Tambov, arose in the 17th century as the village of *Slobodskoye*, from Russian *sloboda*, "sloboda" (a settlement exempt from normal state obligations). In 1702 Peter the Great granted it to his closest associate, General Menshikov, who built a fortress here and called it *Oranienburg*, for the German city of this name. This, simplified to *Ranenburg* (Раненбýрг), became the official name of the town established here in 1779. In 1948 the town was given its present name in honor of the Soviet mechanical engineer Sergey Alekseyevich *Chaplygin* (1869-1942), who was born here.

Chardzhou (Чарджо́у) *City, eastern Turkmenistan*. The city, southwest of Bukhara, arose in the 1880s as a Russian military post in the Bukhara khanate. Its name represents the Turkic words *chor*, "four," and *dzhou*, "stream," referring to the confluence of three small rivers with the great Amudarya here. The name was originally spelled *Chardzhuy* (Чарджуй), but in 1940 was altered to reflect the actual pronunciation.

Chardzhuy See **Chardzhou**.

Charentsavan (Чаренцаван) *Town, northeast central Armenia.* The town, northeast of Yerevan, arose in 1948 when a hydroelectric power station was built here. It was originally known as *Lusavan* (Лусаван), "Lusa's settlement." In 1967 it was renamed as now for the Armenian revolutionary poet Yegishe Abgarovich *Charents* (real name Sogomonyan) (1897–1937). (His pseudonym means "of frenzied lineage.")

Chashniki (Чашники) *Town, north central Belarus.* The town, northwest of Orsha, has a name that is said to derive from the local pottery trade (Russian *chashka*, "cup," "bowl").

Chatyr Dag (Чатырдаг) *Mountain, southern Crimea, southern Ukraine.* The mountain, one of the highest in the Crimean chain, has a Turkic name meaning "tent mountain," from *chatyr* (modern Turkish *çadır*, Russian *shatyor*), "tent," and *dag* (modern Turkish *dağ*, "mountain"). The mountain is trapezoid in shape, with a long, flat summit like a tent ridge. Classical writers actually referred to it as *Trapezus*, from Greek *trapeza*, "table."

Chaykovsky (Чайковский) *Town, western Russia.* The town, on the Kama River east of Izhevsk, arose in 1955 as a settlement for workers engaged on construction of the hydroelectric dam here. As such, until 1962 it was known simply as *posyolok stroiteley Kamskoj GES*, "settlement of workers on the Kama Hydroelectric Station." In that year it was renamed for the Russian composer Pyotr Ilyich *Tchaikovsky* (1840–1893), who was born in the neighboring town of Votkinsk.

Chebarkul (Чебаркуль) *Lake, west central Russia.* The lake, just east of the Southern Urals, west of Chelyabinsk, has a name that may derive from Turkic words *chybar*, "speckled," and *kul*, "lake," referring to the variegated colors of the water. The town of *Chebarkul* on the northern shore of the lake is named for it.

Cheboksary (Чебоксары) *Town, western Russia.* The town, on the Volga in Chuvashia, west of Kazan, has a name of disputed origin. It probably derives from the name of a stream that enters the Volga here, and that itself comes from the Chuvash name *Chebak*. The present Chuvash form of the town's name is *Shupashkar*.

Chechenia (Чечения) *Republic, southwestern Russia.* The republic, north of the Caucasus, and until 1992 combining with **Ingushetia** as *Checheno-Ingushetia*, takes its name from its indigenous *Chechen* people. They are named for the village of *Chechen* here, but their own name for themselves is *Nakhcho*, from *nakh*, "people."

Chekalin (Чекалин) *Town, western Russia.* The town, west of Tula, was originally known as *Likhvin* (Лихвин), a name recorded as early as 1565. In 1944 it was renamed as now for a 16-year-old Komsomol partisan, Aleksandr Pavlovich *Chekalin* (1925–1941), tortured and hanged here by the Germans.

Chekanovsky Ridge (Чекановского кряж) *Mountain ridge, northern Russia.* The ridge, in northern Yakutia, is named commemoratively for the Russian geologist Aleksandr Lavrentyevich *Chekanovsky* (1833–1876), who explored the mineral resources of Eastern Siberia in 1873–75 and who found coal and graphite deposits here.

Chekhov[1] (Чехов) *Town, eastern Russia.* The town, on the southwestern coast of the island of Sakhalin, is named for the Russian writer Anton Pavlovich *Chekhov* (1860–1904), who visited Sakhalin in 1890 and described the lives of convicts and political exiles here. Before 1946 the town had the Japanese name of *Noda*.

Chekhov[2] (Чéхов) *Town, western Russia*. The town, south of Moscow, was so named in 1954 to mark the 50th anniversary of the death of the Russian writer Anton Pavlovich *Chekhov* (1860–1904), who from 1892 to 1898 lived on an estate at Melikhovo, 7 miles (12 km) from here. Its name previous to this was *Lopasnya* (Лопáсня).

Cheleken (Челекéн) *Peninsula, western Turkmenistan*. The peninsula, on the eastern coast of the Caspian Sea, has a name that may derive from a Turkic word related to modern Turkish *çël*, "plain," "desert." The town of *Cheleken* at the western end of the peninsula is named for it.

Chelkar (Челкáр) *Town, west central Kazakhstan*. The town, north of the Aral Sea, takes its name from the standard Kazakh word *shalkar*, "lake," referring to the one on which the town stands.

Chelyabinsk (Челя́бинск) *City, west central Russia*. The city, south of Yekaterinburg just east of the Middle Urals, was founded in 1736 as a fortress in a forest named *Chelyabi-Karagay*, and takes its name from the first part of this. The forest name represents two Turkic words: *karagay*, "pinewood," and *chelyabi*, "ancestor," so that the overall sense is "ancestral forest." The present form of the name was adopted in 1786 when the original settlement gained town status.

Chelyuskin, Cape (Челю́скин мыс) *Cape, northern Russia*. The cape is the northernmost point of the Taymyr Peninsula, opposite North Land. It is named for the Russian polar explorer Semyon Ivanovich *Chelyuskin* (c. 1707–1764), who discovered it in 1742. He himself named it *Severo-Vostochny mys*, "Northeastern Cape." The name was given in 1842 to mark the centennial of his discovery.

Chembar See **Belinsky**.

Cherdyn (Чéрдынь) *Town, western Russia*. The town, just west of the Northern Urals, north of Solikamsk, has a name that was first recorded in 1451. The second part of the name is almost certainly Komi-Permyak *dyn*, "mouth," although the origin of the first part is problematical. It may be the former name of a stream here, perhaps itself meaning simply "tributary." The town is the oldest in the Urals.

Cheremkhovo (Черемхóво) *Town, southern Russia*. The town, northwest of Irkutsk, takes its name from the river on which it stands. The river's own name is based on Russian *cheryomukha*, "bird cherry."

Cherepovets (Череповéц) *City, western Russia*. The city, west of Vologda, has a name first recorded in the 15th century in the form *Cherepoves*. The final part of this is believed to be Old Finnish *vesi*, "water." The main part of the name has yet to be satisfactorily explained.

Cherkassy (Черкáссы) *City, central Ukraine*. The city, southeast of Kiev, takes its name from a group of *Cherkess* (Circassian) people who had come from the Northern Caucasus to settle here in the 13th century. Cf. **Cherkessk**, **Novocherkassk**.

Cherkessk (Черкéсск) *Town, southwestern Russia*. The town, north of the Caucasus and northwest of Kislovodsk, is the capital of the Karachayevo-Cherkess republic, and is named for the *Cherkess* (Circassian) people who are the indigenous inhabitants of the territory. The town was founded as a military post in 1804 and was originally known as *Batalpashinskaya*. This name relates to a victory of Russian forces in 1789 over a Turkish army commanded by *Batal Pasha*. As such, it is a rare example of a name commemorating a defeated leader instead of a victorious one, as is more usual. The name was modified to *Batalpashinsk* (Баталпашинск) in 1880 and in 1930 changed altogether to *Sulimov* (Сулимов), in honor of the local Communist party activist Daniil Yegorovich *Sulimov* (1890–1937). Following his death the name became *Yezhovo-Cherkessk* (Ежово-Черкесск), for the Communist and security police official Nikolay Ivanovich *Yezhov* (1894–1939?), before gaining its present name in 1939. Cf. **Cherkassy, Novocherkassk**.

Chern (Чернь) *Village, western Russia*. The village, northeast of Mtsensk, has a basic name meaning "black" (Russian *chyornyj*), from the old word *chern* used of a deciduous forest, with its blackwood trees, as distinct from a coniferous, with its redwoods.

Chernenko See **Sharypovo**.

Chernigov (Чернигов) *City, northern Ukraine*. The city, northeast of Kiev, has the same name as that of the medieval principality here. The name is first recorded in 907, and is believed to represent Old Russian *cherniga*, "chernozem" (literally "black earth," a geographical term for a type of very fertile soil).

Chernobyl (Чернобыль) *Town, northern Ukraine*. The town, north of Kiev, and notorious for the nuclear power plant disaster of 1986, has a name representing Russian *chernobyl'nik*, a plant of the mugwort family (*Artemisia vulgaris*), found locally.

Chernogorsk (Черногорск) *Town, southern Russia*. The town, east of Novokuznetsk, has a name meaning simply "black mountain," from Russian *chyornyj*, "black," and *gora*, "mountain."

Chernoistochinsk (Черноисточинск) *Town, western Russia*. The town, southwest of Nizhny Tagil, is named for the *Chernoistochinsky* Lake here, itself so named for the "black spring" (Russian *chërnyj istok*), that enables the waters of the Chyornoye ("Black") Lake to flow through the Chyornaya River into the Tagil.

Chernomorskoye (Черноморское) *Village, western Crimea, southern Ukraine*. The village takes its name from the **Black Sea** (Russian *Chyornoye more*), on which it is situated. Before 1945 it was known as *Ak-Mechet* (Ак-Мечеть), from Turkic words meaning "white mosque" (modern Turkish *ak*, "white," and the Arabic word *masjid* that gave the English word *mosque*).

Chernovtsy (Черновцы) *City, southwestern Ukraine*. The city, southwest of Kamenets-Podolsky near the Romanian border, was formerly familiar under the German name of *Czernowitz* and (from 1918 to 1944) under the Romanian name of *Cernăuți*. The name appears to be based on a personal name or nickname, *Chernyj*, "black."

Chernyakhovsk (Черняховск) *City, western Russia*. The city, east of Kaliningrad, derives its present name from that of the Red Army general Ivan Danilovich *Chernyakhovsky* (1906–1945), who commanded the third Byelorussian front in 1944 and who died in this region after recapturing key cities taken by the Germans. Until 1946 the city was known by the German name of *Insterburg*, from its location at the mouth of the *Instruch* River.

Chernyayevo See **Yangiyer**.

Chernyshyov Ridge (Чернышёва кряж) *Hill ridge, northwestern Russia*. The ridge runs west of, and parallel to, the Northern Urals, and is named for the Russian geologist who explored the region, Feodosy Nikolayevich *Chernyshyov* (1856–1914).

Chersky (Чёрский) *Town, northeastern Russia*. The town, a port on the Kolyma River southwest of Ambarchik, takes its name from the Russian explorer of Siberia, Ivan Dementyevich *Chersky* (1845–1892), for whom the extensive **Chersky Range** is also named.

Chersky Range (Чёрского хребёт) *Mountain range, eastern Russia*. The range, in Yakutia, north of the Sea of Okhotsk, was discovered in 1926 and named commemoratively for the Russian explorer of Siberia, Ivan Dementyevich *Chersky* (1845–1892), who perished during an expedition here. His name is also borne by the *Chersky Range* in southern Russia, between Lake Baykal and the border with Mongolia.

Cherven (Чёрвень) *Town, central Belarus*. The town, southeast of Minsk, was originally known as *Igumen* (Игумен). This is the title of the head of a monastery, roughly the equivalent of English "Father Superior." In 1925 the present name was adopted, from Byelorussian *chervony*, "red," presumably in a revolutionary sense. (However, a sense "beautiful" or "warm" is perhaps also implied, since Byelorussian *cherven'* means "June," the month of flowering and warmth.)

Chervonoarmeysk (Червоноармёйск) *Town, western Ukraine*. The town, southwest of Rovno, was originally known as *Radzivilov* (Радзивилов), for the Polish prince *Radziwill* who owned estates here. In 1940 it was renamed as now for the *Red Army*, the first part of the name representing Ukrainian *chervonyj*, "red." Cf. **Krasnoarmeysk**.

Chervonograd (Червоногра́д) *Town, western Ukraine*. The town, southwest of Lutsk near the Polish border, was originally known by the name of *Kristinopol* (Кристинополь), "Christina's town," presumably for a woman of local or national importance. In 1953 it received its present name, meaning "red town," from Ukrainian *chervonyj*, "red" (in the Communist sense), together with the common element *-grad*, "town." Cf. **Krasnograd**.

Chervonopartizansk (Червонопартиза́нск) *Town, eastern Ukraine*. The town, southeast of Krasny Luch, has a Soviet-style name meaning "red partisan," from Ukrainian *chervonyj*, "red," and *partizan*, "partisan."

Cheryomushki (Черёмушки) *District, Moscow, western Russia*. The southwestern district of Moscow stands on the site of the 16th-century village of the same name, itself so called for its bird cherry trees (Russian *cheryomukha*, diminutive plural *cheryomushki*). To the south lies the modern development of **Novyye Cheryomushki**.

Chesma (Чёсма) *Village, southwestern Russia*. The village, southwest of Troitsk, was founded in 1842 and named commemoratively for the victory of the Russian fleet over the Turks in 1770 at the Battle of *Chesma* (modern Çeşme, western Turkey). For similar names of this type, see **Varna**.

Chesnokovka See **Novoaltaysk**.

Chibyu See **Ukhta**.

Chikhachyov Range (Чихачёва хребёт) *Mountain range, southern Russia*. The range, near the border with China, was discovered in 1928 and named for the Russian geographer and geologist Pyotr Aleksandrovich *Chikhachyov* (1808–1890), who explored this region in 1842.

Chimbay (Чимбай) *Town, western Uzbekistan*. The town, south of the Aral Sea, takes its name from a Turkic people who settled here in the 15th century. The meaning of their own name is uncertain.

Chimishliya (Чимишлия) *Town, south central Moldova*. The town, southwest of Bendery, has a name deriving from the Tatar word *chumech*, "scoop," itself the name of a local Tatar people whose emblem is a large ladle.

Chimkent (Чимкент) *Town, southern Kazakhstan*. The town, north of Tashkent, has a name deriving from Kazakh *chim*, "grassland," and *kent*, "town," so that the overall sense is "green town." Cf. **Tashkent**.

Chirchik (Чирчик) *Town, eastern Uzbekistan*. The town, northeast of Tashkent, takes its name from the river here. The river was earlier known as the *Parak*, perhaps from a Tajik word meaning "fleeting," "rapid." The present river name may be of Turkic origin and similar meaning, from a word that gave modern Turkish *sıkı*, "tight," "severe."

Chishmy (Чишмы) *Village, western Russia*. The village, in Bashkortostan southwest of Ufa, has a name deriving from Bashkir *shishma*, "stream," "source," referring to the small river on which the settlement stands. Names such as *Chishma* and *Chishmy* are common in Bashkortostan, and the Turkic name is found elsewhere in Europe, for example in the Turkish village of *Çeşme*, west of Izmir. (This last gave the name of **Chesma**.)

Chişinău See **Kishinyov**.

Chistopol (Чистополь) *Town, western Russia*. The town, in Tatarstan southeast of Kazan, has a name representing Russian *chistoye pole*, "open field." The final *-pol* misleadingly suggests a Greek-style name (such as **Sevastopol**).

Chistyakovo See **Torez**.

Chita (Читá) *City, eastern Russia*. The city, east of Ulan Ude, takes its name from the river on which it stands. The river's own name represents Evenki *chita*, "clay."

Chkalov See **Orenburg**.

Chkalovsk (Чкáловск) *Town, western Russia*. The town, northwest of Nizhny Novgorod, was originally known by the name of *Vasilyovo* (Василёво). In 1937 it was renamed as now for the Soviet air ace Valery Pavlovich *Chkalov* (1904–1938), who was born here. See also **Orenburg**.

Chu (Чу) *River, southern Kazakhstan*. The river rises in the Tien Shan mountains, Kyrgyzstan, and flows north through the town of the same name to expend itself in the sands of the Betpak-Dala desert. Its name represents Tibetan *chu*, simply meaning "water," "river." (Cf. Turkish *su*, "water," and the possibly related English *sea*.)

Chudskoye, Lake (Чудскóе óзеро) *Lake, eastern Estonia/western Russia*. The lake has an Old Russian ethnic name, *Chud*, applied to various Finno-Ugrian peoples, including those of Estonia. The name itself probably means "stranger," and is related to Russian *chuzhoy*, "alien." This denotes a non-Slavic people. The Estonian name of the lake is *Peipus* (Пéйпус), of uncertain origin.

Chukchi Sea (Чукóтское мóре) *Sea, Arctic Ocean*. The sea, north of the Bering Strait between Russia and Alaska, is named for the *Chukchi* people who are the indigenous inhabitants of the northeasternmost part of Siberia. Their name, more accurately *Chaukchu*, means "rich in deer" in their own language. The sea name was officially adopted only as recently as 1935.

Chukhloma (Чу́хлома) *Town, western Russia*. The town, on a lake of the same name east of Vologda, has a name that is said to mean "to dive" and to derive from a Finnic language. The reference would presumably be to the lake.

Chukot Peninsula (Чуко́тский полуо́стров) *Peninsula, northeastern Russia*. The peninsula in extreme eastern Russia, between the Bering Sea and the Chukchi Sea, opposite Alaska, was so named in 1728 by Bering himself for the *Chukchi* people who are the indigenous inhabitants of the region. See **Chukchi Sea**.

Chulym (Чулы́м) *River, southern Russia*. The river, a tributary of the Ob, which it enters below Tomsk, has a name that may relate to that of the **Chu** and so mean simply "water," "river."

Churubay-Nura See **Abay**.

Chusovaya (Чусова́я) *River, western Russia*. The river, which rises in the Middle Urals and flows west as a tributary of the Kama, has a name of disputed origin. It may originate in a Permian word comprising *chus*, "rapid," and *va*, "river." Popular etymology derives the name from four words of different origin each meaning "river": Tibetan *chu*, Turkic *su*, Komi-Permyak *va*, and Mansi *ya*. See also **Chusovoy**.

Chusovoy (Чусово́й) *Town, western Russia*. The town, on the western slopes of the Central Urals east of Perm, takes its name from the **Chusovaya** River on which it lies.

Chuvashia (Чува́шия) *Republic, western Russia*. The republic, between Nizhny Novgorod and Kazan, takes its name from its indigenous people, the *Chuvash*. Their own name has been associated on rather uncertain grounds with Turkish *su*, "water."

Chuya (Чу́я) *River, east central Russia*. The river, a tributary of the Lena north of Lake Balkhash, has a name that probably means simply "water" and that is thus analogous to the name of the **Chu**.

Chyoshskaya Bay (Чёшская губа́) *Bay, northwestern Russia*. The bay, on the Barents Sea, takes its name from the small *Chyosha* River that flows into it. The river name is of uncertain origin.

Colchis (Колхи́да) *Historic region, western Georgia*. The ancient country on the Black Sea, south of the Caucasus, is familiar from Greek legend as the land that was the home of Medea and magic, and as the place where the Golden Fleece was sought by Jason. It takes its name from the *Colchians*, the people who lived here in the first millennium B.C. and who were overcome by King Mithridates of Pontus in the 1st century B.C. Their own name is possibly of Egyptian origin. Its meaning is unknown.

Commander Islands (Команду́рские острова́) *Island group, eastern Russia*. The islands, east of the Kamchatka Peninsula in the southwestern **Bering Sea**, were discovered by Bering himself in 1744 and were named for him, by his naval rank of *Commander* (Russian *komandor*). Bering died on the main island of the group, now named for him as *Bering Island*.

Communism Peak (Коммуни́зма пик) *Mountain, southeastern Tajikistan*. The mountain peak, the highest in the Pamirs and the highest in the former Soviet Union (hence its name), was discovered in 1928 by an expedition comprising members of the Academy of Sciences of the USSR using phototheodolite reconnaissance. Its height was correctly calculated at 7,495 meters (24,590 feet). By error, however, the details were attributed to Mt. Garmo, 20 km (12 miles) to the south. For this reason, the peak is still featured in some gazetteers as having the earlier or alternate name of *Garmo*. (The worthy *Webster's New Geographical Dictionary* is guilty of this.) In 1932 the error was detected, and the mountain was named *Stalin Peak* (Ста́лина пик). In 1962, following the official demotion of Stalin, the peak was renamed as now.

Courland See **Kurzeme**.

Crimea (Крым) *Peninsula, southern Ukraine*. The peninsula, on the northern coast of the Black Sea, was known to classical writers as the *Tauric Chersonese*, from the *Taurians*, its indigenous inhabitants, and Greek *khersos*, "dry land," and *nēsos*, "island." (Cf. **Kherson, Korsun-Shevchenkovsky**.) As *Taurida* (Таври́да), this name was reintroduced by the Russian government when the Crimea became part of Russia in 1783. The present name first appeared in the 15th century under Turkish rule, and is said to mean "wall," "fortress," as originally applied to the fortified settlement of **Stary Krym** in the southeast of the peninsula. The name then extended to the mountain chain along the south, and finally to the whole peninsula. If this is so, there may be a link between the name of the *Crimea* and that of the *Kremlin*, a former citadel.

Czernowitz See **Chernovtsy**.

Dagestan (Дагеста́н) *Republic, southwestern Russia*. The republic, bordered to the east by the Caspian Sea, to the south by Azerbaijan, and to the west by Georgia, has a name meaning "mountain country," from words corresponding to modern Turkish *dağ*, "mountain," and the Iranian *-stan*, "country," "land," familiar from national Asian names such as *Kazakhstan, Kyrgyzstan, Turkmenistan,* and *Uzbekistan*. The reference is to the Caucasus Mountains here. The name arose in the 17th century.

Dalmatovo (Далма́тово) *Town, southwestern Russia*. The town, southeast of Yekaterinburg, arose from the *Dalmatov* monastery founded here in 1644. Its own name comes from that of its founder, the Cossack Dmitry Ivanovich Mokrinsky, who took the religious name *Dalmat* (Dalmatius) on becoming a priest. The village that grew up around the monastery was at first called *Sluzhnaya*, probably from *sluzhka*, "lay brother." In 1781 it was renamed *Dalmatov* and promoted to town status as a regional capital. It later lost this rank, but became a town again in 1947 and took the present form of its name.

Dalnerechensk (Дальнере́ченск) *City, southeastern Russia*. The city, near the Ussuri River midway between Vladivostok and Khabarovsk, has a name that means "far river," from Russian *dal'nij*, "far," and *reka*, "river." The name also alludes to the *Far Eastern Economic Region* (Russian *Dal'nevostochnyj Ekonomicheskiy Rajon*) in which it is located. Until 1973 the city was known as *Iman* (Има́н), for the river of this name that flows into the Ussuri here. Its own name is of uncertain origin.

Dangauerovka (Данга́уэровка) *District, Moscow, western Russia*. The eastern district of Moscow takes its name from the former factory workers' settlement here. This was itself named for the Dangauer and Kayzer boilerworks and foundry set up as a metal workshop in 1869 by A. K. *Dangauer*.

Danilovka (Даниловка) *District, Moscow, western Russia*. The southern district of Moscow takes its name from the *Danilov* monastery here, itself founded in 1282 by Prince *Daniil* Aleksandrovich.

Dankov (Данков) *Town, western Russia*. The town, northwest of Lipetsk, was founded in 1571 as a defensive post on the *Don* River and is traditionally said to take its name from this. But a more likely origin is in the personal name *Danko*, a diminutive of *Daniil*, "Daniel," so that the name means "Danko's place."

Danube (Дунай) *River, central Europe*. The Danube rises in the Black Forest, Germany, and flows generally east and south to enter the Black Sea southwest of Odessa. Its final course forms the border between Ukraine and Romania. Its German name is the *Donau*, while the Romans knew it as the *Danubius*. Its name ultimately goes back to the Iranian root *don-* or *dan-* meaning simply "river." This also gave the names of the **Dnieper, Dniester,** and **Don**.

Darg-Kokh (Дарг-Кох) *Mountain, southwestern Russia*. The mountain, in the central Caucasus, has an Ossetic name meaning "long mountain," from *darg*, "long," and *khokh*, "mountain."

Darkehmen See **Ozyorsk**.

Darvaz Range (Дарвазский хребет) *Mountain range, central Tajikistan*. The name is said to represent Tajik *dar*, "door," and *boz*, "open," alluding to a pass here.

Daryal Pass (Дарьяльское ущелье) *Gorge, Caucasus Mountains, southwestern Russia*. The gorge lies to the east of Mt. Kazbek at the point where the Terek River crosses the Caucasus. The name is based on Iranian *dar*, "gate," "pass."

Daugavpils (Даугавпилс) *City, eastern Latvia*. The city, southeast of Riga, takes its name from the *Daugava* River on which it lies, this being the Latvian name of the river more generally known as the Western **Dvina**. The last part of the name is Latvian *pils*, "fort." The town was founded in 1275 by Ernest von Ratzeburg, a German knight of the Livonian branch of the Teutonic Order, as the fortress of *Dünaburg*, the original site being some 12 miles (19 km) from the present city. It took this name from a form of *Dvina* and German *Burg*, "fort." In 1656 the fortified town that had developed was captured by the Russians in the Russo-Polish War and was renamed *Borisogleb*, apparently because news of the victory reached Alexis Mikhaylovich, Czar of Russia, on July 24, the feastday of St. *Boris* and St. *Gleb* (cf. **Borisoglebsk**). It retained this name until 1667, when the city passed to Poland. (The name is preserved in that of the Cathedral of St. Boris and St. Gleb, built in 1905.) From 1893 to 1917 the city had the official Russian name of *Dvinsk* (Двинск), also from the river.

David-Gorodok (Давид-Городок) *Town, southern Belarus*. The town, east of Pinsk, is apparently named for one *David*, although his precise identity is uncertain. The name of *David*, Prince of Volynia in the late 11th and early 12th centuries, has been suggested, as has that of the Yatvag prince *David*, who converted to Christianity here. But the name may simply relate this **Gorodok** ("township") to the neighboring village of *Davydovka*.

Davlekanovo (Давлеканово) *Town, southwestern Russia*. The town, southwest of Ufa, derives its name from the Bashkir personal name *Davlekan* (originally *Davletkhan*), meaning "lord of wealth," "lord of happiness."

Degtyarsk (Дегтярск) *Town, west central Russia*. The town, southwest of Yekaterinburg, arose around an ironworks built here in the 1730s. The workings that developed included the manufacture of pitch and coal tar. Hence the present name, based on Russian *dëgot'*, "tar."

De Kastri (Де-Кастри) *Village, eastern Russia*. The village, on the bay of the same name opposite Sakhalin island, is named for the bay. This was itself named in 1787 by the French navigator who discovered it, Jean-François Galaup, Comte de La Pérouse (see **La Pérouse Strait**), for Charles de la Croix, Marquis *de Castries* (1727–1800), navy minister from 1780 to 1787.

De Long Islands (Де-Лонга острова) *Island group, Arctic Ocean, northeastern Russia*. The islands, northeast of the New Siberian Islands, are named for the American naval officer and explorer George Washington *De Long* (1844–1881), leader of an expedition in 1879–81 that discovered some of them. After their ship was trapped in ice north of Siberia, De Long and his crew perished here one by one of exposure and starvation. De Long's expedition was financed by the editor James Gordon Bennett (see **Bennett Island**).

Demidov (Демидов) *Town, western Russia*. The town, northwest of Smolensk near the border with Belarus, was originally known as *Porechye* (Поречье), "river place," for its location on the Kasplya River. In 1918 it was given its present name in honor of Ya. Ye. *Demidov* (1889–1918), a district Communist party secretary killed by counterrevolutionaries here in the Civil War.

Derbent (Дербент) *Town, southwestern Russia*. The town, on the west coast of the Caspian Sea in Dagestan, southwest of Makhachkala, derives its name from Iranian *dar* or *der*, "door," "gate," "pass," and *bend*, "obstacle." The town is situated at a point where the Caucasus Mountains come close to the coast, leaving only a narrow route for traffic between Asia and Europe. The pass was known to other countries by a name translating as "Iron Gate," for example Turkish *Demirkapıcı* or Arabic *Bāb el-Ḥadīd*.

Derpt See **Tartu**.

Desna (Десна) *River, western Russia*. The river rises east of Smolensk and flows generally south into Ukraine to join the Dnieper near Kiev. Its name has been derived from the Slavic root word *desn*, "right," as if by contrast with a river that is *shuy*, "left." However, no such rivers of the latter name are known. Moreover, this *Desna* and others of the same name are mostly left-hand tributaries, not right-hand. Perhaps the name actually links up with those of other rivers such as the **Dniester** and **Don** to mean simply "river."

Detskoye Selo See **Pushkin**.

Deynau (Дейнау) *Town, eastern Turkmenistan*. The town, northwest of Chardzhou, is said to have a name representing Tajik *dekh*, "settlement," and *nau*, "new."

Dezhnyov Cape (Дежнёва мыс) *Cape, eastern Russia*. Russia's easternmost cape, on the Bering Strait opposite Alaska, takes its name from the Russian explorer Semyon Ivanovich *Dezhnyov* (c. 1605–1673), who discovered it in 1648. He himself called it the *Bolshoy Kamenny nos*, "Great Rocky Headland." In 1778 Captain Cook plotted the cape on his chart under the name of *East Cape*. The present name was proposed in 1879 by the Swedish Arctic explorer Adolf Eric Nordenskiöld, who that year was the first to accomplish the Northeast Passage from the Atlantic to the Pacific. *Dezhnyov Cape* did not officially replace *East Cape* until

1898, however, when at the request of the Russian Geographical Society the name was adopted to mark the 250th anniversary of the cape's discovery. Even so, it still appears as an alternate name on some maps and in some gazetteers, e.g. *Webster's New Geographical Dictionary* (see Select Bibliography, p. 251). (Cook also named its "opposite number" in Alaska, not as West Cape, even though it is the westernmost point of North America, but as Prince of Wales Cape.)

Diana Strait (Диáны проли́в) *Strait, Kuril Islands, southeastern Russia.* The strait, almost midway in the Kuril chain, is named for the ship on which a Russian crew discovered it in 1811. The *Diana* was a wooden full-rigged sloop built in 1806 as a timber transporter. The vessel was refitted in St. Petersburg and sailed the Pacific before being unrigged in 1813 to serve as a storeship in Petropavlovsk-Kamchatsky.

Didkovsky (Дидко́вского горá) *Mountain, northern Urals, northwestern Russia.* The mountain, one of the highest in the Polar Urals, takes its name from the revolutionary Boris Vladimirovich *Didkovsky* (1883-1938), who was active in the Northern Urals during the Civil War and who later became a noted geologist.

Dikson (Ди́ксон) *Town and port, northern Russia.* The Arctic port, on the estuary of the Yenisey, takes its name from that originally given in 1875 by the Swedish explorer Adolf Erik Nordenskiöld to a deep inlet on what is now known as *Dikson* Island, about a mile off the coast here. He bestowed it in honor of Oskar *Dikson*, the Scottish born Swedish merchant who had financed his expedition.

Dimitrov (Дими́тров) *Town, eastern Ukraine.* The coal-mining town, in the Donbass northwest of Donetsk, was founded in 1911. From 1937 to 1957 it was known as *Novy Donbass* (Но́вый Донбáсс), "New Donbass," but in the latter year was renamed *Novoekonomicheskoye* (Новоэкономи́ческое), "New Economy." In 1972 it was given its present name, marking the 90th anniversary of the birth of the Bulgarian Communist leader Georgi Mikhailovich *Dimitrov* (1882-1949). Cf. **Dimitrovgrad.**

Dimitrovgrad (Дими́тровград) *Town, western Russia.* The town, east of Ulyanovsk, was so named in 1972 to mark the 90th anniversary of the birth of the Bulgarian Communist leader Georgi Mikhailovich *Dimitrov* (1882-1949). Its earlier name was *Melekess* (Мелекéсс), of uncertain origin. Cf. **Dimitrov.**

Diomede Islands (Диоми́да островá) *Islands, Bering Strait, eastern Russia.* Uniquely, the group of two islands is divided between Russia and America, the International Date Line passing between them. The Russians have Big Diomede, the larger island, while the Americans have Little Diomede, the smaller. The two were discovered and named on August 16, St. *Diomedes'* Day, 1728, by the Danish explorer Vitus Bering (see **Bering Strait**). Alternate names for the islands are respectively **Ratmanov Island** and *Kruzenshtern Island* (see **Kruzenshtern Strait**). An alternate Russian name for both together is *Gvozdev Islands* (Гвóздева островá), for the Russian geodesist and traveler who charted them in 1732, Mikhail Spiridonovich *Gvozdev* (?-1759).

Dmitriyevsk See **Makeyevka.**

Dmitrov (Дми́тров) *Town, western Russia.* The town, north of Moscow, is said to have been named in the mid-12th century by Prince Yury Dolgoruky, founder of Moscow, as the place where he learned of the birth of his son *Dmitry* (later, Grand Prince Vsevolod III).

Dmitry Laptev Strait (Дми́трия Ла́птева проли́в) *Strait, northern Russia*. The strait, between the Lyakhov Islands and the Siberian mainland, is named for the Russian Arctic explorer *Dmitry* Yakovlevich *Laptev* (1701-1767), who discovered it in 1740. The **Laptev Sea** lies to the west. Cf. **Khariton Laptev Coast**.

Dneprodzerzhinsk (Днепродзержи́нск) *City, east central Ukraine*. The city, west of Dnepropetrovsk, was originally known as *Kamenskoye* (Ка́менское), "stony place." In 1936 it was given its present name, for the **Dnieper** River on which it lies, and in commemoration of the Soviet Communist leader Feliks Edmundovich *Dzerzhinsky* (1877-1926). Cf. **Dzerzhinsk**.

Dnepropetrovsk (Днепропетро́вск) *City, east central Ukraine*. The city, southwest of Kharkov, was founded in 1783 as *Yekaterinoslav* (Екатериносла́в), "glory of Catherine," in honor of *Catherine* the Great, Empress of Russia, from *Yekaterina*, "Catherine," and *slava*, "glory." From 1796 to 1802 (when Paul I was emperor) it was renamed *Novorossiysk* (Новоросси́йск), "New Russia," as this part of Russia was then called. (See **Novorossiysk**.) It then reverted to *Yekaterinoslav*, as which it remained until 1926, when it received its present name. This represents the names of the **Dnieper** River, on which it stands, and of the Ukrainian Communist politician Grigory Ivanovich *Petrovsky* (1878-1958).

Dnieper (Днепр) *River, western Russia*. The river rises near Smolensk, then flows generally south through eastern Belarus and Ukraine to enter the Black Sea near Kherson. It is mentioned by the 5th-century B.C. Greek historian Herodotus as the *Boristhenes*, as if meaning "from the north," from Greek *boreas*, "north," and the suffix *-then*, denoting motion from a place. But this could have simply been a form of the name of the river now known as the **Berezina**. This was at one time regarded as the main river, with the upper Dnieper as its tributary, although the opposite is actually the case. In Roman documents of the 6th century A.D. the name appears as *Danapris* or *Danaper*. This could mean "deep river," from the Iranian words *dan* or *don*, "river" (cf. **Danube, Don**) and *apr* or *apara*, "deep."

Dniester (Днестр) *River, western Ukraine*. The river flows generally south through Moldova to enter the Black Sea southwest of Odessa. Greek writers mentioned it under the name of *Tyras*, probably from an Iranian word meaning "rapid." Later writers referred to it as the *Danastris*, which gave the present name, from Scythian *dan* or *don*, "river" (cf. **Danube, Dnieper, Don**), and Thracian *istros*, "current," implying a fast-flowing river. See also **Tiraspol**.

Dobryanka (Добря́нка) *Town, west central Russia*. The town, northeast of Perm, derives its name from the river on which it stands. The river name appears to derive from Russian *dobryj*, "good," but almost certainly has some other origin, as yet undetermined. The name was long familiar locally in the form *Domryanka*.

Dokshitsy (До́кшицы) *Town, northwestern Belarus*. The town, southwest of Polotsk, probably takes its name from the Baltic surname *Dokash* or *Dokish*, itself based on a word meaning "ragged."

Dokuchayevsk (Докуча́евск) *Town, southeastern Ukraine*. The town, south of Donetsk, was founded in 1898 and until 1954 was a settlement named *Yelenovskiye Karyery* (Еле́новские Карье́ры), "Yelenovka quarries," for a nearby village. In 1954 it was raised to town status and given its present name, in honor of the Russian geologist, inventor of the term *chernozem* for rich dark soil, Vasily Vasilyevich *Dokuchayev* (1846-1903).

Dolgoderevenskoye (Долгодеревéнское) *Village, west central Russia.* According to local tradition, the village, north of Chelyabinsk, was founded by a Cossack named *Dolgy*. But this seems unlikely (and would moreover have given a placename such as *Dolgovo*). Instead, the name probably means "long village," from Russian *dolgij*, "long," and *derevnya*, "village," referring to the way it straggles along the road.

Dombay (Домбáй) *Village, southwestern Russia.* The village is a holiday and skiing resort in the Caucasus, near the border with Georgia. It takes its name from the nearby mountain *Dombay Ulgen* (Домбáй-ульгéн). This is of Karachay origin and means "slain bison."

Dombay Ulgen See **Dombay**.

Don (Дон) *River, western Russia.* The river rises south of Moscow and flows generally south to enter the Sea of Azov. The 1st-century B.C. Greek geographer Strabo mentions the Don as the *Tanais*, and the present name represents the first part of this. The name itself is of Scythian (Iranian) origin, and means simply "river." The element that gave the name can be seen behind the names of other rivers, including not only the **Dnieper** in Russia and **Dniester** in Ukraine, but also the **Danube** in central Europe and even the *Don* in England.

Donbass (Донбáсс) *Region, eastern Ukraine.* The region, famous as the largest coalfield in the former Soviet Union, takes its name as an abbreviated form of Russian *Donetskiy bassejn* (Донéцкий бассéйн), "Donets basin," from the **Donets** River that flows through it. Cf. **Kuzbass**.

Donets (Донéц) *River, eastern Ukraine.* The river, also known as the *Northern Donets* or *Seversky Donets* (Сéверский Донéц), rises north of Belgorod and flows into the Don northeast of Rostov-on-Don in southwestern Russia. The suffix *-ets* denotes a diminutive, so that the Donets, as a tributary of the **Don**, is effectively a "Little Don." *Northern* is something of a misnomer, since the river is not in the northern Donbass, nor is there a "Southern Donets." It properly refers to the Slavic people known as *Severians*, who had come from the region of the upper Dniester to settle territory around the source of the Donets. Their name has come to be translated "Northerners," from Russian *sever*, "north." Hence the river's alternate name. Cf. **Novgorod-Seversky**, **Severodonetsk**.

Donetsk[1] (Донéцк) *City, eastern Ukraine.* The city, east of Zaporozhye, takes its name from the *Donetskiy bassejn*, i.e. the **Donbass**, in which it is situated, though not itself on the **Donets** River. The original name of the town was *Yuzovka* (Ю́зовка), representing the name of the Welsh industrialist John James *Hughes*, director of the London-based New Russia Coal, Iron and Rail Company, who in 1869 set up an ironworks here to provide iron for Russia's railroads. The mining settlement gained town status in 1917 and on the death of Lenin in 1924 was renamed *Stalino* (Стáлино), there already being an abundance of places named for Lenin. Following the discrediting of Stalin in the mid–1950s, it was renamed as now in 1961.

Donetsk[2] (Донéцк) *Town, southwestern Russia.* The town, west of Kamensk-Shakhtinsky, takes its name from the *Donets* River, on which it lies. Until 1955 it was known as *Gundorovka* (Гу́ндоровка). This Donetsk and the larger one in Ukraine are only some 93 miles (150 km) apart.

Dorogobuzh (Дорогобу́ж) *Town, western Russia*. The town, east of Smolensk, appears to derive its name from the Old Russian personal name *Dorogobud* (literally "I shall be dear"). It is not certain to what extent this name and that of **Drogobych** are of common origin.

Dorogomilovo (Дорогоми́лово) *District, Moscow, western Russia*. The western district of Moscow takes its name from the boyar Ivan *Dorogomilov*, who owned land here in a bend of the Moskva River in the 13th century.

Dorokhovo (До́рохово) *Town, western Russia*. The town, west of Moscow, is named for the Napoleonic Wars hero Ivan Semyonovich *Dorokhov* (1762–1815), who informed Marshal Kutuzov of the withdrawal of Napoleon from Moscow but who died soon after from his injuries.

Dorpat See **Tartu**.

Drezna (Дрёзна) *River, western Russia*. The river, a tributary of the Klyazma, has a name that appears to derive from Old Slavonic *drezga*, "forest." If so, the name shares a common origin with that of the German city of *Dresden*.

Drissa See **Verkhnedvinsk**.

Drogichin (Дроги́чин) *Town, southwestern Belarus*. The town, east of Brest, dates from the 12th century, and probably takes its name from the *Dregovich*, a Slavic people who once inhabited the region. It is possible, however, that the name may derive from that of an individual who owned land here, himself perhaps called *Dorog*.

Drogobych (Дрого́бич) *City, western Ukraine*. The city, southwest of Lvov, has a name that has been linked with Russian *doroga*, "road," "way," but it may actually originate in a personal name. If so, it may share a common source with **Dorogobuzh**.

Druzhba (Дру́жба) *Town, northern Ukraine*. The town, a railroad junction northeast of Konotop, near the Russian border, was formed in 1962 from the merging of three villages. Its name means "friendship," for the cordial relations deemed to exist between Russia, Ukraine, and Belarus, the latter republic being not far to the west.

Dubna (Дубна́) *Town, western Russia*. The town, north of Moscow, takes its name from the river here. Its own name, found elsewhere in Russia, derives from Russian *dub*, "oak," denoting a river flowing through an oak forest. Cf. **Dubno**, **Dubovka**.

Dubno (Ду́бно) *Town, western Ukraine*. The town, southwest of Rovno, takes its name from Russian (and Ukrainian) *dub*, "oak." (The Slavic word is ultimately related to English *timber*.) Similar names are found elsewhere. Cf. **Dubna**, **Dubovka**.

Dubossary (Дубосса́ры) *Town, eastern Moldova*. The town, on the Dniester southeast of Orgeyev, was founded in 1792 and named for the village of *Dubesar* here. Its own name ultimately goes back to Moldovan *dubas*, the term for a type of large fishing boat, especially one used on the Dniester. The final *-ary* of the name is an occupational suffix, here denoting the people who built such boats. The overall sense is thus "place of boatbuilders," rather than "place of fisherfolk."

Dubovka (Дубо́вка) *Town, western Russia*. The town, on the Volga northeast of Volgograd, arose in the 18th century as a defensive post built in an oak grove. Its name is thus based on Russian *dub*, "oak." Cf. **Dubna, Dubno**.

Dudinka (Дудинка) *Town, northern Russia*. The town, on the Yenisey north of Igarka, arose in 1667 as a wintering place called *Dudino*, probably for a person with first name *Duda* or surname *Dudin*. This gave the present name, which is also that of a river that joins the Yenisey here.

Dünaburg See **Daugavpils**.

Dushanbe (Душанбе) *Capital of Tajikistan*. The city, in the west of the republic, arose around a village with a weekly market. The name denotes the day it was held, and represents Tajik *dushanbe*, "Monday," from *du*, "two," and *shanbe*, "Saturday" (literally "Sabbath"), Monday being two days after this. From 1929 to 1961 the city was renamed *Stalinabad* (Сталинабад), from the name of *Stalin* and the Iranian placename suffix *-abad* meaning "inhabited place," "town."

Dvigatelstroy See **Kaspiysk**.

Dvina (Двина) *River, western Russia*. The name is actually that of two distinct rivers: the *Northern Dvina*, in northwestern Russia, which flows generally north into the White Sea, and the *Western Dvina*, in western Russia, which flows west through Belarus and Latvia into the Gulf of Riga. It is not certain that the names are actually of identical origin. It seems likely, however, that they could share a common source with similar river names such as **Danube, Dnieper**, and **Don**, in which case the basic sense is simply "river." See also **Severodvinsk**.

Dvinsk See **Daugavpils**.

Dvoryanskaya Tereshka See **Radishchevo**.

Dvurechensk (Двуреченск) *Town, west central Russia*. The town, southeast of Yekaterinburg, lies at the confluence of the Sysert and Iset rivers, and is named accordingly "two rivers," from Russian *dvu-*, "two," and an adjectival form of *reka*, "river."

Dyatkovo (Дятьково) *Town, western Russia*. The town, north of Bryansk, has a name that appears to derive from Russian *dyadka*, "uncle," used as a familiar form of address (like English "mister"). This was perhaps the nickname of the founder of the place.

Dykh Tau (Дыхтау) *Mountain, southwestern Russia*. The mountain, one of the loftiest in the central Caucasus, has a Turkic name meaning "steep mountain," from words related to modern Turkish *dik*, "steep," "perpendicular," and *dağ*, "mountain."

Dyurtyuli (Дюртюли) *Village, southwestern Russia*. The village, in Bashkortostan northwest of Ufa, has a Bashkir name meaning "four cottages."

Dzaudzhikau See **Vladikavkaz**.

Dzerzhinsk[1] (Дзержинск) *Town, western Russia*. The town, west of Nizhny Novgorod, was originally a village settlement named *Chernorechye*, "Black River," for its location on the Ob. It was then renamed *Rastyapino* (Растяпино), presumably for a local land-owning family. In 1929 it was given its current name, for the Soviet political leader of Polish origin, Feliks Edmundovich *Dzerzhinsky* (1877–1926). See also the next two entries below.

Dzerzhinsk[2] (Дзержинск) *Town, central Belarus*. The town, southwest of Minsk, was originally known as *Koydanovo* (Койданово), allegedly for Prince *Koydan*, defeated in battle here in medieval times. In 1932 it was renamed as now for the Soviet political leader of Polish origin, Feliks Edmundovich *Dzerzhinsky* (1877–1926), who was born only 19 miles (31 km) from here, on the Dzerzhinovo estate. The root of the name is the same as Russian *derzhat'*, "to hold."

Dzerzhinsk[3] (Дзержи́нск) *Town, eastern Ukraine*. The town, northeast of Donetsk, was originally known by the name of *Shcherbinovka* (Щерби́новка). In 1938 it was given its present name, in honor of the Soviet political leader of Polish origin, Feliks Edmundovich *Dzerzhinsky* (1877–1926).

Dzerzhinsky See **Naryan-Mar**.

Dzhalal-Abad (Джала́л-Аба́д) *Town, southwestern Kyrgyzstan*. The town, near the border with Uzbekistan, has an Arabic name, from *jalāl*, "greatness," "glory," and *ābād*, "inhabited place," "town." The town of *Jalalabad*, Afghanistan, has a name of identical origin.

Dzhalil (Джали́ль) *Town, western Russia*. The town, in Tatarstan northeast of Almetyevsk, is named for the Tatar poet Musa Mustafovich *Dzhalil* (1906–1944), who was captured by the Germans in World War II and who died in Berlin.

Dzhalilabad (Джалилаба́д) *Town, southern Azerbaijan*. The town, northwest of Lenkoran, was originally known as *Astrakhan-Bazar* (Астраха́н-База́р), "Astrakhan market," presumably because it lay on a Transcaucasian trading route south of **Astrakhan**. In 1967 it was renamed as now for the Azerbaijani writer *Dzhalil* Mamedkulizade (1866–1932), *-abad* being the common Iranian suffix meaning "town."

Dzhamantau (Джаманта́у) *Mountain range, southern Kyrgyzstan*. The range, in the Tien Shan northwest of Lake Chatyrkyol, has a Kirgiz name meaning "bad mountains," alluding to the unfavorable natural conditions: rare rainfall, scant snow, and few fertile meadows.

Dzhambul (Джамбу́л) *Town, southeastern Kazakhstan*. The original name of the historic town, near the border with Kyrgyzstan, was *Aulie Ata* (А́улие-Ата́), from Uzbek *aulie*, "holy," and *ata*, "father." In 1936 it was renamed *Mirzoyan* (Мирзоя́н), for the Azerbaijani politician Levon Isayevich *Mirzoyan* (1897–1939), who from 1933 held Communist posts in Kazakhstan. In 1938 it was further renamed as now for the Kazakh folk poet *Dzhambul* Dzhabayev (1846–1945), himself named for the mountain *Dzhambul* near Lake Balkhash where he was born.

Dzhankoy (Джанко́й) *Town, northern Crimea, southern Ukraine*. The town, northeast of Simferopol, takes its name from Turkic words *dzhan* (modern Turkish *yeni*), "new," and *koy* (Turkish *köy*), "village."

Dzhansugurov (Джансугу́ров) *Town, southeastern Kazakhstan*. The town, northeast of Taldy-Kurgan, is named for the Kazakh poet Ilyas *Dzhansugurov* (1894–1937), who was born here at a time when the locality was simply "Village No 4."

Dzharkent See **Panfilov**.

Dzhetysu (Джетысу́) *Historic region, southeastern Kazakhstan*. The region, south of Lake Balkhash, has a Turkic name meaning "seven rivers," from words related to modern Turkish *yedi*, "seven," and *su*, "water." The reference is to the seven rivers Karatal, Koksu, Bien, Aksu, Baksan, Lepsa, and Sarkand. The region is sometimes known by its Russian name, *Semirechye*, translating this.

Dzhezkazgan (Джезказга́н) *Town, central Kazakhstan*. The town, southwest of Karaganda, has a Kazakh name meaning "place where copper is mined." The copper mines here are among the largest in the world.

Dzhulfa (Джульфа́) *Town, southern Azerbaijan.* The town, on the Araks River which here forms the border with Iran, is said to take its name from a Turkic word, *dzhulf*, meaning "weaver." The historic town has been famous for its silk trade since the 16th century.

Dzungarian Ala Tau (Джунга́рский Алата́у) *Mountain range, southeastern Kazakhstan.* The range, which here runs along the border with northwestern China, takes its name from the *Dzungar*, an Oyrat (Mongol) people of the latter country. Their own name means "(those on the) left hand," from Mongolian *züün*, "left," and *gar*, "hand." They were so named because from their point of view, they were to the left, i.e. the north, of the rest of China or of Mongolia itself. For the second half of the name, see **Ala Tau**.

Echmiadzin (Эчмиадзи́н) *Town, western Armenia.* The ancient town, west of Yerevan, is the seat of the Armenian patriarch and dates from the 6th century B.C. In the 2nd century B.C. the settlement here was known as *Vardkesavan*. It then became *Vagarshapat* (Вагаршапа́т), from an Iranian personal name followed by the Iranian suffix *-abad*, "inhabited place," "town." In 1945 it took its present name, that of the ancient monastery nearby, when the latter was enclosed within the territory of the town. The name is said to mean "settlement of the children of God."

Efremov See **Yefremov**.

Egoryevsk See **Yegoryevsk**.

Ekaterinburg See **Yekaterinburg**.

Ekaterinenshtadt See **Marks**.

Ekaterinodar See **Krasnodar**.

Ekaterinopol See **Yekaterinopol**.

Ekaterinoslav See **Dnepropetrovsk**.

Ekibastuz (Экибасту́з) *Town, northeastern Kazakhstan.* The town, southwest of Pavlodar, takes its name from a nearby lake. This is L-shaped, so that it came to be known as the "two-headed lake," from Kazakh *yeki*, "two," *bas*, "head," and *tuz*, "salt lake."

Elabuga See **Yelabuga**.

Elbrus (Эльбру́с) *Mountain, Caucasus, southwestern Russia.* Europe's highest peak, in the western half of the Caucasus chain, has a name that has been variously derived from Iranian, Arabic, Turkic and other languages, with meanings such as "high mountain," "snowy ridge," and the like. It seems probable that the name ultimately goes back to the Indo-European element *alp*, meaning simply "mountain," that lies behind the name of the *Alps* in central Europe and the *Elburz* Mountains in northern Iran.

Elektrogorsk (Электрого́рск) *Town, western Russia.* The industrial town, east of Moscow, arose in 1912 on the construction of a peat-fueled electric power station. It was originally known as *Elektroperedacha* (Электропереда́ча), "electric transmission," this being the name of the power station itself, but in 1946 was renamed as now. The second part of the name represents Russian *gorod*, "town," not *gora*, "mountain." The terrain is level, even marshy here.

Elektroperedacha See **Elektrogorsk**.

Elektrostal (Электроста́ль) *Town, western Russia.* The industrial town, east of Moscow, was originally known by the hardly industrial name of *Zatishye* (Зати́шье), "quiet place." This was the name of the rural site where the company of the present name bought land to build its steelworks. In 1917 Russia's first steel plant with electric furnaces opened here, and in 1925 the railroad station was given the name of the manufacturing company, meaning "electric steel." This subsequently passed to the workers' settlement and to the town to which it was raised in 1938.

Elektrougli (Электроу́гли) *Town, western Russia.* The industrial town, southwest of **Elektrostal**, has a name meaning literally "electric carbons." The reference is to the carbon electrodes for arc lamps and projectors which were the original products of the works that opened here in 1899. From 1903 the factory produced carbon brushes of various types and carbon rods for soldering and welding.

Elektrovoz See **Stupino**.

Elensk See **Balta**.

Elets See **Yelets**.

Elista (Эли́ста) *Town, western Russia.* The Kalmyk capital, southeast of Rostov-on-Don, has a Kalmyk name meaning "sandy," from *ilis*, "sand." From 1944 to 1957 the town was known by the Russian name *Stepnoy* (Степно́й), "(town) of the steppes."

Elizavetgrad See **Kirovograd**.

Elizavetpol See **Gyandzha**.

Elton, Lake (Эльто́н) *Lake, western Russia.* The shallow salt lake, east of Volgograd near the border with Kazakhstan, is said to take its name from Kalmyk *altyn-nor*, "golden lake," supposedly either because its waters took on a golden sheen at sunset, or for the metallic hues of its shores. But it is possible that the name actually derives from an English sea captain called *Elton*, who entered Russian service during the reign of Peter the Great and who was granted rights here. If so, he was probably the adventurer John *Elton* (died 1751), who surveyed this region of Russia and who was engaged by the Russian Company to build ships on the Caspian Sea. (He did build them, but for the shah of Persia, a turnabout of loyalties that gravely offended the Russians and that resulted in his assassination.)

Ema (Эма) *River, Estonia.* The river, flowing east into Lake Chudskoye, has the full name of *Emajogi*. This represents Estonian *ema*, "mother," and *jogi*, "river," so that it is a "mother-river," or a main one.

Emba (Эмба) *River, western Kazakhstan.* The river flows generally southwest into the Caspian Sea. Its name is probably of Turkic origin and may originally have been *Yemboyy*, from Kazakh *yem*, "food," "feed," and *boyy*, "valley," so that it was the "valley of the feeding river," meaning one flowing through fertile land.

Energetik (Энерге́тик) *Town, southwestern Russia.* The town, on the Iriklinsky Reservoir northeast of Orsk, has a name alluding to its hydroelectric power station, from Russian *energetik*, "power engineer."

Engels See **Pokrovsk**.

Enisey See **Yenisey**.

Erevan See **Yerevan**.

Erivan See **Yerevan**.

Ermak See **Yermak**.

Erman Range (Э́рмана хребе́т) *Mountain range, southern Russia.* The range, south of Lake Baykal, is named for the German physicist and traveler Georg Adolf *Erman* (1806–1877), who made measurements of the earth's magnetism on a journey through northern Asia.

Erofey-Pavlovich See **Yerofey-Pavlovich**.

Essentuki See **Yessentuki**.

Estonia (Эсто́ния) *Republic, north central Europe.* The northernmost Baltic republic, bordering

Russia to the east and Latvia to the south, takes its name from its indigenous population, the *Estonians*. Their own name may mean "waterside dwellers," from the Baltic word *aueist*. It is not likely to be related to English *east*, despite the appropriateness of this description for a country on the east coast of the Baltic.

Esutoru See **Uglegorsk**.

Evpatoriya See **Yevpatoriya**.

Eysk See **Yeysk**.

Fabrichny (Фабри́чный) *Town, southeastern Kazakhstan*. The town, southwest of Alma-Ata, has an important cloth mill. Hence its name, as the adjectival form of Russian *fabrika*, "factory," "mill."

Faddeyevsky (Фадде́евский) *Island, New Siberian Islands, northeastern Russia*. The island, in the center of the group, was discovered in 1805 by Yakov Sannikov (see **Sannikov Strait**) and named for a trader, one Stepan *Faddeyev*, who first set up winter quarters here.

Fakel (Фа́кел) *Town, western Russia*. The town, in Udmurtia northwest of Votkinsk, has an ideological name, the Russian word for "torch," as a socialist guiding light. (The word itself is from German *Fackel*.)

Fedchenko Glacier (Федче́нко ледни́к) *Glacier, northeastern Tajikistan*. The glacier, in the western Pamirs, was discovered in 1878 by the Russian entomologist and explorer V. F. Oshanin and named for one of the first explorers of Central Asia, the Russian naturalist Aleksey Pavlovich *Fedchenko* (1844–1873), killed on Mont Blanc in the French Alps. It was Fedchenko who discovered what is now Lenin Peak, in the Transalay range.

Feodosiya (Феодо́сия) *Town and port, southeastern Crimea, southern Ukraine*. The town, on the Black Sea coast southwest of Kerch, was founded as a Greek colony by Milesians in the 6th century B.C. They named it *Theodosia*, "God-given (place)." In the 13th century it became a Genoese trading colony and was known as *Kaffa*, a name of uncertain origin. When the Crimea became part of Russia in 1783 the ancient Greek name was restored.

Fergana (Фергана́) *City, eastern Uzbekistan*. The city takes its present name from the *Fergana* valley in which it lies. The name represents the local Pamir word *pargana*, used for a semicircular mountain valley. The town was founded in 1876 with the name *Novy Margelan* (Но́вый Маргела́н), "New Margelan," for what is now the town of **Margilan**, 13 miles (22 km) to the northwest. In 1910 it was renamed *Skobelev* (Ско́белев), in honor of the Russian general Mikhail Dmitrievich *Skobelev* (1843–1882), who served much of his military career in Central Asia and who commanded forces in this region. The city finally received its present name in 1924.

Fershampenuaz (Фершампенуа́з) *Village, western Russia*. The village, northeast of Magnitogorsk, was founded in 1842 and named for the Russian victory over the French in 1814 at *Fère-Champenoise*, east of Paris. For other names of this type, see **Varna**.

Fersman, Mt. (Фе́рсмана гора́) *Mountain, northern Russia*. The mountain, in the northern Taymyr Peninsula, is named for the Soviet geochemist and mineralogist Aleksandr Yevgenyevich *Fersman* (1883–1945), one of the founders of geochemistry as a distinct science.

Fili (Фили́) *District, Moscow, western Russia*. The western district of Moscow takes its name from the *Fil'ka* River here. The origin of its own name is uncertain. In the closing years of the 17th century the church of the Dormition of the Virgin (Russian *Pokrov*, literally "covering") was built here, as a result of which the village was known as *Pokrovskoye* until the early years of the 20th century. It was incorporated in Moscow proper in the mid-1920s.

Fischhausen See **Primorsk**[2].

Fizuli (Физули́) *Town, southern Azerbaijan*. The town, southeast of Stepanakert, was originally known as *Karyagino* (Каря́гино). In 1959 it was renamed as now for the Azerbaijani poet *Fizuli* (1494–1556).

Floreshty (Флорешты) *Town, northern Moldova*. The town, northeast of Beltsy, has a name deriving from the Moldovan surname *Florya*, recorded in the 15th century. The *-eshty* suffix is possessive, so that the overall sense of the name is "[place] belonging to Florya."

Fokino (Фо́кино) *Town, western Russia*. The town, northeast of Bryansk, arose as the industrial settlement of *Tsementny* (Цеме́нтный), alluding to its cement manufacture (Russian *tsement*, "cement"). In 1964 it received its present name, for the Russian revolutionary Ignaty Ivanovich *Fokin* (1889–1919), who lost his life in Bryansk during the Civil War.

Fort-Aleksandrovsky See **Fort Shevchenko**.

Fort Shevchenko (Форт-Шевче́нко) *Town and port, southwestern Kazakhstan*. The town, northwest of Shevchenko, was founded as a military post on the Caspian Sea in 1716 under the name of *krepost Sv. Petra*, "St. Peter's Fort." The czar then was *Peter* the Great. The fortified settlement that arose around it was named in 1846 as *Novopetrovskoye*, "New St. Peter," and in 1857 as *Fort-Aleksandrovsky* (Форт-Алекса́ндровский), "Fort Alexander." The czar now was *Alexander* II. In 1939 it received its present name, marking the 125th anniversary of the birth of the Ukrainian poet and revolutionary, Taras Grigoryevich *Shevchenko* (1814–1861), in exile at the fortress here from 1850 to 1857. Cf. **Shevchenko**.

Fosforitny (Фосфори́тный) *Town, western Russia*. The town, southwest of Yegoryevsk, arose around a phosphorite (phosphate rock) mine in 1922. Hence its name, from Russian *fosforit*, "phosphorite."

Franz Josef Land (Фра́нца-Ио́сифа Земля́) *Island group, northwestern Russia*. The archipelago lies in the Arctic Ocean north of Novaya Zemlya. It was discovered in 1873 by the Austrian expedition of Julius von Payer and Carl Weyprecht and named by them for the Austrian emperor *Franz Josef* I (1830–1916). For some time it was also known as *Fridtjof Nansen Land* (Russian *Zemlya Frit'ofa Nansena*), for the Norwegian explorer, who visited the islands in 1896. The archipelago was annexed by the Soviet Union in 1926.

Friedland See **Pravdinsk**[1].

Frisches Haff See **Vistula Lagoon**.

Frunze See **Bishkek**.

Fryazino (Фря́зино) *Town, western Russia*. The town, northeast of Shchelkovo, is said to take its name from one Ivan *Fryazin*, owner of estates here in the early 16th century. He was an immigrant Italian (perhaps originally named *Fragino*) who was mintmaster to Czar Ivan III and who undertook various diplomatic missions.

Furmanov (Фу́рманов) *Town, western Russia*. The town, northeast of Ivanovo, was originally known as *Sereda* (Середа́). This name derives from Russian *sreda*, which can mean both "middle" and "Wednesday" (the middle day of the week). Here it has the latter sense, referring to a regular Wednesday market. In 1941 the town was renamed as now for the Soviet writer Dmitry Andreyevich *Furmanov* (1891-1926), who was born here.

Furukamappu See **Yuzhno-Kurilsk**.

Gafurov (Гафу́ров) *Town, northern Tajikistan*. The town, southeast of Khodzhent, was originally known as *Leninabad* (Ленинаба́д), "Lenin's town," for the railroad station here. In 1953 it was renamed *Sovetabad* (Советаба́д), "Soviet town." It kept this name until 1962, when it took over the name of *Khodzhent* (Ходжéнт) from the historic city to the northwest, which had itself been renamed Leninabad in 1936. It kept this name until 1964, when it reverted to Sovetabad. Eventually, in 1978, it was renamed as now for the Tajik Soviet politician Bobodzhan Gafurovich *Gafurov* (1908-1977), who was born near here.

Gagarin[1] (Гага́рин) *Town, western Russia*. The town, west of Moscow, was given its present name in 1968 in honor of the Soviet cosmonaut Yury Alekseyevich *Gagarin* (1934-1968), who was born near here. The town was founded in 1719 and was originally named *Gzhatsk* (Гжатск), for the *Gzhat* River on which it stands.

Gagarin[2] (Гага́рин) *Town, central Armenia*. The town, northeast of Yerevan, was founded in 1961 and named for the Soviet cosmonaut Yury Alekseyevich *Gagarin* (1934-1968), who that same year was the first man in space.

Gagra (Га́гра) *Town and port, northwestern Georgia*. The Black Sea resort, northwest of Sukhumi, has a name of uncertain origin. It is hardly connected with Greek *agrios*, "wild," as if the original people here were savages.

Galich (Га́лич) *Town, western Ukraine*. The town, north of Ivano-Frankovsk, has a name that is said to refer to the natural salt here, and that thus relates to Greek *hals* and Latin *sal*, "salt," and ultimately to *salt* itself. If so, the name is related to that of *Halle*, Germany. There is another *Galich* in western Russia, northeast of Kostroma. This could have the same origin. Whatever the case, it was the Ukrainian town that gave the name of **Galicia**.

Galicia (Гали́ция) *Historic region, east central Europe*. The region, which extends into much of present-day Ukraine, derives its name from the historic Russian town of **Galich**, which see for the origin.

Gancheshty See **Kotovsk**[2].

Gandzha See **Gyandzha**.

Garm (Гарм) *Town, central Tajikistan*. The town, northeast of Dushanbe, takes its name from the Tajik word meaning "hot," presumably referring to the hot springs near which it arose. Cf. **Obigarm**.

Gastello (Гастéлло) *Town, Sakhalin, eastern Russia*. The town, on the east coast of Sakhalin island southwest of Poronaysk, is named for the Soviet suicide pilot Nikolay Frantsevich *Gastello* (1907-1941). When his aircraft was hit during an attack on German tanks in Belorussia, he did not bail out but instead crashed his blazing plane into the enemy convoy, ordering his three-man crew to join him as he did so.

Gastello, imeni (Гастéлло и́мени) *Town, eastern Russia*. The town, northwest of Magadan, is named for the Soviet suicide pilot Nikolay Frantsevich *Gastello* (1907-1941) (see **Gastello**), *imeni*, meaning "named for."

Gatchina (Га́тчина) *Town, western Russia*. The town, southwest of

St. Petersburg, is said to take its name from the local Russian word *gat*, used for a wooden causeway laid over marshland. From 1923 to 1929 the town was known as *Trotsk* (Троцк), for the revolutionary leader Leon *Trotsky* (1879–1940). From 1929 to 1944 it was *Krasnogvardeysk* (Красногвардейск), from Russian *Krasnaya Gvardiya*, "Red Guards," the units of armed factory workers employed by the Bolsheviks to seize power at the time of the Revolution.

Gaurdak (Гаурдак) *Village, eastern Turkmenistan*. The village, northeast of Mukry, arose in 1947 around sulfur deposits and a sulfur processing plant. Its name is a corrupt form of *Kukurtdag*, the original Turkmen name meaning "sulfur mountain."

Gavrilovka See **Taldy-Kurgan**.

Gavrilov Posad (Гаврилов Посад) *Town, western Russia*. The town, southwest of Ivanovo, derives the first part of its name from the personal name *Gavril* ("Gabriel") or from a surname such as *Gavrilov* formed from this. The reference would be to the original landowner here. The second word, as for **Sergiyev Posad**, denotes the trading quarter adjacent to a medieval town.

Gavrilov Yam (Гаврилов Ям) *Town, western Russia*. The town, south of Yaroslavl, derives the first part of its name from the personal name *Gavril* ("Gabriel") or from a surname based on this, as for **Gavrilov Posad**. The second word is Russian *yam*, "mail staging-post." Such locations, where posthorses were changed, played a vital role in the everyday life of pre-revolutionary Russia. The postal service was so important that whole villages were involved in it, and every town had a special coachman's quarter.

Gaz-Achak (Газ-Ачак) *Town, northern Turkmenistan*. The town, on the border with Uzbekistan southeast of Urgench, arose in 1967 when a source of natural gas here was first exploited. Hence the name, from Russian *gaz*, "gas," and *Achak*, the name of the locality.

Gazli (Газли) *Town, southwestern Uzbekistan*. The town, northwest of Bukhara, arose in 1958 on the site of an important source of natural gas. Its name indicates this, and derives from Uzbek (and Russian) *gaz*, "gas," and the Uzbek adjectival suffix *-li*. The overall sense is thus "gas (town)."

Gdov (Гдов) *Town, western Russia*. The town, southwest of St. Petersburg, takes its name from the *Gda* River which here flows into Lake Chudskoye. The meaning of the river name is uncertain. It may be of Baltic origin and have a sense that is simply "damp," "wet."

Gegechkori (Гегечкори) *Town, west central Georgia*. The town, northeast of Samtredia, is named for the Georgian revolutionary Aleksey Aleksandrovich *Gegechkori* (1887–1928).

Gelendzhik (Геленджик) *Town and resort, southwestern Russia*. The Black Sea resort, southeast of Novorossiysk, has a name that is said to be a local word for some kind of tree, perhaps a birch or poplar. According to popular tradition, the name is of Turkish origin and means "little bride," from a word related to Turkish *gelin*, "bride." When the Turks were here in the late 15th century, they used the port to ship good-looking local girls back to Turkey for their harems. The name is supposed to refer to this, but the explanation is almost certainly a romantic fiction.

George Land (Георга Земля) *Island, Franz Josef Land, northwestern Russia*. The island, in the west of the group, was discovered in

1880 by an expedition under the British explorer Leigh Smith. It was named in 1897 by the British explorer F. G. Jackson for Prince *George*, the future King George V (1865–1936).

Georgia (Грузия) *Republic, southwestern Asia*. The republic, with the Caucasus forming its northern border with Russia, is an ancient land that takes its name from its indigenous people, known to eastern countries as *Gurz*. This gave modern Russian *Gruziya*, "Georgia," and *gruzin*, "a Georgian." The origin of the name is disputed, but it became associated with St. *George*, the country's patron saint. Hence its English name. The Georgians' own name for themselves is *Kartveli*, from which comes *Sakartvelo*, their name for the country. The Roman names for the region were **Colchis** and *Iberia*, the latter as for the Iberia that is now Spain and Portugal.

Georgiu-Dezh See **Liski**.

Georgiyevsk (Георгиевск) *Town, southwestern Russia*. The town, northeast of Pyatigorsk, arose around a fortress built in 1777 and named for St. *George*.

Gigant (Гигант) *Town, southwestern Russia*. The town, west of Salsk, grew from the *Gigant* ("Giant") sovkhoz (state farm) set up here in 1928 and is named for it.

Gissar Range See **Hissar Mountains**.

Glubokoye, Lake (Глубокое озеро) *Lake, northern Russia*. The long, narrow lake, east of Norilsk, has a Russian name meaning "deep," so contrasting it with Lake **Melkoye**, to the east.

Golden Horn See **Zolotoy Rog**.

Golden Ring of Russia (Золотое кольцо России) *Group of towns, western Russia*. A touristic name, in use from the 1970s, for a group of medieval towns to the northeast of Moscow. Chief among them are Sergiyev Posad, Pereslavl-Zalessky, Rostov, Yaroslavl, Kostroma, Ivanovo, Suzdal, and Vladimir. The group is so named since the towns lie on a clockwise looping route out from Moscow and back. They are "golden" because they are of unique historical and architectural interest.

Golovino (Головино) *District, Moscow, western Russia*. The northwestern district of Moscow takes its name from the former village here. It was itself so called from the owner of lands here in the mid-15th century, the boyar I. V. Khovrin-*Golova*.

Golovnin, Mt. (Головнина вулкан) *Volcano, Kuril Islands, southeastern Russia*. The active volcano, in the south of Kunashir island, at the southern end of the Kurils, is named for the Russian navigator Vasily Milkhaylovich *Golovnin* (1776–1831), who in 1811 charted a major portion of the Kurils (from Cape Nadzehda to the east coast of Iturup island). Also named for him are a strait in the northern Kurils and a cape in Novaya Zemlya.

Golutvin (Голутвин) *Historic town, western Russia*. The town, now merged with Kolomna southeast of Moscow, takes its name from Old Russian *golutva*, "forest clearing."

Goly Karamysh See **Krasnoarmeysk**[1].

Gomel (Гомель) *City, southeastern Belarus*. The city, southeast of Mogilyov, is named as *Gom* in a document of 1142. This and subsequent forms of the name suggest an origin in a Slavic word *gom*, "hill," related to English *holm*. The local topography appears to confirm this, since the city is located on the raised right bank of the Sozh River.

Gorbatov (Горбатов) *Town, western Russia*. The town, west of

Nizhny Novgorod, takes its name from Prince Andrey *Gorbatov*-Shuysky, owner of estates here in the 16th century.

Gori (Го́ри) *Town, central Georgia.* The ancient town, northwest of Tbilisi, takes its name from Georgian *gori*, "mountain." A medieval fort in the town center is built on a steep slope. At this time the town was known as *Tonti*, said to derive from the Georgian word *tinta* of similar meaning.

Gorki (Го́рки) *Town, western Russia.* The town, southeast of Moscow, has a name found commonly elsewhere meaning simply "hill." For much of the 20th century the town was known as *Gorki Leninskiye* (Го́рки Ле́нинские), "Lenin's Gorki." Lenin first came here in 1918 to recuperate after an assassination attempt. He later vacationed here and spent the last months of his life here, from May 1923 to his death the following January.

Gorki Leninskiye See **Gorki**.

Gorky See **Nizhny Novgorod**.

Gorlovka (Го́рловка) *Town, eastern Ukraine.* The town, in the Donbass north of Donetsk, takes its name from the Russian mining engineer Pyotr Nikolayevich *Gorlov*, who in 1867 sank the first coalshaft here.

Gorno-Altaysk (Го́рно-Алта́йск) *Town, southern Russia.* The town, southeast of Biysk, is located in a mountainous section of the **Altay** region. Hence its name, with the first part representing Russian *gornyj*, "mountainous." The original name of the town was *Ulala*, said to be of Turkic origin and to mean "great one" (modern Turkish *ulu*, "great"). In 1932 this was changed to *Oyrot-Tura* (Ойро́т-Тура́), "Oyrot town," for the local *Oyrot*, a Mongoloid people. The present name was adopted in 1948 at the request of these people, who were aware that their ethnic name literally meant "poor." (They are now known as *Altay*.)

Gornozavodsk[1] (Горнозаво́дск) *Town, west central Russia.* The town, northeast of Perm, arose from a cement works built in 1950 by the railroad station of *Pashnya* ("pasture"). The subsequent workers' settlement was at first called *Novopashiysky* (Новопаши́йский) or *Novaya Pashnya* (Но́вая Па́шня) ("New Pashnya"). When the settlement was raised to town status in 1965 its name was changed as now, from Russian *gornyj*, "of the mountain," and *zavod*, "factory." The name relates to the geographical location of the place in the foothills of the Middle Urals.

Gornozavodsk[2] (Горнозаво́дск) *Town, Sakhalin, eastern Russia.* The town, on the southwest coast of Sakhalin island, is a coal-mining center. The name refers to this activity, from Russian *gornyj*, "mining," and *zavod*, "works." Before 1947 it was known by the Japanese name of *Naihoro*.

Gornyak (Горня́к) *Town, southern Russia.* The town, on the border with Kazakhstan southwest of Barnaul, has a name that is the colloquial Russian word for "miner." This relates to the main industrial activity here in the southwestern Altay, which is metal mining. There are other towns and settlements of the same name in the former Soviet Union.

Gorny Shchit (Го́рный Щит) *District, Yekaterinburg, west central Russia.* The southern district of the city has its origin in the village of *Verkhny Uktus* ("Upper Uktus," for the river here), which arose on this site at the turn of the 18th century. It was important strategically, as it was on the road from Kungur to Siberia. In 1709 it was attacked and destroyed by Bashkir forces. In 1721

V. N. Tatishchev, founder of Yekaterinburg itself, set up a fortified post here against any further "Bashkirian" onslaughts, and gave it its present symbolic name, meaning "mountain shield." In the course of time the route to Siberia was altered to pass through Yekaterinburg, while in Gorny Shchit, to the south of the city center, a complex of fortified factories arose. The fortifications soon became superfluous, and had all disappeared by 1773, when the village of the name alone remained.

Gorodets (Городе́ц) *Town, western Russia*. The town, on the Volga northwest of Nizhny Novgorod, has a name meaning "little town," from Russian *gorod*, "town," with the diminutive suffix *-ets*. In medieval times the settlement here was known as *Radilov*, from the personal name *Radil* with the possessive suffix *-ov*.

Gorodishche (Городи́ще) *Town, west central Belarus*. The town, west of Baranovichi, is just one of a number of this name. The meaning is "place where there was a fort," from Russian *gorod*, "fort" (later, "town"), and the suffix *-ishche* here meaning "remnant." The remains of a former fortification can be seen at many places of this name, especially in Belarus.

Gorodok[1] (Городо́к) *Town, northeastern Belarus*. The town, north of Vitebsk, is one of a number so called. Its name implies the former presence of a fort, from Russian *gorod*, "fort" (later, "town") and the suffix *-ok* which is now usually a diminutive but which here denotes the remnants of something. See also **David-Gorodok**, and cf. **Gorodishche**.

Gorodok[2] (Городо́к) *Village, western Russia*. The village, north of Moscow, has a name denoting an old fortified settlement (cf. **Gorodok**[1]). The allusion is to the historic medieval fortified town of *Radonezh*

(Ра́донеж), itself probably so called from the personal name *Radoneg*.

Gorodovikovsk (Городовико́вск) *Town, southwestern Russia*. The town, southeast of Rostov-on-Don, was originally the settlement of *Bashanta* (Башанта́). In 1971 it was raised to town status and renamed as now for the Soviet military leader Oka Ivanovich *Gorodovikov* (1879–1960), a cavalry commander in this region in World War II.

Gorokhovets (Горохове́ц) *Town, western Russia*. The town, west of Dzerzhinsk, was founded in 1239 on the site of the nearby village of *Gorodishchi*. It was then transferred to its present location. The name is said to derive from Russian *gorokh*, "pea," referring to abundant pea crops here. But perhaps it is simply an alteration of the earlier name, meaning "fort."

Gorshechnoye (Горше́чное) *Village, western Russia*. The village, southwest of Voronezh, was at one time noted for its clay pottery. Hence its name, from an adjectival form of Russian *gorshok*, "pot." The pots or pitchers themselves would have been used for baking pastry, boiling milk, brewing beer, etc.

Goryachevodsky (Горячево́дский) *Village, southwestern Russia*. The village, just southeast of Pyatigorsk, arose in 1819 as a Cossack settlement. It is named for the mineral springs here, from Russian *goryachaya voda*, "hot water."

Goryachy Klyuch (Горя́чий Ключ) *Town, southwestern Russia*. The town, south of Krasnodar in the foothills of the western Caucasus, is a noted spa and health resort. Hence its name, meaning "hot spring." It is also known by the alternate name of *Psekups* (Псеку́пс), that of the river which has its mountain source here.

Gotvald See **Zmiyov**.

Goverla (Говéрла) *Mountain, southwestern Ukraine*. The mountain, in the Carpathians near the Romanian border, takes its name from a South Slavic word *ovrl* or *ovrlina*, to which *g* was prefixed for ease of pronunciation. This is the term for a type of *kichka*, a form of ornamental headdress worn by married women in southern Russia. The mountain's shape is similar to this.

Graham Bell Island (Грéэм-Белл óстров) *Island, Franz Josef Land, northwestern Russia*. The chief easternmost island of the group is named for the Scottish born American inventor of the telephone, Alexander *Graham Bell* (1847-1922), whose scientific experiments excited navigators and explorers in the 1870s, when Franz Josef Land itself was discovered.

Grayvoron (Грáйворон) *Town, western Russia*. The town, southwest of Kursk near the border with Ukraine, derives its name from the dialect word for the cawing of a bird such as a raven, rook, or crow. The name would have been given initially to a stream where such noisy birds gathered, then passed to any nearby settlement. The word itself comprises Russian *graj*, "rook," and *voron*, "raven."

Gremyachinsk (Гремячинск) *Town, west central Russia*. The town, northeast of Perm, arose as a coal-mining settlement in 1941. It was raised to town status in 1949, and takes its name from the *Bolshaya Gremyachaya* ("Great Gremyachaya") River here. The river's own name derives from a dialect form of Russian *gremyashchiy*, "thundering," "roaring," referring to its noisy, turbulent current.

Gresovsky (Грéсовский) *Town, central Crimea, southern Ukraine*. The town, on the Salgir River northeast of Simferopol, takes its name from its power station, from the Russian abbreviation *GRES*, the acronym of *gosudarstvennaya rajonnaya elektrostantsiya*, "state regional electric power station."

Grigoriopol (Григориóполь) *Town, eastern Moldova*. The town, on the Dniester estuary southwest of Odessa, was founded in 1792 to accommodate refugees from Armenia. Its name means "Grigory's town," from *Grigory* Aleksandrovich Potyomkin (1739-1781), a favorite of Catherine the Great, and *-pol*, from Greek *polis*, "town." The name is said to have been given by the empress herself. In the reign of Paul I (1796-1801) the town was renamed *Chyornyj*, "black," for its proximity to the **Black Sea**, but under his successor, Alexander I (1801-25), the old name was restored.

Grodekovo See **Pogranichny**.

Grodno (Грóдно) *City, western Belarus*. The city, near the border with Poland, dates from at least the 12th century and has a name meaning "fortified place," from a word related to modern Russian *gorod*, "town."

Grozny (Грóзный) *City, southwestern Russia*. The city, capital of Chechenia, was founded here north of the Caucasus as the Russian fort of *Groznaya*, "fearsome," in 1818. The name was intended to suggest a stronghold that would intimidate the Turks in the war then going on. The present form of the name was adopted in 1869.

Grumm-Grzhimaylo Glacier (Грумм-Гржимáйло ледни́к) *Glacier, east central Tajikistan*. The glacier, in the Pamirs at the foot of Revolution Peak, is named for the Russian explorer and geographer Grigory Yefimovich *Grumm-Grzhimaylo* (1860-1936), leader of the expedition that discovered it in 1887.

Gryazi (Гря́зи) *Town, western Russia.* The town, southeast of Lipetsk, has a name related to Russian *gryaz'*, "dirt," implying a muddy or marshy place. Cf. **Gryazovets**.

Gryazovets (Гря́зовец) *Town, western Russia.* The town, southeast of Vologda, has a name related to Russian *gryaz'*, "dirt," referring to the marshland here. Cf. **Gryazi**.

Gubkin (Гу́бкин) *Town, western Russia.* The town, northeast of Belgorod, arose in the 1930s on the site of the village of *Korobkovo* when the iron-ore deposits of the Kursk Magnetic Anomaly here were first exploited. The name commemorates Ivan Mikhaylovich *Gubkin* (1871–1939), the Soviet geologist who pioneered research in the region in the 1920s.

Gulistan (Гулиста́н) *Town, central Uzbekistan.* The town, southwest of Tashkent, arose in the late 19th century as the village of *Golodnaya Step'*, "Hunger Steppe," where it is located. (This is also known as *Yuzhnaya Golodnaya Step'*, "Southern Hunger Steppe," to be differentiated from the *Golodnaya Step'* that is the alternate name of the **Betpak-Dala** steppe region in Kazakhstan.) In 1922 the village was raised to settlement status with the name *Mirzachul* (Мирзачу́ль), from Uzbek *mirza*, "edge," and *chul*, "desert," "waterless steppe," also referring to the location. In 1961 it was promoted to full urban rank and given its present name, meaning "place of roses," from a Turkic word related to modern Turkish *gül*, "rose," and the Iranian suffix *-stan* meaning "inhabited place," "town." There is another *Gulistan* in southern Uzbekistan, north of Termez, and yet another in western Pakistan. The name always has the same meaning, and is itself familiar in literature as a classic poem by the 13th-century Persian poet Sa'di.

Gumbinnen See **Gusev**.

Gundorovka See **Donetsk**[2].

Guryev (Гу́рьев) *Town and port, western Kazakhstan.* The town, on the north coast of the Caspian Sea at the mouth of the Ural River, was founded in 1640 by the *Guryev* family of fish merchants, who built a palisaded settlement here as a defense against the Cossacks. The town is still an important center of the fishing industry.

Guryevsk (Гу́рьевск) *Town, western Russia.* The town, northeast of Kaliningrad, was named commemoratively in 1946 for the Soviet Army officer S. S. *Guryev*, killed here in 1945 during the Russian assault on Königsberg (modern Kaliningrad). The former German name of the town was *Neuhausen*.

Gusev (Гу́сев) *Town, western Russia.* The town, east of Chernyakhovsk, was so named in 1946 for the Soviet Army officer S. I. *Gusev*, killed in 1945 defending the town, which was then known by the German name of *Gumbinnen*.

Gusinoozersk (Гусиноозёрск) *Town, southern Russia.* The coal-mining town, southwest of Ulan-Ude, is so named for its location on the northeast coast of Lake **Gusinoye** (Russian *Gusinoye ozero*). Until 1953, when it was raised to urban status, it was known as *Shakhty* (Ша́хты), "pits," "mines."

Gusinoye, Lake (Гуси́ное о́зеро) *Lake, southern Russia.* The lake, south of Lake Baykal, is named for its abundance of wild geese, from Russian *gus'*, "goose." An earlier Turkic name of the lake was *Khulnor*, both parts of which mean "lake" (Turkish *göl* and Buryat *nor*). This came about because the local Buryat people wrongly associated the first part of the name with their own word *khul*, "leg," so took the name to mean "leg lake," as if the lake had at one time been shallow enough to wade across. The town of **Gusinoozersk** and village of *Gusinoye Ozero* are both on the lake and are named for it.

Gus-Khrustalny (Гусь-Хрустáльный) *Town, western Russia*. The town, west of Murom, has a name that appears to mean "crystal goose," from Russian *gus'*, "goose," and *khrustal'nyj*, "crystal." The first part of the name in fact comes from the *Gus* River on which the town lies. The second part does mean "crystal" and refers to the glassworks established here in the 18th century. Cf. **Gus-Zhelezny**. The two towns arose at the same time and are only 40 miles (64 km) apart.

Gus-Zhelezny (Гусь-Желéзный) *Town, western Russia*. The town, northwest of Kasimov, has a name that appears to mean "iron goose," from Russian *gus'*, "goose," and *zheleznyj*, "iron." However, the first part of the name comes from the *Gus* River on which the town lies, while the second part refers to the ironworks that arose here in the 18th century. Cf. **Gus-Khrustalny**.

Guzar (Гузáр) *Town, southeastern Uzbekistan*. The town, southeast of Karshi, takes its name from a Tajik word meaning either "pass" (through a mountain) or "ford" (across a river). The name is found elsewhere in the region.

Gvardeysk (Гвардéйск) *Town, western Russia*. The town, east of Kaliningrad, derives its present name from Russian *gvardiya*, "Guards." This was a title of honor given to Soviet Army units that had won distinction in World War II. Before 1946 the town had the German name of *Tapiau*.

Gvozdev Islands See **Diomede Islands**.

Gyandzha (Гянджá) *City, northwestern Azerbaijan*. The city, in the foothills of the Caucasus, is of ancient origin and takes its name from the river on which it stands. The river name itself is of uncertain origin. In 1804 the settlement that had developed here was renamed *Yelizavetpol* (Елизаветпóль), "Elizabeth's town," for the wife of Czar Alexander I, *-pol* representing Greek *polis*, "town," in the manner of the day. In 1935 it was further renamed *Kirovabad* (Кировабáд), commemorating the Soviet politician Sergey Mironovich *Kirov* (1886–1934), who had been secretary of the Azerbaijan Communist Party in the 1920s. The Iranian *-abad* element here means "town." In 1989 the city reverted to its original name.

Gyoygyol (Гёйгёль) *Lake, western Azerbaijan*. The mountain lake, on the northern slopes of the Murovdag (Mrovdag) Range, northwest of Agdam, has an Azerbaijani name meaning "blue lake."

Gzhatsk See **Gagarin**[1].

Heiligenbeil See **Mamonovo**.

Heinrichswalde See **Slavsk**.

Henrietta Island (Генриéттыóстров) *Island, De Long Islands, northeastern Russia*. The northernmost island in the group takes its name from the *Henrietta*, a ship in De Long's expedition of 1879–81. (See **De Long Islands**.) The ship's own name was that of the mother of James Gordon Bennett (1841–1918), the American editor and philanthropist who had financed the expedition. Cf. **Jeannette Island**.

Herald Island (Герáльд остров) *Island, northeastern Russia*. The island, in the Chukchi Sea east of Wrangel Island, was discovered in 1849 by the British vice admiral Sir Henry Kellett (1806–1875), who named it for his ship, the frigate *Herald*.

Hirochi See **Pravda**.

Hissar Mountains (Гиссáрский хребéт) *Mountain range, northwestern Tajikistan.* The range takes its name from Avar *hisor*, "fort in a plain," the plain in question lying to the south of the range, and the fort mentioned giving its name to it in relatively recent times.

Honto See **Nevelsk**.

Hooker Island (Гýкера óстров) *Island, Franz Josef Land, northwestern Russia.* The island, in the western half of the group, is named for the British botanist Sir Joseph Dalton *Hooker* (1817-1911), one of whose specialties was the study of Arctic plants.

Idritsa (Йдрица) *Village, western Russia.* The village, northwest of Nevel, takes its name from that of the river on which it stands. The river's own name probably means simply "water," from an Indo-European root word related to Greek *hudōr*, "water."

Igarka (Игáрка) *Town, northern Russia.* The town, southeast of Dudinka, arose in 1928 on the site of a winter lodge built here by a hunter named *Yegor*, known to local people by the pet form of his name as *Igarka*. (The name itself corresponds to English *George*.) Hence the name of the town.

Igumen See **Cherven**.

Ik (Ик) *River, southwestern Russia.* The river, also known as the *Bolshoy Ik* ("Great Ik"), is a tributary of the Kama and for some distance forms the boundary between Tatarstan and Bashkortostan. Its name is found for several rivers elsewhere in this region of Russia, the northernmost as a tributary of the Yayva and the southernmost as a tributary of the Sakmara. It is possible that the name is of Finno-Ugrian origin and thus related to Finnish *joki* or Saami (Lapp) *jokk*, both meaning "river." On the other hand, some Turkic root word *yk* or *ek* meaning "river" could also be considered, and Kalmyk *ik*, "great," has further been proposed. Local people have a more colorful explanation: someone plunged into the river one day and the cold or the shock made him hiccup (Russian *iknut'*)!

Ili (Илú) *River, southeastern Kazakhstan.* The river rises in western China and flows through southeastern Kazakhstan into Lake Balkhash. Its name is said to represent Mongolian *ili*, "sparkling," "shining," denoting a rapid current.

Ilich (Ильúч) *Town, southern Kazakhstan.* The town, southwest of Tashkent, has a name found fairly widely in the former USSR. It represents the patronymic (middle name) of Vladimir *Ilich* Lenin (1870-1924). Cf. **Ilichyovsk**.

Ilichyovsk (Ильичёвск) *Town and port, southern Ukraine.* The town arose as docks to the southwest of the main port of Odessa in 1958, taking its name from the patronymic (middle name) of Vladimir *Ilich* Lenin (1870-1924). It became a port independent of Odessa in 1961, and in 1973 was raised to town status.

Ilinsky (Ильúнский) *Town, west central Russia.* The town, on the Obva River at the southern end of the Kamskoye Reservoir, north of Perm, is recorded in a document of 1579 as having a church dedicated to St. *Ilya* (Elias), and that is clearly the origin of the present name.

Ilmen (Úльмень) *Lake, western Russia.* The shallow lake, south of Novgorod, has a name believed to derive from a local dialect word meaning simply "lake." A link with Greek *limnē*, "pool," "marsh," is not impossible, since this (through Turkic languages) itself gave Russian *liman*, "flood plain," "estuary." Cf. **Ilmen Range**.

Ilmen Range (Ильме́нский хребе́т) *Mountain range, west central Russia*. The range, at the northern end of the Southern Urals, west of Chelyabinsk, takes its name from one of the many lakes here. Its own name is probably a corruption of Bashkir *Imänkül*, "oak tree lake." There are no oaks now, except those recently planted in the nature preserve here, but there obviously once were. The region, a popular tourist center, is usually referred to by Russians as *Il'meny*, "the Ilmens."

Ilovaysk (Илова́йск) *Town, eastern Ukraine*. The town, just east of Makeyevka, takes its name from the surname, *Ilovaysky*, of a landowner here in prerevolutionary times.

Ilovlya (Йловля) *River, southwestern Russia*. The river, a tributary of the Don, which it enters northwest of Volgograd, has a name based on Russian *il*, "mud," "silt."

Ilukste (Йлуксте) *Village, southeastern Latvia*. The village, northwest of Daugavpils, takes its name from the river on which it stands. The river's own name comes from a word related to Lithuanian *luksztas*, "reed."

Iman See **Dalnerechensk**.

Imandra (Ймандра) *Lake, northwestern Russia*. The lake, south of Murmansk, is said to take its name from a local (Saamian) word for a lake with a broken shoreline and many islands.

Imeretia (Имере́тия) *Historic region, western Georgia*. The former independent kingdom takes its name from Georgian *imer*, "beyond," and the placename suffix *-eti*, so that it is the "place beyond." It is separated from eastern Georgia by the Likhsky mountain range, between the Great Caucasus and Little Caucasus.

Imperatorskaya Gavan See **Sovetskaya Gavan**.

Indigirka (Индиги́рка) *River, northeastern Russia*. The river, in Yakutia, flows north into the East Siberian Sea. Its name derives from an Evenki people, the *Indigir*, with their own name of uncertain origin. The suffix *-ka* has a possessive function, so that the name overall means "(river) of the Indigir."

Ingermanland See **Izhora**.

Ingoda (Инго́да́) *River, southeastern Russia*. The river, between Lake Baykal and the Mongolian border, is said to take its name from Evenki *ingakte*, "pebbles," referring to its stony bed.

Ingria See **Izhora**.

Ingul (Ингу́л) *River, southern Ukraine*. The river, a tributary of the Bug, is said to take its name from Turkic words meaning "new lake" (modern Turkish *yeni*, "new," and *göl*, "lake"). But this origin is suspect, and a more likely source is in a Turkic word meaning "cave," "pit," related to modern Turkish *in*, "den."

Ingulets (Ингуле́ц) *River, southern Ukraine*. The river, a tributary of the Dnieper, appears to be named for the nearby **Ingul**, with *-ets* the diminutive suffix. It is thus the "Little Ingul."

Ingushetia (Ингуше́тия) *Republic, southwestern Russia*. The republic, until 1992 combining with **Chechenia** as *Checheno-Ingushetia*, lies just north of the Caucasus and takes its name from its indigenous people, the *Ingush*, so named from the mountain village of *Angusht*. Their own name for themselves is *Galgai*, "mountain dwellers."

Inkerman (Инкерма́н) *Village, southwestern Crimea, southern*

Ukraine*. The village, just east of Sevastopol, and famous as the scene of a Crimean War battle (1854), is said to take its name from Turkic words related to modern Turkish *yeni*, "new," and *kerman*, "fort." However, the first part of the name could mean "cave," from a word represented by Turkish *in*, "den," so that the sense is "concealed fort." The name is now that of the railroad station of the town of *Belokamensk* ("white stones") here, formed in 1976.

Insterburg See **Chernyakhovsk**.

Iori (Иори) *River, Georgia*. The river, rising in eastern Georgia and flowing southeast into the Mingechaur Reservoir, has a name said to derive from a Georgian word meaning "double," presumably referring to a characteristic confluence at some point.

Irbit (Ирбит) *Town, west central Russia*. The town, northwest of Tyumen, takes its name from the river on which it arose in about 1631. The river name is of uncertain origin but may derive from some Turkic source (Tatar and Bashkir *ir* mean "man," for example) and be based on a personal name.

Irendyk (Ирендык) *Mountain range, southwestern Russia*. The range, at the southern end of the Southern Urals, has a name that may derive from Bashkir *yyryndy*, "ravine," "gulch," meaning that the chain is intercut with gullies of this type.

Irgiz (Иргиз) *River, central Kazakhstan*. The river, a tributary of the Turgay, is popularly said to have a name meaning "big girl," "young heroine," from its chance resemblance to Turkic words related to modern Turkish *iri*, "big," and *kız*, "girl." However, the meaning "winding" is more plausible, from a word related to Turkish *eğri*, "crooked," "bent." The actual meaning remains uncertain.

Irkutsk (Иркутск) *City, southern Russia*. The Siberian city, north of the southwestern end of Lake Baykal, takes its name from the *Irkut* River on which it lies. The river name is of uncertain origin, but may derive from a people who once lived here.

Irtysh (Иртыш) *River, northeastern Kazakhstan*. The river rises in the Altay Mountains and flows west across the Chinese border to join the Ob, as that river's largest tributary. There have been many attempts to explain the name. One of the more likely derives it from an Iranian element *ir* meaning "rapid," "fast-flowing," and a Turkic form of a Ket word *ses* meaning "river." The upper reaches of the Irtysh are well known for their fast currents.

Isachenko Island (Исаченко остров) *Island, northwestern Russia*. The island, the largest in the Sergey Kirov group, in the Kara Sea, is named for the Soviet microbiologist and botanist Boris Lavrentyevich *Isachenko* (1871–1948), founder of the science of marine microbiology in its particular application to polar seas.

Ishimbay (Ишимбай) *Town, southwestern Russia*. The town, south of Sterlitamak, is an oil-drilling settlement established in 1932 on the site of the old Bashkir village of *Ishimbayevo*, itself recorded in 1633. The name comes from the Bashkir personal name *Ishembay*, meaning "my friend is rich." The name is coincidentally appropriate for the oil wealth gained in modern times.

Issyk-Kul[1] (Иссык-Куль) *Lake, northeastern Kyrgyzstan*. The name has long been said to mean "hot lake," from Kirgiz *ysyk*, "hot," and *kul*, "lake." It is true that the lake does not freeze over in winter, but this is not because its waters are warm; it is because they are salt and constantly agitated by strong winds. For this reason, specialists in Turkic placenames now suggest that a more likely sense is "holy lake," from Kirgiz *yzykh*, "sacred," "hallowed." The lake is still revered by the local Kirgiz, who until recently would not defile its waters by swimming in it or even fishing in it.

Issyk-Kul[2] (Иссы́к-Куль) *Town, northeastern Kyrgyzstan*. The town is at the western end of Lake **Issyk-Kul** and takes its name from it. It arose as the village of *Rybachye* (Рыба́чье), "fishermen's (village)," denoting the chief occupation of its inhabitants. In 1989, however, when the town had clearly grown beyond a fishing village, it adopted the name of the lake.

Istobnoye (Исто́бное) *Village, southwestern Russia*. The village, southwest of Stary Oskol, has a Slavic name related to Russian *izba*, "hut," "cottage," denoting a basic place of habitation. The name is found elsewhere in this part of Russia and in Ukraine, to the south. There is an identically named village around 55 miles (90 km) east of this one.

Istra (И́стра) *Town, western Russia*. The town, west of Moscow, was originally called *Voskresensk* (Воскресе́нск), for its monastery, dedicated to the festival of the *Resurrection* (Russian *Voskreseniye*). In 1930 it was renamed as now for the river on which it lies. The river name is of disputed origin. It has been linked with *Ister*, a former name of the lower Danube, but it may mean simply "water," "river."

Itkul (И́ткуль) *Lake, southwestern Russia*. The lake, south of Yekaterinburg, has a name of Turkic (Tatar or Bashkir) origin meaning "meat lake," from *it*, "meat," and *kul*, "lake." The reference is both to the plentiful fish in the lake and to the abundant game formerly found in the surrounding forests.

Iturup (Итуру́п) *Island, Kuril Islands, southeastern Russia*. The largest of the Kuril Islands, at the southern end of the chain, has a name said to derive from Ainu *etoropa*, "jellyfish," presumably for the abundance of these creatures in the waters off its coasts. The island is claimed by Japan, for whom it is *Etorofu*.

Ivangorod (Иванго́род) *Town, western Russia*. The town, on the Narva River west of St. Petersburg, was founded as a fortress on the Swedish frontier in 1492 during the reign of Czar *Ivan* III and is named for him. The name as a whole thus means "Ivan's town," the latter half being Russian *gorod*, "town."

Ivan Grozny, Mt. (Ива́на Гро́зного вулка́н) *Volcano, Kuril Islands, southeastern Russia*. The volcano, in the center of the island of Iturup, has a Russian name meaning "Ivan the Terrible," as the common byname of Czar Ivan IV. The volcano was given the name in 1946 when the Kurils were being charted for Soviet government purposes.

Ivano-Frankovsk (Ива́но-Фра́нковск) *City, western Ukraine*. The city, southeast of Lvov, was founded in 1662 with the name of *Stanislav* (Станисла́в), for *Stanisław* Potocki, a member of the landed Polish family who owned estates here. In 1962 the city was given its present name, in honor of the Ukrainian writer and journalist *Ivan* Yakovlevich *Franko* (1856–1916), who was born in western Ukraine and spent most of his life there.

Ivanovo (Ива́ново) *City, western Russia*. The city, southeast of Yaroslavl, is a long-established industrial (textile-manufacturing) center which in 1871 merged with the nearby village of *Voznesenskaya* ("Ascension," for its church) to become *Ivanovo-Voznesensk* (Ива́ново-Вознесе́нск). In 1932 it gained town status and acquired its present name. This appears to derive from someone called *Ivan*, but his identity remains uncertain. The derivation may lie in the dedication of an earlier church here to St. John the Evangelist (Russian *Ioann Bogoslov*).

Ivanovo-Voznesensk See **Ivanovo**

Ivashchenkovo See **Chapayevsk**

Ivdel (Ивдель) *Town, west central Russia.* The town, just east of the Northern Urals, north of Krasnoturinsk, takes its name from the river here. The river name is generally said to represent Mansi *ivdel*, "treeless," describing the terrain. However, this interpretation does not accord with the toponymy, since the river flows through forest-clad mountains. Moreover, this particular Mansi word is not found in any other placename. The Mansi themselves call the river *Ivtil* or *Ivlya*. If the *-l* is regarded as a suffix, an exact opposite meaning emerges: "river of trees," with the *-de-* inserted to ease the pronunciation of *vl*.

IvGRES See **Komsomolsk**.

Ivnya (Ивня) *Village, western Russia.* The village, south of Kursk, takes its name from the river on which it stands. The river name is based on Russian *iva*, "willow." Similar names are found elsewhere, but in some cases could derive from the personal name *Ivan*.

Izhevsk (Иже́вск) *Town, western Russia.* The town, northeast of Kazan, takes its name from the *Izh* River, on which it was founded in 1760 as an ironworks. The meaning of the river name is unknown. From 1984 to 1987 the town was renamed *Ustinov* (Усти́нов), for the Soviet defense minister Dmitry Fyodorovich *Ustinov* (1908–1984).

Izhora (Ижо́ра) *River, western Russia.* The river, near St. Petersburg, is said to take its name from a Finnic or Germanic word meaning "winding," perhaps ultimately related to modern German *eng*, "narrow." The river in turn gave the name of the Karelian (Finnish) *Ingrian* people who still inhabit the region, which is also known historically as *Ingria* (И́нгрия) or *Ingermanland* (Ингерманла́ндия). The district was long disputed between Sweden and Russia and was captured in 1703 by Peter the Great, who founded **St. Petersburg** here that same year. It passed permanently to Russia in 1721.

Izmaylovo (Изма́йлово) *District, Moscow, western Russia.* The eastern district of Moscow takes its name from the wealthy *Izmajlov* family, landowners here from the late 14th through mid-16th century.

Izumrud (Изумру́д) *Town, west central Russia.* The town, northwest of Asbest, derives its name from the emeralds discovered here in 1831. Russian *izumrud* and English *emerald* both come from the same ultimate source: Greek *smaragdos*, although the word reached Russia through Turkish *zümrüt*, whereas it passed into English from Old French *esmeralde*.

Izvestia Islands ("Изве́стий" острова́) *Island group, northern Russia.* The islands, in the Kara Sea north of Dikson, are named for the Soviet newspaper *Izvestiya*. Their full Russian name is *Izvestiya TsIK*, or *Izvestiya Tsentral'nogo Ispolnitel'nogo Komiteta*, "News of the Central Executive Committee," which was the paper's official title from 1917 to 1938. (The "Central Executive Committee" was that of the Councils of Workers' and Soldiers' Deputies.)

Izyaslav (Изя́слав) *Town, western Ukraine*. The town, southeast of Rovno, is said to take its name from its founder in the 11th century, Prince *Izyaslav* Yaroslavich (1024–1078), although there were other princes of this name (which means "taking the glory"). The original form of the name was almost certainly *Izyaslavl* (cf. **Yaroslavl, Zaslavl**), where the final *-l* denotes possession.

Jeannette Island (Жанне́тты о́стров) *Island, De Long Islands, northeastern Russia*. The easternmost island of the group takes its name from the ship *Jeannette* in De Long's expedition of 1879–81 (see **De Long Islands**). The ship's own name was that of the daughter of the expedition's sponsor, the American editor James Gordon Bennett (1841–1918). Cf. **Henrietta Island**. (*Jeannette* probably represents a blend of father *James* and mother *Henrietta*.)

Jelgava (Ёлгава) *City, central Latvia*. The city, southwest of Riga, was founded in 1266 when the Livonian knights built a castle here. It came to be called *Mitava*, from Latvian *mit*, "to exchange," as it was a trading place. This name then passed to the town that grew up. The present name gradually took over, however. It derives from Liv *jalgab*, "town." (The Livs were a Finno-Ugrian people who settled on the Baltic coast and gave the name of Livonia.)

Jurmala (Ю́рмала) *Town and resort, northern Latvia*. The town, on the Gulf of Riga west of Riga, was formed in 1959 from a number of existing towns and villages. Its name represents Latvian *jūrmala*, "seaside," from *jūra*, "sea," and *mala*, "shore."

Kabachishche See **Zelenodolsk**.

Kabakovsk See **Serov**.

Kabardino-Balkaria (Кабарди́но-Балка́рия) *Republic, southwestern Russia*. The republic, in the north Caucasus, has *Kabardia* as its northern component, on mainly level terrain, and *Balkaria* as its southern, mountainous part. Both names are of ethnic origin, referring respectively to the *Kabardians* and *Balkarians*. The Kabardians took their name from a place here known as *Kabarda*, itself of uncertain origin. The people's own name for themselves is **Adygey** (which see). The Balkarians have a name believed to be related to that of the *Bulgarians*, in which case it probably represents the Turkic word *bulga* meaning "mixed." Their own name for themselves is *Taulu*, "mountain people," from a Turkic word related to modern Turkish *dağ*, "mountain."

Kacha (Ка́ча) *River, southwestern Crimea, southern Ukraine*. The river, which enters the Black Sea north of Sevastopol, may have a name of Turkic origin related to modern Turkish *göç*, "migration," perhaps referring to its "wandering" course.

Kachkanar (Качкана́р) *Town, west central Russia*. The town, in the Middle Urals northwest of Nizhnyaya Tura, takes its name from the nearby mountain, a rich source of titanomagnetite. The mountain's own name is of uncertain origin. It may be based on Mansi *nër*, "rocky mountain," although the first part of the name has no known Mansi correlative. A source in Turkic *kashka* or *kachka*, "bald," and *nar*, "camel," has also been proposed. The mountain has forest-covered lower slopes but bare rocky peaks, so that "bald camel" is an accurate enough description, even if a rather fanciful one. According to an article by R. Kaptikov in *Uralsky sledopyt* ("Ural pathfinder"), No. 4, 1982, one of the mountain's peaks is actually called "Camel" (Russian, *Verblyud*), for the resemblance of its contour to this animal. If so, this appears to confirm the origin.

Kadiyevka See **Stakhanov**.

Kadom (Ка́дом) *Town, western Russia*. The town, east of Ryazan, has a name of uncertain origin, although Finnish *katomaa*, "lost land," has been proposed. The usual fables exist to explain the name, one being that a Greek settled here and named the place for *Cadmus*, the mythical inventor of writing, another claiming that a cave here, lived in by an anchoress, was warmed from her sanctity *kak dom* (Russian, "like a house").

Kadzherom (Каджеро́м) *Town, northwestern Russia*. The town, southwest of Pechora in the Komi republic, has a name representing Komi *ködzhöröm*, "channel," "reach," "[old] river bed."

Kafirnigan (Кафирнига́н) *River, western Tajikistan*. The river, a tributary of the Amudarya, has a name meaning "hiding the infidels," "concealing the non-Muslims," with the first part of the name identical to the now derogatory English *kaffir*. When Islam spread to this region of Central Asia, inhabitants of this valley were slow to abandon their existing faiths as Buddhists and Mazdaists (Zoroastrians).

Kagul (Кагу́л) *Town, southwestern Moldova*. The town, southwest of Komrat, was founded in 1838 on the site of the village of *Frumoasa* ("Beautiful"). It is named commemoratively for the Russian victory over the Turks in 1770 on the *Kagul* River to the southeast.

Kainsk See **Kuybyshev**[1].

Kakhovka (Кахо́вка) *Town, southern Ukraine*. The town, on the Dnieper northeast of Kherson, takes its name from the *Kakhovsky* family, landowners here in the early 19th century.

Käkisalmi See **Priozyorsk**.

Kala (Кала́) *District of Baku, eastern Azerbaijan*. Originally a separate village, the district takes its name from Persian *kala*, "hill," "hill fort," referring to its elevated location above the Caspian Sea.

Kalach (Кала́ч) *Town, southwestern Russia*. The town, southwest of Uryupinsk, has a name deriving from a dialect term for a sharp bend in a river. The town is on such a bend at the confluence of the Tolucheyevka and Podgornaya. The name is found elsewhere, as for **Kalach-on-Don**.

Kalach-on-Don (Кала́ч-на-Дону́) *Town, southwestern Russia*. The town lies west of Volgograd on a sharp bend of the Don. Its name represents a dialect word for such a bend, with the river name added to distinguish this town from **Kalach**, to the northwest.

Kalarash (Калара́ш) *Town, central Moldova*. The town, northwest of Kishinyov, takes its name from a Moldovan word meaning "horseman," "courier," presumably referring to a former staging post here. The present town is on a road and rail route to Kishinyov and Tiraspol.

Kalata See **Kirovgrad**.

Kalevala (Ка́левала) *Town, northwestern Russia*. The town, in Karelia west of Kem, was originally known as *Ukhta*, a name of uncertain meaning. In 1963 it was renamed as now, for *Kalevala*, a poetic name for Finland and thus also for Karelia, as formerly part of Finland, itself meaning "land of heroes." (The name is familiar from *Kalevala*, the great Finnish epic that was pieced together from oral tradition in the mid-nineteenth century by the Finnish poet Elias Lönnrot.)

Kalinin See **Tver**.

Kaliningrad[1] (Калинингра́д) *City, western Russia*. The city, a

Baltic port between Poland and Lithuania, was given its present name in 1946 in honor of the Communist party leader Mikhail Ivanovich *Kalinin* (1875–1946). Before this it bore the German name of *Königsberg*, "royal mount." The city was founded in 1255 by the Teutonic Knights and given a name that paid tribute to the German emperor Ottokar II, who had aided them in their crusade against the heathens of East Prussia. See also **Tver**.

Kaliningrad[2] (Калининград) *Town, western Russia.* The town, northeast of Moscow, is named in honor of the Communist party leader Mikhail Ivanovich *Kalinin* (1875–1946). It was founded in 1938, when the former village of *Podlipki* (Подлипки), "by the lime trees," was raised to urban status.

Kalmykia (Калмыкия) *Republic, southwestern Russia.* The republic, northwest of the Caspian Sea, takes its name from its indigenous Mongoloid people, the *Kalmyks*. Their name is a corrupt form of their own name for themselves, *Khalmg*, from the Mongolian word meaning "mixed," referring to the mixed races of Mongol nomads who settled in this region from the 17th century.

Kaluga (Калуга) *City, western Russia.* The city, southwest of Moscow, is said to take its name from an identical Slavic geographical term for a raised area in marshland. This describes the original site of the town, which arose as a fort built in the 14th century on land by the Yachenka River. In the early 16th century the fort was moved to the site of the present town, almost two miles (3 km) to the south, on the banks of the Oka.

Kalyazin (Калязин) *Town, western Russia.* The town, north of Moscow, is said to take its name from a dialect word *kalyaga*, "slush," or *kalika*, "mud," "dirt." The town is on low-lying land on the banks of the Volga.

Kama (Кама) *River, western Russia.* The river rises west of the Northern Urals and flows generally south to enter the Volga south of Kazan. A number of theories have been proposed for the name, which probably means simply "river," although some authorities have linked it with Russian *kamen'*, "rock," and others with the **Komi** people who inhabit the region where it rises. Both the latter theories are unlikely, however.

Kamchatka (Камчатка) *Peninsula, eastern Russia.* The peninsula, between the Bering Sea and the Sea of Okhotsk, takes its name from the river here, itself said to be named for Ivan Ivanovich *Kamchaty*, a Russian explorer here in the mid-seventeenth century. But this seems simplistic, although it is an improvement on a local legend about a pair of lovers, *Kam*, son of a mountain, and *Chatka*, daughter of a volcano, who plunged to their deaths from a peak somewhere here.

Kamenets (Каменец) *Town, western Belarus.* The town, north of Brest, dates from at least the 13th century. Its name suggests an origin in Russian *kamen'*, "rock," "stone." (Cf. **Kamenets-Podolsky**.) However, the site is not rocky or stony, so the reference may have been to a stone tower or fort here.

Kamenets-Podolsky (Каменец-Подольский) *City, southern Ukraine.* The city, northeast of Chernovtsy, takes the first part of its name from Russian *kamen'*, "rock," "stone," with the diminutive suffix *-ets*. The reference is to the town's stony site. Since this name is found elsewhere, a distinguishing word was added to locate this particular Kamenets in **Podolia** (which see). See also **Kamen-on-Ob**.

Kamenka (Каменка) *River, southern Russia*. The river, a tributary of the Angara, has a name found widely elsewhere in Russia both for rivers and, as here, for towns and villages on such a river. The derivation is in Russian *kamen'*, "stone," "rock," referring to the river's stony bed or rocky course.

Kamen-on-Ob (Камень-на-Оби) *Town, southern Russia*. The town, southwest of Novosibirsk, has a basic name deriving from Russian *kamen'*, "stone," "rock," "mountain." The name is found in various parts of Russia, especially in mountainous districts, as here, north of the Altay system. This particular Kamen has a distinguishing suffix locating it on the **Ob** River.

Kamenskoye See **Dneprodzerzhinsk**.

Kamensk-Shakhtinsky (Каменск-Шахтинский) *Town, southwestern Russia*. The town, northeast of Rostov-on-Don, arose in 1686 as a Cossack settlement on the Donets River and in 1817 was known as *Kamenskaya*, from Russian *kamen'*, "rock," "stone." It added *Shakhtinskij* when raised to urban status in 1927, from Russian *shakhty*, "mines," "pits," referring both to its manufacture of mining (pitshaft) gear and to the mining town of **Shakhty** to the south, which had existed under this name since 1920.

Kamensk-Uralsky (Каменск-Уральский) *Town, west central Russia*. The town, southeast of Yekaterinburg, is an important industrial center on the banks of the Iset River and its tributary the *Kamenka*, and takes its name from the latter. The settlement was founded in 1682 around an ironworks and was named *Kamensky* until 1935, when it became the town of *Kamensk*. From 1940 *Ural'skij* ("of the Urals") was added to distinguish the town from

Kamensk-Shakhtinsky. The river name itself derives from Russian *kamen'*, "rock," "stone."

Kamo (Камо) *Town, central Armenia*. The town, northeast of Yerevan, was originally known by the name of *Nor-Bayazet* (Нор-Баязёт). In 1959 it received its present name, representing the party pseudonym of the Armenian revolutionary *Kamo*, real name Simon Arshakovich Ter-Petrosyan (1882–1922).

Kamskoye Ustye (Камское Устье) *Town, western Russia*. The town lies south of Kazan on the banks of the Volga opposite the mouth of the **Kama** River, as its present name indicates, from *Kama* and Russian *ust'ye*, "mouth," "estuary." It arose in the 17th century under the name of *Rybnaya sloboda*, "fishing village." It then became *Bogorodskoye* (Богородское), for the dedication of its church to the Virgin Mary (Russian *Bogoroditsa*, literally "God-bearer"). It gained its present name in 1939.

Kamyshin (Камышин) *Town, southwestern Russia*. The town, on the Volga northeast of Volgograd, originally arose in 1667 as the village of *Kamyshinka* on the *Kamyshin* River, its own name deriving from Russian *kamysh*, "reeds," "rushes." Peter the Great then promoted a plan to convert the river into a canal so as to link the Volga with the Don, as a result of which a small fort named *Petrovskaya* (for Peter) was built on the bank opposite the village. When excavation work on the canal was abandoned, villagers were transferred from the left bank to the fort on the right bank, and their village became a town named *Dmitriyevsk*. The inhabitants sided with the Cossack rebel Pugachov (who claimed to be Czar Peter III) in the peasant rebellion of 1773–75, as a result of which the town was renamed *Kamyshin* in 1780 to rid the name Dmitriyevsk of its "rebel" associations.

Kamyshlov (Камышлóв) *Town, southwestern Russia*. The town, east of Yekaterinburg, takes its name from the small *Kamyshlovka* River on which it stands. The river name probably derives from Tatar or Bashkir *kamyshly*, "reeds," "rushes" (Russian *kamysh*).

Kananikolskoye (Кананикóльское) *Town, southwestern Russia*. The town, in the Southern Urals southwest of Magnitogorsk, arose from a copper-smelting works built here in the mid-eighteenth century on the *Kana* River, a tributary of the Belaya. Hence the first part of its name. The rest of the name refers to the dedication of its church to St. *Nicholas* Thaumaturge (Wonderworker) (Russian *Nikolaj*).

Kanash (Канáш) *Town, western Russia*. The town, in Chuvashia southwest of Kazan, has a name deriving from the Chuvash word for "council," i.e. the equivalent of "Soviet." It arose in the 1890s, and until 1925 was known as *Shikhrany*.

Kandagach See **Oktyabrsk²**.

Kandalaksha (Кандалáкша) *Town, northwestern Russia*. The town, a port on the White Sea south of Murmansk, has a Karelian name said to represent *kanta lakhshi*, "corner inlet," referring to the town's location on an inlet (the *Kandalaksha Gulf*) formed by an angle of the White Sea.

Kanev (Кáнев) *Town, central Ukraine*. The town, southeast of Kiev, probably takes its name from the personal name *Kan*, with *-ev* a possessive suffix. The meaning would then be "Kan's place." However, recent research has proposed an alternate origin: in Turkic *kagan*, "prince," "lord." If so, the placename would mean "prince's town."

Kanibadam (Канибадáм) *Town, northern Tajikistan*. The town, east of Khodzhent, takes its name from the Iranian phrase *kent-i-badam*, "town of almonds," from words related to modern Turkish *kent*, "town," and *badem*, "almond." The town has a thriving fruit and vegetable canning industry.

Kanin Peninsula (Кáнин полуóстров) *Peninsula, northwestern Russia*. The peninsula, projecting into the Barents Sea to the east of the White Sea, is said to have a name deriving from the Nenets word *kaninz*, "to freeze." The peninsula is inside the Arctic Circle.

Kansk (Канск) *City, southern Russia*. The city, east of Krasnoyarsk, takes its name from the *Kan* River on which it lies. The river name probably means simply "river" in a local (Tungusic) language.

Kantemirovka (Кантемúровка) *Town, southwestern Russia*. The town, southeast of Rossosh near the Ukrainian border, takes its name from the Moldavian prince Dmitry Konstantinovich *Kantemir* (1673–1723), who signed a secret treaty with Peter the Great agreeing a joint campaign against the Turks and authorizing the annexation of Moldavia by Russia. Peter subsequently appointed him an adviser on eastern affairs and granted him lands in this region, where he founded the present town. See also **Tsaritsyn**.

Kapsukas See **Marijampole**.

Kara See **Kara Sea**.

Karabagish See **Sovetabad**.

Karabakh See **Nagorno-Karabakh**.

Karabash (Карабáш) *Town, western Russia*. The town, in the Middle Urals northwest of Chelyabinsk, takes its name from the mountain here. The name is Turkic and means "black head," from words related to modern Turkish *kara*, "black," and *baş*, "head."

Kara-Bogaz-Gol (Карá-Богáз-Гол) *Lake, western Turkmenistan.* The large shallow lake was an inlet of the Caspian Sea until a dike was built across its entrance in 1979. Its name is Turkic and means "black throat lake," from words related to modern Turkish *kara*, "black," *boğaz*, "throat," and *göl*, "lake." The "throat" is the former narrow entrance. The black color is that of dried salt deposits here.

Karachay-Cherkessia (Карачáево-Черкéсия) *Republic, southwestern Russia.* The republic, at the western end of the Caucasus, takes its name from its two main indigenous peoples: the *Karachay* and the *Cherkess*. The *Karachay* take their name from the *Karachay* River here, with its own name of Turkic origin meaning "black water" (modern Turkish *kara*, "black," and *çay*, "stream"). The *Cherkess*, also known in English as *Circassians*, are said to take their name from an Ossetic word meaning "eagle." Their own name for themselves is **Adygey** (which see).

Karachayevsk (Карачáевск) *Town, southwestern Russia.* The town, south of Cherkessk, is the capital of **Karachay-Cherkessia**, and takes its name from the first part of this. It was founded in 1929 and until 1944 was known as *Mikoyan-Shakhar* (Микоян-Шахáр), "Mikoyan's town," from the Armenian statesman Anastas Ivanovich *Mikoyan* (1895–1978), who was secretary of the North Caucasus Communist party organization at the time of founding, and a Turkic word meaning "town," related to modern Turkish *şehir*, "city." From 1944 to 1947 it was renamed *Klukhori* (Клухóри), for the pass of this name to the south through the Caucasus.

Karadag (Карадáг) *Village, eastern Azerbaijan.* The coastal village, at the eastern end of the Caucasus, takes its name from a nearby mountain. The meaning, both here and wherever else it occurs (frequently in Turkey), is "black mountain," from Turkic words related to modern Turkish *kara*, "black," and *dağ*, "mountain." The reference is to a mountain that loses its snow cover in summer. Cf. **Karatau.**

Karadarya (Карадарья́) *River, southern Kyrgyzstan.* The name is a blend of Turkic *kara*, "black," and Iranian *darya*, "river." There are other identically named rivers in Central Asia.

Karadarya See **Zeravshan.**

Karafuto See **Sakhalin.**

Karaganda (Карагандá) *City, east central Kazakhstan.* The city, southeast of Tselinograd, was founded in 1932 on the site of a coal-mining settlement. Its name comes from a river or some other distinctive feature here, and derives from Kazakh *karagan*, "black acacia," with the adjectival suffix *-dy*.

Karagay (Карагáй) *Village, western Russia.* The village, northwest of Perm, has a name found elsewhere in this region and further south in Bashkortostan. It represents Bashkir *karagay*, "pine."

Karakalpakstan (Каракалпакстáн) *Republic, western Uzbekistan.* The republic takes its name from its indigenous inhabitants, the *Karakalpak*, their own name being of Turkic origin and meaning "black caps," from words related to modern Turkish *kara*, "black," and *kapak*, "cap." The reference is apparently to the people's traditional headdress. The final *-stan* is the Iranian suffix meaning "inhabited place," "land."

Karaklis (Караклис) *Town, northern Armenia.* The town, north of Yerevan, arose in 1826 when the villages of *Bolshoy Karaklis* and *Maly Karaklis* (respectively "Great" and "Little") became the single town of *Karaklis*. The meaning of the name is uncertain. In 1935 the town was renamed *Kirovakan* (Кировакан), "Kirov's town," from the name of Sergey Mironovich *Kirov* (1886–1934), the Communist party leader who established Soviet power in the Caucasus, and Turkic *-kan*, "town" (the equivalent of *-kand* and *-kent* elsewhere, as for **Samarkand** and **Tashkent**). The old name was readopted in 1991.

Karakol See **Przhevalsk**.

Karakul (Каракуль) *Lake, northeastern Tajikistan.* The lake derives its name from Turkic words meaning "black lake," as for modern Turkish *kara*, "black," and *göl*, "lake." The name is found for lakes elsewhere in the Asian republics, and for settlements on them.

Kara Kum (Каракум) *Desert, Turkmenistan.* The desert, which occupies most of Turkmenistan, has a Turkic name meaning literally "black sands," from words related to modern Turkish *kara*, "black," and *kum*, "sand." The name does not imply that the sands are evil or gloomy, but that they are generally dark because covered with vegetation. Cf. **Kyzyl Kum**.

Kara Sea (Карское море) *Sea, northern Russia.* The sea is an arm of the Arctic Ocean extending east of Novaya Zemlya. It takes its name from the *Kara* River that flows into it. Its own name may be that of a Nenets people formerly here.

Kara Strait (Карские ворота) *Strait, northern Russia.* The strait connects the Kara Sea with the Barents Sea, between Novaya Zemlya and the island of Vaygach. It was originally known to Russian merchants simply as *Vorota*, "passage" (now "gateway"). Once the name of the **Kara Sea** had become established, it was known as *Karskiye vorota*, "Kara Strait."

Karasu (Карасу) *River, western Kyrgyzstan.* Wherever the river name occurs in the Asian republics, it means "black water," from Turkic words related to modern Turkish *kara*, "black," and *su*, "water." The name does not refer to the color of the water but to that of its source, from black earth. The name is implicitly contrasted with **Aksu**, "white water." The water of a *Karasu* river is thus usually clearer than in a turbid *Aksu*.

Karasubazar See **Belogorsk**[2].

Karatau (Каратау) *Town, southern Kazakhstan.* The town, northwest of Dzhambul, takes its name from the *Kara Tau* mountains to the south. Their own name is of Turkic origin and means "black mountain," from words related to modern Turkish *kara*, "black," and *dağ*, "mountain." The name refers to mountains that lose their snow cover in summer, by contrast with mountains named *Alatau*, "white mountain," which have permanent snow. Cf. **Karadag**.

Karatobe (Каратобе) *Village, western Kazakhstan.* The village, southeast of Uralsk, has a Turkic name meaning "black hill," from words related to modern Turkish *kara*, "black," and *tepe*, "hill."

Karelia (Карелия) *Republic, northwestern Russia.* The republic, east of the border with Finland, takes its name from the region's indigenous inhabitants, the *Karelians*. The origin of their own name is uncertain, but it may relate to Finnish *karja*, "herd," "livestock." If so, the people were reindeer breeders.

Kargopol (Ка́ргополь) *Town, northwestern Russia*. The town, northeast of Vytegra, is first recorded in the 14th century. Its final *-pol* suggests Greek *polis*, "town," as for places in the Crimea. But in this region a Finnish origin is much more likely. The final source of the name is uncertain, but one proposal is Finnish *karhu*, "bear," and *puoli*, "side." However, the word *karhu* has not been recorded anywhere else east of the Finnish border, and it is possible that the name may actually be a combination of Russian dialect *karga*, "crow," and *pole*, "field."

Karkinit Bay (Каркини́тский зали́в) *Bay, southern Ukraine*. The bay is an inlet of the Black Sea between mainland Ukraine and the Crimea. Its name is an ancient one, and Ptolemy, in the 2nd century A.D., mentions a river here called *Karkinitis*. The ancient Greek settlement of *Kerkinitos* was believed to be near Yevpatoriya (Eupatoria). The Romans knew the bay as *Carcinites sinus*. The origin of the name is uncertain. According to one source, it derives from Scythian *karkana*, "cock." The significance of this is obscure, however.

Karl Marx Peak (Ка́рла Ма́ркса пик) *Mountain, southern Tajikistan*. The mountain, the highest in the south of the country, was first climbed by Soviet mountaineers in 1946 and named for *Karl Marx* (1818–1883), the German founder of modern Communism.

Karlo-Libknekhtovsk (Ка́рло-Ли́бкнехтовск) *Town, eastern Ukraine*. The town, northeast of Artyomovsk, takes its name from the German socialist leader *Karl Liebknecht* (1871–1919), assassinated in an unsuccessful Communist uprising.

Karpinsk (Карпи́нск) *Town, western Russia*. The town, in the Middle Urals west of Krasnoturinsk, was given its present name when raised to urban status in 1941 for the Soviet geologist Aleksandr Petrovich *Karpinsky* (1846–1936), who was born locally. Before this the name of the settlement was *Bogoslovsk* (Богосло́вск), for the church here dedicated to St. John the Evangelist (Russian *Ioann Bogoslov*). The present town was formed when this settlement combined with the neighboring one of *Ugol'nyj* (Russian *ugol'*, "coal").

Karsakpay (Карсакпа́й) *Village, central Kazakhstan*. The village, west of Dzhezkazgan, appears to derive its name from the Turkic personal name *Karsak*.

Karshi (Карши́) *Town, southern Uzbekistan*. The town, southwest of Samarkand, arose in the 14th century on an ancient caravan route from Samarkand and Bukhara to Afghanistan. Its name is of Turkic origin and means "fortress," "citadel."

Kartaly (Карталы́) *Town, southern Russia*. The town, southeast of Magnitogorsk near the border with Kazakhstan, has a name of Turkic origin, from *karta*, "hedge," with the suffix *-ly*, a possessive suffix, so that the overall sense is "place with a hedge."

Karyagino See **Fizuli**.

Kashira (Каши́ра) *Town, western Russia*. The town, southwest of Moscow, may derive its name from a south Russian dialect word *koshira*, "cattle pen," itself of Turkic origin. The town is on a high bank overlooking the Oka River, and this could have been a suitable site for such an enclosure.

Kashkadarya (Кашкадарья́) *River, southeastern Uzbekistan*. The second part of the river name is Iranian *darya*, "river," found elsewhere, as for the **Amudarya**. The first part appears to be of Turkic origin, from *kashka*, literally "bald," "bare." This could imply a river with clear water.

Kasimov (Касимов) *Town, western Russia*. The town, northeast of Ryazan, was founded in 1152 and until 1471 was known as *Gorodets-Meshchersky*, for the *Meshcher* people who inhabited this region. (*Gorodets* means "town.") It took its present name when Grand Prince Vasily II Tyomny ("The Dark") of Moscow assigned it to the Tatar khan *Kasym*, who had deserted the Golden Horde to enter Russian service. It is thus named for him.

Kasli (Касли) *Town, western Russia*. The town, in the Middle Urals southeast of Yekaterinburg, has a name that may represent Mansi *khasli*, "moss."

Kaspiysk (Каспийск) *Town, southwestern Russia*. The town, in Dagestan southeast of Makhachkala, is on the western coast of the *Caspian* Sea (Russian *Kaspiyskoye more*), and is named for it. It was originally an industrial settlement called *Dvigatelstroy* (Двигательстрой), for the engineering works here, from Russian *dvigatel'*, "engine," "motor," and *stroy*, "construction." It acquired its present name in 1947.

Kastornoye (Касторное) *Village, southwestern Russia*. The village, west of Voronezh, has a name that may derive from the local word *kaster'*, the term for a type of rough plant used in scutching (dressing flax or hemp by beating it). It is hardly likely to come from Latin *castor*, "beaver," as proposed by some.

Kasum-Ismailov (Касум-Исмайлов) *Town, west central Azerbaijan*. The town, west of Yevlakh, takes its name from the Azerbaijani revolutionary *Kasum Ismailov*.

Katav-Ivanovsk (Катав-Ивановск) *Town, western Russia*. The town, southwest of Bakal in the Southern Urals, takes the first part of its name from the *Katav* River on which it stands. The river name may derive from the Bashkir word *katyu*, meaning "drying up," "muddying." The second part of the name relates to the merchant *Ivan* Tverdyshev and his factory-owner brother-in-law *Ivan* Myasnikov, who had founded an ironworks here in 1755.

Kataysk (Катайск) *Town, southwestern Russia*. The town, southeast of Kamensk-Uralsky, arose in 1655 as a fortified post on the small *Katayka* River, and takes its name from it. The river name derives from that of a local Bashkir people, the *Katay*. The origin of their own name is uncertain.

Kattakurgan (Каттакурган) *Town, eastern Uzbekistan*. The town, northwest of Samarkand, takes its name from two Iranian words: *kanta*, a term for an enclosed place, related to *kan* and *kent*, "town" (as for **Tashkent**), and *kurgan*, "burial mound," "tumulus." The overall sense is thus of a fortified place built on a hill.

Katun (Катунь) *River, southern Russia*. The river, in the Altay mountains, is believed to have an old Turkic name meaning simply "river." Attempts to derive the name from a Turkic word meaning "woman" (modern Turkish *kadın*) have not been supported, since the many rivers with a name element *kat* or *khat* are more likely to have a sense that is simply "river." Cf. **Khatanga**.

Katyk See **Shakhtyorsk**[2].

Kaufman Peak See **Lenin Peak**.

Kaunas (Каунас) *City, south central Lithuania*. The city, northwest of Vilnius, was founded in the late 10th or early 11th century, and until 1917 was officially known as *Kovno* (Ковно). The meaning of the name remains uncertain, although there have been attempts to relate the earlier name to Russian *kovat'*, "to forge," as if the place arose around a blacksmith's forge. A Baltic origin would be more likely. Local legend derives the name from that of the city's founder, the son of Milda, the Lithuanian goddess of love.

Kazakhstan (Казахстáн) *Republic, central Asia*. The republic, lying chiefly between southwestern Russia and Mongolia, takes its name from its indigenous inhabitants, the *Kazakhs*. Their own name probably derives from the Turkic word *kazak*, meaning "nomad." The final *-stan* is an Iranian element meaning "inhabited place," "land." The word that gave the ethnic name also gave the name of the *Cossacks*.

Kazalinsk (Казалийнск) *Town, southern Kazakhstan*. The town, on the lower reaches of the Syr-Darya River, east of the Aral Sea, takes its name from Kazakh *kaz*, "goose," with the possessive suffix *-ly*. The overall sense is thus "place of wild geese."

Kazan (Казáнь) *City, western Russia*. The city, the Tatar capital, east of Nizhny Novgorod, has a name said to derive from a Turkic word related to modern Turkish *kazan*, "cauldron," referring to the pits and hollows of the terrain here. This also presumably gave the name of the *Kazanka* River, on which the city stands. But a connection with the Muslim personal name *Hassan* is also possible.

Kazandzhik (Казанджи́к) *Town, western Turkmenistan*. The town, east of Nebit-Dag, has a name said to derive from Turkmen *kazan*, "cauldron," doubtless referring to the terrain here. Cf. **Kazan**.

Kazbegi (Казбéги) *Village, northern Georgia*. The village, a mountain resort in the central Caucasus, takes its name from the Georgian writer Aleksandr *Kazbegi* (1848–1893), who was born here and who owned substantial estates locally. The name was given only in 1921, before which the village was known as *Stepantsminda* (Степáнцминда), for the nearby medieval church of St. Stephen. It was Kazbegi that gave the Russian name of **Kazbek**, the mountain rising to the west.

Kazbek (Казбéк) *Mountain, central Caucasus, southwestern Russia*. The mountain, an extinct volcano, takes its name from the village of **Kazbegi** that lies at its eastern foot in northern Georgia. The Georgian name of the peak is *Mkinvartsveri*, from *mkinvari*, "glacier," and *tsveri*, "mountain." Its Ossetic name is *Urskhokh*, "white mountain," with reference to its permanent (and abundant) snow cover.

Keksgolm See **Priozyorsk**.

Kellomäki See **Komarovo**.

Kem (Кемь) *Town, northwestern Russia*. The town, a port in Karelia on the White Sea north of Belomorsk, takes its name from the river at the mouth of which it stands. The river name is of uncertain origin, but may mean simply "river."

Kemerovo (Кéмерово) *City, southern Russia*. The city, east of Novosibirsk, has a name that probably represents the family name *Kemerov*, owners of coal workings here. The present town arose in 1918 from the merging of two villages: *Kemerovo*, founded in 1863, and *Shcheglovo*, founded in 1720. The latter gave the earlier name of the town to 1932, *Shcheglovsk* (Щеглóвск).

Kentau (Кентáу) *Town, southern Kazakhstan*. The town, northeast of Turkestan, was founded in 1955 on the site of iron ore workings and has a Kazakh name meaning "broad mountain," from words related to Turkish *geniş*, "wide," and *dağ*, "mountain."

Kerch (Керчь) *City and port, eastern Crimea, southern Ukraine.* The city, northeast of Feodosiya, is one of the oldest in the former Soviet Union. It was founded in the 6th century B.C. by Milesians as the colony of *Panticapaeum*. The origin of this name is uncertain. As it stands it suggests a Greek source, beginning with *pan*, "all." However, it is almost certainly a distortion of some earlier name, perhaps Iranian in origin. The present name is first recorded in the 11th century (in an inscription on the famous Tmutarakan Stone of 1068), and may ultimately derive from the early Slavic root element *krch*, meaning "metalworker," related to modern Russian *kuznets*, "blacksmith." The city is still well known for its iron mines.

Kerchevsky (Ке́рчевский) *Town, west central Russia.* The town, northwest of Solikamsk, stands at the point where the small *Kerchevka* River enters the Kama, and takes its name from it. The river name may derive from Komi-Permyak *kerch*, "marsh ledum" (*Ledum palustre*), a species of wild rosemary.

Kerki (Керки́) *Town, southeastern Turkmenistan.* The town, southwest of Amudarya, has a name that may be based on Persian *kerk*, "building." The town is ancient, and was known to exist in the 10th century.

Ket (Кеть) *River, south central Russia.* The river, a tributary of the Ob, has a name that could be linked to that of the *Ket* people who inhabit this region. Their own name probably means simply "people."

Kexholm See **Priozyorsk**.

Khabarovsk (Хаба́ровск) *City, southeastern Russia.* The city, on the Amur River northeast of Vladivostok, was founded in 1858 as the military post of *Khabarovka*, so named commemoratively for the Russian explorer and navigator Yerofey Pavlovich *Khabarov* (c. 1610–after 1667), who made several expeditions to various parts of the Amur. The present form of the name was adopted in 1893. Cf. **Yerofey-Pavlovich**.

Khakassia (Хака́сия) *Republic, southern Russia.* The republic, north of northwestern Mongolia, takes its name from its indigenous inhabitants, the *Khakass*. Their own name derives from the word *khas*, "person," "man."

Khalilovo (Хали́лово) *Town, southwestern Russia.* The town, northwest of Orsk, derives its name from the well-known Muslim personal name *Khalil* ("bosom friend").

Khalturin (Халту́рин) *Town, western Russia.* The town, northeast of Kotelnich, was founded in the 11th century under the name *Orlov* (Орло́в). In 1923 it was renamed for the revolutionary Stepan Nikolayevich *Khalturin* (1856–1882), who was born near here.

Khamza (Хамза́) *Town, eastern Uzbekistan.* The town, southwest of Margilan, was originally a village named *Shakhimardan*. It was then known as *Vannovsky* until 1963, when it was renamed *posyolok imeni Khamzy Khakimzade* (посёлок и́мени Хамзы́ Хакимзаде́), "settlement named for Khakimzade Khamza," in honor of the Uzbek poet and revolutionary *Khakimzade* Niyazi *Khamza* (1889–1929), murdered here by religious fanatics. It received its present name in 1974 on being raised to town status.

Khamzy Khakimzade, posyolok imeni See **Khamza**.

Khankendy (Ханкенды́) *Town, southwestern Azerbaijan.* The town, the capital of Nagorno-Karabakh, has a name of Turkic origin meaning literally "khan's town," from words related to modern Turkish *han*, "khan," and *kent*, "town." In 1923 it was renamed *Stepanakert* (Степанакéрт), "Stephen's town," in honor of the Soviet revolutionary active in the Caucasus, Stepan Georgiyevich Shaumyan (1878–1918) (cf. **Stepanavan**). In 1991 the town reverted to its original name.

Khanlar (Ханлáр) *Town, west central Azerbaijan.* The town, south of Gyandzha, was originally a German colony called *Yelenendorf* ("Helen's village"). In 1938 it was renamed as now for the Bolshevik *Khanlar* Safaraliyev (1885–1907), a worker revolutionary active in Azerbaijan.

Khan-Tengri (Хан-Тéнгри) *Mountain, eastern Kyrgyzstan/ southeastern Kazakhstan.* The mountain, in the central Tien Shan range, stands at the meeting point of the borders of Kyrgyzstan, Kazakhstan, and China. Its name represents words common to Mongol and Turkic languages: *khan*, "lord," and *tengri*, "heaven" (Turkish *Tanrı*, "God," "heaven"). The peak is thus the "lord of heaven." See also **Pobeda Peak**.

Khanty-Mansiysk (Ханты́-Мансий́ск) *Town, west central Russia.* The town, north of Tobolsk, takes its name from the two indigenous peoples of the region: the *Khants* (formerly known as the *Ostyaks*) and the *Mansi* (formerly known as the *Voguls*). The town was founded as a worker's settlement in 1931 and was originally known as *Ostyako-Vogulsk* (Остя́ко-Вогу́льск), for the earlier names of these peoples. The present name was adopted in 1940. Both the ethnic names amount to a meaning "person," "kin." The earlier names *Ostyak* and *Vogul* were respectively from *As* (the Khant name for the Ob River), and the root of Russian *voda*, "water," similarly.

Khariton Laptev Coast (Харитóна Лáптева бéрег) *Coastal region, Taymyr Peninsula, northern Russia.* The region, on the northwestern Taymyr Peninsula, between the Pyasina and Taymyra rivers, is named for the Russian Arctic explorer *Khariton* Prokofyevich *Laptev* (1700–1763), who charted it in 1740. Cf. **Dmitry Laptev Strait**, **Laptev Sea**.

Kharkov (Хáрьков) *City, northeastern Ukraine.* The city, northeast of Dnepropetrovsk, was founded in the mid-seventeenth century as a fortified post against the Crimean Tatars. The name is said to derive from that of an early Cossack settler, one *Kharko*, this being a diminutive form of the name *Khariton*, itself from Greek *kharis*, "grace," "favor," the source of English *charisma*.

Khaypudyrskaya Inlet (Хайпуды́рская губá) *Inlet, northwestern Russia.* The inlet, in Pechora Bay west of the Polar Urals, takes its name from the *Khaypudyra* River that flows into it. The river in turn takes its name from the forest that surrounds its upper reaches, as a Russian form of the Nenets name *Khebidyapedara*, meaning "Sacred Forest." The reference is said to be to a Samoyed cemetery, located on a raised site in a pinewood clearing by these upper reaches. However, the name could equally allude to the bear (Nenets *khebidya*), so named because it is a sacred animal.

Khem-Beldyr See **Kyzyl**.

Kherson (Херсóн) *City and port, southern Ukraine.* The city, a port on the Dnieper northeast of Odessa, was founded in 1778 as a fortress serving as a base for a future Black Sea fleet. It was named for the Greek colony in the Crimea known as *Chersonese*, from Greek *khersos*, "dry land," and *nēsos*, "island," i.e. "land island," otherwise "peninsula." (The Crimea was properly the Tauric Chersonese, while the better known one in the Greek world was the Thracian Chersonese, or Gallipoli Peninsula.) The name was simply a modish classical one for the city, since there is no actual peninsula there.

Khibinogorsk See **Kirovsk**.

Khiva (Хива́) *Town, western Uzbekistan*. The town, southwest of Urgench, is a very old one, dating back to the early Christian era. It takes its name from an ancient well here called *Kheyvak*. The meaning of this is uncertain. The town gave the name of the former khanate of *Khiva*, later familiar as the exclave of **Khorezm**, and was the capital of each in turn until 1920. See also **Caspian Sea, Khvalynsk**.

Khmelnitsky (Хмельни́цкий) *Town, west central Ukraine*. The town, west of Vinnitsa, was already a fortified post in the 15th century with the name of *Ploskurov*, from its location in the valley of the *Ploskaya* River. When Poland was partitioned in 1793, the settlement that had arisen passed to Russia and the name settled as *Proskurov* (Проску́ров). It stayed as such until 1954, when the present name was adopted, to mark the tercentennial of the union of Ukraine and Russia. It honored the Ukrainian leader and patriot Bogdan Mikhaylovich *Khmelnitsky* (c. 1595–1657), who favored such a union.

Khodzhent (Ходже́нт) *City, northwestern Tajikistan*. The city, on both banks of the Syrdarya River near the border with Uzbekistan, is one of the oldest in Central Asia. In 329 A.D. Alexander the Great built a fortress here by the name of *Alexandria Eskhata*, "farthest Alexandria," as the Alexandria that was the farthest from Macedonia. Even earlier than this, however, there was a Persian fortress on the site that was destroyed by Alexander and that was known to the Greeks in the 6th and 5th centuries B.C. as *Cyropolis*, "Cyrus's city," or *Cyreskhata*, "farthest (city of) Cyrus." *Cyrus* was Cyrus the Great, the 6th-century B.C. king of Persia. The present name is first recorded in the 7th century A.D. (with regard to the Great Silk Road that passed through here from China to Europe). The meaning of this is not known. In 1936 the town was renamed *Leninabad* (Ленинаба́д), for *Lenin*, with -*abad* the common Iranian suffix meaning "inhabited place," "town." In 1991 the former name was readopted.

Khodzhent See **Gafurov**.

Kholm (Холм) *Town, western Russia*. The town, northeast of Velikiye Luki, has a name found widely elsewhere, representing Russian *kholm*, "hill" (English *holm*).

Khoni (Хо́ни) *Town, western Georgia*. The town, northwest of Kutaisi, takes its name from the original small settlement here. This was made a town in 1921 and in 1936 was renamed *Tsukulidze* (Цукули́дзе), for the Georgian revolutionary Aleksandr Grigoryevich *Tsukulidze* (1876–1905), who was born here and who is buried here. The town reverted to its original name in 1991.

Khorezm (Хоре́зм) *Historic region, northwestern Uzbekistan*. The region, known also as **Khwarism**, has a name of uncertain origin. Some authorities have seen the final *zm* as an element related to Russian *zemlya*, "land," and the initial *khor* as akin to the name of *Hor*, the Egyptian sky god. But this is somewhat fanciful, and the name has yet to be satisfactorily explained. As a former khanate, the region was long familiar under the name of **Khiva**. See also **Caspian Sea, Khiva, Khvarynsk**.

Khorog (Хорóг) *Town, southern Tajikistan.* The town, on the border with Afghanistan, has a name deriving from a local word *kharag*, meaning simply "settlement."

Khovrino (Хóврино) *District, Moscow, western Russia.* The northwestern district of Moscow takes its name from the former village here, itself so called from an estate owned in the 15th century by G. S. Safarin, a rich merchant known by the Russian dialect nickname *Khovra*, "Sloven." Hence the present name.

Khoyniki (Хóйники) *Town, southeastern Belarus.* The town, southeast of Mozyr, has a name found elsewhere in Belarus and Poland, deriving from a Slavic word (Russian *khvoya*, Polish *choja*) meaning "pine branches."

Khuzhir See **Ust-Ordynsky**.

Khvalynsk (Хвалы́нск) *Town, western Russia.* The town, on the right (west) bank of the Volga southwest of Syzran, arose in 1556 as a fortified post on the Volga island of Sosnovy ("Pine"). In 1606 the settlement that had developed was moved to its present site and began to be called *Sosnovy Ostrov* ("Pine Island"). In 1780 it was raised to town status and named as now for the Old Russian name of the **Caspian Sea** (into which the Volga flows).

Khwarism (Хорéзм) *Historic region, Central Asia.* The region corresponds approximately with ancient *Chorasmia*, a northern province of ancient Persia, and with the **Khorezm** region of Uzbekistan. See also **Khiva**, **Khvalynsk**.

Kiev (Ки́ев) *Capital of Ukraine.* The city, in north central Ukraine, is one of the oldest in the former USSR, and has been prominent so long that it is known as the "mother of Russian cities." Its name has long been traditionally associated with its legendary founder, one *Kiy*, but this is simply an attempt to explain the name, which may actually derive from the Slavic word *kuyava*, meaning "hill," "peak." The city is located on rising ground on the west bank of the Dnieper.

Kikvidze (Киквúдзе) *Village, western Russia.* The village, northeast of Novoanninsky, takes its present name from the Civil War commander Vasily Isidorovich *Kikvidze* (1895–1919), who was killed in armed combat here. Before 1936 the village was known as *Preobrazhenskaya* (Преображéнская), for the dedication of its church to the Transfiguration (Russian *Preobrazheniye*).

Kiliya (Килия́) *Town, southwestern Ukraine.* The town takes its name from the *Kiliya* River on which it lies, and which here forms the border with Romania. The river's own name may be of Turkic origin and mean "clayey," from a word related to modern Turkish *kil*, "clay."

Kimovsk (Ки́мовск) *Town, western Russia.* The town, southeast of Novomoskovsk, was established as a town in 1952 from the former village of *Mikhaylovka*. It took its present name, in this industrial region, from the Russian acronym *KIM*, representing *Kommunisticheskiy internatsional molodyozhi*, "Communist Youth International," a youth organization that existed from 1919 to 1943 as a junior branch of the Comintern (Communist International).

Kineshma (Ки́нешма) *City, western Russia.* The industrial city, on the Volga southeast of Kostroma, takes its name from the small *Kineshma* River that enters the Volga here. The river's own name is of uncertain origin, but is somewhat similar to that of the nearby village of *Reshma*. A fabulous tale is told of a captive Persian princess who was taken up the Volga past these places by the 17th-century Cossack rebel leader Stenka Razin, and who first cried *Rezh mya* ("Kill me!"), then sobbed *Kinesh mya* ("Don't leave me!").

Kingisepp (Кӥнгисепп) *Town, western Russia.* The town, southwest of St. Petersburg near the border with Estonia, was founded in 1384 as the fortress of *Yam*, so named from the Finno-Ugrian *Yam* people who inhabited the region. In 1707 this name became *Yamburg* (Я́мбург), with Germanic *burg*, "fort," added. The present name was given in 1922 for the revolutionary leader in Russia and Estonia, Viktor Eduardovich *Kingisepp* (1888–1922), executed in Tallinn by the Estonian military. There is another *Yamburg* as a village on the Taz River estuary, in northwestern Siberia. But its name is probably a corruption of local words meaning "big swamp."

Kingisepp See **Kuressaare**.

Kirgizia See **Kyrgyzstan**.

Kirillov (Кирӥллов) *Town, western Russia.* The town, northeast of Cherepovets, takes its name from St. *Kirill* Belozersky (1337–1427), the medieval monk and writer who founded the Belozersky monastery here in 1397. The town grew around the monastery, which is itself named for the *Beloye ozero*, "white lake," to the north.

Kirov (Ки́ров) *Town, western Russia.* The town, east of Roslavl, takes its present name from the Communist party leader Sergey Mironovich *Kirov* (original name Kostrikov) (1886–1934), a leading aide of Stalin. Until 1936 it was known as *Pesochnya* (Песо́чня), from the river here. Its own name, found in various forms elsewhere, is based on Russian *pesok*, "sand."

Kirov See **Vyatka**.

Kirovabad See (1) **Gyandzha**, (2) **Pyandzh**.

Kirovakan See **Karaklis**.

Kirov Bay (Ки́рова зали́в) *Bay, southern Azerbaijan.* The bay of the Caspian Sea, south of Lenkoran, is named for the Communist party leader Sergey Mironovich *Kirov* (1886–1934). Its alternate name, still occasionally in use, is *Kyzylagach*, "red tree," from Turkic words related to modern Turkish *kızıl*, "red," and *ağaç*, "tree." The reference must be to a conspicuous tree or group of trees of this color by the coast here.

Kirovgrad (Кировгра́д) *Town, western Russia.* The town, in the Middle Urals south of Nizhny Tagil, derives its name from the Communist party leader Sergey Mironovich *Kirov* (1886–1934). Before it was renamed in 1936 it was known as *Kalata* (Калата́).

Kirovograd (Кировогра́д) *City, central Ukraine.* The city, north of Nikolayev, was founded in 1764 near St. *Elizabeth's* fortress, built in 1754 as a defense against the Turks and Tatars. It was so named by order of the reigning empress of Russia, *Elizabeth* Petrovna (*Yelizaveta Petrovna*) (1709–1762). The town that arose was thus named *Yelizavetgrad* (Елизаветгра́д), "Elizabeth's town." In 1934 the city was renamed *Kirovo*, for the Communist party leader Sergey Mironovich *Kirov* (1886–1934). In 1936 it was further renamed *Zinovyevsk* (Зино́вьевск), for the Communist politician Grigory Yevseyevich *Zinovyev* (original name Ovsel Gershon Aronov Radomyslsky) (1883–1936), who was born here. The previous name was readopted in modified form (adding *-grad*) in 1939.

Kirovsk (Ки́ровск) *Town, northwestern Russia.* The town, at the base of the Kola Peninsula, east of Apatity, derives its present name from the Communist party leader Sergey

Mironovich *Kirov* (1886–1934). Before 1934 it was known as *Khibinogorsk* (Хибиногорск), so named for the nearby mountain (Russian *gora*) of *Khibina*. Its own name is based on Saamian *khiben*, "hills."

Kirovsky (Кировский) *Town, southwestern Russia*. The town, a fishing port in the Volga delta south of Astrakhan, is named for the Soviet politician Sergey Mironovich *Kirov* (1886–1934), a leading aide of Stalin. Until 1934 it was known as *Nikitinskiye Promysly* (Никитинские промыслы), "Nikitin's Fisheries." The name *Kirovsky* is (or was) found for several other towns.

Kirsanov (Кирсанов) *Town, western Russia*. The town, east of Tambov, was founded in the 18th century around an ironworks by a settler named Khrisanf Zubakhin. His first name, *Khrisanf* (from Greek *Chrysanthos*, "golden flower"), had a pet form *Kirsan*, and this gave the name of the town.

Kirzhach (Киржач) *Town, western Russia*. The town, northeast of Moscow, takes its name from the river on which it stands. The river's own name may be of Finno-Ugrian origin and mean "left," perhaps because it is a left-hand (northern) tributary of the Klyazma.

Kishinyov (Кишинёв) *Capital of Moldova*. The city, in the center of the republic, has its name recorded in a document of 1466. Until 1818 it was a minor trading center in Bessarabia. Its name probably represents Old Moldovan *kishineu*, "artesian well," "spring," related to Vulgar Latin *pissiare*, "to urinate," and so to English *piss*. The Moldovan form of the name is *Chişinău*.

Kislovodsk (Кисловодск) *City, southwestern Russia*. The city is a large health resort in the foothills of the northern Caucasus, southwest of Pyatigorsk. Its name refers to its mineral waters, from Russian *kislaya voda*, "sour water," as a popular form of *uglekislaya voda*, literally "carbonic water," otherwise the type of curative mineral water known to Russians as "Narzan."

Kivach (Кивач) *Waterfall, northwestern Russia*. The waterfall, on the Suna River in Karelia, has a name that probably represents Finnish *kiivas*, "violent," "turbulent," referring to the force of the falls.

Kiviõli (Кивиыли) *Town, northern Estonia*. The town, east of Rakvere, is an important center of shale oil production, and the name indicates this activity, from Estonian *kivi*, "rock," and *õli*, "oil."

Kizel (Кизел) *Town, west central Russia*. The town, northeast of Perm, arose around an ironworks established here to the west of the Middle Urals in the 1780s. It was not iron that promoted the growth of the present town, however, but coal, discovered not far from the iron mine in 1786. The first coalpit was dug in 1797, and the settlement that arose was raised to town status in 1926. The name derives from the *Kizel* River on which the town lies. Its own name is said to represent Tatar *kyzyl*, "red," referring to the red berries of the dogrose and elder bushes that grow on its banks.

Kizhi (Кижи) *Island, Lake Onega, northwestern Russia*. The island, in the northern part of Lake Onega, and famous for its 18th-century wooden churches, has a name said to derive from Karelian *kiät*, "singing and dancing," as if the former site of youthful celebrations. But an origin in Finnish *kesä*, "summer," has also been proposed, in the transferred sense "south," as if by contrast with a more northerly place.

Kizlyar (Кизляр) *Town, southwestern Russia*. The town, in Dagestan northeast of Grozny, is said to take its name from a Turkic word *kyz*, "girl" (modern Turkish *kız*) and the plural indicator *-lar*. This is said to refer to an incident in which a number of girls drowned in the Terek River here. But this is almost certainly an invented story. Nor is an apparently plausible source in Turkic words meaning "red precipice" (Turkish *kızıl*, "red," and *yar*, "precipice") supported by the low-lying deltic terrain here.

Klaipeda (Клайпеда) *City and port, western Lithuania.* The Baltic port was founded in 1252 by the Teutonic knights as the fort of *Memel* (Мемель), this being a German alteration of the name of the **Neman**, the river that enters the Baltic to the south of the city. The city's present Lithuanian name represents *klai*, a term of unknown meaning, and *pėda*, "territory." The earlier name was reinstated during periods of German occupation, from 1919 to 1923 and again from 1941 to 1944.

Klin (Клин) *Town, western Russia.* The town, northwest of Moscow, has a name representing Russian *klin*, "wedge." This could have various senses, depending on the toponymy, such as a corner of land or a wood in the angle of a river. Klin is on the Sestra River, but the precise application of the name here remains uncertain. The name is first recorded in a document of 1234.

Klintsy (Клинцы́) *Town, western Russia.* The town, southwest of Bryansk near the border with Belarus, derives its name from Russian *klin*, "wedge," "corner of land." Cf. **Klin**. The town is on the north bank of the small Turosna River.

Klukhori See **Karachayevsk**.

Klyazma (Кля́зьма) *River, western Russia.* The river rises just north of Moscow and flows generally east to join the Oka at Nizhny Novgorod. Its name remains undeciphered, and attempts to derive it from Greek *klasma*, "fragment," "bit broken off" (as if it were a "piece" of the Oka) are ingenious but also ingenuous. It is probably of Finno-Ugrian origin.

Klyuchevskaya Sopka (Ключевска́я Со́пка) *Volcano, eastern Russia.* The volcano, in the east central Kamchatka Peninsula, is Siberia's highest mountain. It takes its name from the nearby village of **Klyuchi**, with *sopka* a local word for an active or extinct volcano (this one is active).

Klyuchi (Ключи́) *Village, eastern Russia.* The village lies at the foot of the **Klyuchevskaya Sopka**, to which it gave its name. The name itself is widely found in Russia and means "spring." (The word is actually plural but this is a characteristic of certain placenames and does not denote the presence of several springs.)

Knyaginino (Княги́нино) *Village, western Russia.* The village, southeast of Nizhny Novgorod, was so named on its founding in the 16th century by Princess Vorotinskaya, from Russian *knyaginya*, "princess." From 1779 to 1926 it enjoyed town status as *Knyaginin*.

Kobrin (Ко́брин) *Town, southwestern Belarus.* The town, east of Brest, is known to have existed in the 11th century and is said to take its name from a personal name, *Cobrunus*, itself ultimately of Celtic origin.

Kohtla-Järve (Ко́хтла-Я́рве) *Town, northern Estonia.* The town, near the Gulf of Finland coast west of Narva, has an Estonian name meaning "lake place," from *koht*, "place," and *järv*, "lake."

Koivisto See **Primorsk**[1].

Kokand (Коканд) *City, eastern Uzbekistan.* The city, southwest of Andizhan, dates from at least the 10th century and was the chief town of the Kokand khanate in the 18th century. Its name appears to be based on Iranian *kan* or *kent*, "town," but the initial *Ko-* is unexplained.

Kokchetav (Кокчетав) *Town, northern Kazakhstan.* The town, south of Petropavlovsk, was founded in 1824 as a Cossack village and has a Turkic name meaning "green mountain." The reference is to the hills here with pine-covered slopes which stand out among the steppes.

Koksovy (Ко́ксовый) *Town, southwestern Russia.* The town, in the Donbass southeast of Kamensk-Shakhtinsky, arose in 1932 when coal was first mined here. Hence its name, from Russian *koks*, "coke."

Koktash (Кокта́ш) *Village, western Kyrgyzstan.* The village, northwest of Dzhalal-Abad on the border with Uzbekistan, has a Turkic name meaning "blue stone" (or "green stone"). Cf. **Kokchetav**.

Koktebel See **Planyorskoye**.

Kola (Ко́ла) *River, northwestern Russia.* The river joins the Tuloma south of Murmansk at the historic town of *Kola*, named for it. The name itself is probably based on a Finno-Ugrian root word, *kol* or *kul*, meaning "fish." See also **Kola Peninsula**.

Kola Peninsula (Ко́льский полуо́стров) *Peninsula, northwestern Russia.* The peninsula projects eastwards between the Barents Sea to the north and White Sea to the south. Its name comes from the **Kola** River at its western end.

Kolchugino See **Leninsk-Kuznetsky**.

Kolguyev (Колгу́ев) *Island, Barents Sea, northwestern Russia.* The island, southwest of Novaya Zemlya, has a name of uncertain origin. It has been linked not too convincingly with Finnish *kolkka*, "corner," as if referring to its location in a corner of the Barents Sea. More likely would be a derivation in a North Russian dialect word such as *kolga*, "ski." The island is inside the Arctic Circle.

Kologriv (Кологри́в) *Town, western Russia.* The town, northeast of Kostroma, has an Old Russian name representing modern Russian *okolo grivy*, "by the *griva*." *Griva* (literally "mane") is a term for a wooded ridge.

Kolokol (Ко́локол) *Volcano, Kuril Islands, southeastern Russia.* The volcano, on Urup island, has a Russian name meaning "bell." The reference is to its shape, which is that of a cone with a narrow level platform atop as the consequence of a crumbled crater.

Kolomna (Коло́мна) *City, western Russia.* The city, southeast of Moscow, may derive its name from the Finno-Ugrian word *kolm*, meaning "grave," "cemetery." Some authorities, however, prefer an origin in the Russian dialect word *kolomen*, "neighborhood." The name does not derive from Russian *kolonna*, "column," "pillar," despite suggestions to this effect. The city dates from at least 1177.

Kolomyya (Коломы́я) *City, southwestern Ukraine.* The city, southeast of Ivano-Frankovsk, has a name that appears to represent what in modern Russian would be *okolo Myi*, "by the *Myya*," this being the name of a small river that joins the Prut here. If so, the name is similar to that of **Kologriv**.

Kolpino (Ко́лпино) *Town, western Russia.* The town, southeast of St. Petersburg, may have a name based on the Slavic word *kolp*, the term for a type of heron. The town arose on the Izhora River here in the early 18th century.

Kolyma (Колымá) *River, northeastern Russia*. The river, rising in the mountains of the same name, flows generally north into the Arctic Ocean. The origin of its name is uncertain. It is perhaps an alteration of *Kulu*, its Evenki name. This in turn is said to represent the Evenki word *kula*, used as a term for a north-facing river bank. This would be appropriate for a river whose course is mainly northwards.

Kolyvan (Колывáнь) *Town, southern Russia*. The town, northwest of Novosibirsk, has a name that is said to be a transference of the historic alternate name of **Tallinn**. There is another town of the same name 280 miles (450 km) south of this one, near the border with Kazakhstan.

Komandorsky Islands See **Commander Islands**.

Komarno (Комáрно) *Town, western Ukraine*. The town, southwest of Lvov, has a name that probably derives from Russian and Ukrainian *komar*, "mosquito," denoting a place infested with these insects. The name is found elsewhere in Slav countries, for example at *Komárno* in southern Slovakia, near the Hungarian border.

Komarovo (Комáрово) *Village, western Russia*. The village is a resort on the Gulf of Finland northwest of St. Petersburg. It received its present name in 1946 in honor of the Soviet botanist and geographer Vladimir Leontyevich *Komarov* (1869–1945), who was born in St. Petersburg. Before this it had the Finnish name of *Kellomäki*, literally "bell hill," from Finnish *kello*, "bell," and *mäki*, "hill."

Komi (Кóми) *Republic, northwestern Russia*. The republic, west of the Northern Urals, takes its name from its indigenous *Komi* people, whose own name probably means simply "person." The people use this name for themselves as well as *Mort*, with the same meaning, and of Iranian origin. (Cf. **Mordovia, Udmurt**.) In prerevolutionary Russia the Komi were known as the *Zyrians* (Russian *zyryane*), a name perhaps related to Finnish *syrjä*, "edge," denoting people who live in a relatively remote region, as here.

Kommunarsk (Коммунáрск) *Town, eastern Ukraine*. The town, southwest of Lugansk, arose in 1895 when a metalworks was constructed here. The settlement that grew from it was named *Alchevsk* (Алчéвск), for one *Alchevsky*, founder of the construction company. In 1931 it was renamed *Voroshilovsk* (Ворошúловск), for the Soviet military leader, later president of the Soviet Union, Kliment Yefremovich *Voroshilov* (1881–1969). It received its present name in 1961, following Voroshilov's involvement in the attempt to oust Khrushchev. It derives from Russian *kommunar*, "communard," a term historically related to a member or supporter of the Paris Commune of 1871 set up in opposition to the National Assembly, but in more recent times applied to the member of any commune, such as an agricultural collective of the early Soviet era. The word also has associations with *Communism*.

Kommunizma Pik See **Communism Peak**.

Komsomolets (Комсомóлец) *Island, North Land, northern Russia*. The island, the northernmost of the four largest in the group, has a name meaning "*Komsomol* member," for the former Communist Youth League. A group of members came here on an Arctic expedition in 1931. Cf. **Pioneer**.

Komsomolets See **Myortvy Kultuk**.

Komsomolsk (Комсомо́льск) *Town, western Russia*. The town, west of Ivanovo, received its current name in 1951, for the *Komsomol*, the Communist Youth League. It arose in 1931 on construction of the Ivanovo electric power station here, and was at first accordingly named *IvGRES* (ИвГРЭС), the acronym of *Ivanovskaya gosudarstvennaya rajonnaya elektrostantsiya*, "Ivanovo state regional electric power station."

Komsomolsk-on-Amur (Комсомо́льск-на-Аму́ре) *City, eastern Russia*. The city, on the *Amur* River northeast of Khabarovsk, was founded in 1932 on the site of the village of *Permskoye* (Пе́рмское), itself settled in 1860 by peasants who had come from the *Perm* region. Construction of the new city was undertaken by members of the *Komsomol*, the Communist Youth League, who were drafted here from all parts of the former Soviet Union, and the name was given in their honor. The river name was added subsequently to distinguish this *Komsomolsk* from others. Cf. **Komsomolsk**.

Komsomol 20th Anniversary Peak See **Pobeda Peak**.

Konakovo (Конако́во) *Town, western Russia*. The town, southeast of Tver, was originally known as *Kuznetsovo* (Кузнецо́во), so named for M. S. *Kuznetsov*, who bought the porcelain factory here in 1870. In 1930 it was renamed as now for a local revolutionary, P. P. *Konakov*.

Kondopoga (Ко́ндопога) *Town, northwestern Russia*. The town, in Karelia north of Petrozavodsk, probably derives its name from Russian dialect *konda*, "pitch pine," a word of Finnish origin, and Finnish *pohja*, "bottom," "ground," referring to its location at the end of an inlet. Cf. **Lakhdenpokhya**.

Königsberg See **Kaliningrad**.

Konotop (Конотоп) *City, northeastern Ukraine*. The city, west of Belopolye, has a name found elsewhere in Slav countries. It is said to derive from *kon*, "horse," and *topit'*, "to sink," implying a difficult passage by horse-drawn transport over soft ground, as along a miry road or across a muddy ford.

Konstantinograd See **Krasnograd**.

Konstantinovka (Константи́новка) *Town, eastern Ukraine*. The town, in the Donbass southeast of Kramatorsk, arose in 1869 when a railroad station was built here on the line south from Kharkov. It was presumably named for Grand Duke *Konstantin* (Constantine) (1827–1892), son of Czar Nicholas I and brother of Alexander II.

Konstantinov Kamen (Константи́нов Ка́мень) *Mountain, northwestern Russia*. The mountain, at the northernmost end of the Urals, was climbed in 1848 by E. K. Gofman, leader of an expedition sponsored by the Russian Geographical Society. He gave it the name by which it is now known, "Mt. Constantine," for the son of Czar Nicholas I and brother of Alexander II, Grand Duke *Konstantin* (Constantine) (1827–1892), then the Society's president. (He was only nominally president, since the Society's actual executive head was its vice president, Admiral Litke.)

Konzhakovsky Kamen (Конжако́вский Ка́мень) *Mountain, west central Russia*. The mountain, one of the highest in the Middle Urals, has a name meaning "Mt. Konzhakov." It was given this name in the 19th century for *Konzhakov*, a prominent local hunter and member of the

Vogul tribe, who lived in a yurt (tent made of skins) at the foot of the mountain.

Kopet-Dag (Копетдáг) *Mountain system, southwestern Turkmenistan.* The mountains extend along the border between northeastern Iran and Turkmenistan. Their name derives from the Turkic words *kop*, "many," and *dag*, "mountain." The name originally applied only to the smallish chain west of Ashkhabad, but was later extended to the whole system.

Kopeysk (Копéйск) *Town, southwestern Russia.* The town, just southeast of Chelyabinsk, is noted for its coal mines and takes its name from Russian *kopi*, "mines." It was actually known as *Kopi* from its establishment in 1907 as a coal-mining settlement until 1933, when it was raised to town status.

Korf Bay (Кóрфа залúв) *Bay, eastern Russia.* The bay, an inlet of the Bering Sea on the northeast coast of the Kamchatka Peninsula, takes its name from the first governor general of the Amur District, Aleksandr Nikolayevich *Korf* (1833–1903). The town of *Korf* on the bay here arose in the mid-1920s.

Korkino (Кóркино) *Town, southwestern Russia.* The town, south of Chelyabinsk, arose as a coal-mining settlement in 1932 on the site of the village of the same name, said to have been founded in the mid-eighteenth century by an escaped exile, Afanasy *Korkin*.

Korosten (Кóростень) *Town, northwestern Ukraine.* The ancient Russian town, northwest of Kiev, was originally known as *Iskorosten*, a name probably based on a local word *korost*, used for a winter stack of sheaves of flax.

Korotoyak (Коротоя́к) *Village, western Russia.* The village, a former town southeast of Liski, takes its name from the river on which it stands. The meaning of its own name is uncertain, but it is probably Turkic in origin. A once popular account of the name, proposed by the 19th-century Russian priest and historian Yevgeny Bolkhovitinov, was that it came from the exclamation *Kruto yak* ("How steep!"), made by Ukrainian farmers as they urged their carts up the hill here.

Korsakov (Корсáков) *Town, southeastern Russia.* The town and port, at the southern end of Sakhalin island, was so named in 1946, on the return of this part of Sakhalin by Japan to Russia, for the Russian hydrographer Voin Andreyevich Rimsky-*Korsakov* (1822–1871), who charted the Tatar Strait between Sakhalin and mainland Russia. It was founded as the military post *Muravyovsky*, and was then renamed *Korsakovsky* until its annexation by Japan in 1905. The Japanese name for the port was *Otomari*.

Korsun-Shevchenkovsky (Кóрсунь-Шевчéнковский) *Town, north central Ukraine.* The ancient town, west of Cherkassy, was founded in 1032 by Prince Yaroslav the Wise. It was originally just *Korsun*, as an Old Russian form of the name of what is now the seaport city of **Kherson**, in southern Ukraine. It was through that port that the ancient state of Kievan Rus traded with Byzantium, and that Christianity came to Russia. The second part of the name was added in 1944 to honor the Ukrainian national poet, Taras Gregoryevich *Shevchenko* (1814–1861), who was born in the village of Morintsy, some 21 miles (34 km) away.

Koryak (Коря́к) *Autonomous region, northeastern Russia.* The region, at the northern end of the Kamchatka Peninsula, takes its name from its indigenous people, the *Koryaks*. Their name means "place of reindeer," otherwise "reindeer people," from *kor*, "reindeer," and the placename suffix *-ak*.

Korzhenevskaya Peak (Корженёвской пик) *Mountain, northern Tajikistan*. The mountain, in the Academy of Sciences Range, was discovered in 1910 and named for the wife of the Soviet geographer and glaciologist Nikolay Leopoldovich *Korzhenevsky* (1879–1958). Cf. **Korzhenevsky Glacier**.

Korzhenevsky Glacier (Корженёвского ледни́к) *Glacier, southern Kyrgyzstan*. The glacier, in the Transalay range east of Lenin Peak, is named for the Soviet geographer and glaciologist Nikolay Leopoldovich *Korzhenevsky* (1879–1958), who discovered it in 1928.

Kostroma (Кострома́) *Town, western Russia*. The town, northeast of Yaroslavl, takes its name from the *Kostroma* River on which it stands. The river name has been the subject of considerable speculation, partly because the final *-ma* suggests a Finno-Turkic origin. Those who favor a wholly Slavic source derive it from *kostra*, "bast," "fiber." The popular etymology of the name is in Russian *kostër*, "bonfire," as if timber were transported over the river by being floated on huge "bonfires."

Kotelnich (Коте́льнич) *Town, western Russia*. The town, southwest of Vyatka, probably takes its name from Russian *kotyol*, "cauldron," referring to a hollow or depression here, by the Vyatka River.

Kotelny Island (Коте́льный о́стров) *Island, New Siberian Islands, northern Russia*. The largest of the New Siberian Islands, east of the Laptev Sea, was discovered in 1773 by an expedition led by the Russian trader Ivan Lyakhov (see **Lyakhov Islands**). By mistake, the team left behind a cauldron. In 1775, one Khvoynov, a topographer surveying the island, came across the large kettle (Russian *kotyol*), a distinctive object on an otherwise uninhabited island. Hence the name.

Kotlas (Ко́тлас) *Town, western Russia*. The town, northwest of Vyatka, has a name that remains of uncertain origin. It is not likely to derive from Russian *kotyol*, "hollow."

Kotlin (Ко́тлин) *Island, western Russia*. The island, in the Gulf of Finland, is said to have a Finnish name deriving from *kattila*, "hollow," "depression," referring to a deep stretch of water nearby. But this etymology must be regarded as no more than tentative.

Kotovsk[1] (Кото́вск) *Town, western Russia*. The town, southeast of Tambov, was until 1940 officially part of the city of Tambov itself. When it was separated off, it was named for the Civil War hero and military commander Grigory Ivanovich *Kotovsky* (1881–1925). Cf. **Kotovsk**[2] and **Kotovsk**[3].

Kotovsk[2] (Кото́вск) *Town, central Moldova*. The town, southwest of Kishinyov, was until 1940 a village called *Gancheshty* (Ганче́шты), derived from a personal name. That year it was renamed *Kotovskoye* and when raised to town status in 1965, *Kotovsk*. The name honors the Civil War hero and military leader Grigory Ivanovich *Kotovsky* (1881–1925), who was born here. Cf. **Kotovsk**[1] and **Kotovsk**[3].

Kotovsk[3] (Кото́вск) *Town, southern Ukraine*. The town, southwest of Balta, was founded in the early 19th century and was originally known as *Birzula* (Би́рзула). In 1935 it was renamed as now for the Civil War hero and military commander Grigory Ivanovich *Kotovsky*

(1881-1925), who fought in the Ukraine and who is buried in the town. Cf. **Kotovsk**[1] and **Kotovsk**[2].

Kotsyubinskoye (Коцюби́нское) *Town, northern Ukraine.* The town, west of Kiev, and originally the settlement of *Berkovets*, is named commemoratively for the Ukrainian revolutionary and fiction writer Mikhail Mikhaylovich *Kotsyubinsky* (1864-1913).

Kounradsky (Коунра́дский) *Town, east central Kazakhstan.* The town, north of Balkhash, takes its name from the nearby mountain *Kounrad.* Its Kazakh name, *Konyrad,* means "gray horse," alluding to a group of peaks whose outline bears a fanciful resemblance to a horse.

Kovda (Ко́вда) *Village, northwestern Russia.* The village, in Karelia south of Kandalaksha, takes its name from the river here. Its own name is said to derive from Saamian *govdag,* "broad."

Kovel (Ко́вель) *Town, northwestern Ukraine.* The town, northwest of Lutsk, dates from the 14th century and is said to take its name from a personal name or nickname meaning "traitor," "ambusher."

Kovno See **Kaunas**.

Kovrov (Ковро́в) *Town, western Russia.* The town, northeast of Vladimir, arose in the 12th century on the site of a village then known as *Yepifanovka,* said to be named for a hunter, *Yepifan* (from Greek *Epiphanes,* "notable"). The village was then renamed *Rozhdestvennoye,* for the dedication of its church to the Nativity (Russian *Rozhdestvo*). Its present name comes from the princely *Kovrov* family, landowners here in the 16th century.

Koydanovo See **Dzerzhinsk**[2].

Kozelsk (Козе́льск) *Town, western Russia.* The town, southwest of Kaluga, is said to take its name from Old Russian *kozel,* "granary."

Kozhva (Ко́жва) *Village, northwestern Russia.* The village, southwest of Pechora, takes its name from the river on which it lies. The river name represents local words *kozh,* "pool," and *va,* "river."

Kozlov See **Michurinsk**.

Kozmodemyansk (Козьмодемья́нск) *Town, western Russia.* The town, on the Volga east of Nizhny Novgorod, takes its name from the two 3rd-century saints and martyrs honored widely by the Orthodox Church, the brothers *Cosmas* and *Damian.* A popular tale tells how Ivan the Terrible spent the night here in 1552 on their feastday (October 27) after conquering Kazan, and liking the place ordered a fort to be built and named for them. But a village in fact already existed then.

Kramatorsk (Краматорск) *City, eastern Ukraine.* The industrial city, just south of Slavyansk, arose in the second half of the 19th century when the railroad reached here. It gained industrial importance with the opening of the *Kramatorsk* metalworks in 1887. For this reason, the name has been popularly derived from French *crématoire,* "crematory," purportedly referring to its furnaces. However, the factory was built in an already existing village named *Krematorka,* and the name therefore derives from this. Its origin is thought to be in dialect *kroma,* "edge," and *Tor,* the latter being the river here now known as the *Kazyonny Torets.* The overall sense is thus "(town by the) edge of the Tor."

Krasnaya Polyana (Кра́сная Поля́на) *Town, western Russia.* The town, north of Moscow, has a name found elsewhere meaning "beautiful glade," from obsolete Russian *krasnyj,* "beautiful," and *polyana,* "glade."

Krasnaya Presnya See **Presnya**.

Krasnoarmeysk[1] (Красноармéйск) *Town, western Russia*. The town, southwest of Saratov, was founded in 1766 and was originally known as *Goly Karamysh* (Гóлый Карамы́ш), for the river on which it stands, Russian *golyj* meaning "bare." In the late 18th century German settlers renamed it *Baltser* (Бáльцер), presumably for one of their number named *Balzer*. This name existed in parallel with the earlier one until 1926, when it became the sole official name. In 1942 it was superseded by the present name, for the Soviet *Red Army* (Russian *Krasnaya Armiya*). Many other places bear (or bore) this name, such as the two below.

Krasnoarmeysk[2] (Красноармéйск) *Town, western Russia*. The town, northeast of Moscow, was originally a village named *Voznesensky*, for the dedication of its church to the Ascension (Russian *Vozneseniye*). A textile factory here was thus known as *Voznesenskaya manufaktura*. In early Soviet times this was renamed *imeni Krasnoj Armii i Flota*, "named for the Red Army and Navy," or acronymically *Kraft* (which many Russians would associate with the German word meaning "strength"). In 1928 the residential development here was officially raised to a workers's settlement, and in 1946 it gained urban status, when it was renamed more succinctly as now.

Krasnoarmeysk[3] (Красноармéйск) *District of Volgograd, southwestern Russia*. The southern district of Volgograd, on the Volga, was founded in 1765 as a Moravian settlement called *Zarephath*, a name adopted from the biblical village that was the home of Elijah (1 Kings 17:9). The German settlers doubtless had regard for the literal sense of the Hebrew name, which means "workshop for refining metals," perhaps also interpreting this figuratively as "melting pot." The name settled to the form *Sarepta* (Сарéпта), now also in use (as well as *Sarafand*) for the original village, on the Mediterranean coast just south of Sidon (Saïda), Lebanon. In 1920 the town that had evolved on the Volga was renamed as now for the Red Army. Cf. the two entries above.

Krasnodar (Краснодáр) *City, southwestern Russia*. The city, northeast of Novorossiysk, was founded in 1793 as a military encampment named *Yekaterinodar* (Екатеринодáр), "Catherine's gift," from Russian *Yekaterina*, "Catherine," and *dar*, "gift." The name paid tribute to Catherine the Great, who had brought Cossacks here from the Black Sea to serve in a strategically important region. The lands she gave them here were her "gift." In 1920 the city was renamed as now, with the "gift" element unchanged, but "Red" (Russian *krasnyj*) substituted for the name of Catherine.

Krasnodon (Краснодóн) *Town, eastern Ukraine*. The town, southeast of Lugansk, arose in 1912 as a coal-mining settlement in the Donbass. It was originally known as *Sorokino* (Сорóкино), for a family of settlers named *Sorokin*. In 1938 it was given its present name. This translates literally as "red Don," from Russian *krasnyj*, "red," and the river name *Don*. However, the reference is more likely to be to the *Don*bass, not the Don, as this river is over 60 miles (100 km) away. "Red," too, does not refer to the color of any local object, but is the symbolic revolutionary hue.

Krasnograd (Красногрáд) *Town, northeastern Ukraine*. The town, southwest of Kharkov, was founded in 1782 during the reign of Catherine the Great and originally named

Konstantinograd (Константиноград), "Constantine's town," for her grandson, Grand Prince *Konstantin* Pavlovich (1779-1831), who was the heir to the throne (but who did not succeed because of his morganatic marriage to a Polish countess). In 1922 the town received its present name, translating as "red city," from Russian *krasnyj*, "red," and the common Slavic placename suffix *-grad*, "town," "city." "Red" is here the revolutionary color.

Krasnogvardeysk (Красногвардейск) *Town, eastern Uzbekistan*. The town, northeast of Samarkand, has a name honoring the Red Guards (Russian *Krasnaya Gvardiya*), the units of armed factory workers employed by the Bolsheviks to seize power at the time of the 1917 Revolution. The name is found elsewhere.

Krasnogvardeysk See **Gatchina**.

Krasnokamsk (Краснокамск) *Town, western Russia*. The town, northwest of Perm, arose from a settlement founded in 1929 around a cellulose plant. Its name translates as "red Kama," from Russian *krasnyj*, "red," here the revolutionary color, and *Kama*, the river on which it stands.

Krasnokokshaysk See **Yoshkar Ola**.

Krasnooktyabrsky (Краснооктябрьский) *Town, southwestern Russia*. The town, on the Volgograd Reservoir north of Volzhsky, has a revolutionary name meaning "Red October" (Russian *Krasnyj Oktyabr'*).

Krasnopolye (Краснополье) *Town, eastern Belarus*. The town, southeast of Mogilyov, has a name meaning "fair field," from obsolete Russian *krasnyj*, "fair" (now meaning "red"), and *pole*, "field."

Krasnoselkup (Красноселькуп) *Village, northern Russia*. The village, in the Yamalo-Nenets autonomous area southwest of Igarka, has a name based on that of the *Selkup* (Ostyak Samoyed) people who inhabit the region. The first part of the name represents Russian *krasnyj*, "red," in the revolutionary sense.

Krasnoshchyokovo (Краснощёково) *Village, southern Russia*. The village, on the Ob River southwest of Barnaul, takes the second part of its name from Russian *shchyoki*, "cheeks," here used in a local (Siberian) sense for steep banks that narrow the course of a river. The first part of the name is Russian *krasnyj*, "red," literally rather than metaphorically, referring to the color of the soil.

Krasnoslobodsk (Краснослободск) *Town, southwestern Russia*. The town, on the eastern bank of the Volga opposite Volgograd, was originally a village named *Krasnaya Sloboda*, "beautiful sloboda," a *sloboda* being a settlement exempt from usual state obligations in return for certain services. The first word is Russian *krasnyj*, now meaning "red" but formerly "beautiful." In 1955 the settlement was raised to town status and the two words of the name blended as now.

Krasnoturinsk (Краснотурьинск) *Town, west central Russia*. The town, northwest of Serov to the east of the Middle Urals, arose round a coppermine opened beside the *Turya* River here in 1758. The miners' settlement that developed was at first known as *Turinskiye Rudniki* (Турьинские Рудники), "Turya Mines." It received its present name in 1944, when it gained urban status, with *Krasno-*, "red," the common revolutionary symbol (but also perhaps alluding to the color of the copper). The river name is said to derive from Mansi *tur*, "river," and *ya*, "lake," thus meaning "river of lakes," descriptive of its upper reaches.

Krasnoufimsk (Красноуфимск) *Town, western Russia.* The town, west of Yekaterinburg, was founded in 1736 by the **Ufa** River, in a location then known as *Krasny Yar*, "beautiful bank" or "red bank," as a defensive post against Bashkir raids. The settlement that arose was at first known as either *Krasnoyarskaya* or *Ufimskaya*. Both names were subsequently combined to give *Krasnoufimskaya*. The present form of the name was adopted on gaining town status in 1781. The *Krasno-* element here thus predates any revolutionary symbolism. Cf. **Krasnoyarsk**, **Krasny Yar**.

Krasnouralsk (Красноуральск) *Town, western Russia.* The town, in the Northern Urals east of Verkhnyaya Tura, arose in 1925 as a settlement around copper workings. The original name of the plant was *Uralmedstroy* (Уралмедьстрой), a Soviet-style abbreviation comprising *Ural*, "Urals," *med'*, "copper," and *stroy*, short for *stroitel'stvo*, "construction site." The present name, meaning "red Urals," was given in 1932. "Red" is here the revolutionary color, and "Urals" is the mountain name used in an industrial context.

Krasnousolsky (Красноусольский) *Town, southwestern Russia.* The town, northwest of Sterlitamak, takes its name from the *Usolka* River on which it stands. The river's own name is based on Russian *sol'*, "salt," referring to its saltpans, which were used for the saltworks that existed here in the 16th and 17th centuries. The town actually arose in 1752 around the copper-smelting plant that had been set up here, and which in 1893 was converted into a glassworks. The revolutionary prefix *Krasno-*, "red," was added subsequently.

Krasnov, Mt. (Краснова гора) *Mountain, Sakhalin, eastern Russia.* The mountain, in central Sakhalin island northwest of Makarov, is named for the Russian botanist and geographer Andrey Nikolayevich *Krasnov* (1862–1914).

Krasnovidovo (Красновидово) *Village, western Russia.* The village, on the west bank of the Volga south of Kazan, has a name referring to the panoramic view from its elevated site, from obsolete Russian *krasnyj*, "fine," "beautiful," and modern *vid*, "view." Other places of the same name will have the same meaning.

Krasnovishersk (Красновишерск) *Town, west central Russia.* The town, east of Cherdyn to the west of the Middle Urals, developed from the cellulose plant set up here in 1930. It takes its name from the *Vishera* River on which it stands, with *Krasno-*, "red," added subsequently in its revolutionary sense. It is not certain to what extent the name of this *Vishera* relates to the identically named river in western Russia on which **Malaya Vishera** stands.

Krasnovodsk (Красноводск) *Town and port, northwestern Turkmenistan.* The town, a port on the Caspian Sea northwest of Nebit Dag, was founded in 1869 as a military post. Its name translates as "red water," from Russian *krasnyj*, "red," and *voda*, "water." Despite appearances, this is not a revolutionary name, but derives from an earlier name of the bay here, *Krasnyye Vody*, "red waters." The reason for this particular name remains uncertain. In 1994 Krasnovodsk was renamed *Turkmenbashy*, "Turkmen headland," for the peninsula here.

Krasnoyarsk (Красноярск) *Town, southern Russia.* The town, east of Achinsk at the point where the Transsiberian Railway crosses the Yenisey, was founded in 1628 as a military post named *Krasnyj*, "red," and soon after *Krasnyj Yar*, "red bank." This was probably a Russian translation of an earlier Turkic name. The reference is to the red soil or rocks on the river bank here. The present form of the name was adopted in 1822 when the settlement became a town. Cf. **Krasny Yar**.

Krasnoye Selo (Кра́сное Село́) *Town, western Russia*. The town, southwest of St. Petersburg, arose as a village in 1730 and has a name meaning "beautiful village," from obsolete Russian *krasnyj*, "beautiful" (now meaning "red"), and *selo*, "village." The village was incorporated into Leningrad (as St. Petersburg then was) in 1973.

Krasnoznamensk (Краснозна́менск) *Town, western Russia*. The town, southeast of Neman, was founded in 1734 and originally had the German name of *Lasdehnen*. In 1945 it was renamed as now. The name translates as "red banner," from Russian *krasnyj*, "red," and *znamya*, genitive *znameni*, "banner." The reference is to Red Army units that were awarded the Order of the Red Banner for their stand against German forces here in World War II.

Krasny Klyuch (Кра́сный Ключ) *Town, southwestern Russia*. The town, northeast of Chernikovsk, has a name translating as "beautiful spring." *Krasnyj* can mean both "beautiful" and "red," but here clearly means the former. The town, which at one time was known as *Bely Klyuch*, "white spring," is located in a picturesque setting by the spring that has this name.

Krasny Kut (Кра́сный Кут) *Town, southwestern Russia*. The town, southeast of Saratov, has a name meaning "red corner." The first word is Russian *krasnyj*, "red," in its revolutionary sense. The second is a south Russian dialect or Ukrainian word used for a narrowing stretch of land or water, such as the end of a headland or an inlet, or any angular piece of land. (It is related to Greek *kanthos*, "angle where the eyelids meet.") There is a village of the same name in western Ukraine, northwest of Krasny Luch.

Krasny Liman (Кра́сный Лима́н) *Town, eastern Ukraine*. The town, northeast of Slavyansk, has a name meaning "red lake." Russian *krasnyj*, "red," here has its revolutionary sense. *Liman* is a regional word applied to a lake without reeds or waterweeds. (It is related to Greek *limnē*, "lake.") The name is found elsewhere, as further north, in Russia, for a village southeast of Voronezh.

Krasny Luch (Кра́сный Луч) *Town, eastern Ukraine*. The town, east of Donetsk, was founded in the 1890s as the settlement of *Krindachyovka* (Криндачёвка). It became a town in 1926 and took its present Soviet name, meaning "red ray," from Russian *krasnyj*, "red," and *luch*, "ray." The name is suitably symbolic for a major coal-mining center.

Krasny Mayak (Кра́сный Мая́к) *Town, western Russia*. The town, east of Vladimir, has a Russian revolutionary name meaning "red lighthouse," from *krasnyj*, "red," and *mayak*, "lighthouse." Cf. **Mayachny**. Until 1925 the settlement was known as *Yakunchikov* (Яку́нчиков), presumably for a local factory owner or other entrepreneur of this name.

Krasny Oktyabr (Кра́сный Октя́брь) *Village, western Russia*. Wherever it is found, the name means "Red October," commemorating the Russian Revolution of 1917, which in the Old Style calendar occurred in October. There are or were several places with this name in the former Soviet Union. This particular one is northeast of Moscow.

Krasny Yar (Кра́сный Яр) *Village, south central Russia*. The village, northwest of Tomsk on the Ob River, has a name translating as "red bank," from Russian *krasnyj*, "red," and *yar*, "bank," "slope," a word of Turkic origin, related to modern Turkish *yar*, "precipice." There are many places with this name, all by rivers. The reference is to the red-colored soil or rock of a steep river bank. Cf. **Krasnoufimsk, Krasnoyarsk**.

Kremenchug (Кременчу́г) *City, east central Ukraine.* The city, northwest of Dnepropetrovsk, has a name that could derive from Russian *kremen'*, "flint" (cf. **Kremenets**), but that is possibly of Turkic origin, from *kermen*, "fort." Cf. **Inkerman**.

Kremenets (Кре́менец) *Town, western Ukraine.* The medieval town, southeast of Rovno, appears to take its name from Russian *kremen'* or Ukrainian *kremin'*, "flint."

Krenytsin, Mt. (Крени́цына вулка́н) *Volcano, Kuril Islands, southeastern Russia.* The active volcano, on Onekotan island, near the northern end of the Kuril chain, is named for the Russian navigator Pyotr Kuzmich *Krenitsyn* (1728–1770), leader of an expedition that in 1764–70 charted all of the Aleutian Islands and explored the west coast of Alaska.

Krestovsky Island (Кре́стовский о́стров) *Island, St. Petersburg, western Russia.* The island is one of the largest of the ten on which St. Petersburg stands. The name derives in some way from Russian *krest*, "cross," perhaps because there was a cross-shaped lake here at one time, or because a cross was discovered buried here, or because a building such as a chapel had a prominent cross. One theory claims that the original cart routes here formed a crisscross pattern.

Krestovy Pereval (Кресто́вый перева́л) *Mountain pass, northern Georgia.* The pass, in the central Caucasus, has a name meaning "cross pass," from Russian *krest*, "cross," and *pereval*, "pass." The pass was given its name in 1824 for the large stone cross here that marks the route over the Caucasus.

Kresttsy (Крестцы́) *Village, western Russia.* The village, southeast of Novgorod, has an Old Russian name meaning "crossroads." The village is on the Moscow to St. Petersburg highway at a point where it is crossed by another road.

Krindachyovka See **Krasny Luch**.

Kristinopol See **Chervonograd**.

Krivaya Kosa See **Sedovo**.

Krivoy Rog (Криво́й Рог) *City, south central Ukraine.* The city, southwest of Dnepropetrovsk, arose from a post station founded in 1775 by a bend in the Ingulets River. Its name indicates this location, and translates literally as "crooked horn," from Russian *krivoj*, "crooked," and *rog*, "horn." The latter word is used for various geographical sites with a rounded contour or curving course, such as a cape, a ravine, or a river bend, as here.

Kronshtadt (Кроншта́дт) *Town and port, western Russia.* The town, on Kotlin Island in the Gulf of Finland west of St. Petersburg, was founded by Peter the Great in 1704 as a fort to guard the sea approaches to St. Petersburg, laid out the previous year. The original fort was called *Kronshlot*, otherwise Swedish *Kronslott*, "crown castle." In 1723 it received its present name, from German *Krone*, "crown," and *Stadt*, "town." Unusually for a "royalist" name, it never underwent a Soviet name change.

Kropachyovo (Кропачёво) *Town, southwestern Russia.* The town, west of Zlatoust, takes its name from

A. P. *Kropachyov*, a merchant contractor who took part in the construction of the Samara to Zlatousk railroad.

Kropotkin (Кропо́ткин) *Town, southwestern Russia.* The town, northwest of Armavir, arose in the late 19th century as the village of *Romanovsky Khutor* (Рома́новский Ху́тор), "Romanov's village." In 1921 it was renamed as now for the Russian revolutionary and geographer Pyotr Alekseyevich *Kropotkin* (1842–1921).

Kropotkin Range (Кропо́ткина хребе́т) *Mountain range, southern Russia.* The range, northeast of Lake Baykal, is named for the Russian revolutionary and geographer Pyotr Alekseyevich *Kropotkin* (1842–1921), who explored this region in 1866.

Kruber Range (Кру́бера хребе́т) *Mountain range, Kuril Islands, southeastern Russia.* The chain of extinct volcanoes, at the northeastern end of Iturup island, is named for the Soviet physical geographer Aleksandr Aleksandrovich *Kruber* (1871–1941).

Kruzenshtern Strait (Крузенште́рна проли́в) *Strait, Kuril Islands, southeastern Russia.* The strait is one of the largest in the chain, between the small Lovushka Islands to the north and Raykoke Island to the south. It takes its name from the Russian navigator Admiral Ivan Fyodorovich *Kruzenshtern* (in Western sources usually known as Adam Johann Krusenstern) (1770–1846), who commanded the first Russian circumnavigation of the world in 1803–06 on board the *Nadezhda* (see **Nadezhda Strait**) and who charted this region of the North Pacific during the course of it.

Krylatskoye (Крыла́тское) *District, Moscow, western Russia.* The western district of Moscow has a name dating from at least the 15th century. Its precise meaning is uncertain, although it appears to be connected in some way with Russian *krylo*, "wing." Perhaps there was some wing-shaped natural object here, such as a gully.

Kryukovo (Крю́ково) *Town, western Russia.* The town, northwest of Moscow, has a name that appears to derive from a personal name or nickname (based on Russian *kryuk*, "hook"). In the 14th and 15th centuries there were boyars named Ivan *Kryuk* and Boris *Kryuk*, and it is possible the village belonged to one or other of them.

Kryzhin Range (Кры́жина хребе́т) *Mountain range, southern Russia.* The range, in the Eastern Sayan north of the Mongolian border, honors one *Kryzhin*, a topographer member of the Siberian expedition of 1855–58 sponsored by the Russian Geographical Society.

Kuban (Куба́нь) *River, southwestern Russia.* The river rises in the Caucasus, in Georgia, and flows generally north and northwest to divide into three mouths, two on the Sea of Azov and one on the Black Sea. More than 200 variants of its name have been recorded over the past 2,500 years. The present name is generally explained as deriving from the *Kuman*, a Polovtsian people who inhabited the Black Sea region in the 11th century. The Greeks knew the river as the *Hypanis*, which is clearly an earlier form of the name. This has led some authorities to see a source in Greek *hippos*, "horse," although this is almost certainly an ingenuous attempt to explain the name.

Kudelka See **Asbest**.

Kudirkos-Naumiestis (Куди́ркос-На́уместис) *Town, southwestern Lithuania.* The town, southwest of Kaunas, was founded in 1643 and was originally known as *Vladislavov*. In 1917 it was renamed *Naumiestis* and in 1934 as now. The first part of the name honors the Lithuanian writer and patriot Vincas *Kudirka* (1858–1899), who died here.

Kudymkar (Кудымкáр) *Town, western Russia*. The town, capital of the Komi republic, southwest of Berezniki, has a name that is said to be a combination of the personal name *Kudym*, of Turkic origin but uncertain meaning, and Komi *kar*, "town." The town had its beginnings in the 16th century.

Kukarka See **Sovetsk**[2].

Kultuk (Култýк) *Town, southern Russia*. The town, at the western end of Lake Baykal, has a name of Turkic origin, from *kultyk*, "corner," "nook," denoting a concealed inlet.

Kulyab (Куля́б) *Town, southwestern Tajikistan*. The town, southeast of Dushanbe, is said to take its name from Turkic *kul*, "lake" (modern Turkish *göl*), and Iranian *ab*, "water." The town is in the valley of the Yakhsu River, although there is no obvious lake here.

Kuma (Кумá) *River, southwestern Russia*. The river rises in the Caucasus and flows east to the Caspian Sea. Its name derives from Turkic (and modern Turkish) *kum*, "sand." The waters of the Kuma reach the sea only in the dry season.

Kumayri (Кумáйри) *City, northwestern Armenia*. The city, northwest of Yerevan, is one of the oldest in Armenia, with a settlement recorded here in the 5th century B.C. The present name, also in the form *Gumri*, emerged subsequently. In 1837 a Russian fortified settlement was built nearby and in 1840 was raised to town status and given the Greek-style name, as was then fashionable, of *Aleksandropol* (Александрóполь), so to say *Alexandropolis*, "Alexandra's town," for Empress *Alexandra* Fyodorovna, wife of Czar Nicholas I. In 1924 the town, which by then had absorbed Kumayri, was renamed *Leninakan* (Ленинакáн) in memory of *Lenin*, who had died earlier that year. The final *-kan* is the Iranian element meaning "town," as does the *-kand* of **Samarkand** and *-kent* of **Tashkent**. The former name *Kumayri* was readopted in 1990. The meaning of this is uncertain. It may relate to Turkish *gümrük*, "customs," since the earlier settlement was a post for the collection of imposts from merchants' caravans.

Kumertau (Кумертáу) *Town, southwestern Russia*. The town, in Bashkortostan southeast of Orenburg, has a Bashkir name meaning "coal mountain," from *kumer* (Turkish *kömür*), "coal," and *tau* (Turkish *dağ*), "mountain." The town arose in 1953 at the center of an already flourishing coal-mining region.

Kunashir (Кунашúр) *Island, Kuril Islands, southeastern Russia*. The southernmost of the Kuril Islands, and the closest to Japan, has a name of Ainu origin meaning "black island," from *kuna*, "black," and *shiri*, "island." The reference is either to the dark-colored soil on the island or to its dense coniferous forest, by contrast with the barren tundra of the northern Kurils. The Japanese name for the island, *Kunashiri*, is based on this.

Kungrad (Кунгрáд) *Town, western Uzbekistan*. The town, northwest of Nukus, is said to derive its name from the *Kongrat*, an Uzbek tribe who settled in the area from the 15th century. The second part of the name may have been influenced by Russian *-grad*, "town," as in *Volgograd*, although Kungrad is some way south of Russia. Until 1969 the settlement was named *Zheleznodorozhny* (Железнодорóжный), the adjectival form of Russian *zheleznaya doroga*, "railroad."

Kungur (Кунгу́р) *Town, southwestern Russia*. The town, southeast of Perm, was founded as a defensive post in 1648 on the right bank of the Iren River, near the point where it is joined by a tributary, the *Kungur*. Following repeated raids by Bashkirs and Kungur Tatars, however, the fort was moved in the 1660s to a new site on the estuary of the Iren, where defense was easier. The original fort was apparently named for the river, which itself gave the name of the Tatar tribe. The precise meaning of the name remains uncertain. It may be Tatar *kongyr*, "rapid," alluding to the swift current.

Kuntsevo (Ку́нцево) *District, Moscow, western Russia*. The western district of Moscow was an independent town from 1926 to 1960. It takes its name from the village first recorded here in the 15th century. Its own name is said to derive from Old Russian *kunet'*, "to look pleasant," or *kunka*, "pleasant," "agreeable." The reference would have been to the natural beauty of the place, west of the Moskva River.

Kuokkala See **Repino**.

Kura (Кура́) *River, Georgia/Azerbaijan*. The river rises in northeastern Turkey and flows north into Georgia then southeast through Azerbaijan to the Caspian Sea. Greek geographers knew it as the *Cyrus*, which is a form of the same name. The name itself probably derives from some ancient Caucasian language and simply means "river."

Kurchatov (Курча́тов) *Town, western Russia*. The town, southwest of Kursk, arose in 1971 when the Kursk atomic electric power station was built here. The name honors the Soviet nuclear physicist Igor Vasilyevich *Kurchatov* (1903–1960), who guided the development of the Soviet Union's first atomic electric power station (at Obninsk, 1954).

Kuressaare (Ку́рессааре) *Town and port, western Estonia*. The town, on the southern side of the island of Saaremaa, was founded in the mid-fourteenth century around a castle that stood on the site of an earlier fortress built by Livonian knights and named *Arensburg*, "Arnold's fort." The Estonian name of the town, which gradually superseded the German one, derives from the personal name *Kure* and Lithuanian *saare*, "island." In 1952 the town was renamed *Kingisepp* (Ки́нгисепп), in honor of the Estonian revolutionary leader, active in Russia, Viktor Eduardovich *Kingisepp* (1888–1922), who was born on the island. The town reverted to its earlier name in 1988.

Kurgan (Курга́н) *City, southwestern Russia*. The city, southeast of Yekaterinburg, arose in 1662 on the site of an ancient fortified settlement named *Tsaryovo Gorodishche*, "royal fort" (cf. **Gorodishche**), itself founded in 1553. Near this fort was a burial mound called *Tsaryov Kurgan*, "royal tumulus." The settlement was destroyed in 1738 when a road was built here, but was later re-established and on gaining town status in 1782 took the second and main word of this as its official name. Cf. **Kurgan-Tyube**.

Kurgan-Tyube (Курга́н-Тюбе́) *Town, southwestern Tajikistan*. The town, south of Dushanbe, was described in a 17th-century document as follows: "On a high hill there still stand the ruined walls of a once impressive fortress." The description is borne out by the name, which derives from two Turkic words: *kurgan*, "burial mound," "fort," and *tyube*, "height," "hill." The sense is thus "fort on a hill." Cf. **Kurgan**.

Kuril Islands (Кури́льские острова́) *Island group, southeastern*

Russia. The islands, off the east coast of Russia, extend from the southern tip of the Kamchatka Peninsula to Hokkaido, the northernmost island of Japan (who occupied them from 1875 to 1945, and who still claims the two southernmost islands, Iturup and Kunashir). The name has been popularly associated with Russian *kurit'*, "to smoke," as if referring to the many volcanoes on the islands. But a much more likely origin is in the Ainu word *kur*, "person," denoting their indigenous inhabitants. The Ainu formerly lived in the Japanese islands, but were gradually pushed northwards by the Japanese. There are still a few Ainu on Hokkaido, but they are mostly now found in Sakhalin and the Kuril Islands. The Japanese name for the Kurils is *Chishima*, "thousand islands." (There are actually 56.)

Kurilsk (Курńльск) *Town, Kuril Islands, southeastern Russia*. The town is the "capital" of the Kuril Islands and is on the largest of them, Iturup. It was so named, for the **Kuril Islands** themselves, in 1946, when Japan returned the islands to Russia. Under Japanese occupation the town was known as *Syana*.

Kurisches Haff See **Kursky Zaliv**.

Kurland See **Kurzeme**.

Kursk (Курск) *City, western Russia*. The city, northwest of Belgorod, takes its name from the small *Kur* River here on which a fortress of Kievan Rus was built in the 10th century. The river's own name derives from a local word, *kurya*, for a river inlet or channel.

Kursky Zaliv (Кýрский залńв) *Inlet, western Russia/southern Lithuania*. The inlet of the Baltic Sea has a name meaning "inlet of the *Kuri*," from Russian *zaliv*, "inlet," and the name of the *Kuri* people who at one time inhabited the southeast Baltic coast. Before 1946 the inlet was more familiar under its German name of *Kurisches Haff*, the latter word meaning "lagoon." Cf. **Kurzeme**.

Kurzeme (Кýрземе) *Historic region, western Latvia*. The name means "land of the *Kuri*," from Latvian *zeme*, "land," and the name of the *Kuri* people who once inhabited the region. The region is also known as *Courland* or *Kurland*. Cf. **Kursky Zaliv**.

Kushka (Кýшка) *Town, southeastern Turkmenistan*. The town, near the border with Afghanistan south of Mary, takes its name from the Iranian word *keshk* or *kushk*, "tower," "fort."

Kushnarenkovo (Кушнарёнково) *Village, southwestern Russia*. The village, northwest of Ufa, was so named in 1937 for the political head of the local Bashkir *narkomzem* (people's commissariat for agriculture), one *Kushnarenko*.

Kushva (Кýшва) *Town, western Russia*. The town, in the Middle Urals southwest of Krasnouralsk, takes its name from the river on which it lies. The river name has been derived from Finno-Ugrian words meaning "bare water," but it is more likely to represent a blend of *kush*, "forest glade," and *va*, "water."

Kustanay (Кустанáй) *Town, northern Kazakhstan*. The town, west of Kokchetav, was founded in 1883 by Russian and Ukrainian settlers on an existing site of this name. Its original form seems to have been *Kostana*, which has been derived from Kazakh *kos*, "two," and the name of the *Tana* people who formerly lived here. But it is not clear what there were "two" of. When the original settlement was raised to town status in 1893, it was at first known as *Nikolayevsk* (Николáевск). The old name was restored two years later.

Kusye-Aleksandrovsky (Кусье-Александровский) *Town, west central Russia*. The town, in the Middle Urals east of Chusovoy, is located at the confluence of the *Kusya* and Koyva rivers and takes the first part of its name from the former. The second part represents the name of *Aleksandr* Grigoryevich Stroganov, who in 1715 built an iron foundry at the mouth of the Ustya, naming it for the river and its owner. The river name is of uncertain origin, although the final *ya* is probably the Mansi word for "river."

Kutaisi (Кутаиси) *City, western Georgia*. The city, northwest of Zestafoni, was the chief town of ancient Colchis, when it was known by the name of *Aea*. Its present name comes from Old Georgian *kuato*, "rocky," describing the terrain in the oldest part of the city.

Kuvandyk (Кувандык) *Town, southwestern Russia*. The town, northwest of Orsk, is generally said to have a name based on Kazakh *kuan*, "parched," "scorched," alluding to hot, dry terrain. But this hardly accords with the toponymy, since the town is surrounded by picturesque woodland and meadows. The name is thus more likely to derive from Kazakh *kuanu* or Bashkir *kyuanyu*, "to rejoice," which itself could be the basis of a personal name or else directly describe the location as a "place of joy."

Kuybyshev[1] (Куйбышев) *Town, southern Russia*. The town, west of Novosibirsk, was founded in 1722 under the name of *Kainsk* (Каинск). In 1935 it was renamed as now for the Bolshevik leader Valerian Vladimirovich *Kuybyshev* (1888–1935), who was banished here in 1907 for his revolutionary activities.

Kuybyshev[2] (Куйбышев) *Town, western Russia*. The town, capital of Tatarstan, south of Kazan, was founded in 1781 and was originally known as *Spassk* (Спасск), for its church, dedicated to the Savior (Russian *Spas*). (See **Spassk**.) In 1926 it was renamed *Spassk-Tatarsky* (Спасск-Татарский), "Tatar Spassk," to be distinguished from other places of this name. In 1935 it received its present name, commemorating the Bolshevik leader Valerian Vladimirovich *Kuybyshev* (1888–1935), who was active in this region, notably in **Samara**.

Kuybyshev See **Samara**.

Kuybyshevka-Vostochnaya See **Belogorsk**[1].

Kuybyshevsky (Куйбышевский) *Town, northern Kazakhstan*. The town, west of Kokchetav, is named for the Russian Bolshevik leader Valerian Vladimirovich *Kuybyshev* (1884–1935). Until 1969 the workers' settlement was known as *Trudovoy* (Трудовой), the adjectival form of Russian *trud*, "labor."

Kuzbass (Кузбасс) *Industrial region, southern Russia*. The important coal-mining region, in the basin of the Tom River, extends approximately from Mezhdurechensk in the south to Kemerovo in the north, and includes the industrial towns of Novokuznetsk and Leninsk-Kuznetsky. The name is an abbreviation of *Kuznetskij bassejn* (Кузнецкий бассейн), "Kuznetsk basin," and arose on an analogy with the **Donbass**, of which it is an eastern counterpart. But whereas the Donbass derived its name from the Donets River, the Kuzbass takes its name from the *Kuznetsy*. This was a nickname, meaning "smiths," given by Russians in the 17th and 18th centuries to the Tatars in this region, who were noted metalworkers. See also **Kuznetsk, Leninsk-Kuznetsky, Novokuznetsk**.

Kuznetsk (Кузнецк) *City, western Russia*. The city, east of Penza, arose in 1780 on the site of a village named *Naryshkino*, so called from the boyars named *Naryshkin* who owned estates here from the mid-17th century. The present name appears to derive from Russian *kuznets*, "smith," "blacksmith." This would allude to a smithy or metalworks here. However, there is little archive material regarding the early history of the town.

Kuznetsk See **Novokuznetsk**.

Kuznetsk Basin See **Kuzbass**.

Kuznetsovo See **Konakovo**.

Kuznetsovsk (Кузнецóвск) *Town, northwestern Ukraine*. The town, on the Styr River northwest of Rovno, arose in 1977 when an atomic electric power station was built here. It is named for the Soviet reconnaissance agent Nikolay Ivanovich *Kuznetsov* (1911-1944), killed by Ukrainian nationalists in World War II when working behind enemy lines.

Kyrgyzstan (Кыргызстáн) *Republic, Central Asia*. The republic, south of Kazakhstan, has a name meaning "land of the *Kirgiz*," from its indigenous population. Their name is of Mongol origin but uncertain meaning. It may be related to that of the *Khakass* (see **Khakassia**). Until the republic gained independence in 1991, it was generally more familiar as *Kirgizia*.

Kyshtym (Кышты́м) *Town, southwestern Russia*. The town, northwest of Chelyabinsk, stands on the *Kyshtym* River. The name perhaps derives from Bashkir *kyshky*, "winter," alluding to some type of winter quarters here. The present town was founded on the site of such quarters in 1757 and raised to town status in 1934. Meanwhile the winter settlement itself had given the name of the river.

Kyzyl (Кызы́л) *Town, southeastern Russia*. The town, the capital of Tuva, west of Irkutsk, has a Tuvan name meaning "red" (related to Turkish *kızıl*). The revolutionary name was given in 1926 in marked contrast to its original name of *Belotsarsk* (Белоцáрск). This means "white czar," from Russian *belyy*, "white," and *tsar'*, "czar," and was given the town on its founding in 1914 in order to "promote" the Russian czar in this eastern land. In 1918 this Russian royalist name was superseded by the indigenous name of *Khem-Beldyr* (Хем-Белды́р), from *khem*, "river," the Tuvan name of the Yenisey, and *beldyr*, "confluence." Kyzyl is located at the point where the Bolshoy Yenisey ("Big Yenisey," Tuvan *Biy-Khem*) and Maly Yenisey ("Little Yenisey," Tuvan *Ka-Khem*) join to form the Verkhny Yenisey ("Upper Yenisey").

Kyzyl See **Suvorovo**.

Kyzylagach See **Kirov Bay**.

Kyzyl-Kiya (Кызы́л-Кия́) *Town, southwestern Kyrgyzstan*. The town, southwest of Osh near the border with Uzbekistan, has a Kirgiz name meaning "red rock," from words related to Turkish *kızıl*, "red," and *kaya*, "rock." The color is literally descriptive of the rocky soil here.

Kyzyl Kum (Кызылкýм) *Desert, Uzbekistan/Kazakhstan*. The desert, between the Amudarya and Syrdarya rivers, has a Turkic name meaning "red sands," from words related to modern Turkish *kızıl*, "red," and *kum*, "sand." The desert overall is not noticeably red, and differs little in hue from the Kara-Kum ("black sands") to the west. However, certain areas have reddish or brick-colored sands, so that the name probably at first applied to these, then spread to apply generally to the desert as a whole.

Kyzyltash (Кызылтáш) *Lake, southwestern Russia*. The lake, at the southern end of the Middle Urals, northwest of Chelyabinsk, has a Bashkir name meaning "red rock," from *kyzyl*, "red," and *tash*, "rock," "stone." The reference is to *Krasnyj Kamen'* (Russian, "Red Rock"), a cape on the northern shore of the lake, from which the lake itself took its name.

Kzyl-Orda (Кзыл-Орда́) *Town, southern Kazakhstan.* The town, east of the Aral Sea, was founded in 1820 as a fort of the Kokand khanate called *Ak-Mechet*, "white mosque" (cf. **Chernomorskoye, Simferopol**). In 1853 it was captured by Russian forces under the command of General V. A. *Perovsky* and was renamed for him as *Perovsky*, and subsequently as the town of *Perovsk* (Перо́вск). It was again *Ak-Mechet* from 1917 to 1925, when it acquired its present Turkic name, meaning "red fort," from words related to modern Turkish *kızıl*, "red," and *ordu*, "army" (English *horde*). "Red" has its revolutionary sense here, and in this instance the name additionally suggests a reference to the *Red* Army.

Labiau See **Polessk**.

Labytnangi (Лабытна́нги) *Town, northwestern Russia.* The town, across the Ob River from Salekhard to the east of the Polar Urals, has a Khanty name meaning "seven larches," from *lapyt*, "seven," and *nangk*, "larch." There must have been a prominent group of these trees here at some time. The present town dates from 1975 and developed when the railroad from the Vorkuta line was extended over the Urals to here.

Lacha (Ла́ча) *Lake, northwestern Russia.* The lake, south of Kargopol, takes its name from the northern dialect word *lach*, used for an area of marshland with small hills.

Ladoga, Lake (Ла́дожское о́зеро) *Lake, northwestern Russia.* The large lake, northeast of St. Petersburg, takes its name from the ancient town of *Ladoga* (now *Staraya Ladoga*, "Old Ladoga"), 7 miles (12 km) south of it on the Volkhov River. (See also **Novaya Ladoga**.) The town took its name from the *Ladoga*, a tributary of the Volkhov, and the river takes its own name from Finnish *Alodejoki*, "low place river," from *alode*, "low place," and *joki*, "river." The lake's historic Russian name was *Nevo*, probably related to the name of the **Neva** River.

Ladushkin (Ла́душкин) *Town, western Russia.* The town, southwest of Kaliningrad, originally bore the German name of *Ludwigsort*, "Ludwig's place." In 1946 it was renamed as now for the Red Army soldier I. M. *Ladushkin*, killed in combat nearby in 1945.

Lakhdenpokhya (Лахденпо́хья) *Town, northwestern Russia.* The town, on the northwestern shore of Lake Ladoga southeast of Sortavala, has a name of Finnish origin meaning "bottom of the inlet," from *lahden*, genitive of *lahti*, "bay," "inlet," and *pohja*, "bottom," "end." The town is located at the end of a long narrow inlet. The Finnish border is only 15 miles (24 km) away.

Lakinsk (Ла́кинск) *Town, western Russia.* The town, southwest of Vladimir, was originally the village of *Undol*, a name not yet satisfactorily explained. It takes its present name from the Russian revolutionary M. I. *Lakin*, killed here in 1905 for his subversive propaganda.

Lama (Ла́ма) *River, western Russia.* The river, northwest of Moscow, flows north into the Ivankov Reservoir. Its name has been linked with Lithuanian *loma*, "depression," and Latvian *lama*, "pool." Both descriptions suit the low-lying terrain here.

La Pérouse Strait (Лаперу́за проли́в) *Strait, southeastern Russia.* The strait, between the Russian island of Sakhalin and Japanese island of Hokkaido, is named for the French navigator Jean François Galaup, comte de *La Pérouse* (1741–1788), who passed through it in 1787 (although he was not the first to do so).

Laptev Sea (Ла́птевых мо́ре) *Sea, northern Russia.* The sea, in the Arctic Ocean between the Taymyr Peninsula and New Siberian Islands, was so named in 1913 by the Russian Geographical Society at the suggestion of the geographer and cartographer Yu. M. Shokalsky in honor of naval officers Dmitry Yakovlevich *Laptev* (1701–1767) and his cousin Khariton Prokofyevich *Laptev* (1700–1763), who led Arctic expeditions over land and sea here. Earlier names for the sea include *Tatar Sea* (Тата́рское мо́ре), *Lena Sea* (Ле́нское мо́ре) (for the **Lena**, which enters it), *Nordenskiöld Sea* (Норденше́льда мо́ре) (see **Nordenskiöld Archipelago**), and *Siberian Sea* (Сиби́рское мо́ре).

Larga (Ла́рга) *Village, northern Moldova.* The village, near the border with Ukraine, takes its name from the river on which it stands. The river name means "broad," from a Moldovan word related to French *large* in the same sense.

Lasdehnen See **Krasnoznamensk**.

Latvia (Ла́твия) *Republic, northern Europe.* The republic, on the Baltic Sea between Estonia to the north and Lithuania to the south, takes its name from its indigenous people, the *Latvians*, formerly often known as *Letts*. Their own name is said to derive from the small *Lata* River which flows close to the border with Lithuania.

Lazarev (Ла́зарев) *Town, southeastern Russia.* The town, on the cape of the same name south of Nikolayevsk-on-Amur, is named for the Russian admiral and Black Sea Fleet commander Mikhail Petrovich *Lazarev* (1788–1851). Cf. **Lazarev Island**.

Lazarev Island (Ла́зарева о́стров) *Island, Aral Sea, western Uzbekistan.* The island, in the southern part of the sea, is named for the Russian admiral and Black Sea Fleet commander Mikhail Petrovich *Lazarev* (1788–1851). Cf. **Lazarev**.

Lazarevskoye (Ла́заревское) *Resort, southwestern Russia.* The Black Sea resort, southeast of Tuapse, is named for the Russian general I. P. *Lazarev*, a leader of the war fought in the late 18th century to free the Caucasus from the Turks.

Lazovsk (Лазо́вск) *Town, north central Moldova.* The town, southeast of Beltsy, was originally the village of *Synzhereya* (Сынжере́я), a name based on the Moldovan word meaning "cornel" (a tree related to the dogwood). It was raised to the status of urban settlement in 1965 and renamed for the Moldovan Civil War hero Sergey Georgiyevich *Lazo* (1894–1920), who with other revolutionaries was captured by the Japanese in Vladivostok, then tortured and burned to death in a locomotive firebox. The Moldovan village of his birth, formerly *Pyatry*, and the Far Eastern railroad station of his death, originally *Muravyovo-Amurskaya*, were both renamed *Lazo* in his honor.

Lbishchensk See **Chapayev**.

Lebedin (Лебеди́н) *Town, northeastern Ukraine.* The town, southwest of Sumy, is said (without much foundation) to take its name from Russian *lebed'*, "swan." It may well derive from the personal name *Lebed'*, however. The town was founded in 1653.

Lebedyan (Лебедя́нь) *Town, western Russia.* The town, northwest of Lipetsk, is said to take its name from the many swans here, from Russian *lebed'*, "swan." But, like **Lebedin**'s, the actual origin may be in the personal name.

Lefortovo (Лефо́ртово) *Historic region, Moscow, western Russia.* The eastern region of Moscow takes its name from the Lefortov regiment based here in the late 17th century under the command of the Swiss born Russian army officer Frants Yakovlevich *Lefort* (1655–1699), a comrade-in-arms of Peter the Great.

Lemberg See **Lvov**.

Lena (Ле́на) *River, east central Russia.* The river rises west of Lake Baykal then flows generally east and north to enter the Laptev Sea in the Arctic Ocean. The origin of the name has not been conclusively established. However, a source in Evenki *yene*, "river," is possible. Its Yakut name is *Ulakhan-Yuryakh*, "big river."

Lena Sea See **Laptev Sea**.

Lenin (Ле́нин) *Village, southern Belarus.* The village, southeast of Soligorsk, cannot be named for Lenin since it is recorded as early as 1582. The origin of the name is uncertain, although it may well have come from a personal name. The placename was reinterpreted at the time of the Revolution, when a local Bolshevik cell was centered here, and it has even been suggested that V. I. Ulyanov took his party pseudonym from it (although it predated the 1917 Revolution).

Leninabad See (1) **Gafurov**, (2) **Khodzhent**.

Leninakan See **Kumayri**.

Leningrad See **St. Petersburg**.

Lenino (Ле́нино) *Village, eastern Crimea, southern Ukraine.* The village, southwest of Kerch, received its present name, for *Lenin*, in 1957. Before that it was known as *Sem Kolodezey* (Семь Коло́дезей), "seven springs," from the small railroad station of this name built here in 1900 on the main line to Kerch. The name was significant in this arid region of the Crimea.

Lenino-Dachnoye (Ле́нино-Да́чное) *District, Moscow, western Russia.* The southern district of Moscow takes the first part of its name from the workers' settlement of *Lenino*, set up here in 1939 and named for *Lenin*. The second part relates to the *dachas* that were here in the 19th century, as well as in neighboring **Tsaritsyn**, as country cottages in a suburban setting.

Leninogorsk[1] (Ленинго́рск) *City, eastern Kazakhstan.* The city, northeast of Ust-Kamenogorsk, was originally named *Ridder* (Ри́ддер), for the Englishman Philip *Ridder*, who in 1786 discovered a small mine here containing gold, silver, copper, and lead. Mining began in 1791 and remained in English hands until World War I, during which (until the Revolution) production was in the hands of the concessionnaire John Leslie Urquhart. In 1941 the town was renamed as now for *Lenin*, with *-gorsk* implying both "town" (Russian *gorod*) and, adjectivally, "mining" (Russian *gornyj*).

Leninogorsk[2] (Ленинго́рск) *Town, western Russia.* The town, in Tatarstan northwest of Bugulma, was originally known by the name of *Novaya Pismyanka* (Но́вая Письмя́нка), "New Pismyanka." In 1955 the settlement, with its established coal and gas industry, was raised to town status and given its present name for *Lenin*, with *-gorsk* implying both "town" (Russian *gorod*) and, adjectivally, "mining" (Russian *gornyj*).

Lenin Peak (Ле́нина пик) *Mountain, southwestern Kyrgyzstan/*

northeastern Tajikistan. The mountain, in the Transalay range, was discovered in 1871 by the Russian naturalist A. P. Fedchenko (see **Fedchenko Glacier**), and named by him *Kaufman Peak* (пик Ка́уфмана) for the then governor general of Turkestan, Konstantin Petrovich *Kaufman* (1818–1882). On the death of *Lenin* in 1924, it was proposed (through the newspaper *Izvestia*) that his name be given to what was then believed to be the highest mountain in the Soviet Union. (It was later found that Communism Peak was higher.) This was accordingly acted on in 1928 by the Academy of Sciences of the USSR, then extensively exploring the Pamirs, to the south of the range.

Leninsk[1] (Ле́нинск) *Town, southwestern Russia*. The town, on an arm of the Volga east of Volgograd, was originally known as *Prishib* (При́шиб). In 1919 it was renamed as now for *Lenin*. As such, it was the first Soviet town to be named for the Communist leader in his lifetime.

Leninsk[2] (Ле́нинск) *Town, eastern Uzbekistan*. The town, south of Andizhan, was originally a village named *Assake* (Ассаке́). In 1934 this was raised to the status of "settlement of urban type" and renamed *Zelensk* (Зе́ленск), "green place." The following year it was renamed as now for *Lenin*. The settlement was raised to town status in 1937.

Leninsk-Kuznetsky (Ле́нинск-Кузне́цкий) *Town, southern Russia*. The coal-mining town, southeast of Kemerovo, was originally known as *Kolchugino* (Кольчу́гино). The meaning of this is unknown. In 1925 it was renamed as now for *Lenin*, who had died the previous year, with the second part of the name added to distinguish this *Leninsk* from others and to refer to the town's location in the **Kuzbass** (*Kuznetsky bassejn*).

Lenkoran (Ленкора́нь) *Town and port, southeastern Azerbaijan*. The port, on the southwest shore of the Caspian Sea southwest of Baku, is one of the oldest towns in Azerbaijan. It is not known when it was founded, but it takes its name from the river on which it stands. The name is said to derive from an Iranian word meaning "anchor," referring to the historic importance of the site as a place of anchorage. The town is less than 20 miles (32 km) from the Iranian border.

Lepel (Ле́пель) *Town, north central Belarus*. The town, south of Polotsk, takes its name from the lake here, its own name said to derive from Latvian *liepa*, "lime (tree)." Cf. **Liepāja**.

Lermontovo (Ле́рмонтово) *Village, western Russia*. The village, southwest of Penza, was so named in 1917 for the Russian poet Mikhail Yuryevich *Lermontov* (1814–1841), who after being orphaned as a child was raised here by his grandmother. The previous name of the place was *Tarkhany* (Тарха́ны), from Tatar *tarkhan*, "tax-free," a name found for other villages that were free of imposts. (Cf. Turkish *tarh*, "imposition of taxes.")

Leselidze (Лесели́дзе) *Resort, northwestern Georgia*. The Black Sea resort, northwest of Gagra on the border with Russia, was originally known as *Yermolovsk* (Ермоло́вск). In 1944 it was renamed as now for the Georgian military commander Konstantin Nikolayevich *Leselidze* (1903–1944).

Leskhimstroy See **Severodonetsk**.

Lesnyye Polyany (Лесны́е Поля́ны) *Town, western Russia*. The town, with its timber industry northwest of Kirov, has a name translating from the Russian as "forest glades."

Lesogorsk (Лесого́рск) *Town, Sakhalin, eastern Russia*. The town, on the west coast of Sakhalin island, takes its name from that of the *Lesogorka* River, at the mouth of which it lies. The river's own name is a modern Russian one, from *les*, "forest," and *gora*, "mountain," referring to the timber industry here and the mountains to the east in which the river rises. Before 1946, under Japanese occupation, the town was known as *Nayoshi*. Cf. **Uglegorsk**, to the south.

Lesopilnoye (Лесопи́льное) *Town, southeastern Russia*. The town, northeast of Dalnerechensk, is named for its timber industry. Its name translates as "sawmill," from the adjectival form of Russian *lesopil'nya*, itself from *les*, "timber," and *pila*, "saw."

Lesozavodsk (Лесозаво́дск) *Town, southeastern Russia*. The town, southwest of Dalnerechensk near the border with China, has an important timber industry. Hence its name, meaning "timber mill," from Russian *les*, "timber," and *zavod*, "factory," "mill."

Letny Bereg (Ле́тний бе́рег) *Coast, northwestern Russia*. The coast is that of the southern shore of the White Sea, west of Arkhangelsk. Its name means "summer shore," by contrast with the more northerly **Zimny Bereg**.

Lev Tolstoy (Лев Толсто́й) *Town, western Russia*. The town, west of Chaplygin, was so named in 1927 for the famous Russian writer *Lev* (Leo) Nikolayevich *Tolstoy* (1828–1910), who died at the railroad station here, then known as *Astapovo* (Аста́пово).

Lgov (Льгов) *Town, southwestern Russia*. The town, west of Kursk, was originally known as *Olgov*, and is said to have been founded by one of the princes of Kievan Rus named *Oleg*.

Libava See **Liepāja**.

Lida (Ли́да) *City, western Belarus*. The city, northeast of Grodno, takes its name from Baltic *lydimas*, a term for an area of cleared woodland.

Liepāja (Ли́епая) *City and port, western Latvia*. The city, on the Baltic Sea north of Klaipeda, dates from at least the 13th century, and was formerly familiar under the German form of its name as *Libava*. The name is said to derive either from Latvian *liepa*, "lime (tree)," or from Estonian *liva*, "sand," with reference to its sandy shore.

Likhoslavl (Лихосла́вль) *Town, western Russia*. The town, northwest of Tver, has a name that appears to be based on the personal name *Likhoslav*, this presumably being the individual (perhaps a prince) who founded it. The final *-l* has a possessive force, so that the name as a whole means "Likhoslav's (town)."

Likhvin See **Chekalin**.

Lipetsk (Ли́пецк) *Town, western Russia*. The town, north of Voronezh, is mentioned in records dating from the 13th century. It was originally a village known as *Lipovka*, so called from the small river of this name. The river name derives from Russian *lipa*, "lime tree."

Lisichansk (Лисича́нск) *Town, eastern Ukraine*. The town, on the Donets east of Proletarsk, arose in 1710 as a Cossack defensive post in the south of Russia. The fort was set up on a wooded riverside slope known as *Lis'ya Balka* or *Lisichij Bajrak*, "fox gully." The latter subsequently developed to the present name.

Liski (Ли́ски) *Town, western Russia*. The town, southeast of Voronezh, arose in 1870. It takes its name from the small *Lyska* River which here enters the Don. The meaning of the river name is unknown. The original village was also known at one time as *Novopokrovka* (Новопокро́вка), from *novo-*, "new," and the dedication of its church to the Feast of the *Protection* of the Virgin (Russian *Pokrov*, literally "covering"). In 1928 the growing settlement was renamed *Svoboda* (Свобо́да), "freedom," a name it kept until 1943. It then reverted to *Liski* before being further renamed in 1965 as *Georgiu-Dezh* (Георгиу-Деж). This name commemorated the Romanian Communist leader and president Gheorghe *Gheorghiu-Dej* (1901–1965). The town reverted to its original name in 1991, following the abolition of Communism in Romania.

Lisyansky Peninsula (Лися́нского полуо́стров) *Peninsula, eastern Russia*. The peninsula, on the north coast of the Sea of Okhotsk east of Okhotsk, is named for the Russian navigator Yury Fyorodovich *Lisyansky* (1773–1837), who explored this region during the first Russian circumnavigation of the world in 1803–06.

Lisy Nos (Ли́сий Нос) *Town, western Russia*. The town and resort, on the Gulf of Finland northwest of St. Petersburg, takes its name from that of the cape here. It means "fox's nose," alluding to its pointed shape.

Lithuania (Ли́тва) *Republic, northern Europe*. The republic, on the Baltic Sea south of Latvia, is said to take its name from the *Letavka* River, a tributary of the Neris, itself a tributary of the Neman. The river's own name may mean "flooding one."

Litke Strait (Ли́тке проли́в) *Strait, eastern Russia*. The strait between Kamchatka peninsula and the island of Karaginsky was so named by the Geographical Society of the USSR in honor of the Russian navigator and geographer Fyodor Petrovich *Litke* (1797–1882), who discovered it in 1827. His name was also given to various geographical entities within the Arctic Circle, such as an island in the Kara Sea and another in Franz Josef Land.

Little Russia See **Ukraine.**

Litvino See **Sosnovoborsk.**

Livadiya (Лива́дия) *Town and resort, southern Crimea, southern Ukraine*. The Black Sea resort, southwest of Yalta, is said to derive its name from Greek *leimōn*, "damp grassy place," "meadow." (The 1945 Yalta Conference, despite its name, took place at Livadiya, which is nearly 2 miles from Yalta. Russians usually refer to it as the Crimean Conference.)

Livonia (Ливо́ния) *Historic region, Estonia/Latvia*. The region, a former government in Russia's Baltic Provinces, takes its name from the *Livs*, a Finnish people here. Their own name means "dwellers in the muddy place," from a Finno-Ugrian word related to modern Finnish *liefu*, "mud." The region, also known as *Livland*, was ceded to Russia in 1721 but later freed from it. The northern part became part of Estonia and the southern part joined to Latvia in 1918.

Lobva (Ло́бва) *Town, west central Russia*. The town, south of Serov, takes its name from the small *Lopva* River on which it stands, as a tributary of the Lyalya. The river's own name probably derives from Komi-Permyak *löp*, "driftwood," "river refuse," and *va*, "water."

Lodeynoye Pole (Лоде́йное по́ле) *Town, western Russia*. The town, on the Svir River southwest of Podporozhye, was originally a village of boatbuilding people named *Mokrishvitsa*, where Peter the Great had founded a boatyard called *Olonetskaya*. In 1785 the village became a town under its present name, from Russian *lad'ya*, "boat," and *pole*, "field."

Lokhvitsa (Лóхвица) *Town, north central Ukraine*. The town, east of Kiev, takes its name from the river on which it stands. The river name derives from a Slavic word *lokva*, "swamp."

Lomonosov (Ломонóсов) *Town, western Russia*. The town, on the Gulf of Finland west of St. Petersburg, was given its present name in 1948 in honor of the Russian scientist and man of letters Mikhail Vasilyevich *Lomonosov* (1711-1765), who is buried in St. Petersburg. Before this the town had the German name of *Oranienbaum* (Ораниенбáум), "orange tree," for the orangery that was a feature in the palace and park here owned by the aristocratic Menshikov family.

Long Strait (Лóнга пролúв) *Strait, northeastern Russia*. The strait, between Wrangel Island and the Siberian mainland, is named for the American ship's captain Thomas *Long*, who passed through it to the Chukchi Sea on board the whaler *Nile* in 1867.

Lopasnya See **Chekhov**[2].

Lopatin, Mt. (Лопáтина горá) *Mountain, Sakhalin, eastern Russia*. The mountain, in central Sakhalin island, is the island's loftiest and is named for the Russian geologist and geographer Innokenty Aleksandrovich *Lopatin* (1839-1909), whose investigations revealed the industrial potential of Sakhalin's rich coal deposits.

Lopatino See **Volzhsk**.

Lopatka, Cape (Лопáтка) *Cape, Kamchatka, eastern Russia*. The cape, the southern tip of the Kamchatka peninsula, takes its name from Russian *lopatka*, "shovel," "shoulder blade," describing its shape.

Losinoostrovsk See **Babushkin**[2].

Lozovaya (Лозовáя) *Town, eastern Ukraine*. The town, south of Kharkov, has a name found elsewhere deriving from Russian *loza*, "rod," "withy," "vine," meaning a group of bushes or a shrubbery of some kind.

Lubny (Лубны́) *Town, north central Ukraine*. The town, west of Mirgorod, takes its name from Slavic *lub*, "bast" (the inner bark of lime used for fiber and matting).

Ludwigsort See **Ladushkin**.

Luga (Лýга) *Town, western Russia*. The town, south of St. Petersburg, takes its name from the river on which it lies. The river's own name is of uncertain origin. It is not likely to be linked with Russian *lug*, "meadow."

Lugansk (Лугáнск) *City, eastern Ukraine*. The city, east of Kadiyevka, takes its name from the *Lugan* River on which it stands. The river name is of uncertain origin, but could possibly derive from Russian *lug*, "meadow." The town was founded in 1795 around an iron foundry, and gained the present form of its name in 1882. In 1935 it was renamed as *Voroshilovgrad* (Ворошиловгрáд), for the Soviet soldier and politician Kliment Yefremovich *Voroshilov* (1881-1969), who had been active for some time as a revolutionary in Lugansk. Following his fall from favor after his unsuccessful attempt (with others) to oust Khrushchev from office, the name reverted to *Lugansk* in 1958. After his death, however, the town again became *Voroshilovgrad* in 1970, finally reverting to *Lugansk* in 1990.

Lugovoy (Луговóй) *Town, southern Kazakhstan*. The town, east of

Dzhambul, takes its name from Russian *lug*, "meadow," denoting a place with grass in an otherwise barren or inhospitable region.

Lukhovitsy (Луховицы) *Town, western Russia*. The town, southeast of Kolomna, has a name that is an altered form of *Lukhovichi*, with the final *-ichi* denoting an inhabited place. The first part of the name may derive from the Slavic word *lokva*, "swamp" (as for **Lokhvitsa**). An origin in Russian *luka*, "river bend" (cf. **Lutsk**) would be possible if the town were on a river with a noticeable bend.

Lukoyanov (Лукоянов) *Town, western Russia*. The town, southeast of Arzamas, takes its name from one Ivashko *Lukoyanov*, who built a mill here in the 16th century.

Lusavan See **Charentsavan**.

Lutsk (Луцк) *City, northwestern Ukraine*. The city, northwest of Rovno, takes its name from Russian *luka*, "river bend." The town is on a raised defensive site at a marked bend in the Styr River. The former Polish name of the city was *Łuck*.

Lutugino (Лутугино) *Town, eastern Ukraine*. The coal-mining town, southwest of Lugansk, was founded in 1896 and named for the Russian geologist Leonid Ivanovich *Lutugin* (1864–1915), who made a special study of the coal-bearing strata of the Donbass region.

Luzhniki (Лужники) *District, Moscow, western Russia*. The southwestern district of Moscow lies in a loop of the Moskva River and was long subject to flooding, so that to the early 20th century much of its territory consisted of water meadows. Hence its name, from Russian *lug*, "meadow."

Lvov (Львов) *City, western Ukraine*. The city, northwest of Ternopol, arose in the 13th century as a fortress built by order of the Galician prince Daniil Romanovich, who is said to have named it for his son *Lev* (Leo). When in Austria (from 1772 to the collapse of Austria-Hungary after World War I) the city was known by the German name of *Lemberg*, "Lev's fortress."

Lyakhov Islands (Ляховские острова) *Islands, northeastern Russia*. The islands lie east of the Laptev Sea and south of the New Siberian Islands. (Some geographers include them in this group.) The two islands, *Bolshoy Lyakhovsky* ("Big Lyakhov") and *Maly Lyakhovsky* ("Little Lyakhov"), were so named in the 1770s by order of Catherine the Great for the Yakut ivory trader Ivan *Lyakhov* (?–c. 1800), who explored them in 1770. It was Lyakhov who discovered **Kotelny**.

Lysva (Лысьва) *City, western Russia*. The city, west of Nizhny Tagil in the Middle Urals, takes its name from the river on which it lies. The river name is said to be from a Permian language and to mean "pine-needle water," from *lys*, "pineneedles," and *va*, "water."

Lysyye Gory (Лысые Горы) *Town, western Russia*. The town, west of Saratov, has a name transferred from the nearby hills, and translates from the Russian as "bald hills." The region here is located in the central Volga Heights.

Lyuban (Любань) *Town, south central Belarus*. The town, east of Soligorsk, probably has a descriptive name based on the Slavic element *lyub* meaning "favored," "favorite" (Russian *lyubit'*, "to like"). Names with this element are found widely in Slavic countries, and include *Lyubljana*, capital of Slovenia, and *Lublin*, Poland. See also **Lyubech**.

Lyubech (Любеч) *Town, northern Ukraine*. The town, northwest of

Chernigov, is on the Dnieper, which here forms the border with Belarus. It is one of the oldest in historic Russia, mentioned in a document dated 882. Its name probably derives from the Slavic element *lyub* meaning "favored," "favorite," denoting a desirable location. Cf. **Lyuban**.

Lyubertsy (Люберцы) *Town, western Russia*. The town, southeast of Moscow, is said to take its name from a proper name *Libor* or *Lyubor*, presumably that of its founder or an early landowner.

Lyudinovo (Людиново) *Town, western Russia*. The town, north of Bryansk, takes its name from the Old Russian personal name *Lyudin*, with the final *-ovo* a possessive suffix, so that the sense is "Lyudin's (town)." An absurd attempt to derive the name from Russian *lyudi novyje*, "new people," was supposed to refer to the foundry workers who came from the Urals to set up a factory here in the 18th century.

Madona (Мадона) *Town, east central Latvia*. The town, east of Riga, probably takes its name from the personal name *Made*. Until 1926 it was known as *Birzhi* (Биржи).

Magadan (Магадан) *City and port, northeastern Russia*. The port, on the northern coast of the Sea of Okhotsk, was founded in the 1930s. Although of recent origin, the meaning of its name remains obscure. A source in the Evenki word *mongodan*, "alluvium," has been proposed.

Magnitka (Магнитка) *Town, west central Russia*. The town, at the southern end of the Central Urals, north of Zlatoust, has a name derived from Russian *magnit*, "magnet," referring to the iron ore extraction that is its chief industry.

Magnitnaya (Магнитная) *Mountain, southwestern Russia*. The mountain, in the Southern Urals south of Magnitogorsk, has a name meaning "magnetic." The deposits of magnetite iron ore here are powerful enough to deflect a compass needle. Hence the name. The mountain gave the name of neighboring **Magnitogorsk**.

Magnitogorsk (Магнитогорск) *City, southwestern Russia*. The industrial city, in the Southern Urals southwest of Chelyabinsk, arose around an ironworks set up here in 1929. It took its name from the nearby Mt. **Magnitnaya**. The name passed from the plant to the town, with the *-gorsk* representing Russian *gora*, "mountain."

Makarov (Макаров) *Town and port, Sakhalin, eastern Russia*. The port, on the southeast coast of Sakhalin island, was named for the Russian naval commander and polar explorer Stepan Osipovich *Makarov* (1848–1904), killed off Port Arthur during the Russo-Japanese War. Before 1946, under Japanese occupation, the town was known as *Shiritoru*.

Makaryev (Макарьев) *Town, western Russia*. The town, east of Kostroma, arose around a monastery founded in 1439 in the forest here by the Nizhny Novgorod monk *Makary* (Macarius) after the Tatars had destroyed his earlier monastery at what is now **Makaryevo**. It is thus named for him. For some time before the settlement was raised to town status in 1778 its name was officially *Podmonastyrskaya sloboda*, "village by the monastery."

Makaryevo (Макарьево) *Village, western Russia*. The village, on the Volga east of Nizhny Novgorod, arose from a monastery built here in the late 14th century by the Nizhny Novgorod monk *Makary* (Macarius), and is named for him. The monastery became an important stronghold, and as such was destroyed by the Tatars in the early 15th century. A new monastery of the same name was built in 1620 and the village that developed around it, known at first as *Makaryevskaya*, became a town in 1779, but subsequently reverted to village status as a worker's settlement. The site here was also earlier known as *Zhyoltyye peski*, "yellow sands." See also **Makaryev**.

Makeyevka (Макéевка) *City, southeastern Ukraine*. The city, just east of Donetsk, takes its name from a former village here that was itself named for a coal mine owned in the late 18th century by one *Makeyev* (or according to some sources by a Scot named *Mackay*). From 1898 to 1931 the settlement that had developed from the metallurgical works here was known as *Dmitriyevsk* (Дмúтриевск).

Makhachkala (Махачкалá) *City and port, southwestern Russia*. The city, capital of Dagestan, on the northwestern coast of the Caspian Sea, was founded in 1844 as the fortified post of *Petrovskoye* (a military camp of *Peter* the Great was said to have stood here). In 1857 this name was altered to *Petrovsk-Port* (Петрóвск-Порт), emphasizing the town's role as a port. In 1922 the city was renamed as now for the Dagestani revolutionary leader Magomed Ali Dakhadayev (1882-1918), killed in the Civil War. *Makhach* is a pet form of *Magomed* (Mahomet), and *kala* means "fort," "town."

Makharadze See **Ozurgeti**.

Malakhov (Малáхов) *Fortification, southwestern Crimea, southern Ukraine*. The fortification, on a height southeast of Sevastopol, was captured in the Crimean War by the French in 1855 after a long siege, so deciding the fate of Sebastopol. There are conflicting accounts regarding the origin of its name, which appears to be from the personal name *Malakhov*. One story tells of a drunken skipper of the name who opened a store here. Another mentions a skipper, one A. A. Malakhov, who lived nearby and set up a market. But perhaps these were one and the same person. The French victory here is commemorated in France in the name of *Malakoff*, a southern suburb of Paris, and it also gave the title of the French victor at Sebastopol himself, Marshal Pélissier, Duc de *Malakoff* (1794-1864).

Malaya Vishera (Мáлая Вúшера) *Town, western Russia*. The town, southeast of St. Petersburg, takes its name from the river on which it lies. The river name means "Little Vishera," so called to distinguish it from the nearby *Bolshaya Vishera*, "Big Vishera," now actually the smaller of the two. The origin of the river name is uncertain. Some toponymists have linked it to the name of the *Weser*, in Germany, itself perhaps based on Indo-European root elements *veik*, "to flow," and *aha*, "water." If so, the sense could be the same here.

Maloarkhangelsk (Малоархáнгельск) *Town, western Russia*. The town, southeast of Oryol, was formed in 1778 from the village of *Arkhangelskoye*, so named for its church, dedicated to St. Michael the *Archangel*. The prefixing element *Malo-*, "little," was added to avoid confusion with the much better known **Arkhangelsk**.

Malorita (Малорúта) *Town, southwestern Belarus*. The town, southeast of Brest, has a name derived from that of the small river here, the *Malaya Rita*, "Little Rita."

Maloyaroslavets (Малоярослáвец) *Town, western Russia*. The town, southwest of Moscow, was founded in the late 14th century by Prince Vladimir Andreyevich Serpukhov and named *Yaroslavets* for his son *Yaroslav*. In 1485 it became part of the grand principality of Moscow and was given its present name, with the prefixing element *Malo-*, "little." This was doubtless to distinguish it from the better known **Yaroslavl**.

Maloyaz (Малоя́з) *Village, west central Russia*. The village, in Bashkortostan west of Zlatoust, takes its name from the *Malayaz* River on which it is located. The river name means "cattle clearing," from Bashkir *mal*, "cattle," and *ayaz*, "clearing," "glade." The present form of the name has been influenced by Russian *Malo-*, "little," as for **Maloyaroslavets** (above).

Malygin Strait (Малы́гина проли́в) *Strait, northwestern Russia*. The strait, between the Yamal peninsula and Bely island, was named in honor of the Russian Arctic explorer Stepan Gavrilovich *Malygin* (?–1764), who visited and described the region in 1737.

Mamadysh (Мамады́ш) *Town, western Russia*. The town, in Tatarstan east of Kazan, is said to have been founded by one *Mamadysh*, who fled here following the defeat of the Golden Horde by Timur (Tamerlane) in 1395. But there is no firm evidence for this. For some time in the 18th century the village here was known as *Troitskoye*, for the dedication of its church to the *Trinity* (Russian *Troitsa*). However, the earlier name prevailed.

Mamonovo (Мамо́ново) *Town, western Russia*. Russia's westernmost town, southwest of Kaliningrad near the border with Poland, was founded in 1301 and originally had the German name of *Heiligenbeil*. It was given its present name in 1951 in honor of a Soviet national hero, N. V. *Mamonov*, killed here in World War II while defending the approaches to East Prussia.

Manglisi (Мангли́си) *Village, central Georgia*. The village, west of Tbilisi, has an Akkadian (Sumer) name meaning "fortress."

Mangyshlak (Мангышла́к) *Peninsula, Caspian Sea, southwestern Kazakhstan*. The peninsula, on the northeast coast of the Caspian Sea, has a name for which various explanations have been proposed. One of the most likely is an origin in Kazakh *kyshlag*, "kishlak" (a type of village in Central Asia), with the name of the Nogay people *Menk* prefixed. The overall sense could thus be "Menk kishlak," "village inhabited by the Menk."

Manych (Ма́ныч) *River, southwestern Russia*. The river, a tributary of the lower Don, which it enters east of Rostov-on-Don, takes its name from Turkic *manach*, "bitter." Further east, between the lower Don and the lower Kuma, is the *Manych* depression, where a series of salt lakes explains the sense of the name.

Marganets (Ма́рганец) *Town, southeastern Ukraine*. The town, southwest of Zaporozhye, arose in the 1880s as a settlement around the manganese ore workings here, and takes its name from them, from Russian *marganets*, "manganese."

Margilan (Маргила́н) *Town, eastern Uzbekistan*. The town, east of Kokand, is one of the oldest in the Fergana Valley. The origin of its name remains uncertain. Cf. **Fergana**.

Mari (Мари́) *Republic, western Russia*. The republic, to the east of Nizhny Novgorod, takes its name from its indigenous people, the *Mari*, whose name in their own language means "man." In the past they were often known as the *Cheremis*, a name of unknown meaning.

Maria Pronchishcheva Bay See **Pronchishchev Bay**.

Mariinsk (Мари́инск) *Town, southern Russia*. The town, east of

Tomsk, arose in the early 18th century from the village of *Kiyskoye*, so named because it was on the Trans-siberian route from the *Kiy* River. In 1856 it was raised to town status as *Kiysk*, and in 1857 was named as now for *Maria* Alexandrovna (1824-1880), wife of Czar Alexander II. Cf. **Mariinsky Posad**.

Mariinsky (Мариинский) *Village, southwestern Russia*. The village, south of Revda in the Middle Urals, was originally *Mariinsky Zavod*, the latter word meaning "works," "factory." The factory itself was set up in 1840 and is said to have been named for the owner of several local factories at that time, *Maria* Denisovna Demidova.

Mariinsky Posad (Мариинский Посад) *Town, western Russia*. The town, in the Chuvash republic on the Volga east of Cheboksary, arose from the early 17th-century village of *Sundyr*. In 1856 this village merged with others here to form the town of *Mariinsky Posad*, "Maria's quarter," for *Maria* Alexandrovna (1824-1880), wife of Czar Alexander II. Cf. **Mariinsk**. The name is locally shortened to *Marposad*.

Marijampole (Мариямполе) *Town, southwestern Lithuania*. The town, southwest of Kaunas, arose as a monastic center in the 18th century and originally had the Slavic name *Starapole*, "old field." This was later modified to the present name, meaning "Mary's field," for the dedication of the monastery to the Virgin *Mary*. In 1955 the town was renamed *Kapsukas* (Капсукас), for the Lithuanian revolutionary leader Vincas Simanovič Mickēvičius-*Kapsukas* (1880-1935). It reverted to its earlier name in 1989.

Maritime Kray See **Primorsky Kray**.

Mariupol (Мариуполь) *City and port, southeastern Ukraine*. The city, southwest of Donetsk, was founded in 1779 by Greeks who had fled here to escape Turkish repression. They gave the settlement a Greek name, "Mary's town," either in honor of *Maria* Fyodorovna, wife of the heir to the Russian throne, the future czar Paul I, or for the Virgin *Mary*. (According to some accounts, the Greeks brought an ancient icon of the Virgin with them from the Crimea.) In 1948 the city was renamed **Zhdanov** (Жданов), for the Soviet Communist party leader Andrey Aleksandrovich *Zhdanov* (1896-1948), who was born here. The original name was readopted in 1989.

Marks (Маркс) *Town, western Russia*. The town, on the Volga northeast of Saratov, arose in 1767 when Catherine the Great planted settlers from Germany and Switzerland in the lower Volga region. The town came to be called *Yekaterinenshtadt* (Екатериненштадт), "Catherine's town," with the "town" as the German suffix -*stadt*. (Catherine herself was German in origin.) However, the original name *Baronsk* (Баронск) was widely used. This related to the Dutch founder, *Baron* Cano de Berehard. In 1920 the town was renamed *Marksshtadt* (Марксштадт), "Marx's town," for the German founder of Communism, Karl *Marx* (1818-1883). The German suffix was equally suitable for him. It was dropped, however, in 1941, when the present form of the name was adopted. The town of *Engels* (now **Pokrovsk**) is only 30 miles (48 km) away to "pair" the German Communist name.

Marksshtadt See **Marks**.

Martsialnyye Vody (Марциальные Воды) *Resort, northwestern Russia*. The health resort, in Karelia northwest of Petrozavodsk, is Russia's earliest spa. Mineral springs were discovered here in 1714 and in 1719 Peter the Great founded the resort proper. Its name literally means "Martial Waters," i.e. waters of *Mars*, the god of war and iron, personified by the health and strength of the springs.

Mary (Мары́) *Town, southeastern Turkmenistan*. The town, southwest of Chardzhou, has a name of ancient origin. In the 3rd century B.C. Antiochus the Great, king of the Seleucid kingdom of Syria, founded a fortified settlement in the region, naming it *Antiochia Margiana*, "boundary Antioch," so called to distinguish it from the biblical *Antioch*, now the Syrian city of *Antakya*. Over the centuries, this name gradually altered and shortened to *Merv* (Мерв). In 1884 the present town was founded some 19 miles (30 km) west of Merv, and took its name. In 1937 the town took the Turkic form of the name, as now.

Matochkin Shar (Ма́точкин Шар) *Channel, Novaya Zemlya, northwestern Russia*. The channel lies between the two main islands of Severny ("northern") and Yuzhny ("southern"). *Shar* is a local Komi word meaning "strait." *Matochkin* probably derives from a personal name, but it is not certain what this was. Alternately, an origin in Russian *matka*, "mother," has been suggested, as an ancient term among seafarers for Novaya Zemlya, which for them was a rich source of food.

Matsesta (Маце́ста) *Village, southwestern Russia*. The Black Sea resort, east of Sochi, is famous for its hot springs. Its name is traditionally explained with reference to this in the sense "fire water," from Abaza *mtsa*, "fire," and Adygey *psy*, "water."

Mayachny (Мая́чный) *Town, southwestern Russia*. The town, in Bashkortostan northeast of Orenburg, has a name that is the adjectival form of Russian *mayak*, "lighthouse." The presence of such a name in the forests and steppes of the Urals may seem strange, but apart from its familiar sense, *mayak* was also used for any kind of landmark or distinctive feature, such as a pole, post, earth mound, cairn (heap of stones), watchtower, signal beacon, or the like, and one such must have been here. The name exists elsewhere, and in some cases carries the word's later revolutionary associations. Cf. **Krasny Mayak**.

Mayakovsky See **Bagdadi**.

Maykop (Майко́п) *Town, southwestern Russia*. The town, capital of Adygey, southeast of Krasnodar, was founded in 1857 as a Russian fortress. Its name is said to represent an Adygey original form *Myekuape*, from *miye*, "apple tree," *ko*, "valley," and *pe*, "river mouth," so that the overall sense is "mouth of the apple-tree valley." But some authorities prefer an origin in Turkic *may*, "oil," and *kopa*, "marsh," referring to a site where crude oil underground seeps up to the surface.

Maykor (Майко́р) *Town, west central Russia*. The town, on the western shore of the Kamskoye Reservoir, arose from the iron and steelworks constructed here in 1811. The name is said to mean "beaver town," from Komi-Permyak *moy*, "beaver," and *kor*, "town," "settlement." It is possible, however, that even if the interpretation is right, the first part of the name may represent a personal name, itself deriving from the riverine animal.

Mednogorsk (Медного́рск) *Town, southwestern Russia*. The town, northwest of Orsk, arose in 1939 when a copper mine here was first worked and a copper smelting plant built. Hence its name, from Russian *med'*, "copper," and *gora*, "mountain." The town is between spurs of the Guberlinskiye

Mountains at the southern end of the Urals.

Medvedkovo (Медвёдково) *District, Moscow, western Russia*. The northern district of Moscow arose from a village that itself developed from an estate owned here in the early 16th century by the boyar V. F. Pozharsky. He was known by the nickname *Medved'* (Russian, "Bear"). Hence the present placename.

Medvezhyegorsk (Медвежьегорск) *Town, northwestern Russia*. The town, at the northern end of Lake Onega, north of Petrozavodsk, was known until 1938 as *Medvezhya Gora* (Медвёжья Горá), "Bear Mountain," from the adjectival form of Russian *medved'*, "bear," and *gora*, "mountain." The mountain may have been so named from its resemblance to a bear (cf. **Ayu Dag**), or the name may have originally had some totemic reference, to an animal both feared and revered in Russia and Finland alike.

Megrega (Мéгрега) *Village, northwestern Russia*. The village, in Karelia southwest of Petrozavodsk, takes its name from the river on which it lies. The river name is said to mean "badger river," from Karelian words related to Finnish *mäyrä*, "badger," and *joki*, "river."

Megrelia See **Mingrelia**.

Melekess See **Dimitrovgrad**.

Melenki (Мéленки) *Town, western Russia*. The town, on the Unzha River southeast of Gus-Khrustalny, takes its name from the Slavic root word that gave modern Russian *mel'nitsa*, "mill."

Meleuz (Мелеýз) *Town, southwestern Russia*. The town, south of Sterlitamak, takes its name from the *Meleuz* River on which it stands. The river name is of uncertain origin, but has been explained as deriving from Turkic words *mana*, "to watch," "to guard," and *ukuz*, "river." A river with such a name may have been liable to flood.

Melitopol (Мелитóполь) *Town, southern Ukraine*. The town, near the southwest shore of the Sea of Azov, arose in the early 19th century on the site of the village of *Novo-Aleksandrovka*. It was raised to town status in 1841 and given a Greek-style name meaning "honey town," from Greek *meli*, genitive *melitos*, "honey," and *polis*, "town." The name had been intended for a town here in the second half of the 18th century, when the fashion for such names was at its height, but the town was never built. Melitopol is on the **Molochnaya** River, whose name means "milky." It is not clear to what extent the names are intended to interrelate, as if the region were a sort of biblical "land flowing with milk and honey."

Melkoye, Lake (Мéлкое óзеро) *Lake, northern Russia*. The lake, east of Norilsk, has a Russian name meaning "shallow," contrasting with that of Lake **Glubokoe** to the south. Its average depth is only 12 ft. 10 in. (3.9 m), its maximum 72 ft. (22 m).

Memel See **Klaipeda**.

Mendeleyev, Mt. (Менделéева вулкáн) *Volcano, Kuril Islands, southeastern Russia*. The active volcano, in central Kunashir island, at the southern end of the Kurils, was so named in 1946 for the Russian chemist Dmitry Ivanovich *Mendeleyev* (1834–1907), deviser of the original periodic table of elements.

Mendeleyevo (Менделéево) *Village, west central Russia*. The village, northwest of Perm, is named for the Russian chemist Dmitry Ivanovich *Mendeleyev* (1834–1907), who in 1899 visited this region of the Urals to investigate the mineral-producing potential of the mountains.

Mendeleyevsk (Менделеевск) *Town, western Russia.* The town, in Tatarstan northwest of Naberezhnyye Chelny, arose from the chemical works founded here in the mid-nineteenth century. It was originally known as *Bondyuzhsky* (Бондюжский), presumably for the works founder or owner. In 1967 it was renamed as now for the Russian chemist Dmitry Ivanovich *Mendeleyev* (1834–1907), who had worked at this factory.

Merv See **Mary**.

Meshchovsk (Мещо́вск) *Town, western Russia.* The town, southwest of Kaluga, although known since the 13th century, takes its name from the *Meshchersky* princes to whom it passed in the 16th century.

Meshchyora (Мещёра) *Lowland, western Russia.* The lowland, an extensive area of marshland along the Oka River east of Moscow, takes its name from the *Meshchera*, the people who were its indigenous inhabitants in the first millennium B.C. Their own name is of uncertain origin but has been associated by some authorities with that of the *Magyars* of Hungary.

Mezen (Мезе́нь) *Town, northwestern Russia.* The town, northeast of Arkhangelsk, takes its name from the river on which it stands. The river name is itself of uncertain origin.

Mezhdurechensk (Междуре́ченск) *Town, southern Russia.* The town, east of Novokuznetsk, is located at the point where the Usa River enters the Tom. Hence its name, which means "between the rivers," from Russian *mezhdu*, "between," and *reka*, "river." The name is found elsewhere, and in classical terms corresponds to *Mesopotamia*.

Mezhevaya Utka See **Novoutkinsk**.

Mglin (Мглин) *Town, western Russia.* The town, southwest of Bryansk, has a name that dates from at least the 14th century and that appears to derive from a Slavic word related to modern Russian *mgla*, "mist." However, it is possible the origin may lie in a personal name.

Miass (Миа́сс) *Town, southwestern Russia.* The town, southeast of Zlatoust, arose from a copper-smelting plant built here by the *Miass* River in 1773. The town is thus named for the river, whose own name is of uncertain origin.

Michurinsk (Мичу́ринск) *City, western Russia.* The city, northwest of Tambov, arose in 1636 and until 1932 was known as *Kozlov* (Козло́в), presumably from a personal name. It was then renamed as now for the Russian horticulturist Ivan Vladimirovich *Michurin* (1855–1935), who lived and worked here, and who died here.

Mikha-Tskhakaya See **Senaki**.

Mikhaylov (Миха́йлов) *Town, western Russia.* The town, southwest of Ryazan, dates back to the 11th century. Its present name is first recorded in 1546, however, when builders are said to have found an icon of St. *Michael* (Russian *Mikhail*) buried here. But the real origin may be in a personal name.

Mikhaylovsk (Миха́йловск) *Town, west central Russia.* The town, in the Middle Urals southwest of Nizhniye Sergi, arose as an ironworks built in 1805 by the Moscow merchant and industrialist *Mikhail* Konstantinovich Gubin, and is named for him. The former settlement of *Mikhaylovsky* gained town status in 1961.

Mikoyan Bay (Микоя́на зали́в) *Bay, North Land, northern Russia.* The bay, on the north coast of Bolshevik island, was named in 1932 for the Soviet deputy premier Anastas Ivanovich *Mikoyan* (1895–1978). His fall from favor following the removal of Khrushchev (1964) resulted in the renaming of major places that bore his name.

Mikoyan-Shakhar See **Karachayevsk**.

Mineralnyye Vody (Минера́льные Во́ды) *Town, southwestern Russia*. The town, a spa north of Pyatigorsk, has a straight Russian name meaning "mineral waters," referring to the many natural springs here, north of the Caucasus. The town arose in 1875 as a railroad station serving other spas in the region, especially Pyatigorsk, Kislovodsk, and Yessentuki. The construction of an airport for flights to other resorts made the name (first given in 1920) even more appropriate.

Mingechaur (Мингеча́ур) *Town, north central Azerbaijan*. The name of the town, northwest of Yevlakh, is said to derive from that of an Arab military commander, *Minkojavar*, who invaded Transcaucasia in the 9th century. A popular etymology takes it from an Azerbaijani phrase meaning "no way ahead," "turn back," supposedly referring to a previously impassable ravine in the Kura River here.

Mingrelia (Мингре́лия) *Historic region, northwestern Georgia*. The former Russian province, in the Caucasus, has a name of Turkic origin meaning "[place of a] thousand springs," with the first part of the name related to modern Turkish *bin*, "thousand." An alternate form of the name is *Megrelia* (Мегре́лия).

Minsk (Минск) *Capital of Belarus*. The city, in the center of the republic, has a name found in historical records dating back to 1067 as *Menesk* and *Mensk*. The town is on the Svisloch, but is said to take its name from another river, the *Meni*, southwest of the present site. The river name may be related to that of the *Main* in Germany. If so, it could mean "slow water," and be of Celtic origin.

Minusinsk (Минуси́нск) *Town, southern Russia*. The town, just east of Abakan, arose in 1739 and takes its name from the *Minus* River on which it stands. It was originally a village named *Minusy*, and adopted its present name when raised to town status in 1822. The river name is said to derive from Turkic *min*, "many" (literally "thousand"), and Mongolian *us*, "water," "river." The reference is to its rapid current. It joins the Yenisey here.

Minyar (Миньяр) *Town, southwestern Russia*. The town, in Bashkortostan northeast of Chernikovsk, arose from the factory founded here in 1784 on the *Minyar* River and takes its name from the latter. The river's own name is said to mean "thousand banks," from Turkic *meng*, "thousand" (modern Turkish *bin*), and *yar*, "bank," "precipice." The river's course winds through steep banks and rocks.

Miory (Мио́ры) *Town, northern Belarus*. The town, northwest of Novopolotsk, has a name derived from the Germanic family name *Meyer* or *Mayer*, who must have been landowners here at one time. The present form of the name may have arisen by false association with Russian *major*, "major" (the military rank).

Mir-Bashir (Мир-Баши́р) *Town, central Azerbaijan*. The town, southwest of Yevlakh, is named for the Azerbaijani revolutionary and Communist party official *Mir Bashir* Fattakh ogly Kasumov (1879–1949).

Mirny (Ми́рный) *Town, east central Russia*. The town, in Yakutia northwest of Lensk, arose in 1955 when diamonds were discovered here. Its name is a Soviet ideological one, meaning "peaceful."

Mirzachul See **Gulistan**.

Mirzoyan See **Dzhambul**.

Mitau See **Jelgava**.

Mogilyov (Могилёв) *City, eastern Belarus*. The city, east of Minsk, is first mentioned in records dated 1267. The name suggests Russian *mogila*, "grave," and is said to refer to an ancient burial mound on which the city arose. But the origin may actually be in a personal name. (Cf. **Mogilyov-Podolsky**.) There is no mound here now.

Mogilyov-Podolsky (Могилёв-Подо́льский) *Town, southwestern Ukraine*. The town, on the Dniester, which here forms the border with Moldova, arose in the 16th century on the site of a castle built by a member of the wealthy Polish Potocki family and named by him for his father-in-law, Peter *Mogila*. This name then passed to the town, with *Podolsky* added (for its location in **Podolia**) for distinction from the **Mogilyov** now in Belarus.

Moldavia See **Moldova**.

Moldova (Молдо́ва) *Republic, southeastern Europe*. The republic, between Ukraine and Romania, and long familiar as *Moldavia*, takes its name from the historic territory of *Moldova*, itself named for the *Moldova* River, a tributary of the Siret, now in eastern Romania. The river name itself may be of Germanic origin from a word related to modern German *Mulde*, "hollow," although a source in Romanian *molid*, "larch," or Indo-European *mel*, "dark," has also been proposed. Much of the region is in plainland, to the east of the Carpathians.

Molochnaya (Моло́чная) *River, southern Ukraine*. The river, known as the *Tokmak* in its upper reaches, flows into the Sea of Azov south of Melitopol. Its name represents Russian *molochnaya*, "milky," for its cloudy waters.

Molodechno (Молоде́чно) *Town, northwestern Belarus*. The town, northwest of Minsk, has a name derived from Russian *molodets*. This, from *molodoy*, "young," now means "fine fellow," but originally was the term for a young warrior in a prince's armed force.

Molodogvardeysk (Молодогварде́йск) *Town, eastern Ukraine*. The coal-mining town, southeast of Lugansk, has a name meaning "Young Guard" (Russian *Molodaya gvardiya*), this being a subversive section of the Komsomol. It is not far from Krasnodon, where in 1942 the Young Guard were active as saboteurs during the German occupation of the Donbass, and where many of them were tortured and executed.

Molokovo (Мо́локово) *Village, western Russia*. The village, southwest of Cherepovets, is named for the Soviet air pilot and Arctic explorer Vasily Sergeyevich *Molokov*. He was born here in 1895, when it was known as *Irininskoye*.

Molotov See **Perm**.

Molotovsk See (1) **Nolinsk**, (2) **Severodvinsk**.

Monchegorsk (Мончего́рск) *Town, northwestern Russia*. The town, south of Murmansk, was earlier a village named *Moncha-Guba*, from the *Monchetundra* mountains in this region, and Russian *guba*, "river mouth." (The town is on Lake Imandra.) The mountains have a Saamian (Lapp) name meaning "beautiful tundra." The village took the present form of its name when raised to town status in 1937, with the second part representing Russian *gora*, "mountain."

Monchetundra See **Monchegorsk**.

Monetny (Моне́тный) *Town, west central Russia*. The town, northeast of Yekaterinburg, lies on land that formerly belonged to the Yekaterinburg Mint (Russian *monetnyj dvor*, literally "coin yard"), founded in 1735. It was thus named for the mint, and the forests and lands here were at first known as *Monetnaya dacha*, "mint portion." The mint closed in 1875 but the name remained.

Mordovia (Мордо́вия) *Republic, western Russia.* The republic, known also in English as *Mordvinia*, is in the middle Volga region south of Nizhny Novgorod and takes its name from its indigenous *Mordovian* (*Mordvin*) people. They speak a Finno-Ugrian language, and their name is believed to derive from a Finno-Ugrian word of Iranian origin, *mortyo*, "person." For a similar source word, cf. **Komi, Udmurt**.

Mordvinia See **Mordovia**.

Morozova imeni (Моро́зова и́мени) *Town, western Russia.* The town, on the Neva River east of St. Petersburg, takes its name from the Russian revolutionary, writer, and scientist Nikolay Aleksandrovich *Morozov* (1854–1946). *Imeni* means "named for."

Moscow (Москва́) *Capital of Russia.* Russia's best-known city, in the west of the federation southwest of St. Petersburg, takes its name from the *Moskva* River on which it stands. The origin of the river name has not yet been precisely established, and there have been many theories purporting to explain it. They include the following: (1) from a root word meaning "to wash" related to Latin *mergere*, "to dip," and so to English *immerse*; (2) from a Slavic word *moskva* meaning "damp," "marshy"; (3) from a Slavic phrase *most-kva* meaning "bridge-water"; (4) from Finno-Ugrian words *moska* meaning "calf" and *va* meaning "river," so "calf ford" (something like English *Oxford*); (5) from Finno-Ugrian *mos*, "to darken," and *ka*, "water." Probably the basic meaning, whatever its exact origin, is no more than "water," as for many ancient river names. See also **Muscovy**.

Mosty (Мосты́) *Village, western Belarus.* The village, southeast of Grodno, stands on the Neman River. Its name relates to this location, and means "(place by the) bridge" (Slavic *most*, "bridge").

Mozdok (Моздо́к) *Town, southwestern Russia.* The town, northeast of Nalchik, was founded in 1763 as a fortified settlement in the northern foothills of the Caucasus. It took the name of the natural site here, from Kabardian words meaning "thick wood."

Mozhaysk (Можа́йск) *Town, western Russia.* The town, west of Moscow, has a name of Baltic origin. A source in Latvian *mežs*, "forest," is possible.

Mozyr (Мо́зырь) *Town, southeastern Belarus.* The town, southwest of Gomel, is first recorded in 1155 and probably has a name of ethnic origin, deriving from the *Mazovian* (*Masurian*) people.

Mramorsky (Мра́морский) *Settlement, southwestern Russia.* The settlement, southeast of Yekaterinburg, derives its name from Russian *mramor*, "marble." Marble was discovered here in the early 18th century and was first quarried in 1738, when the settlement arose.

Msta (Мста) *River, western Russia.* The river, flowing generally west into the northern end of Lake Ilmen southeast of St. Petersburg, takes its name from the Baltic word *musta* meaning "black," "dark," referring to the color of its water. Cf. **Mustvee**.

Mstislavl (Мстисла́вль) *Town, eastern Belarus.* The town, east of

Mogilyov, is an ancient one, first mentioned in 1156. It takes its name from its founder, Prince *Mstislav* Vladimirovich of Smolensk (1076–1132), son of Grand Prince Vladimir II of Kiev (who gave the name of **Vladimir**) and Gytha, daughter of Harold II, king of England. The final *-l*, as in similar names elsewhere, has a possessive force, so that the overall sense is "Mstislav's (town)."

Mtsensk (Мценск) *Town, western Russia.* The town, northeast of Oryol, takes its name from that of the *Metsna* River, although it is actually on the Zusha. The origin of the river name is uncertain. It is unlikely to derive from Finnish *määhna*, "fish roe," as has been proposed by some.

Mtskheta (Мцхета) *Town, central Georgia.* The town, north of Tbilisi, is very old, dating from the first millennium B.C. The origin of its name is uncertain. Local tradition derives it from one *Mtskhetos*, supposedly the son of its founder.

Mudyuga (Мудъюга) *Village, northwestern Russia.* The village, southwest of Arkhangelsk, takes its name from the river on which it lies. Its own name probably represents Finnic words related to Finnish *muta*, "mud," and *joki*, "river." It is not certain in what way, if any, this name is related to that of *Mundyugsky* Island, in the White Sea north of Arkhangelsk.

Muhu (Муху) *Island, western Estonia.* The island, in the Baltic Sea between Saaremaa island and the mainland, has a name of Balto-Finnic origin, from a word related to Finnish *muhku*, "lump," "bump," referring to the island's appearance (although it is not noticeably elevated). It was long familiar as *Moon*, the German form of the name.

Mukachevo (Мукачево) *Town, western Ukraine.* The town, west of Chernovtsy, derives its name from the personal name *Mukach*, with the final *-evo* a possessive suffix.

Murmansk (Мурманск) *City and port, northwestern Russia.* The city, a port on the Barents Sea, was founded in 1916 as a naval base at the northern terminus of the newly constructed railroad to the Arctic Ocean. It was at first named *Romanov-on-Murman* (Романов-на-Мурмане), for the *Romanov* dynasty of czars then reigning (in the person of Nicholas II), and *Murman*, the Russian name for the coastland here. This itself originated as an altered form of *Norman*, i.e. *Norseman* ("northerner"), since the coast here was sporadically raided by Scandinavians (Vikings). The present form of the name was adopted in 1917.

Murom (Муром) *Town, western Russia.* The town, southeast of Vladimir, is one of the most ancient in Russia, first mentioned in a monastic document of 862. It takes its name from the *Muroma*, a local people, whose name is of Finno-Ugrian origin but uncertain meaning. It does not appear to be related to the *Mordvins* who gave the name of **Mordovia**.

Murzinka (Мурзинка) *Village, west central Russia.* The village, northeast of Yekaterinburg, arose in 1639, and is said to take its name from a Tatar *murza* (tribal chief) who lived here and who raised a small army of local men to counter Russian forces. *Murza* is itself a word of Turkic origin, meaning literally "lord," "chief," that was adopted from Persian *mirza* in the same sense.

Muscovy (Московия) *Historic region, western Russia.* The name is that of the principality founded in the late 13th century by Daniel, son of Alexander Nevsky. It took its name from **Moscow**, then a fortified village at its center. The name was later used for **Russia** itself, until the latter name superseded it in the 17th century. The English form of the name derives from modern Latin *Moscovia*, itself based on Russian *Moskova* (now *Moskva*).

Mushketov, Mt. (Мушкётова горá) *Mountain, southern Russia*. The mountain, in the Vitim Tableland southeast of Lake Baykal, takes its name from the Russian geologist and geographer Ivan Vasilyevich *Mushketov* (1850–1902), who made a special study of the rocks and minerals of Central Asia. The *Mushketov* Glacier in the Tian Shan, Kyrgyzstan, is also named for him.

Mustla (Мýстла) *Town, southern Estonia*. The village, west of Tartu, derives its name from a Finnic word related to Finnish *musta*, "black." The Germans knew the town as *Mustel*. Cf. **Mustvee**.

Mustvee (Мýствээ) *Town, eastern Estonia*. The town, on the western shore of Lake Chudskoye, north of Tartu, takes its name from the *Chyornaya* River that flows into the lake here. The river's name is Russian for "black," the Estonian for which is *must*, genitive *musta*. (The river has dark water.) The second part of the name means "water" (modern Estonian *vesi*). Cf. **Msta**.

Muyezersky (Муéзерский) *Town, northwestern Russia*. The town, in Karelia southwest of Belomorsk, takes its name from the nearby lake *Muyezero*. Its own name means "whitefish lake," from Karelian *muje*, "whitefish" (here the species *Coregonus sardinella*), and Russian *ozero*, "lake."

Muyunkum (Муюнкýм) *Desert, southern Kazakhstan*. The desert, north of Dzhambul, has a name deriving from Kazakh *moyun*, "neck," and the Turkic *kum*, "desert," found in many Asian desert names (such as **Kara Kum**). "Neck" describes the outline of the desert, which curves in a gradually widening strip from west to east.

Myortvy Kultuk (Мёртвый Култýк) *Mud flat, western Kazakhstan*. The extensive mud flat, on the northeast coast of the Caspian Sea, has a half-Russian, half-Turkic name meaning "dead corner," from Russian *mërtvyj*, "dead," and *kultuk*, a word related to Turkish *koltuk*, "armpit." The flat is "dead" since it is devoid of vegetation and almost uninhabited. The name appears on some maps preceded by *Sor*, a Kazakh word meaning "arid marshland." The name is also used as an alternative for the bay here, which in Soviet times became *Komsomolets*, "Komsomol member," and in prerevolutionary days was *Tsesarevich*, "cesarevitch." The two correspond in their compliment to youth: the Komsomol was the Communist Youth League, while the cesarevitch was the czar's eldest son and heir to the throne.

Mysovsk See **Babushkin**[1].

Myt (Мыт) *Village, western Russia*. The village, southeast of Ivanovo, is one of a number of the name, which denoted a place where in medieval times a levy was imposed on travelers and their goods for the benefit of a local landlord or government authority. Cf. **Mytishchi**.

Mytishchi (Мытúщи) *Town, western Russia*. The town, just northeast of Moscow, is on the site of a medieval portage that extended for about 4 miles (7 km) to the Yauza River on the river route from the Moskva to the Klyazma. It was here that a levy was raised from travelers and their goods using the portage. The word for such a levy was *myt* (cf. **Myt**) and this gave the present name. The suffix *-ishche* (here in the plural) denotes something formerly existing (cf. **Gorodishche**): the river route was abandoned in the 14th century, when the levy ceased.

Naberezhnyye Chelny (Набережные Челны) *City, western Russia.* The city, on the Kama River northwest of Ufa, was originally a fishing village known as *Chelny*, from the plural form of Russian *chelno*, "boat." When it was raised to town status in 1930, it added the first word of the present name, meaning "quayside," from *na*, "on," and the adjectival form of *bereg*, "bank," "shore." In 1982 it was renamed *Brezhnev* (Брежнев), in commemoration of the Soviet head of state Leonid Ilich *Brezhnev* (1906-1982). In 1988, however, following Gorbachev's reforming of the so-called Brezhnev Doctrine, the city reverted to its previous name.

Nadezhda Strait (Надежды пролив) *Strait, Kuril Islands, eastern Russia.* The strait, one of the most favorable through the island chain, takes its name from the *Nadezhda* (Russian, "Hope"), the ship on which Kruzenshtern (see **Kruzenshtern Strait**) discovered it in 1805. The ship was a wooden, full-rigged sloop that began life in England in 1803 as the *Leander*. The sloop was lost off Denmark in 1808.

Nadezhdinsk See **Serov**.

Naftalan (Нафталан) *Town and resort, central Azerbaijan.* The health resort, southwest of Yevlak, uses a local natural source of *naphthalan* (Russian *naftalan*), a variety of petroleum, for treating skin diseases, rheumatism, and arthritis. Hence the name.

Nagayev Bay (Нагаева бухта) *Bay, eastern Russia.* The bay, on the Sea of Okhotsk just south of Magadan, is named for the Russian hydrographer Aleksey Ivanovich *Nagayev* (1704-1781), who charted the region in 1745.

Nagorno-Karabakh (Нагорно-Карабах) *Region, western Azerbaijan.* The autonomous region (oblast), in territory disputed by Azerbaijan and Armenia, has a name that is part-Russian, part-Azerbaijani. *Nagorno* means "mountainous," literally "on the mountain," from Russian *na*, "on," and *gora*, "mountain," alluding to its location in the southern Caucasus. *Karabakh* means "black garden," from Turkic words related to modern Turkish *kara*, "black," and *bahçe*, "garden." Although "black" could have a literal sense here, perhaps referring to the black grapes of the vineyards, it is more likely to serve as a plural indicator. The sense would thus be "[place of] many gardens."

Naihoro See **Gornozavodsk**[2].

Nakhichevan (Нахичевань) *Town, southwestern Azerbaijan.* The town, capital of the *Nakhichevan* autonomous republic, named for it, is an ancient one, dating back to the 6th century B.C., when it was known to classical writers as *Naxuana*, a form of the present name. The name probably derives from that of the *Nakhtcha*, the people who were the original inhabitants here, with *-van* meaning "land," "settlement." The origin of the ethnic name is not known.

Nakhodka (Находка) *Town and port, southeastern Russia.* The port, on the Sea of Japan southeast of Vladivostok, takes its name from the Bay of *Nakhodka* here. The bay was discovered in 1859 and given a name meaning "find," "discovery," referring to its suitability for ships in this far region of Russia. The bay is calm and sheltered, and would be a welcome "find" for a ship seeking a haven from stormy seas.

Nalchik (Нáльчик) *Town, southwestern Russia.* The capital of Kabardino-Balkaria, north of the Caucasus, has a name explained as deriving from Balkarian and Kabardino-Cherkess meaning "little horseshoe." However, the relevance of this is obscure.

Narimanov (Наримáнов) *Town, southwestern Russia.* The town, on the Volga northwest of Astrakhan, was originally known as *Nizhnevolzhsk* (Нижневóлжск), "lower Volga," for its location near the Volga delta. In 1984 the settlement was raised to town status and renamed as now for the Georgian born Soviet politician and writer Nariman Kerbalay Nadzhaf ogly *Narimanov* (1870–1923), who was exiled to Astrakhan in 1909.

Narodnaya (Нарóдная) *Mountain, northwestern Russia.* The mountain, in the Northern Urals, and the highest in the range overall, was discovered in 1927, on the eve of the tenth anniversary of the October Revolution. Its name thus means "of the people," from Russian *narodnyj*, the adjective of *narod*, "people," "race." However, the mountain's discoverer, A. N. Aleshkov, apparently based this on its local name of *Narodaiz*, with the final *-iz* a Komi word meaning "rock," "mountain," but the main part of unknown meaning. He therefore adapted the existing name for ideological purposes. In deference to the actual origin, the name is frequently spoken and printed in Russian with the stress on the first syllable (Нáродная), and in many reference sources this is the recommended pronunciation.

Narva (Нáрва) *City, northeastern Estonia.* The city, east of Kohtla-Järve, takes its name from the river on which it stands. The river name is of uncertain origin. It is not likely to derive from German *Narbe*, "scar," as sometimes explained.

Naryan-Mar (Нарьян-Мар) *Town, northwestern Russia.* The town, west of Vorkuta, is the capital of the Yamal-Nenets republic and takes its name from Nenets *naryan*, "red," and *mar*, "town," with a revolutionary symbolism. The town was founded in 1929 on the site of a locality called *Beloshchelye* (Белощéлье), "white slope," and originally bore this name. In 1933 construction of industrial estates began and the name was changed to *Dzerzhinsky* (Дзержúнский) for the Soviet Communist politician and Cheka head, Feliks Edmundovich Dzerzhinsky (1877–1926). In 1935 the settlement was raised to town status and the present name was adopted. The change from "white" (implying anti-Communist) to "red" was therefore not simply cosmetic.

Narym (Нарым) *Village, central Russia.* The village, on the Ob River northwest of Tomsk, is named for the low-lying region here, itself so called from Khanty *narym*, "swamp."

Naryn (Нарын) *Town, southeastern Kyrgyzstan.* The town, south of Rybachye, takes its name from the river on which it lies. The origin of the river name is uncertain. Some authorities derive it from Mongolian *nariyn*, "narrow," with reference to the river's upper reaches, where its course is restricted. Others take it from the general element *nar*, "water," "river," found behind other names relating to rivers in Europe and Asia, such as *Narbonne* in France. This seems more likely.

Naumiestis See **Kudirkos-Naumiestis**.

Navlya (Нáвля) *Village, western Russia.* The village, southeast of Bryansk, takes its name from the river on which it lies. The river name has been linked with Slavic *nava*, "mermaid," as if alluding to some water goddess. But the name probably means simply "river."

Navoi (Навой) *Town, eastern Uzbekistan*. The town, northeast of Bukhara, was originally a settlement named *Kermine*. In 1958 it was raised to town status and renamed as now for the Uzbek poet and philosopher Alisher *Navoi* (1441–1501).

Navoloki (Наволоки) *Town, western Russia*. The town, on the Volga west of Kineshma, has a name found elsewhere in western and northwestern Russia, deriving from Russian *navolok*, "water meadow."

Nayoshi See **Lesogorsk**.

Nebit-Dag (Небит-Даг) *Town, western Turkmenistan*. The town, southeast of Krasnovodsk, arose in 1933 as a settlement for oil workers when oil extraction began here. Its name derives from Turkmen *nebit*, "oil," "petroleum," and *dag*, "mountain," this being the name of the mountain just northeast of the town.

Neftabad (Нефтеабад) *Town, northern Tajikistan*. The town, east of Khodzhent, has a name meaning "oil town," from Russian *neft'*, "oil," "petroleum," and the Iranian suffix *-abad* meaning "inhabited place," "town." Oil is extracted locally.

Neftchala (Нефтечала) *Town, southeastern Azerbaijan*. The town, south of Baku, is an oil workers' settlement, as the first part of the name indicates, from Russian *neft'*, "oil," "petroleum." The second part of the name is Azerbaijani *chala*, "hollow," "gully," so that the name as a whole means "hollow land where there is oil."

Neftegorsk[1] (Нефтегорск) *Town, southwestern Russia*. The town, at the western end of the Caucasus south of Apsheronsk, has a name meaning "oil mountain," from Russian *neft'*, "oil," "petroleum," and *gora*, "mountain." Oil is extracted here.

Neftegorsk[2] (Нефтегорск) *Town, Sakhalin, eastern Russia*. The town, in northern Sakhalin island south of Okha, is an oil workers' settlement known until 1970 as *Vostok* (Восток), "east." Its present name means "oil town," from Russian *neft'*, "oil," with *-gorsk* here more likely to represent Russian *gorod*, "town," rather than *gora*, "mountain," since the region is not mountainous. The town was devastated by an earthquake in 1995.

Neftekamsk (Нефтекамск) *Town, western Russia*. The town, in Bashkortostan southeast of Izhevsk, takes its name from the **Kama** River on which it stands, with the first part of the name relating to its oil industry, from Russian *neft'*, "oil," "petroleum." The original settlement arose following the discovery of oil here in 1956. In 1963 it was raised to town status.

Neftekumsk (Нефтекумск) *Town, southwestern Russia*. The town, east of Budyonnovsk, arose in 1961 as an oil and gas terminal on the *Kuma* River. Hence the latter part of the name, with the first part representing Russian *neft'*, "oil," "petroleum."

Nefteyugansk (Нефтеюганск) *Town, central Russia*. The town, just south of the Ob River southwest of Surgut, arose in the 1960s on the site of a natural oil field. The first part of its name derives from Russian *neft'*, "oil," "petroleum." The second part represents Khanty *yugan*, "river." Oil extracted here is transported to Baku by sea.

Neftyanyye Kamni (Нефтяные Камни) *Town, Caspian Sea, eastern Azerbaijan*. The Russian name means "oil rocks," and refers to a site in the Caspian Sea, 26 miles (42 km) east of the Apsheron Peninsula, where oil rises from the seabed to the surface. Extraction of oil from the seabed here began in 1949, using derricks. As the work progressed, a colony of oil workers developed, living in accommodation on platforms around the derricks, with a linking road. In 1952 the colony was granted the official status of "urban settlement," so became a town on a lake. However, it has no permanent population.

Nekrasovskoye (Некрáсовское) *Town, western Russia.* The town, on the Volga east of Yaroslavl, was originally known as *Bolshiye Soli* (Большие Со́ли), "big salts." In 1938 it was renamed as now in honor of the Russian poet Nikolay Alekseyevich *Nekrasov* (1821-1878), who spent his childhood years in the locality on his father's estate and who went to school in Yaroslavl.

Neman (Нéман) *River, Lithuania.* The river rises in central Belarus, then flows west and north into Lithuania, forming its southern border with Russia before entering the Baltic Sea. The name is of Lithuanian origin and represents *nemunas*, "river." Its former German name was *Memel*, an altered form of this.

Nenets See **Yamal-Nenets**.

Nerchinsk (Нéрчинск) *Town, southeastern Russia.* The town, east of Chita, takes its name from the *Nercha* River on which it lies. The river name probably derives from the root element *ner* or *nar*, "river," found elsewhere in Europe and Asia. Cf. **Naryn**.

Nerekhta (Нéрехта) *Town, western Russia.* The town, southwest of Kostroma, takes its name from the river on which it lies. The origin of the river name itself is uncertain. It is not likely to derive, as claimed by some, from Russian *ne*, "not," and a form of the verb *regotat'*, "to shout," as if meaning "quiet river."

Neryungri (Нерюнгри́) *Town, eastern Russia.* The town, in Yakutia northwest of Nagorny, takes its name from the river on which it lies. The river has an Evenki name meaning "grayling," for these fish in its waters.

Nesterov[1] (Нéстеров) *Town, western Russia.* The town, east of Chernyakhovsk, takes its present name from the Red Army officer S. K. *Nesterov* (1906-1944), killed here in World War II. Its German name before 1946 was *Stallupënen*.

Nesterov[2] (Нéстеров) *Town, western Ukraine.* The town, north of Lvov, takes its present name from the Russian pilot Pyotr Nikolayevich *Nesterov* (1887-1914), killed in the early days of World War I when engaged in aerial combat over the town. Its original name was *Vinniki*; then from 1598 to 1951, *Zholkva* (Жóлква).

Nesvizh (Нéсвиж) *Town, west central Belarus.* The town, northeast of Baranovichi, appears to have a name deriving from Russian *ne-*, "not," and the dialect term *svid'*, denoting woods along a river. If so, the name describes a place by a river in a location cleared of trees and thickets.

Neuhausen See **Guryevsk**.

Neukuhren See **Pionersky**.

Neva (Невá) *River, western Russia.* The river, flowing from Lake Ladoga to the Gulf of Finland, has a name of Finnish origin. It was originally *Nevajoki*, "swampy river," from *neva*, "marsh," "swamp," and *joki*, "river." The reference would either have been to the delta (where St. Petersburg now stands) or to Lake Ladoga itself. The latter is actually named in Old Russian sources as *Nevo*. However, it is possible the name went "upriver," being extended from the delta to the river as a whole, and from the river to the lake that was its source.

Nevelsk (Невельск) *Town and port, Sakhalin, southeastern Russia.* The town, on the southwest coast of Sakhalin island, was known under Japanese occupation as *Honto*. In 1946 it received its present name, given in honor of Gennady Ivanovich *Nevelskoy* (1813–1876), the Russian admiral who explored this region. Cf. **Nevelskoy Strait**.

Nevelskoy Strait (Невельского пролив) *Strait, southeastern Russia.* The strait is the narrowest part of the Tatar Strait, between Sakhalin island and the mainland. It was named in 1909, on the suggestion of the Russian geologist N. N. Tikhonovich, in honor of Gennady Ivanovich *Nevelskoy* (1813–1876), the Russian admiral and explorer who discovered the strait in 1849, proving that Sakhalin was an island, not simply a peninsula, like Kamchatka. Cf. **Nevelsk**.

Nevyansk (Невьянск) *Town, western Russia.* The town, in the Middle Urals southeast of Nizhny Tagil, takes its name from the *Neyva* River on which it lies. Although rather far east, it is tempting to derive the river name from Finnish *neva*, "marsh," "swamp," as for the **Neva**.

New Land See **Novaya Zemlya**.

New Russia See **Novorossiysk**.

New Siberian Islands (Новосибирские острова) *Island group, northeastern Russia.* The islands, between the Laptev Sea and East Siberian Sea, were discovered in the early 18th century and take their name from one of their number, **Novaya Sibir**. Some geographers include the **Lyakhov Islands** in the group.

Nezametny See **Aldan**.

Nezhin (Нежин) *Town, northern Ukraine.* The town, southeast of Chernigov, has a name of uncertain origin. It was recorded in a monastic document of 1147 as *Unenezh*. It may ultimately derive from a personal name.

Nikel (Никель) *Town, northwestern Russia.* Russia's northwesternmost town, on the border with Norway northwest of Murmansk, derives its name from its mining activity, from Russian *nikel'*, "nickel."

Nikitinskiye Promysly See **Kirovsky**.

Nikolayev (Николаев) *City and port, southern Ukraine.* The city, on the estuary of the Bug northeast of Odessa, dates back to a fort built in 1784. The port itself developed from the shipyard founded here in 1788 by order of Field Marshal G. A. Potyomkin. He called it *Nikolayev*, a name confirmed by Catherine the Great in 1790. According to historians, the name commemorates the storming of the Black Sea port of Ochakov by Russian troops in 1788, during the Russo-Turkish War. This took place on December 6, the feast-day of St. *Nicholas*. Moreover, Nikolayev originated as a shipyard, and St. Nicholas is the patron saint of sailors. As if to settle the matter, the first ship launched at Nikolayev, in 1790, was the 44-gun frigate *St. Nicholas*.

Nikolayevsk See (1) **Kustanay**, (2) **Pugachyov**.

Nikolayevsk-on-Amur (Николаевск-на-Амуре) *Town and port, eastern Russia.* The port, at the mouth of the **Amur** River facing the northwest coast of Sakhalin island, arose as a trading post in 1852, during the reign of Czar *Nicholas* I, and is named for him. The river name was added in 1926 to distinguish this town from others identically named, such as the Nikolayevsk that is now **Pugachyov** in western Russia.

Nikolsk-Ussuriysky See **Ussuriysk**.

Nikolsky Khutor See **Sursk**.

Nikopol (Нікополь) *Town, east central Ukraine.* The town, on the Dniester southwest of Dnepropetrovsk, was founded in 1782 on the site of the village of *Nikitino.* It was at first named *Slavyansk,* in honor of the southern *Slavs* who were at war with the Turks (cf. **Slavyansk**). The name did not catch on, however, since the fashion at that time was for Greek-style names. The village name was therefore adapted to suggest the Greek name *Nicopolis,* meaning either "town of Nike" (the goddess of victory) or simply "town of victory," from Greek *nikē,* "victory," and *polis,* "town." This name already existed in the classical world, for example for the city of *Nicopolis* in northwestern Greece, or the *Nicopolis* that gave the name of modern *Nikopol* in northern Bulgaria. The original village name of *Nikitino* came from the personal name *Nikita,* which itself derives from the Greek name *Aniketos,* "unconquered." The sense of "victory" explicit in the present name was thus also implicit in the original.

Nizhnevolzhsk See **Narimanov**.

Nizhniye Sergi (Нижние Серги) *Town, west central Russia.* The town, southwest of Yekaterinburg, had its beginnings in the two metalworks founded here by the Demidov family in 1741 on territory bought from the Bashkirs by the *Serga* River, a tributary of the Ufa. The two factories were respectively named for their relative locations on the lower and upper reaches of the river as *Nizhneserginsky,* "Lower Serga," and *Verkhneserginsky,* "Upper Serga," the distance between the two being about 10 miles (16 km). Construction of the former works was completed in 1743, and that of the latter a year earlier. *Nizhniye Sergi* became a town in 1943, while *Verkhniye Sergi* remained a "settlement of urban type." The name for both is actually plural in Russian, indicating that there are two places named for the river. Its own name is of uncertain origin.

Nizhny Agdzhakend See **Shaumyanovsk**.

Nizhnyaya Salda (Нижняя Салда) *Town, west central Russia.* The town, northeast of Nizhny Tagil, arose as one of two ironworks built here on the *Salda* River. The one that gave the present name, meaning "Lower Salda," was constructed in 1760. The other, which gave the name of modern *Verkhnyaya Salda,* "Upper Salda," was opened in 1778. The two places are approximately 10 miles (16 km) apart, respectively on the lower and upper reaches of the Salda, whose own name may be related to Mansi *salt,* "bast," implying the former importance of this material. The settlements that arose around the two ironworks both became towns in 1938.

Nizhnyaya Tavda See **Tavda**.

Nizhnyaya Tunguska See **Tunguska**.

Nizhnyaya Tura See **Verkhnyaya Tura**.

Nizhny Novgorod (Нижний Новгород) *City, western Russia.* The city, on the Volga east of Moscow, was founded in 1221 by Prince Yury Vsevolodovich of Vladimir as *Novgorod,* "new town" (see **Novgorod**). *Nizhny,* meaning "lower," was added as early as the 14th century. The reference is probably not a geographical one (although this Novgorod is further south than the other), but refers to its status, which was "lower" than "Novgorod the Great," as the other ancient city was known. In 1932 it was renamed *Gorky* (Гóрький), for the Russian writer Maksim *Gorky* (original name Aleksey Maksimovich Peshkov) (1868-1936), who was born here, although he himself opposed the renaming. In 1990 the city reverted to its former name.

Nizhny Tagil (Нúжний Тагúл) *City, west central Russia.* The city, in the Middle Urals northwest of Yekaterinburg, has a name meaning "lower Tagil," from Russian *nizhniy*, "lower," and the *Tagil* River on which it lies. It is thus further down the river than **Verkhny Tagil**, "upper Tagil," to the north. It developed around the ironworks that was founded here in 1725. The river's own name is said to be of Ugric origin and to mean simply "stream," "river."

Nizhny Ufaley See **Verkhny Ufaley**.

Noda See **Chekhov**[1].

Noginsk (Ногúнск) *City, western Russia.* The city, east of Moscow, arose in the 16th century as the village of *Rogozha* (for the river of this name on which it stands, itself perhaps from Russian *rogoz*, "reed mace"). It gradually grew, and gained town status in 1781 when it was renamed *Bogorodsk* (Богорóдск), for its church, dedicated to the Virgin (Russian *Bogoroditsa*, literally "God-bearer"). In 1930 it was renamed as now for the revolutionary and Communist party official, Viktor Pavlovich *Nogin* (1878-1924), who had worked at the Glukhov textile factory here in the early 20th century.

Nolinsk (Нолúнск) *Town, western Russia.* The town, south of Vyatka, takes its name from the *Nolya* River here. The river name is of uncertain origin. From 1940 to 1957 the town was known as *Molotovsk* (Мóлотовск), for the Soviet statesman Vyacheslav Mikhaylovich *Molotov* (1890-1986). It reverted to its original name when he joined the "antiparty" group that tried to depose Khrushchev.

Nor-Bayazet See **Kamo**.

Nordenskiöld Archipelago (Норденшéльда архипелáг) *Archipelago, northern Russia.* The island group, in the southeastern Kara Sea, takes its name from the Swedish geologist and Arctic explorer Nils Adolf Erik *Nordenskiöld* (1832-1901), who went on several expeditions to Spitsbergen and who accomplished the Northeast Passage in 1878-80. A bay and glacier in Novaya Zemlya are also named for him. The largest island in the group is **Russky Island**.

Nordenskiöld Sea See **Laptev Sea**.

Nordvik (Нóрдвик) *Bay, northern Russia.* The bay, on the Laptev Sea east of the Taymyr Peninsula, has a Norse name simply meaning "northern bay," from *north*, "northern," and *vík*, "bay." There is a bay of similar name and meaning in northern Norway.

Norilsk (Норúльск) *Town, northern Russia.* The town, one of the northernmost in the world, east of Dudinka, arose in 1935 when a nickel production plant was built here. It based its name on the root element *nor* or *nar* meaning "water" that was already in local use for the lakes and rivers here. This same element lies behind the names of **Naryn** and **Nerchinsk**.

North Land (Сéверная Земля́) *Island group, northern Russia.* The islands, dividing the Laptev Sea from the Kara Sea, are still often known by their Russian name of *Severnaya Zemlya* (Сéверная Земля́). They were discovered in 1913 by an expedition led by the Russian explorer B. A. Vilkitsky (see **Vilkitsky Strait**) and the following year were named *Zemlya imperatora Nikolaya II*, "Emperor Nicholas II Land," in honor of the reigning czar. In 1926 they were given their present, non-royalist name. The chief four islands were later accorded individual Soviet names: **October Revolution Island, Bolshevik, Komsomolets,** and **Pioneer.**

North Ossetia See **Ossetia.**

Novabad[1] (Новабáд) *Town, central Tajikistan.* The town, northeast of Dushanbe, has a name meaning "new town," from Russian *novyj*, "new," and the Iranian *-abad* suffix found commonly elsewhere in Asia to mean "inhabited place," "town." Until 1950 the former village here was named *Shulmak*.

Novabad[2] (Новабáд) *Town, western Tajikistan.* The town, just northwest of Dushanbe, has a name meaning "new town," from Russian *novyj*, "new," and the Iranian *-abad* suffix found commonly elsewhere in Asia to mean "inhabited place," "town." This *Novabad* is only 80 miles (129 km) from the one in the entry above.

Novaya Ladoga (Нóвая Лáдога) *Town, western Russia.* The town, on the southern shore of Lake **Ladoga**, north of Volkhov, has a name meaning "new Ladoga." It was founded by order of Peter the Great in 1703 to house the transferred population of *Staraya Ladoga* ("old Ladoga") further south. (This still exists, but only as a village.)

Novaya Lyalya (Нóвая Ляля) *Town, west central Russia.* The town, northeast of Nizhnyaya Tura, takes its name from the *Lyalya* River on which it lies. The river's own name is of uncertain origin, and it is hardly from Mansi *lyal'*, "enemy," as has been suggested. *Novaya* means "new," and the town arose in 1938, its name as a whole contrasting it with the existing smaller *Staraya Lyalya*, "old Lyalya," some 27 miles (43 km) upstream to the west.

Novaya Pashnya See **Gornozavodsk**[1].

Novaya Pismyanka See **Leninogorsk**[2].

Novaya Sibir (Нóвая Сибúрь) *Island, New Siberian Islands, northeastern Russia.* The main easternmost island of the New Siberian Islands has a name meaning "new Siberia." It was discovered by Russian hunters in 1806 and named by the Russian polar explorer Matvey Matveyevich Gedenshtrom (c. 1780–1845), who led an expedition here in 1809-10. It was this island that gave the name of the group as a whole.

Novaya Zemlya (Нóвая Земля) *Island group, northeastern Russia.* The islands, extending northwards between the Barents Sea and Kara Sea, have a Russian name meaning "new land." They may have received this name from 12th-century Russian hunters who regarded them as "new land" by contrast with the "old land," or mainland, where their trade had hitherto been conducted. The islands were rediscovered in 1553 by the English sea captain Sir Hugh Willoughby, who led an expedition along the Siberian coast. His journal refers to them by their Russian name, in the form *Nova-Zemla*. (The islands were long referred to in Western texts as *Nova Zembla*, and the French name for them is still *Nouvelle-Zemble*.) The two main islands of the group are respectively *Severny* ("northern") and *Yuzhny* ("southern").

Nova Zembla See **Novaya Zemlya.**

Novgorod (Нóвгород) *City, western Russia.* The city, southeast of

St. Petersburg, just north of Lake Ilmen, is one of the oldest in Russia, and is mentioned in a document of 859. This appears to contradict its name, which means "new town." However, it was "new" by contrast with an even earlier settlement on the site: that is to say, a "new town" arose where an "old town" had been. It is not known what the earlier settlement was called. The city was the second most important (after Kiev) in Kievan Rus, and in medieval times was the capital of the principality of the same name. Its status earned it the title of "Novgorod the Great" (Russian *Novgorod Velikij*). (Cf. **Nizhny Novgorod**.) Medieval Scandinavian records refer to the city as *Holmgard*, "island city," from Scandinavian *holm*, "land by water," "island," and *gard*, "enclosed place." This refers to the city's location on both banks of the Volkhov River. It is possible that Novgorod existed as early as the 6th century.

The contemporary Gothic historian Jordanes has the following (Latin) passage: "Sclaveni a civitate Novietunense et laco qui appellatur Mursiano usque ad Danastrum et in boream Viscla tenus commorantur; hi paludes silvasque pro civitatibus habent" ("The Sclaveni live from the town of Novietunum and a lake called Mursianus [to the south] to the Danastris, and to the north to the Viscla; instead of towns they have swamps and forests"). In this, *Novietunum* is a Latin-style exact Celtic equivalent to *Novgorod*, translating as "new town" (Celtic *novio-*, "new," and *dūnos*, "town"). Lake *Mursianus* would thus be Lake Ilmen. (The *Danastris* is the Dniester, and the *Viscla* is the Vistula.) Cf. **Novgorod Seversky, Novograd-Volynsky**.

Novgorod-Seversky (Нóвгород-Сéверский) *Town, northern Ukraine.* The town, northeast of Chernigov, has a name meaning "new town (in the land of the) *Severians*," the latter being the name of a people who lived in this region. Their name is of disputed origin. It is not clear whether it relates to Russian *sever*, "north," so that they are "Northerners." If it does, it is strange that there are no Slavic people named "Easterners," "Westerners," or "Southerners." The same people probably gave the alternate name of the Donets River (see **Donets**). It is not known when this Novgorod was founded, but it was already the capital of the Severian principality in 1096.

Novoaltaysk (Новоалтáйск) *Town, southern Russia.* The town, northeast of Barnaul, was originally known as *Chesnokovka* (Чеснокóвка). In 1962 it received its present name, meaning "new Altay (town)," referring to its location in the **Altay** region.

Novobelokatay (Новобелокатáй) *Village, southwestern Russia.* The village, northwest of Zlatoust, has a name representing Russian *Novo-*, "new," added to the Bashkir place-name *Belokataj*, itself a blend of *bala*, "child," and *Kataj*, the name of a local people. "Child" here serves as an adjective meaning "small," "lesser." The present form of the name was influenced by Russian *belo-*, "white" (cf. **Beloretsk**). The village of *Starobelokataj*, "old Belokatay," lies some 22 miles (35 km) to the northeast.

Novocheboksarsk (Новочебоксáрск) *Town, western Russia.* The town, a port on the Volga, arose in 1960 as a satellite town for **Cheboksarsk**, 19 miles (30 km) to the west. Hence its name, meaning "new Cheboksary."

Novocherkassk (Новочеркáсск) *City, southwestern Russia.* The city, northeast of Rostov-on-Don, was founded in 1805 when the original settlement of *Cherkasskaya*, capital of the Don Cossacks, on the Don, was moved here because the former site was frequently flooded. Hence its present name, "new Cherkassk." The original town (now known as *Starocherkassk*, "old Cherkassk") takes its name from the *Cherkess* (Circassians), the Caucasian people who had gone to settle there from Turkish-controlled territory in the northern Caucasus. Cf. **Cherkassy, Cherkessk**.

Novodvinsk (Новодвинск) *Town, northwestern Russia*. The town, southeast of Arkhangelsk, arose in modern times as the industrial settlement of *Pervomaysky* (Первомайский), "First of May." In 1977 it was renamed as now, "new Dvina," for its location on the Northern **Dvina** River.

Novoekonomicheskoye See **Dimitrov**.

Novograd-Volynsky (Новоград-Волынский) *Town, western Ukraine*. The town, northwest of Zhitomir, is first mentioned in 1257 under the name *Zvyagel*. The origin of this is unknown. It then passed to Poland, but as capital of **Volynia** (hence the second part of the name), it became part of the Russian empire in 1793. It was renamed as now in 1795, with the first part of the name meaning "new town" and Slavic, as was then the fashion, rather than specifically Russian.

Novogrudok (Новогрудок) *Town, western Belarus*. The town, east of Grodno, has a Polish name meaning "new little town," from *nowy*, "new," and a diminutive of *gród*, "fort," "town." The town is said to have been founded in 1116, when it must have been "new" in relation to some earlier town or fortified place.

Novokuybyshevsk (Новокуйбышевск) *Town, western Russia*. The town, just southwest of Samara, arose in 1952 when an oil refinery and petrochemical plant came into operation. Its name means "new Kuybyshev," referring to **Samara,** which at that time was called *Kuybyshev* (Куйбышев).

Novokuznetsk (Новокузнецк) *City, southern Russia*. The city, southeast of Novosibirsk, is famous for its iron and steel industry, as its name indicates. It arose in 1617 as a fortified settlement known as *Kuznetsky ostrog*, "ironworkers' village," from Russian *kuznets*, "smith," "ironworker," and *ostrog*, "stockade." The local people were well known for their work with iron: they extracted and smelted iron ore and made objects such as cooking pots, trivets, arrows, and steel weapons of various kinds. The town that developed here was at first known simply as *Kuznetsk* (Кузнецк). It received its present name, meaning "new Kuznetsk," in 1931, the prefix distinguishing it from the **Kuznetsk** in western Russia, east of Penza. In 1932 it was renamed *Stalinsk* (Сталинск), for *Stalin* (whose name appropriately means "steel"). In 1961, following his fall from favor, it reverted to its earlier name.

Novo-Mariinsk See **Anadyr**.

Novomichurinsk (Новомичуринск) *Town, western Russia*. The town, south of Ryazan, has a name translating as "new Michurin." This is not so much for *Michurinsk* (Мичуринск), which is some 84 miles (135 km) to the southeast, as for that city's eponym, the Soviet biologist Ivan Vladimirovich *Michurin* (1855-1935), who was born in this locality near the village of Dolgoye (now renamed for him as *Michurovka*).

Novomoskovsk (Новомосковск) *City, western Russia*. The city, southeast of Moscow, arose in 1929 when a new chemical works and electric power station were built here. It was first known as *Bobriki* (Бобрики), for the village then here. This name came from the small *Bobrik* River on which it stood, itself deriving from Russian *bobr*, "beaver." In 1934 the town was renamed *Stalinogorsk* (Сталиногóрск), for *Stalin*, with the last part of the name representing Russian *gorod*, "town." Following his fall from favor, it was given its present name in 1961. The meaning is "new Moscow," referring to its location in the Moscow coal basin.

Novonikolayevsk See **Novosibirsk**.

Novopashenny Island See **Zhokhov Island**.

Novopashiysky See **Gornozavodsk**[1].

Novopokrovka See **Liski**.

Novopolotsk (Новополóцк) *Town, northern Belarus*. The town, immediately west of **Polotsk**, arose much later than that historic city and is named for it, with Russian *Novo-* meaning "new."

Novorossiysk (Новоросси́йск) *City and port, southwestern Russia*. The city, on the Black Sea coast northwest of Tuapse, was founded in 1838 as a fortified post on the ruins of the former Turkish fortress of *Sudjuk-Kale* ("fortress of Sudjuk"). The name derives from Russian *Novorossiya* (Новоро́ссия), "New Russia." This was the name given to the region along the Black Sea coast from the end of the 18th century when Russian territory was extended to the Black Sea during the course of the Russo-Turkish wars. The name alludes not so much to the late incorporation of this region into Russia as to the relatively slow economic growth of a new and sparsely populated area. The name was also formerly that of **Dnepropetrovsk**, Ukraine.

Novorossiysk See **Dnepropetrovsk**.

Novorzhev (Новоржéв) *Town, western Russia*. The town, southeast of Pskov, was originally known as *Arsho*. This is probably an alteration of a river name such as *Rzha* or *Rzhev*, itself from Russian *rzha*, "rust," referring to its rusty-colored water (from ore deposits or clay). The settlement became a town in 1777 and took the present name, "new Rzhev," so called to be distinguished from the **Rzhev** northwest of Moscow.

Novoshakhtinsk (Новоша́хтинск) *Town, southwestern Russia*. The town, northeast of Rostov-on-Don, has a name meaning "new pits," from Russian *shakhta*, "pit," "coalmine." The reference is both to the coalmining city of *Shakhty*, to the east, and to the miners' settlements from which it was formed as a new town in 1939.

Novosibirsk (Новосиби́рск) *City, southern Russia*. The major Siberian city, east of Omsk, arose in 1893 as *Novaya derevnya* ("new village") when a railroad bridge was built over the Ob here during construction of the Transsiberian Railway. In 1894 the village was renamed *Aleksandrovsky*, for the czar then reigning, *Alexander* III. In 1895 the growing settlement was renamed *Novonikolayevsky*, "new Nicholas," for the new czar, *Nicholas* II. The *Novo-* ("new") was to distinguish this Nikolayevsk from others, such as **Nikolayevsk-on-Amur** or the Nikolayevsk that is now **Pugachyov**. The settlement was raised to town status in 1903 and became *Novonikolayevsk* (Новоникола́евск). After the October Revolution the newspaper *Sovetskaya Sibir* ("Soviet Siberia") invited readers to propose a new name for the city. Suggestions included *Oktyabrgrad* ("October town"), *Obgorod* ("Ob town"), *Sibgrad* ("Siberia town"), *Krasnosibirsk* ("red Siberia"), *Sibkraygrad* ("Siberia region town"), *Krasnograd* ("red town"), and *Krasnokuznetsk* ("red Kuznetsk"). But the majority preferred *Novosibirsk*, "new Siberia," and the name was duly adopted in 1926.

Novosibirsky Islands See **New Siberian Islands**.

Novosil (Новосиуль) *Town, western Russia*. The town, southeast of Mtsensk, appears at first sight to have a name deriving from Russian *novoye selo*, "new village." But this is unlikely, and the true origin is probably in the personal name *Novosil*. The town dates from 1155.

Novosineglazovsky (Новосинеглазовский) *Town, southwestern Russia*. The town, just south of Chelyabinsk, is named with *Novo-*, "new," to distinguish it from the village of *Sineglazovo*, which arose here in the 18th century. The basic name is the surname *Sineglazov* ("Blue-Eyes"), that of one of the original settlers.

Novo-Starobinsk See **Soligorsk**.

Novotroitsk (Новотроицк) *Town, southwestern Russia*. The town, on the Ural River west of Orsk, arose around a metalworks constructed here in 1939 on the site of mineral and gemstone deposits discovered in 1928. The settlement developed by the existing village of *Novotroitsk*, its own name combining *Novo-*, "new," with **Troitsk**, the latter said to be the town from which its original settlers had come (unless they were from one of the places named *Troitskoye* or *Troitskij*).

Novoulyanovsk (Новоульяновск) *Town, western Russia*. The town, on the west bank of the Kuybyshev Reservoir, south of **Ulyanovsk**, was founded in 1967 and named for the larger city, with Russian *Novo-* meaning "new."

Novoutkinsk (Новоуткинск) *Town, west central Russia*. The town, northwest of Pervouralsk, takes its name from the *Utka* River (formerly *Verkhnyaya Utka*, "upper Utka") on which it lies, at the point where the river enters the larger Chusovaya. Both this town, "new Utkinsk," and *Staroutkinsk*, "old Utkinsk," farther to the north, on another Utka River (originally *Srednyaya Utka*, "middle Utka"), arose as workers' settlements in the first half of the 18th century. The river name itself, which happens to coincide with the Russian word for "duck," probably derives from Mansi dialect *utya*, "water." As well as the two Utka rivers mentioned, there is a third, *Mezhevaya Utka* (formerly *Nizhnyaya Utka*, "lower Utka"). The first word is the adjectival form of Russian *mezha*, "boundary," referring to the border that the river formed, originally between the czar's lands and those of the wealthy Stroganov family, and later between those of the Stroganovs and the equally distinguished Demidov dynasty.

Novouzensk (Новоузёнск) *Town, southwestern Russia*. The town, southeast of Krasny Kut, has a name meaning "new Uzen," the latter being the *Uzen* River on which it lies. In the 18th century the settlement here was known by the Turkic name of *Chertanla*, from the word for "pike" (the fish). In 1835 it became the town of *Novy Uzen*, "new Uzen," a name later altered to its present form. The river name is also Turkic in origin, and is a term for a minor river.

Novy Afon (Новый Афон) *Town and resort, northwestern Georgia*. The resort, on the Black Sea coast northwest of Sukhumi, arose near a monastery of this name founded in 1875. The name means "new Athos," for Mount *Athos* ("holy mountain") in northeastern Greece, the center of Orthodox monasticism.

Novy Donbass See **Dimitrov**.

Novy Margelan See **Fergana**.

Novy Oskol (Но́вый Оско́л) *Town, western Russia.* The town, northeast of Belgorod, was founded in 1637 as a fortified site on the front that ran from Belgorod to Simbirsk. In 1647 it was given the name *Tsaryov-Alekseyev*, for *Czar Aleksey* (Alexis) I Mikhailovich (1629–1676), then reigning. In 1655 it gained its present name, "new Oskol," for the *Oskol* River on which it stands. It was "new" by comparison with the town of *Oskol* (now *Stary Oskol*, "old Oskol"), founded in 1593, some 22 miles (35 km) to the north. The river's own name is of uncertain origin.

Novyye Cheryomushki (Но́вые Черёмушки) *District, Moscow, western Russia.* The southwestern district of Moscow arose in the 1960s as a massive housing development that was a southern extension of the existing settlement of **Cheryomushki**, itself so called for its bird cherry trees (Russian *cheryomukha*, diminutive plural *cheryomushki*). The present name thus means "New Cheryomushki."

Nukha See **Sheki**.

Nukus (Нуку́с) *Town, southwestern Uzbekistan.* The town, south of the Aral Sea near the border with Turkmenistan, is the capital of the Kara-Kalpak autonomous republic. It was founded in 1932 on a village of the same name that had itself arisen in the 1860s. The name is said to be a former designation of the Uzbeks, although its meaning is obscure. Some sources relate the name to the village itself, and interpret it as *Nuzkaz*, "new estate," or *Nukesh*, "nine houses."

Nuratau (Нурата́у) *Mountain range, eastern Uzbekistan.* The mountains, north of Samarkand, appear to take their name from Mongolian *nuru*, "ridge," and Turkic *tau* (modern Turkish *dağ*), "mountain."

Nurek (Нуре́к) *Town, western Tajikistan.* The town, southeast of Dushanbe, arose in 1960 when a hydroelectric station was constructed on the Vakhsh River here. The town took the name of the former village on the site, itself said to derive from Tajik *anor*, "garnet." However, once the hydroelectric station was completed, the name came to be associated with Tajik *nur*, "light," "ray," so that it was equated with Russian names of similar meaning, such as **Svetogorsk**.

Nyazepetrovsk (Нязепетро́вск) *Town, southwestern Russia.* The town, west of Verkhny Ufaley, arose around the metalworks founded here in 1747 by the merchant *Pyotr* Osokin, and his forename provides the second part of its name. The first part is the name of the *Nyazya* River, a tributary of the Ufa, on which the town stands. The river name may derive from Turkic *nazy*, "fir."

Nyrob (Ны́роб) *Town, western Russia.* The town, on the Kolva River west of Ivdel across the Urals, is recorded as existing here in 1579. Its name is a blend of Komi-Permyak *nyr*, "nose," and *yb*, "field," presumably describing the shape of a former field here. It is possible that *nyr* translates Russian *nos* in a personal name such as *Nos* or *Nosov*, that of the original owner of the field.

Nyukhcha (Ню́хча) *Village, northwestern Russia.* The village, in Karelia west of Onega, has a name deriving from Saami *nûhč*, "swan." There is another place of the same name further east, on the Pinega River southeast of Arkhangelsk.

Ob (Обь) *River, central Russia.* The great Siberian river rises in the Altay Mountains, near the border with Mongolia, and flows generally northwest then north to enter the Kara Sea east of Novaya Zemlya. Its name almost certainly derives from Iranian *ob*, "water," itself coming from the Indo-European root element *ap*, "water," "river." (Cf. **Apsheron**.)

Obdorsk See **Salekhard**.

Obigarm (Обигарм) *Resort, western Tajikistan*. The health resort, northeast of Dushanbe, is noted for its natural springs. Its name denotes this attribute, and represents the Tajik words for "hot water." Cf. **Garm**.

Obiralovka See **Zheleznodorozhny**.

Obninsk (Обнинск) *Town, western Russia*. The town, southwest of Moscow, arose from an estate here owned in the 19th century by the *Obninsky* family. Hence its name.

Obruchev, Mt. (Обручева гора) *Mountain, southern Russia*. The mountain, in the Khamar-Daban range, south of Lake Baykal, is named for the Russian geographer and geologist Vladimir Afanasyevich *Obruchev* (1863–1956), who explored the region in the 1890s.

Obruchevo See **Ulyanovo**.

Obshchy Syrt (Общий Сырт) *Plateau, southwestern Russia*. The plateau, to the west of the southern end of the Urals, between the Volga and Ural rivers, has a name that means "general Syrt." *Syrt* is a local geographical term for a tableland intersected by river valleys, as here. It is "general" because it was long only sparsely inhabited and served as common pastureland for both Kazakhs and Russians.

Ochakov (Очаков) *Town and port, southern Ukraine*. The town, on the northern shore of the Dnieper estuary southwest of Nikolayev, stands on the site of the ancient Greek colony of *Alektor* (a name that happens to be the Greek word for "cock"). In 1492 the Crimean khan Mengli Giray built here, on the site of the ruined Polish fortress of *Dashev*, a fort called *Kara-Kermen*, a Turkic name meaning "black fort." The fort soon passed to the Turks, who called it *Achi-Kale*, "angled fort" (Turkish *açı*, "angle," and *kale*, "fort"). This gave the present form of the name, as if deriving from a Russian personal name. The town that developed passed to Russia only in 1791.

October Revolution Island (Октябрьской Революции остров) *Island, North Land, northern Russia*. The island, the largest in the group, was separately charted in 1931 and named for the 1917 *October Revolution*.

Odessa (Одесса) *City and port, southwestern Ukraine*. The Black Sea port, southwest of Nikolayev, was founded in 1795 on the site of the Turkish village of *Khadzhibey*, from Turkish *hacı*, "hajji" (a Muslim who has made a pilgrimage to Mecca), and *bey*, "lord." The name of *Odessa* was proposed by the Russian Academy of Sciences with the intention of commemorating the ancient Greek colony of *Odessos*, which was believed to have been on this site. (It was actually not here but farther east, on the Bug estuary.) Because of the Greek connection, the name has also been (wrongly) associated with that of the famous mythical hero *Odysseus*, although his Odyssey never took him to the Black Sea region. There was another *Odessos* on the western Black Sea coast, at what is now the Bulgarian port of Varna. The origin of the Greek placename itself is uncertain.

Odintsovo (Одинцово) *Town, western Russia*. The town, west of Moscow, takes its name from the former estate owner here, the boyar A. I. *Odinets*-Domotkanov.

Oka (Ока) *River, western Russia*. The river rises near Kursk then flows generally north and northeast to join the Volga, as its longest tributary, at Nizhny Novgorod. Various explanations have been proposed for the name, which has been related to Finnish *joki*, "river," Lithuanian *aka*, "source," and Slavic *oko*, "eye" (in the sense of an open expanse of water). No doubt the basic sense, in whatever language it was, amounted simply to "water," "river." There are other rivers of the name, such as the Siberian *Oka* that flows north from the Sayan Mountains to the Angara River. Some authorities also link the name with that of the *Okata* (see Sea of **Okhotsk**).

Okhansk (Оха́нск) *Town, western Russia*. The town, southwest of Perm at the northern end of the Votkinskoye Reservoir (formed from the Kama River), arose in the mid-seventeenth century by an established fishing site. The wealthy Stroganov family are known to have had nets here in 1663. Hence fishing as the prime occupation of the original settlement's inhabitants. Hence also the name of the town, which derives from *okhan*, the term for a special type of wide-meshed net for catching beluga (white sturgeon). Such nets formerly appeared in the town's coat of arms. The settlement was raised to town status in 1781.

Okhotsk, Sea of (Охо́тское мо́ре) *Sea, eastern Russia*. The sea, an inlet of the Pacific west of the Kamchatka Peninsula, has a name that dates only from the mid-eighteenth century. It comes from the town and port of *Okhotsk* on its northern shore, which was founded as a Cossack wintering settlement in 1647, becoming a town and port in 1731. The settlement took its own name from the *Okhota* River that flows into the sea here. It was originally known as the *Okata*, an Evenki name probably meaning simply "river" (cf. **Oka**). It was altered to its present Russian form by association with Russian *okhota*, "hunt." This would be an apt association, if a linguistically incorrect one, for a region already favored by hunters. In the 17th and 18th centuries the sea was also known as the *Tungus*, for a former name of the Evenki (cf. **Tunguska**), the *Lama*, from Evenki *lama*, "sea," the *Kamchatka*, for the peninsula, and the *Penzhina*, for the river that enters it between Kamchatka and the mainland.

Oktemberyan (Октемберя́н) *Town, southwestern Armenia*. The town, west of Echmiadzin, has an Armenian name meaning "October." It was so named in 1947 to mark the 30th anniversary of the *October* Revolution. Its earlier name was *Sardarabad* (Сардараба́д), from Iranian words meaning "sirdar's town." A *sirdar* was a commander-in-chief in Persia and Turkey in medieval times. The *-abad* is the common Iranian suffix meaning "inhabited place," "town."

Oktyabrsk[1] (Октя́брьск) *Town, western Russia*. The town, on the Volga west of Samara, was formed in 1956 from the settlements of Batraki, Pravaya Volga, and Pervomaysky and named for the *October* Revolution, from Russian *oktyabr'*, "October."

Oktyabrsk[2] (Октя́брьск) *Town, west central Kazakhstan*. The town, southeast of Aktyubinsk, was given its present name in 1967 to mark the 50th anniversary of the *October* Revolution, from Russian *oktyabr'*, "October." Its earlier name was *Kandagach* (Кандага́ч), from the Kazakh word meaning "alder thicket."

Oktyabrsky (Октя́брьский) *Town, western Russia*. The town, in Bashkortostan southwest of Ufa, is just one of the many places formerly (or still) of this name, which is the adjectival form of Russian *oktyabr'*, "October," commemorating the

October Revolution of 1917. The town arose following the discovery of oil here in 1937.

Olga Bay (Ольги залив) *Bay, southeastern Russia.* The bay, on the Sea of Japan northeast of Nakhodka, was charted in 1857 and named for St. *Olga* (c. 890–969), widow of Grand Prince Igor of Kiev.

Olgopol (Ольгополь) *Village, southwestern Ukraine.* The village, southeast of Vinnitsa, was originally known as *Chechel'nik*. In 1795 it was raised to the status of district capital, and in the fashion of the day was given the Greek-style name of *Olgopol*, "Olga's town," perhaps in honor of St. *Olga* (c. 890–969), widow of Grand Prince Igor of Kiev, but more likely for Princess *Olga* Pavlovna, one of Catherine's granddaughters. (Cf. **Balta, Yekaterinopol**.) It was subsequently realized, however, that the capital had been established in the wrong place, and in 1812 it was transferred some 6 miles (10 km) to the intended site, *Roguzka-Chechel'nitskaya*, which was thus in turn renamed *Olgopol*, while the earlier Olgopol reverted to Chechel'nik. *Roguzka* came from the river of the same name here, this itself deriving from Russian *rogoz*, "reed mace" (a type of marsh plant). There is another village *Olgopol* north of Nikolayev, about 130 miles (209 km) southeast of this one.

Olkhon (Ольхон) *Island, Lake Baykal, southern Russia.* Lake Baykal's largest island, in its center, takes its name from the Buryat word for "dry." The island has little rain and is parched by strong winds.

Olkhovatka (Ольховатка) *Town, southwestern Russia.* The town, northwest of Rossosh, has a name found commonly in western Russia and northern Ukraine, deriving from Russian *ol'kha*, "alder." The name is found for rivers and populated places, and also occurs as *Olkhovka*.

Olonets (Олонец) *Town, western Russia.* The town, near the eastern shore of Lake Ladoga, southwest of Petropavlovsk, takes its name from the *Olonka* River on which it lies. The river name may derive from Finnish *alanko*, "plain." The town is mentioned in 1137 and was known in historic times as *Aunus*.

Olviopol See **Pervomaysk²**.

Olympic Village (Олимпийская деревня) *District, Moscow, western Russia.* The southwestern residential district of Moscow arose from the 18 16-storied buildings erected for participants in the 1980 Olympic Games. The name is an exact translation of the *Olympic Village* that was built for a similar purpose in Los Angeles at the time of the 1932 Olympics. Russian *derevnya* "village" is normally used for a small populated place in the country, and a more appropriate word for this urban complex would have been *posyolok*, "settlement." However, this word was not in general use in the modern sense in the 1930s, when the Russian equivalent for *Olympic Village* first entered the language.

Omsk (Омск) *City, southern Russia.* The city, west of Novosibirsk, was founded as a fortified post in 1716 at the confluence of the *Om* and Irtysh rivers, taking its name from the former. The river name is said to derive from a Tatar word *om* meaning "quiet," referring to its slow-moving current.

Onega (Онега) *River, northwestern Russia.* The river rises some distance east of Lake Onega and flows north into the White Sea. Its name has been explained as deriving from Finnish *enojogi*, "main river," but this may simply be an attempt to explain a much older name. It may derive from the same ultimate source as that of Lake **Onega**.

Onega, Lake (Онёжское о́зеро) *Lake, northwestern Russia*. The lake, east of Lake Ladoga, has a name recorded in early documents as *Onego*. The origin of this is unknown. It may derive from the same source as that of the **Onega** River.

Opochka (Опо́чка) *Town, western Russia*. The town, northwest of Velikiye Luki, is said to take take its name from Russian *opoka*, "silica clay," used as a building material.

Oranienbaum See **Lomonosov**.

Oranienburg See **Chaplygin**.

Ordubad (Ордуба́д) *Town, southern Azerbaijan*. The town, in Nakhichevan near the border with Iran, has a name deriving from Turkic *orda*, "military camp" (English *horde*), and the common Iranian suffix *-abad* meaning "inhabited place," "town."

Ordzhonikidze See (1) **Vladikavkaz**, (2) **Yenakiyevo**.

Ordzhonikidzeabad (Орджоникидзеаба́д) *Town, western Kyrgyzstan*. The town, east of Dushanbe, was originally known as *Yangibazar* (Янгибаза́р), from Uzbek words meaning "new market." (Cf. **Yangibazar**.) In 1936 it was renamed as now, with Iranian *-abad*, "town," for the Georgian born Soviet politician Grigory Konstantinovich *Ordzhonikidze* (1886–1937).

Ordzhonikidzegrad See **Bezhitsa**.

Orekhovo-Zuyevo (Оре́хово-Зу́ево) *City, western Russia*. The city, east of Moscow, arose in 1917 when the two villages of *Orekhovo* (on the right bank of the Klyazma River) and *Zuyevo* (on the left bank) were combined with three other villages to form a single town. The origins of these two names are uncertain.

Orekhovo is mentioned in an 18th-century document as *Arekhov*, which could derive either from a personal name or from a form of *orekh*, "hazel nut," referring to a grove of such trees. *Zuyevo* is more likely to come from a personal name.

Orel See **Oryol**.

Orenburg (Оренбу́рг) *City, southwestern Russia*. The city, on the Ural River southeast of Samara, was originally founded in 1735 as a fortress on the site where **Orsk** stands today, some 155 miles (250 km) to the southeast, at the point where the *Or* River enters the Ural. It was given the German-style name of *Orenburg*, "fortress on the *Or*." But the location proved unsuitable: it flooded every spring and there was no local supply of timber. In 1740 it was thus moved west to the Ural River. But this also proved unacceptable, so that in 1743 it was moved even further west, to its present site on the same river. It kept the name of the *Or* even though it is now far from that river. (Possibly the similarity between *Or* and *Ural* helped, although their names are not related.) The river name itself is of Turkic origin, and means "channel," "ditch," or more generally "valley," and hence "river." In 1938 Orenburg was renamed *Chkalov* (Чка́лов), for the Soviet aviator Valery Pavlovich *Chkalov* (1904–1938), killed that year testing a new aircraft (cf. **Chkalovsk**). It reverted to its original name in 1957.

Orgeyev (Орге́ев) *Town, central Moldova*. The town, north of Kishinyov, has a name of Hungarian origin, from *var*, "town," and *hely*, "place," indicating a settlement. The second word here gave the Slavic-style ending *-yev*.

Orgtrud (Оргтру́д) *Town, western Russia*. The town, northeast of Vladimir, has an early Soviet name that is the abbreviated form of *organizatsionnyj trud*, "organizational labor."

Orlov See **Khalturin**.

Orsha (Орша) *Town, eastern Belarus*. The town, northeast of Minsk, is mentioned in records of 1067 as *Rsha*. It takes its name from the *Orshitsa* River which enters the Dnieper here. The river name is of uncertain meaning, but may be of Baltic origin.

Orsk (Орск) *Town, southwestern Russia*. The town, southeast of **Orenburg** (which see) near the border with Kazakhstan, was founded as a fortress in 1735 at the point where the *Or* River enters the Ural. It takes its name from the former, with the river name itself probably representing Kazakh *or*, "channel," "ditch."

Oryol (Орёл) *City, western Russia*. The city, north of Kursk, was founded in 1564 by the wealthy Stroganov family as a fortress against Tatar attacks. It stands at the confluence of the Oka and its tributary, the *Orlik*, and takes its name from the latter. Its own name is said to derive from the Turkic word *ayyr* meaning "fork," referring to this confluence, which is at an acute angle. The fact that the town's name is exactly the same as the Russian word for "eagle" is thus a coincidence. Even so, it was enough for the town's historic coat of arms to depict an eagle (originally one-headed, but later two-headed).

Osa (Оса́) *Town, western Russia*. The town, on the Votkinskoye Reservoir southwest of Perm, has a name that happens to coincide with the Russian word for "wasp." (Hence the town's historic coat of arms showing a beehive surrounded by flying bees.) Its name actually derives from the small *Osinka* River, which here flows into the Kama, at the point where the town was founded as the village of *Novaya Nikolskaya* ("new [St.] Nicholas") in 1591. The name was later changed to *Osinskaya*, and then to *Osa*. The place was raised to town status in 1781. The origin of the river name is unknown.

Osh (Ош) *Town, southern Kyrgyzstan*. The town, on the border with Uzbekistan southwest of Dzhalal-Abad, has a very old name dating from at least the 9th century. It has been linked with the *Ush* people, speaking an Iranian language, who inhabited the southeastern region of Central Asia in historic times.

Oshmyany (Ошмя́ны) *Town, western Belarus*. The town, northwest of Minsk near the border with Lithuania, has a name that may derive from Lithuanian *akmenas*, "rock," "stone," describing its location. *Akmyane*, in northern Lithuania itself, has a name of this origin.

Osinniki (Оси́нники) *Town, southern Russia*. The town, southeast of Novokuznetsk, takes its name from Russian *osinnik*, "aspen wood."

Osintorf (Осинто́рф) *Town, eastern Belarus*. The town, northeast of Orsha, arose around a peatworks (Russian *torf*, "peat") on the former *Osinovsky* marsh, and is named for both accordingly.

Osipenko See **Berdyansk**.

Oskol (Оско́л) *River, northeastern Ukraine*. The river, a tributary of the Donets, is believed to have a name of Turkish origin, with the first part representing the tribal name *As*, a division of the ancient Alani people, and the second part meaning "arm," "valley" (modern Turkish *kolu*, "sleeve"), otherwise basically "river." The name as a whole would thus mean "river of the As."

Ossetia (Осе́тия) *Region, southwestern Russia/northern Georgia*.

The region, in the central Caucasus, gave the names of the Russian republic of *North Ossetia* and the former region (oblast) of *South Ossetia* in Georgia. The basic name is that of the people indigenous to this territory, the *Ossetians* or *Ossetes*. Their own name is probably of Iranian origin and may derive from a root element *os* meaning "speedy," related to Greek *ōkus*, "rapid."

Ostankino (Останкино) *District, Moscow, western Russia.* The northern district of Moscow takes its name from the former village and estate here, first recorded in 1558. The name is of uncertain origin but probably derives from an early landowner, one *Ostan*. This personal name is itself a Russified form of the Greek name *Eustathios*, "healthy" (literally "well based").

Ostrog (Острог) *Town, western Ukraine.* The town, southwest of Rovno, is first mentioned in 1100. It takes its name from Old Russian *ostrog*, originally "stake," "palisade" (the word is related to Russian *ostryj*, "sharp"), then "stockade," "fortified place." Many well known Siberian placenames began as a compound with this word. *Omsk*, for example, was originally *Omsky ostrog*, "fortified place on the Om River," and *Irkutsk* was *Irkutsky ostrog* similarly.

Ostrogozhsk (Острогожск) *Town, southwestern Russia.* The town, southwest of Liski, is named for the small *Ostrogoshcha* River that flows into the larger Tikhaya Sosna here. Since the town arose (in 1652) on the site of an old fortification, it is possible that the river name may derive from Russian *ostrog*, "fort" (cf. **Ostrog**), although normally a structure takes its name from a river, not the other way round.

Ostrov (Остров) *Town, western Russia.* The town, south of Pskov, takes its name from Russian *ostrov*, "island." The reference is not just to land surrounded by water, but to a wooded region on a plain or in the steppes, a raised dry place in a swampy area, an oasis in a barren region, or a glade in a forest. This *Ostrov* is on low-lying land by two rivers. The name is found elsewhere in Slavic lands, for example for the Polish town of *Ostrów Mazowiecka*, northeast of Warsaw.

Ostyako-Vogulsk See **Khanty-Mansiysk**.

Otdykh See **Zhukovsky**.

Otomari See **Korsakov**.

Otradnoye (Отрадное) *District, Moscow, western Russia.* The northern district of Moscow developed from a 19th-century rural suburb consisting of holiday cottages (dachas). The name means "pleasing," "comforting" (Russian *otradnyj*).

Otvazhnoye See **Zhigulyovsk**.

Ovidiopol (Овидиополь) *Town, southern Ukraine.* The town, on the Dniester estuary southwest of Odessa, was so named in 1793 when the vogue for Greek-style names was at its height. The name means "Ovid's town," for the Roman poet *Ovid*, who was banished to this region by the Black Sea in 8 A.D. (The second part of the name represents Greek *polis*, "town.") Before 1789 there was a Turkish fortress here named *Hadzhi-dere*, from *hacı*, "hajji" (a Muslim who has made a pilgrimage to Mecca) and *dere*, "stream," "valley."

Ovinishche (Овинище) *Village, western Russia.* The village, northwest of Yaroslavl, has a name based on Russian *ovin*, a term for a barn used for drying crops. The *-ishche* means "place of."

Ovruch (Овруч) *Town, northern Ukraine.* The town, northwest of Kiev, has a name recorded in a document dated 971 as *Vruchy*. The Slavic root word behind this is probably *vreti*, "to boil," "to seethe," referring to a spring or fast-flowing stream here.

Oyrot-Tura See **Gorno-Altaysk**.

Ozurgeti (Озургéти) *Town, western Georgia*. The town, northeast of Batumi, bases its name on Georgian *zurgi*, "back," "ridge," referring to the mountain chain to the east of it. In 1934 it was renamed *Makharadze* (Махарáдзе), for Filipp Iyeseyevich *Makharadze* (1868-1941), a noted Georgian Communist, who was born near here. It reverted to its original name in 1991.

Ozyorsk (Озёрск) *Town, western Russia*. The town, southeast of Chernyakhovsk near the border with Poland, bases its name on Russian *ozero*, "lake." The town is on the Angrapa River, which flows south to Lake Mamry, northern Poland, in a region with many lakes. Until 1946 the town had the German name of *Darkehmen*.

Paide (Пáйде) *Town, north central Estonia*. The town, southeast of Tallinn, was founded in the 13th century and has a name apparently based on Finnish *paas*, "paving stone."

Pakhtusov Island (Пáхтусова óстров) *Island, northern Russia*. The island, off the east coast of Novaya Zemlya, takes its name from the Russian navigator and hydrographer Pyotr Kuzmich *Pakhtusov* (1800-1835), leader of expeditions to Novaya Zemlya from 1832 to 1835.

Paldiski (Пáлдиски) *Town and port, northwestern Estonia*. The town, west of Tallinn, was founded in 1718 by order of Peter the Great as a settlement by the naval port on the Baltic here. In 1723 it was named *Rogervik*, then in 1783 *Baltiysky port* (Балтийский порт), a Russian name meaning "Baltic port." Its present name, adopted in 1917, is an Estonian form of this. Cf. **Baltiysk**, its Russian southern counterpart.

Palekh (Пáлех) *Village, western Russia*. The village, southeast of Ivanovo, has one of several similar names in the area, along the Klyazma River. Their language of origin is unknown. The names have certain features in common: they all end in *-kh*, they are all stressed (accented) on the first syllable, they all have similar vowels, and they all have liquid consonants (such as *l* or *r*). Other names of this type include *Landekh*, *Lyulekh*, and *Vondukh*.

Palmnicken See **Yantarny**.

Pamirs (Памир) *Mountains, eastern Tajikistan*. The mountainous region, which extends into China and Afghanistan, has a name traditionally said to represent Iranian *Pa-i-Mihr*, "foot of Mithra," referring to the ancient Persian god of light, identified with the sun. This sounds fanciful, but could be interpreted to describe a place that lay at the eastern extremity (where the sun rises) of the region peopled by the Persians. However, the name has more prosaically been derived from the local word *pamir*, used for a glacial valley. But it is possible that this word came from the name, and not the name from the word.

Pamyati 13 Bortsov (Пáмяти 13 Борцóв) *Town, southern Russia*. The town, northwest of Krasnoyarsk, has a Russian name translating as "in memory of the 13 fighters." The reference is to 13 revolutionary factory workers who were executed here in 1919 in the Civil War by the counterrevolutionary forces of Admiral Kolchak.

Pamyat Parizhskoy Kommuny (Пáмять Парúжской Коммýны) *Town, western Russia*. The town, on the Volga southeast of Nizhny

Novgorod, has a Russian name translating as "[in] memory of the Paris Commune," alluding to the council set up in Paris in 1871 in opposition to the French National Assembly. It was crushed with great bloodshed by Assembly troops. Communists regarded it as the first proletarian revolution and the first working class government.

Panevėžis (Паневежйс) *Town, north central Lithuania.* The town, northeast of Vilnius, takes its name from the *Nevėžis* River on which it lies, with the initial *Pa-* performing the same function as Russian *Po-*, meaning "on," "along," in such names as **Podolia**.

Panfilov (Панфйлов) *Town, southeastern Kazakhstan.* The town, northeast of Alma-Ata near the border with China, was originally known by the name of *Dzharkent* (Джаркéнт). In 1942 it was renamed as now for the Red Army officer Ivan Vasilyevich *Panfilov* (1893-1941), who died in combat near Moscow and who before the war had been a military commander in Central Asia.

Papanin, Cape (Папáнина мыс) *Cape, northern Russia.* The cape, on the Taymyr Peninsula, takes its name from the Russian Arctic explorer and geographer Ivan Vasilyevich *Papanin* (1894-1986), who carried out wide-ranging research in the region in the 1930s.

Paramushir (Парамушйр) *Island, Kuril Islands, southeastern Russia.* The largest of the Kuril Islands, at the northern end of the chain, has an Ainu name meaning "broad island," from *para*, "wide," and *mushir*, "island."

Parma (Пáрма) *Town, northwestern Russia.* The town, north of Pechora, has a Komi name meaning "fir forest height."

Pärnu (Пярну) *Town and port, western Estonia.* The town, on the Gulf of Riga south of Tallinn, derives its name from Estonian *pärn*, "lime tree." The original form of the name may have been *Pärnjo*, with the *-jo* representing Estonian *jõgi*, "river." The town is at the mouth of the river of the same name.

Partizansk (Партизáнск) *Town, southeastern Russia.* The town, east of Vladivostok, was originally known as *Suchan* (Сучáн), for the river on which it lies. In 1972 it was renamed as now from Russian *partizan*, "partisan," meaning a guerrilla fighting in a revolutionary cause.

Pashiya (Пашйя) *Town, western Russia.* The town, in the Central Urals northeast of Chusovoy, arose from the ironworks founded here in 1785. It takes its name from the *Pashiya* River on which it stands. The river name is said to derive from Mansi *pash*, a type of fishing tackle, and *ya*, "river."

Pavlodar (Павлодáр) *Town, northeastern Kazakhstan.* The town, southeast of Omsk, was founded in 1720 as a military outpost called *Koryakovsky forpost*. In 1861 it became a town and gained its present name, modeled on that of *Yekaterinodar* (see **Krasnodar**). The meaning is thus "Paul's gift," from Russian *Pavel*, "Paul," and *dar*, "gift." The reference is presumably to *Paul* (Russian *Pavel*) (1754-1801), emperor of Russia from 1796 to his death, since the czar reigning in 1861 was Alexander II. Just as Yekaterinodar was "Catherine's gift," named for Catherine the Great, so Pavlodar was named similarly (but commemoratively) for her son.

Pavlograd (Павлогрáд) *Town, east central Ukraine.* The town, east of Dnepropetrovsk, was founded here in 1779 as the village of *Luganskoye*. The following year a fort was built nearby and named for the heir to the throne, the future emperor of Russia,

Paul (Russian *Pavel*) (1754–1801), who succeeded in 1796. This name replaced the original one in 1784, with *-grad* added in 1797 when the settlement gained town status.

Pavlovo (Па́влово) *Town, western Russia.* The town, southwest of Nizhny Novgorod, was founded in 1566. Its name clearly refers to one *Pavel* (Paul), but his identity remains unknown. Perhaps he was the owner of a ferry across the Oka River here.

Pavlovsk[1] (Па́вловск) *Town, western Russia.* The town, south of St. Petersburg, was founded in 1777 on the site of an estate granted by Catherine the Great to her son *Paul* (Russian *Pavel*) (1754–1801), heir to the throne, who became emperor of Russia in 1796. He built a grand palace and gardens here, basing them on *Vauxhall* Gardens, London, as a result of which the dance hall became known as a *vokzal* (partly by association with Russian *zal*, "hall"). When the railroad was built to here from St. Petersburg in 1837, this word was extended to the station buildings, so that today *vokzal* is the standard Russian word for "railroad station."

Pavlovsk[2] (Па́вловск) *Town, southwestern Russia.* The town, southeast of Voronezh, arose from the fortress built here in 1709 by order of Peter the Great. When the fort of St. *Paul* (Russian *Pavel*) further south near the Black Sea coast was destroyed in one of the Russo-Turkish wars, its garrison was transferred here and brought its name with it.

Pavlovsky Posad (Па́вловский Поса́д) *Town, western Russia.* The town, east of Elektrostal, is recorded in 14th-century documents as the village of *Pavlovo*. This comes from the personal name *Pavel* or *Pavlov*. If the former, the origin may be in a church dedication to St. *Paul* (Russian *Pavel*). *Posad*, a word denoting a trading or manufacturing quarter (cf. **Mariinksy Posad, Sergiyev Posad**), was added in 1844 when this village combined with others to form a wool, cotton, and silk manufacturing town.

Pay-Khoy (Пай-Хой) *Mountain range, northwestern Russia.* The range, at the northern end of the Urals, has a Nenets name meaning "mountain tundra," from *pe*, "rock," "mountain," and *khoy*, "tundra." Cf. **Pay-Yer**.

Pay-Yer (Па́йер) *Mountain, northwestern Russia.* The highest mountain in the Polar Urals has a name of Nenets origin meaning "master mountain," from *pe*, "rock," "mountain," and *yerv*, "master." The overall sense is thus something like "Lord of the Urals." Cf. **Pay-Khoy**.

Pechenga (Пе́ченга) *Town, northwestern Russia.* The town, northwest of Murmansk near the Norwegian border, has a name that may derive from a Finno-Ugrian word meaning "pine tree" (Finnish *petaja*). The Finnish name of the town is *Petsamo*, by which it was known from 1920 to 1944, when part of Finland. This is basically the same name.

Pechora (Печо́ра) *River, northwestern Russia.* The river rises in the Middle Urals and flows generally west and north into Pechora Bay, an inlet of the Barents Sea. Its name has long baffled toponymists, who have been inclined to derive it from an ethnic name, a Nenets or Komi people called the *Pechera* or *Pechora*, who inhabited this part of Russia. But the name is probably a very old one, in a so far undetermined language. Attempts to derive it from Russian *peshchera*, "cave," are almost certainly misguided.

Pechory (Печо́ры) *Town, western Russia.* The town, west of Pskov near the Estonian border, has a name said to derive from Russian *peshchera*, "cave." But this may simply be an attempt to explain the name, as for the **Pechora** River.

Peipus, Lake See Lake **Chudskoye**.

Pendzhikent (Пенджикéнт) *Town, western Tajikistan*. The ancient town, northwest of Dushanbe, has a name that on the face of it means "five towns," from Iranian *panj*, "five," and *kent*, "town." However, this may have evolved from an earlier form of the name with a slightly different meaning, such as *Pandzhikat*, "five houses," or *Pyandshambe*, "fifth day." This last would have referred to the fifth day of the week, i.e. Thursday, when a regular weekly market was held. Cf. **Dushanbe**.

Penza (Пéнза) *City, western Russia*. The city, northwest of Saratov, was founded in 1663 as a fortress on what was then the southeastern border of Russia and took its name from the *Penza* River on which it stood. The river name may itself derive from a word related to Nenets *penzya* or Komi *pendzey*, both of which apply to a dried-up river.

Perekop (Перекóп) *Town, northern Crimea, southern Ukraine*. The town is on the isthmus of the same name that joins the Crimean peninsula to the mainland. In prehistoric times a defensive trench was dug across the isthmus, and a wall built alongside it. Hence its name, from Russian *perekop*, literally "dug across," as a term for a transverse ditch or wall. At its narrowest point, the Perekop isthmus is only 5 miles (8 km) wide.

Peremoga (Перемóга) *Village, north central Ukraine*. The village, east of Kiev, has a name that is the Ukrainian word for "victory,"

intended in the Soviet sense (the triumph of Communism).

Pereslavl-Zalessky (Переслáвль-Залéсский) *Town, western Russia*. The town, southwest of Yaroslavl, was founded in 1152 by Prince Yury Dolgoruky as a fortified post on the border of the Rostov-Suzdal principality. Until the 15th century it was known as *Pereyaslavl*, a name that appears to have been adopted from one or other of the towns that are now respectively **Pereyaslav** and **Ryazan** (earlier *Pereyaslavl-Ryazansky*). The reason for the adoption of the name is uncertain, although it may be no coincidence that all three towns are on an identically named river, the Trubezh. The second part of the name was then added to distinguish this particular Pereyaslav (or Pereslavl, as it became). It means "beyond the forest," from Russian *za*, "beyond," and *les*, "forest." (Cf. Romania's *Transylvania*.)

Pereyaslav (Переяслав) *Town, central Ukraine*. The town, near the northern bank of the Dnieper southeast of Kiev, has a name recorded in a document of 906. Its precise origin remains uncertain. It is probably based on some Slavic personal name ending in *-slav*, although there may be a link with the Bulgarian town of *Preslav*. A folk etymology derives the name from Russian *proslavit'*, "to glorify," claiming that the place was famous for its leather goods (or some other feat or fact). In 1953 the town was renamed *Pereyaslav-Khmelnitsky* (Переяслав-Хмельни́цкий), the second word being the name of the famous hetman (Cossack leader) Bogdan *Khmelnitsky* (c. 1595-1657), who in 1654 brought about an agreement here making the Ukraine part of Russia, with his Cossacks swearing an oath of allegiance to the Russian czar, Alexis. Understandably, this addition was dropped when

Ukraine regained its independence in 1991.

Pereyaslav-Khmelnitsky See **Pereyaslav**.

Perlovka (Перлóвка) *Town, western Russia*. The small town, north of Moscow, was so named in the late 19th century for the owner of the estate here, a rich Russian tea trader named *Perlov*.

Perm (Пермь) *City, western Russia*. The city, just west of the Middle Urals, stands on the site of the former village of *Bryukhanovo*, which arose here in 1568. In 1723 the *Yagoshikha* copper-smelting works was built here, taking its name from the river on which it stood. The settlement that grew around it was renamed as now in 1780. Its origin is believed to be in the Vepsian name *Perya maa*, "rear land." The Veps, speaking a Finno-Ugrian language, inhabited territory between Lakes Ladoga and Onega, northeast of St. Petersburg, so that for them the "rear land," or far region, would have been that to the east, in and beyond the basin of the Northern Dvina. From 1940 to 1957 the city was renamed *Molotov* (Мóлотов), for the Soviet statesman Vyacheslav Mikhaylovich *Molotov* (1890–1986), minister for foreign affairs from 1939 to 1949 and 1953 to 1956. The old name was readopted following his dismissal in 1956 and his membership of the "antiparty" group that tried to depose Khrushchev the following year.

Permskoye See **Komsomolsk-on-Amur**.

Perovsk See **Kzyl-Orda**.

Pershotravensk (Першотрáвенск) *Town, eastern Ukraine*. The town, east of Dnepropetrovsk, was founded in 1954 and has a Ukrainian name meaning "first of May," in the revolutionary sense. Cf. **Pervomaysk**, the Russian equivalent.

Pervomaysk[1] (Первомáйск) *Town, western Russia*. The town, east of Ryazan, was originally a village called *Tashino* (Тáшино). This arose in 1853 when an ironworks was built here. It was named by the factory's owner, A. M. Karamzin, son of the famous historian N. M. Karamzin, for his wife *Tasha* (as a pet form of *Natasha*). In 1941 it was renamed as now for the May Day workers' holiday, from Russian *Pervoye maya*, "first of May."

Pervomaysk[2] (Первомáйск) *Town, south central Ukraine*. The town, north of Odessa, was founded in 1744 as a fortified post on the Southern Bug River. This was originally known as *Orel*, from the existing name of the site, itself representing a Turkic word related to modern Turkish *ayır*, "corner," "remote spot." In 1773 the settlement that had developed was raised to town status and given the Greek-style name *Olviopol* (Ольвиóполь), following the fashion of the day. The first part of this represents *Olbia*, an ancient Greek colony that was also on the Bug, but much farther south, almost at the confluence with the Dnieper. (Its ruins can still be seen at the village of Parutino, near Nikolayev.) The Greek name itself comes from *olbios*, "happy," "blessed," "rich." The second part represents Greek *polis*, "town." In 1920 the town was given its present name, commemorating the May Day workers' holiday, from Russian *Pervoye maya*, "first of May."

Pervomaysk[3] (Первомáйск) *Town, eastern Ukraine*. The town, west of Lugansk, arose around a coal mine here and was originally known as *Petro-Maryevka* (Пéтро-Мáрьевка). The meaning of this is transparent: from Russian *Pyotr*, "Peter," and *Mariya*, "Mary," but the reason for the name is uncertain. It may have represented the first names of the mine owner and his wife. In 1920 the settlement was renamed as now, for the May Day workers' holiday, from Russian *Pervoye maya*, "first of May."

Pervomaysky See **Novodvinsk**.

Pervouralsk (Первоуральск) *Town, western Russia*. The town, just south of Yekaterinburg in the Middle Urals, arose in 1732 when an ironworks was built. The original name of the settlement was *Shaytanka* (Шайтанка), for the small river here. In 1933 the town was given its present name, meaning "first (in the) Urals," from Russian *pervyj*, "first," and *Ural*, "Urals." The reference is to the ironworks, which were the first to be constructed in the Urals.

Pesochnya (Песочня) *Village, western Russia*. The village, west of Bryansk, takes its name from the river here. Its own name means "sandy," from Russian *pesok*, "sand." There are similar names in various parts of the country, such as *Peschanka* and *Peski*.

Pesochnya See **Kirov**.

Petergof See **Petrodvorets**.

Peterhof See **Petrodvorets**.

Peter Islands (Петра острова) *Island group, Laptev Sea, northern Russia*. The islands, off the northeast coast of the Taymyr Peninsula, were discovered in an expedition of 1735-36 by the Russian navigator V. V. Pronchishchev (see **Pronchishchev Coast**) and named for *Peter* the Great (1672-1725).

Petersburg See **St. Petersburg**.

Peter the First Range (Петра Первого хребет) *Mountain range, northern Tajikistan*. The range, between the Surkhob and Obikhingou rivers, is named for *Peter I*, better known as the czar Peter the Great (1672-1725).

Peter the Great Bay (Петра Великого залив) *Bay, eastern Russia*. The bay, an inlet of the Sea of Japan south of Vladivostok, was so named in 1859 by the Russian army officer, explorer, and governor general of Eastern Siberia Nikolay Nikolayevich Muravyov-Amursky (1801–1881) in commemoration of the czar *Peter the Great* (1672-1725), creator of the Russian navy.

Petro-Aleksandrovsk See **Turtkul**.

Petrodvorets (Петродворец) *Town, western Russia*. The coastal town, on the Gulf of Finland west of St. Petersburg, has a name that means "Peter's palace," from Russian *Pyotr*, genitive *Petra*, "Peter," and *dvorets*, "palace." In 1704 *Peter* the Great had a summer residence built here where he could stay the night in the course of his many journeys from St. Petersburg to Kronshtadt (Cronstadt) and back during construction of the fortress at the latter place. The palace at first had the Dutch name of *Pieterhof*, "Peter's palace." The settlement that he built here from 1709 to 1711, with its palace, ornamental gardens and harbor, had the same name, but in the 1840s this was modified slightly to its German equivalent, *Peterhof* (Петергоф). In 1944, when the war with Germany was at its height, the present Russian version of the name was adopted.

Petrograd See **St. Petersburg**.

Petrograd Island (Петроградский остров) *Island, St. Petersburg, western Russia*. Petrograd Island is the largest of the four islands that together make up the city's so-called *Petrograd Side* (Петроградская сторона). Before the founding of St. Petersburg in 1703 the island was known as *Beryozovy*, "Birch (Island)." In the early 18th century it became *Gorodskoy*, "City (Island)," as this was where the city had its beginnings. In the 1730s it began to be called *Petersburg*, as for some time it was the city's central district. The present name came when St. Petersburg was renamed *Petrograd* in 1914.

Petrokamenskoye (Петрокáменское) *Village, western Russia*. The village, southwest of Alapayevsk to the east of the Middle Urals, arose around a factory founded here on the *Kamenka* River in 1788. The place is thus partly named for the river, and partly for the factory owner, *Pyotr* Yakovlev. The factory subsequently closed.

Petrokrepost (Петрокрéпость) *Town, western Russia*. The town, at the southwestern corner of Lake Ladoga, east of St. Petersburg, was founded by settlers from Novgorod in 1323 as a fortress on *Orekhovy* ("Nut") Island, with the fort itself named from this as *Oreshek*. In 1611 the fort was captured by the Swedes and renamed *Nöteborg*, from Swedish *nöt*, "nut," and *borg*, "fort." The fort was stormed by Russian forces in 1702 under Peter the Great (he wrote: "this nut was very hard, but, thank God, we cracked it") and he gave it the German name of *Schlüsselburg*, "key fort," from *Schlüssel*, "key," and *Burg*, "fort." The name refers to its key position on the eastern flank of St. Petersburg. The town that grew by the fort, across the Neva River, had the same name until 1944, when it was given its present name, "Peter's stronghold," commemorating the Russian victory in the Great Northern War (against Sweden) of 1700–21.

Petro-Maryevka See **Pervomaysk**[3].

Petropavlovsk (Петропáвловск) *City, northern Kazakhstan*. The city, west of Omsk, was founded in 1752 as the military post of St. *Peter* (Russian *Pyotr*) and St. *Paul* (Russian *Pavel*), taking this name from the church within its walls. (Significantly, the city was founded during the reign of Elizabeth *Petrovna*, daughter of *Peter* the Great. Cf. **St. Petersburg**.) In 1807 the settlement gained town status and the present form of the name was adopted.

Petropavlovsk-Kamchatsky (Петропáвловск-Камчáтский) *Town and port, eastern Russia*. The town, at the southern end of the Kamchatka peninsula, was founded in 1740 as *Petropavlovskaya gavan'*, "Petropavlovsk harbor," taking this name from the two ships, *St. Peter* and *St. Paul*, that had anchored here during the second expedition of the Danish explorer in Russian service Vitus Bering. (The expedition had been commissioned by *Peter* the Great, so that the first ship's name has added significance. Cf. **St. Petersburg**.) In 1822 the name was modified to *Petropavlovsky port*, "Petropavlovsk port." The town took its present name in 1924, with the second word locating it on the *Kamchatka* peninsula and distinguishing it from **Petropavlovsk** in Kazakhstan. For more on Bering, see **Bering Strait**.

Petrov Glacier (Петрóва леднúк) *Glacier, eastern Kyrgyzstan*. The glacier, in the Tien Shan mountains southeast of Lake Issyk-Kul, is named for one *Petrov*, a member of the expedition here in 1869 led by A. V. Kaulbars.

Petrovsk (Петрóвск) *Town, western Russia*. The town, northwest of Saratov, was founded in the late 17th century by *Peter* the Great as a defensive post at the edge of the steppes and named for him.

Petrovskoye See **Svetlograd**.

Petrovsk-Port See **Makhachkala**.

Petrovsky Zavod See **Petrovsk-Zabaykalsky**.

Petrovsk-Zabaykalsky (Петро́вск-Забайка́льский) *Town, southern Russia*. The town, southeast of Ulan-Ude, arose from the ironworks founded here in 1789. This was at first called *Petrovsky Zavod* (Петро́вский заво́д), "Petrov's factory" (or "Peter's factory"), presumably for its owner rather than for any of the czars named Peter. (But cf. **Petrozavodsk**.) The present name was adopted in 1926, with the second word meaning "beyond Baykal," denoting its location to the south of this lake, and distinguishing this Petrovsk from the many others.

Petrov Val (Петро́в Вал) *Town, western Russia*. The town, southwest of Saratov, is named for the earthworks (Russian *val*, "bank," "rampart") that are the remains of a canal which *Peter* the Great dug here in 1697 to link the Volga and Don rivers by joining their tributaries, the Kamyshinka and Ilovlya. Work on the canal was abandoned early.

Petrozavodsk (Петрозаво́дск) *City, northwestern Russia*. The city, the capital of Karelia, on the northwestern shore of Lake Onega, was founded by Peter the Great in 1703 as an ironworks (making cannon and armament) and named for him, originally as *Petrovsky zavod*, "Peter's factory." The settlement that arose was then called *Petrozavodskaya sloboda*, "Peter's factory settlement." In 1777 it was raised to town status by order of Catherine the Great and given its present name, a shortened form of this.

Petsamo See **Pechenga**.

Petushki (Петушки́) *Town, western Russia*. The town, northeast of Orekhovo-Zuyevo, is probably so called from the folkname *petushki* (a plural diminutive of *petukh*, "cock"), for various plants of the Iris family. This must have grown here at some time.

Pillau See **Baltiysk**.

Pinega (Пи́нега) *River, northwestern Russia*. The river, a tributary of the Northern Dvina, has a name explained as deriving from Finnish *pieni*, "small," and *joki*, "river." But the river, with a length of 484 miles (779 km), is hardly "small" even by Russian standards, and an origin in some pre-Finnish name seems much more likely. The final *-ga* suggests a link with river names such as **Ladoga**, **Onega**, and possibly **Volga**. The meaning of this may be simply "river."

Pinsk (Пинск) *Town, southern Belarus*. The town, east of Brest, takes its name from the *Pina* River, on which it lies. The origin of the river name is uncertain. It can hardly derive from Russian *pena*, "foam."

Pioneer (Пионе́р) *Island, North Land, northern Russia*. The westernmost and smallest of the group's four main islands is named for a member of the *Pioneers*, the junior branch of the Komsomol, the Communist Youth League. (The neighboring larger island, the northernmost of the group, is **Komsomolets**.)

Pionersky (Пионе́рский) *Town, western Russia*. The town, on the Baltic coast northwest of Kaliningrad, is named for the *Pioneers*, the junior branch of the Komsomol, the Communist Youth League. Until 1947 the town had the German name of *Neukuhren*.

Pirita (Пи́рита) *District, Tallinn, northwestern Estonia*. The northeastern district of Tallinn, on Tallinn Bay, takes its name from a 14th-century monastery formerly here. It was founded after the death of her husband by a Swedish nun, *Birgitta*, and the present placename is a corruption of this.

Piryatin (Пиря́тин) *Town, central Ukraine*. The town, southeast of

Kiev, dates from the 12th century. Its name derives from the personal name *Piryat*, with the possessive suffix *-in*. The sense is thus "Piryat's place."

Pishpek See **Bishkek**.

Pitkyaranta (Питкяранта) *Town, northwestern Russia*. The town, on the northern shore of Lake Ladoga, east of Sortavala, has a Finnish name meaning "long shore," from *pitkä*, "long," and *ranta*, "shore." The town extends for some miles along the lake here.

Planyorskoye (Планёрское) *Town and resort, southeastern Crimea, southern Ukraine*. The town, southwest of Feodosiya, was noted in the 1920s and 1930s for its gliding contests. Hence its name, from the adjectival form of Russian *planër*, "glider" (a word borrowed from French *planeur*). Until 1944 the town was named *Koktebel* (Коктебéль).

Plast (Пласт) *Town, western Russia*. The town, southwest of Chelyabinsk on the eastern slopes of the Southern Urals, arose in the mid-19th century on the site of a goldfield. The gold itself was present in the sandy subsoil in layered deposits, and the central mining area was thus known as the "Great Layer" (Russian *Bolshoy Plast*). Hence the name of the town, which grew from the workings here.

Pleshcheyevo, Lake (Плещéево óзеро) *Lake, western Russia*. The lake, northeast of Moscow, is the one on which Pereslavl-Zalessky stands, for which reason its alternate name is Lake *Peryaslavskoye* (Переяслáвское). Its more usual name may derive from Russian *plesk*, "splash," rather than *plyos*, "stretch of water," although this leaves the final *-ev* unexplained. It usually denotes possession, following a personal name.

Plyos (Плёс) *Village, western Russia*. The village, on the Volga northeast of Ivanovo, has a name meaning "reach (of a river)."

Pobeda Peak (Побéды пик) *Mountain, eastern Kyrgyzstan*. The mountain, the highest in the Tien Shan range, on the border with China, has a name meaning "Victory Peak." It was first climbed by Soviet mountaineers in 1938 and originally named "Komsomol 20th Anniversary Peak" (20 лет ВЛКСМ пик), commemorating the founding of this organization in 1918. Its height of 24,406 feet (7,439 m) was first calculated in 1943 by a team of Soviet topographers, and it was given its present name then, marking the victories gained, and to be gained, by Soviet forces in World War II. (Their first counteroffensive gained momentum in 1943 and Soviet troops entered Berlin two years later.) It is believed that the local name **Khan-Tengri** ("lord of the sky") was originally given to this mountain. However, in 1857 the Russian topographer P. P. Semyonov applied that name to another, lower peak, some distance to the north, and it is that mountain which has borne the name ever since.

Pochinok (Почи́нок) *Town, western Russia*. The town, southeast of Smolensk, has a name denoting a settlement that arose in a clearing or that grew from a single farm, from Russian *pochin*, "beginning." There are other places with similar names, such as the villages of *Pochinok*, northwest of Yekaterinburg, and *Pochinki*, southeast of Nizhny Novgorod.

Podkamennaya Tunguska See **Tunguska**.

Podkumok (Подку́мок) *River, southwestern Russia*. The river is a tributary of the *Kuma*, which it enters north of the Caucasus. Its name is a virtual double diminutive, denoting this status, with *pod-* meaning "under," "lesser," and *-ok* meaning "little."

Podlipki See **Kaliningrad**[2].

Podolia (Подо́лия) *Historic region, western Ukraine.* The region, between the Dniester and Southern Bug rivers, takes its name from the Russian dialect word *podol*, a term for a plain below higher ground, from *po-*, "along," and Slavic *dol*, "lower region" (related to modern Russian *dolina*, "plain," "valley"). The region here lies below the Carpathians. It was this region that gave the name of **Kamenets-Podolsk**. See also **Podolsk**.

Podolsk (Подо́льск) *Town, western Russia.* The town, south of Moscow, takes its name from the former village of *Podol* here. It in turn has a name meaning "lower land," from *po-*, "along," and Slavic *dol*, "lower region" (related to modern Russian *dolina*, "plain," "valley"). (Cf. **Podolia**.) The terrain here is lower and more level than the hill country to the south and west.

Podushkino (Поду́шкино) *District, Moscow, western Russia.* The northern district of Moscow takes its name from the former village here, its own name coming from that of I. V. *Podushkin*, a merchant who owned lands here in the 15th century.

Pogranichny (Пограни́чный) *Town, southeastern Russia.* The town, northwest of Ussuriysk, is on a road that leads to the Chinese border. Hence its name, from the adjectival form of Russian *granitsa*, "border," "frontier." Until 1958 the town was known as *Grodekovo* (Гроде́ково).

Pokrov (Покро́в) *Town, western Russia.* The town, east of Moscow, takes its name from its church, dedicated to the Feast of the Protection of the Virgin (Russian *Pokrov*, literally "covering"). The village here apparently arose in the 14th century, becoming a town in 1778.

Pokrovsk (Покро́вск) *Town, western Russia.* The town, on the left (east) bank of the Volga opposite Saratov, is named for its church, dedicated to the Feast of the Protection of the Virgin (Russian *Pokrov*, literally "covering"). (Cf. **Pokrov**.) The site here is said to have been originally called *Bakury*. The church was then built that gave the present name. In the late 18th century it was known for a while by the German name of *Kazakstadt*, "Cossack town," following the settlement in the region of some 27,000 Germans in 1760 by special decree of Catherine the Great. This name did not last, however. In 1931 the town was renamed *Engels* (Э́нгельс), for the German socialist leader and founder of Marxism, Friedrich *Engels* (1820–1895). The name was appropriate for the town that was now the capital of the Volga German Republic, abolished in 1941. Matching **Marks** is only some 30 miles (48 km) further up the Volga. Engels reverted to its earlier name in 1991.

Pokrovskoye-Streshnevo (Покро́вское-Стре́шнево) *District, Moscow, western Russia.* The northwestern district of Moscow takes the first part of its name from the church of the Protection of the Virgin (Russian *Pokrov*, literally "covering"), built in 1629. In 1664 the village passed to the *Streshnev* family of boyars. Hence the second part of the name. An alternate name is *Pokrovskoye-Glebovo*, the second part of which refers to a later landowner, Princess Shakhovskaya-*Glebova*-Streshneva.

Polessk (Поле́сск) *Town, western Russia.* The town, northeast of Kaliningrad, has a name implying its wooded location, from Russian *poles'ye*, "woodland" (cf. **Polesye**). Until 1946 it had the German name of *Labiau*.

Polesye (Поле́сье) *Region, southern Belarus/northwestern Ukraine.*

The region, an extensive marshland, takes its name from the standard Russian word meaning "woodlands," from *po-*, "along," and *les*, "forest." The term came to apply in particular to a region of plains intersected by woods and marshes, as here. The more common English name for this region is *Pripet Marshes* (see **Pripyat**).

Pologi (Пологи) *Town, southeastern Ukraine*. The town, southeast of Zaporozhye, probably takes its name from Russian *po-*, "along," and Slavic *log*, "valley," so that it is a "town in the valley." The town is on the Konka River, a tributary of the Dnieper.

Polonnoye (Полонное) *Town, west central Ukraine*. The town, west of Zhitomir, has a name that may derive from the old Ukrainian dialect word *polonina*, "meadow." It is not likely to come from Russian *polon*, "captivity," as has been suggested by some.

Polotnyany (Полотняный) *Town, western Russia*. The town, northwest of Kaluga, takes its name from the *polotnyanyj zavod*, "linen mill," first operating here in the 18th century. The earlier name of the place was *Zgomoni*.

Polotsk (Полоцк) *City, northern Belarus*. The city, northwest of Vitebsk, takes its name from the *Polota* River that joins the Northern Dvina here. The river name probably comes from the Slavic root word *pal*, "marsh."

Poltava (Полтава) *City, east central Ukraine*. The city, southwest of Kharkov, is one of the oldest in Ukraine, with a name recorded as *Ltava* in a document of 1174. The present form of the name is first noted in 1430. Its origin remains unclear, however, and it is not certain whether the initial *Po-* is a prefix or part of the main name. A source in a Slavic root word *pal*, "marsh," has been suggested. Cf. **Polotsk**.

Poltoratsk See **Ashkhabad**.

Polunochnoye (Полу́ночное) *Town, western Russia*. The town, north of Ivdel, arose in 1942 when manganese workings opened here on the *Polunochnaya* River. The name thus comes from that of the river, whose own name, literally meaning "midnight," must be interpreted as "northern." (The converse would be *Poludennaya*, "midday," otherwise "southern.")

Polyarny (Поля́рный) *Town, northwestern Russia*. The town, a fishing port on the Barents Sea northeast of Murmansk, has a name meaning "polar," for its location inside the Arctic Circle (Russian *Severnyj polyarnyj krug*, "northern polar circle"). Other towns and settlements north of the Arctic Circle have the same name.

Porechye See **Demidov**.

Poronaysk (Поронайск) *Town, Sakhalin, eastern Russia*. The town stands on Terpeniya Bay in central Sakhalin island at the mouth of the *Poronay* River, from which it takes its name. The river name means "big river," from Ainu *poro*, "big," and *nay*, "river." Until 1946 the town had the Japanese name of *Shikuka*.

Port-Ilich (Порт-Ильич) *Town and port, southeastern Azerbaijan*. The town, north of Lenkoran, is a fishing *port* on the Caspian Sea named for Vladimir *Ilich* Lenin (1870–1924). It was raised to town status in 1971.

Poshekhonye-Volodarsk (Пошехонье-Володарск) *Town, western Russia*. The town, on the eastern shore of the Rybinsk Reservoir northeast of Rybinsk, was originally a village named *Pertoma*, for the *Pertomka* River here. In 1777 the village was raised to town status and renamed *Poshekhonye*. In 1918 the second part of the name was added, in honor of the revolutionary V. *Volodarsky* (real name Moisey Markovich Goldshtein) (1891–1918), murdered in Petrograd when on his way to address a public meeting.

Posyet (Посьёт) *Town, southeastern Russia*. The town, near the border with North Korea, southwest of Vladivostok, is a port on the bay of the same name, in the western part of Peter the Great Bay. The name is that of the Russian naval officer Konstantin Nikolayevich *Posyet* (1819–1899), who in 1852-54 explored the coast here on board the frigate *Pallada*.

Poti (Поти) *Town and port, western Georgia*. The town, on the Black Sea north of Batumi, has an ancient name recorded by the Greek geographer Strabo in the 1st century BC in the form *Phasis*. The meaning of this is unknown. The present form of the name arose under Georgian influence.

Povenets (Повенец) *Town, northwestern Russia*. The town, at the northern end of Lake Onega, west of Medvezhyegorsk, has a name that appears to derive from some sense of Russian *venets*, "crown," "wreath," perhaps alluding to its location at the head of the lake. In the 18th century the town's coat of arms had a representation of a mountainous coastline on a blue background with seven fishes in a semicircle.

Poyarkovo (Поярково) *Town, southeastern Russia*. The town, southeast of Blagoveshchensk near the border with China, is named for the Yakut Cossack explorer Vasily Danilovich *Poyarkov* (?-?), leader of an expedition in this region in 1643-46.

Pravda (Правда) *Town, Sakhalin, eastern Russia*. The town, on the southwest coast of Sakhalin island, is named for the Russian newspaper *Pravda*. Before 1946, it had the Japanese name of *Hirochi*.

Pravdinsk[1] (Правдинск) *Town, western Russia*. The town, southeast of Kaliningrad, is named for the Russian newspaper *Pravda*. Before 1946 it had the German name of *Friedland*.

Pravdinsk[2] (Правдинск) *Town, western Russia*. The town, on the Volga River northwest of Nizhny Novgorod, arose around the Balakhin paper mill, first operating in the 1920s. This supplied the newsprint for *Pravda*, so the settlement that developed was duly named for that newspaper in 1932.

Preobrazhenskaya See **Kikvidze**.

Preobrazhenskoye (Преображенское) *District, Moscow, western Russia*. The northeastern district of Moscow takes its name from the former village here, itself taking its name from the 17th-century church of the Transfiguration (Russian *Preobrazheniye*).

Presnya (Пресня) *River, western Russia*. The river is a short tributary of the Moskva in western Moscow, where it is channelled undergound. The river name derives from Russian *presnyj*, now meaning "fresh" (as distinct from "salt"), but earlier meaning more like "sweet." Its water must have seemed pleasant to the taste, not bitter. It gave its name to the street *Presnya*, which in 1918 was renamed *Krasnaya Presnya* (Красная Пресня), "Red Presnya," to commemorate the Decembrist uprising of 1905 in Moscow, when demonstrators barricaded it. This name then passed to the surrounding district.

Preussisch Eylau See **Bagrationovsk**.

Priargunsk (Приаргу́нск) *Town, southern Russia.* The town, southeast of Chita near the border with China, takes its name from the *Argun* River, near which it lies. The prefix *pri-*, meaning "by," "near," denotes its location. Until 1962 it was known as *Tsurukhaytuy* (Цурухайту́й).

Prikumsk See **Budyonnovsk**.

Priluki (Прилу́ки) *Town, east central Ukraine.* The town, east of Kiev, stands on a bend of the River Uday. Hence its name, from the prefix *pri-*, "by," and Russian *luka*, "river bend."

Primorsk[1] (Примо́рск) *Town, western Russia.* The town, northwest of St. Petersburg, stands on the Gulf of Finland. Hence its name, meaning "maritime," "seaside," from the prefix *pri-*, "by," and Russian *more*, "sea," in its (shortened) adjectival form. It was formerly in Finland, and until 1949 had the Finnish name of *Koivisto* (Ко́йвисто), from Finnish *koivu*, "birch tree."

Primorsk[2] (Примо́рск) *Town, western Russia.* The town, west of Kaliningrad, stands on the Baltic coast. Hence its name, meaning "maritime," "seaside," from the prefix *pri-*, "by," and Russian *more*, "sea," in its (shortened) adjectival form. It was formerly in East Prussia, and until 1946 had the German name of *Fischhausen*, "fish building," referring to its role as a fishing port.

Primorsky Kray (Примо́рский край) *Region, eastern Russia.* The name is that of the autonomous territory, with capital Vladivostok, which extends north along the coast of the Sea of Japan from the border with North Korea in the south and with China in the southwest to a point parallel with Khabarovsk. The self-descriptive meaning is "Maritime Kray," and the territory is designated on some English maps in this translated form. The unofficial Russian name for the region is *Primorye* (Примо́рье). *Kray* means literally "edge," implying a delimited territory. (Cf. **Ukraine**.)

Priozyorsk (Приозёрск) *Town, western Russia.* The town, on the western shore of Lake Ladoga, north of St. Petersburg, has a name that describes its location, meaning "by the lake," from the prefix *pri-*, "by," and Russian *ozero*, "lake." It arose as a Swedish fortress in 1295, and until 1948 had the Swedish name of *Kexholm* (Кексго́льм). The second half of this appears to represent Swedish *holm*, "island," but the name is actually a corruption of Karelian *kekkisaari*, "cuckoo's island," or *kekkisalmi*, "cuckoo's strait." When under Finnish rule from 1918 to 1940 the town had the Finnish form of the name, *Käkisalmi*.

Pripet Marshes See **Polesye**.

Pripyat (При́пять) *River, southern Belarus.* The river rises in northwestern Ukraine and flows north across the border into Belarus, then generally east to join the Dnieper north of Kiev. The meaning of its name is uncertain, and it is not even clear whether the initial *pri-* is the prefix (meaning "by") found in many Russian names. One theory derives the name from a local word *pripech'* used for a sandy river bank. It was this river that gave the name of the region usually known in English as the *Pripet Marshes* and in Russian (also occasionally in English) as **Polesye**.

Prishib See **Leninsk**[1].

Pristan-Przhevalsk (При́стань-Пржева́льск) *Town, eastern Kyrgyzstan.* The town has a landing stage (Russian *pristan'*) on the east coast of Lake Issyk-Kul, north of **Przhevalsk**. Hence the two parts of its name.

Privokzalny (Привокза́льный) *Town, western Russia.* The town, south of Volokolamsk, is on a rail route to Moscow. Hence its name, from Russian *pri-*, "near," "by," and *vokzal*, "railroad station." (The latter word is an English import, representing *Vauxhall.* See **Pavlovsk**[1].) The name is found elsewhere for settlements that have developed around a railroad station.

Privolzhsk (Приво́лжск) *Town, western Russia.* The town, southeast of Yaroslavl, lies on the Shacha River, a tributary of the Volga. Hence its name, meaning "(place) near the Volga," from *pri-*, "near," and an adjectival form of *Volga*. The town grew from the village of *Yakovlevskoye* (Яковлевское), and had this name until 1941. It in turn probably derives from the surname *Yakovlev*.

Progress (Прогре́сс) *Town, southeastern Russia.* The town, southeast of Blagoveshchensk, has a Soviet name alluding to the *progress* of Communism. (Cf. English *progressive* in the sense "favoring social and political change.")

Proletarsk (Пролета́рск) *Town, southwestern Russia.* The town, southeast of Rostov-on-Don, was originally a village called *Velikoknyazheskaya* (Великокня́жеская), "Grand Duke." Following the 1917 Revolution, it became *Proletarskaya*, for the key role assigned to the *proletariat*, or laboring class. It took the present form of its name in 1970 on gaining urban status. There are other places with similar names.

Promyshlenny (Промы́шленный) *Town, northern Russia.* The coal-mining town, at the northern end of the Urals northwest of Vorkuta, has a name meaning "industrial" (Russian *promyshlennyj*).

Pronchishchev Bay (Про́нчищевой бу́хта) *Bay, northern Russia.* The name is that of a bay in the Laptev Sea on the **Pronchishchev Coast** of the Taymyr Peninsula. It commemorates Tatyana Fyodorovna *Pronchishcheva* (1713–1736), wife of the Russian explorer V.V. Pronchishchev, who accompanied her husband on his expeditions and who died only 14 days after him. (It was long believed that Pronchishcheva's first name was Maria. Hence the name of *Maria Pronchishcheva Bay* on the east coast of the Taymyr peninsula. Her maiden name was Kondyreva.)

Pronchishchev Coast (Про́нчищева бе́рег) *Coast, northern Russia.* The name is that of the east coast of the Taymyr Peninsula. It commemorates the Russian explorer Vasily Vasilyevich *Pronchishchev* (1702–1736), who investigated the shoreline here in 1736 in the months before his death from scurvy. Cf. **Pronchishchev Bay**.

Pronsk (Пронск) *Town, western Russia.* The town, east of Tula, takes its name from the *Pronya* River on which it stands. The river name is of uncertain origin.

Propoysk See **Slavgorod**.

Proskurov See **Khmelnitsky**.

Provideniya (Провиде́ния) *Town, eastern Russia.* The town, at the southern end of the Chukot Peninsula, takes its name from the bay here. The bay's name means "providence" (Russian *provideniye*). It was so called in 1848 by the British sea captain Thomas Moore, who recorded the "happy providence" that had enabled his ship to winter here. The bay was first discovered by a Russian expedition in 1660.

Prut (Прут) *River, western Moldova.* The river rises in the Carpathians, in southwestern Ukraine, then flows generally southeast along the border between Romania and Moldova into the Danube. Its name has long been thought to derive from an Indoeuropean root word meaning "ford," to which English *ford* and Russian *brod* are themselves related.

Przhevalsk (Пржевáльск) *Town, northeastern Kyrgyzstan*. The town, east of Lake Issyk-Kul, was founded in 1869 and was originally known as *Karakol* (Каракóл), a Turkic name meaning "black lake," from words related to modern Turkish *kara*, "black," and *göl*, "lake." In 1889 it was renamed as now for Nikolay Mikhaylovich *Przhevalsky* (1839-1888), Russian explorer of Central Asia, who died near here at the start of his fifth expedition. (It was he who discovered the rare wild horse known for him as Przewalski's horse.) The town reverted to its original name of *Karakol* from 1921 to 1939.

Psekups See **Goryachy Klyuch**.

Pskov (Псков) *City, western Russia*. The city, southwest of St. Petersburg, is an old one, dating from at least the early 10th century, with its name recorded in a document of 947 as *Pleskov*. This form of the name has led some authorities to derive it from Russian *plyos*, "reach," "stretch of water," or rather from the diminutive form of this, *plesok*. This would then refer to the *Pskova* River (named for the town) which flows into the larger Velikaya ("Great") here. The precise origin of the name remains uncertain.

Puchezh (Пýчеж) *Town, western Russia*. The town, southeast of Kineshma, has a name said to derive from Russian *puchina*, "gulf," "abyss." But this does not seem to be relevant here, and the actual origin may be in a pre-Russian word. Mary *puchy*, "deer," has been proposed.

Pudozh (Пýдож) *Town, northwestern Russia*. The town, in Karelia to the east of Lake Onega, has a name that may derive from Karelian *puvas* (Finnish *pudas*), "inlet," "river arm." Local topography appears to support this origin, since the town is on an arm of the Vodla River.

Pugachyov (Пугачёв) *Town, western Russia*. The town, northeast of Saratov, arose from a village which in the 18th century was known as *Mechetnaya*, from Russian *mechet'*, "mosque." In 1835 it was raised to town status and renamed *Nikolayevsk* (Николáевск), for the reigning czar, *Nicholas* I (1796-1855). In 1918 it was given its present name, for the Cossack soldier Yemelyan Ivanovich *Pugachyov* (c. 1742-1775), who stopped here in 1772 when organizing his famous Cossack and peasant rebellion against Catherine the Great. The name was proposed by the Civil War commander V.I. Chapayev, for whom **Chapayev** is named.

Pushkin (Пýшкин) *Town and resort, western Russia*. The town, south of St. Petersburg, was originally a Finnish village taken by the Russians under Peter the Great in 1708 and presented to his wife Catherine as a summer residence. The name of the site was *Saari*, from the Finnish word for "island," implying a place on raised ground. This then became *Sarskoye selo*, "Saari village." But as the place was the residence of the czar, the name was reinterpreted as *Tsarskoye selo*, "czar's village." The village grew and in 1808 was officially named *Tsarskoye Selo* (Цáрское Селó) accordingly. In 1918, after the Revolution, the royal residence and its grounds were commandeered as a holiday resort for children from worker and peasant families, and the name was changed to *Detskoye Selo* (Дéтское Селó), "children's village." In 1937 the town was given its present name, marking the centennial of the death of the Russian poet Aleksandr Sergeyevich *Pushkin* (1799-1837), who was at school here and who penned his earliest works here.

Pushkino (Пу́шкино) *Town, western Russia*. The town, northeast of Moscow, dates from the 15th century, and takes its name from the boyar Grigory *Pushkin*, said to be an ancestor of the famous Russian poet, for whom **Pushkin** is named.

Pushkinskiye Gory (Пу́шкинские Го́ры) *Town, western Russia*. The town, northwest of Velikiye Luki, has a name meaning "Pushkin hills." The poet Alexander *Pushkin* is buried here in the Svyatogorsk monastery.

Putivl (Пути́вль) *Town, northern Ukraine*. The town, on the Seym River northwest of Belopolye, dates from at least the 12th century. Its name probably derives from Russian *put'*, "way," "route," referring not so much to the town but to the river, as a waterway to the west and ultimately, via the Desna, south to Kiev.

Putyatin (Путя́тин) *Island, eastern Russia*. The island, in Peter the Great Bay southeast of Vladivostok, takes its name from the Russian admiral Yefim Vasilyevich *Putyatin* (1803–1883), who explored the coast here on board the frigate *Pallada* in 1852-55, while conducting a diplomatic mission to Japan.

Pyandzh (Пяндж) *Town, southwestern Tajikistan*. The town, southwest of Kulyab, takes its name from the *Pyandzh* River on which it lies, the river here forming the border with Afghanistan. Its own name appears to derive from Iranian *panj*, "five," as if referring to five tributaries. But it is not certain which these are, or even if this is the correct origin. Until 1931 the town was known as *Saray Komar* (Сара́й Кома́р), and from 1931 to 1936 *Baumanabad* (Баумана́бад), for the Latvian-born Communist official Karl Yanovich *Bauman* (1892–1937), *-abad* being the Iranian element meaning "town." In 1936 it was further renamed *Kirovabad* (Кировоба́д), for the Soviet politician and aide of Stalin, Sergey Mironovich *Kirov* (1888–1934). Following the discrediting of Stalin, the town reverted to its original name in 1963.

Pyatigorsk (Пятиго́рск) *Town and health resort, southwestern Russia*. The town, northwest of Nalchik, was founded in 1830 and given a Russian name equivalent to that of the nearby mountain of **Beshtau**. Its Turkic name means "five mountains," from words related to modern Turkish *beş*, "five," and *dağ*, "mountain." (The mountain has five peaks.) The Russian name thus derives from *pyat'*, "five," amd *gora*, "mountain."

Pyatikhatki (Пятиха́тки) *Town, east central Ukraine*. The town, west of Dneprodzerzhinsk, has a name representing Ukrainian *pyat' khat*, "five houses," referring to an original village that comprised this number of dwellings.

Pyshma See **Verkhnyaya Pyshma**.

Radekhov (Раде́хов) *Town, western Ukraine*. The town, northeast of Lvov, takes its name from the medieval owner of an estate here, one *Radekh*. The final *-ov* is a possessive suffix.

Radishchevo (Ради́щево) *Village, western Russia*. The village, southwest of Syzran, was originally known as *Dvoryanskaya Tereshka* (Дворя́нская Тере́шка), "nobleman's Tereshka," from the *Tereshka* River here. In 1918 it was renamed as now for the Russian revolutionary writer Aleksandr Nikolayevich *Radishchev* (1749–1802), who lived here in 1798.

Radomyshl (Ра́домышль) *Town, west central Ukraine*. The town, west of Kiev, is mentioned in a document of 1150 under the name of *Mykgorod*. It takes its present name from the personal name *Radomysl*.

Radonezh See **Gorodok**[2].

Radovitsky (Радовицкий) *Town, western Russia*. The town, north of Ryazan, takes its name from marshland here, itself known as *Radovitsky mokh*, the latter word denoting an area of swamp or marsh overgrown with moss. The marshland presumably has a personal name.

Radzivilov See **Chervonoarmeysk**.

Rakhya (Рахья) *Town, western Russia*. The town, northeast of St. Petersburg, has a name honoring the Russian revolutionary Ivan (originally Jukka) Abramovich *Rakhya* (1887–1920), active in Finland at the time of the Revolution. He was killed in the Civil War during a counterrevolutionary attack on a Communist club in Petrograd.

Ramenskoye (Ра́менское) *Town, western Russia*. The town, southeast of Moscow, dates from at least the 14th century and bases its name on the Russian dialect word *ramen'*, "forest," "settlement by a forest."

Ranenburg See **Chaplygin**.

Rassvet (Рассве́т) *Town, eastern Russia*. The town, north of Okhotsk, has a Soviet name meaning "dawn," implying the beginning of a new age (of Communism).

Rastyapino See **Dzerzhinsk**[1].

Ratmanov Island (Ратма́нова о́стров) *Island, Bering Strait, northeastern Russia*. The island, Russia's easternmost territory, is the larger of the group of two known collectively as the **Diomede Islands**. The name was originally misapplied in 1816 to Cape **Dezhnyov** by the Russian navigator O. Ye. Kotsebu, who took it to be a fourth island in the group. It was correctly assigned to the present island in the late 1820s by the British naval officer and geographer Frederick William Beechey. The name itself is that of Lieutenant Makar Ivanovich *Ratmanov* (1772–1833), a member of Kruzenshtern's expedition (see **Kruzenshtern Strait**).

Razdolnoye (Раздо́льное) *Town, southeastern Russia*. The town, south of Ussuriysk, takes its name from the *Razdolnaya* River on which it lies. The river name means "broad valley," The settlement name is found elsewhere, not necessarily on a river so called, and in some cases evokes the secondary sense of the word, which is "carefree." One such town is in northwestern Crimea, southern Ukraine.

Rechitsa (Ре́чица) *Town, southeastern Belarus*. The town, southwest of Gomel, derives its name from Slavic *reka*, "river," with the Old Slavonic suffix *-itsa*. Rechitsa is a river port on the Dnieper.

Red Russia (Черво́нная Русь) *Historic region, western Ukraine/ eastern Poland*. The name is that of a former territory corresponding to eastern Galicia. It is found in a 15th-century document in the Medieval Latin form of *Rossia rossa*, but the present Ukrainian form of the name, *Chervona Rus'* (Russian *Chervonnaya Rus'*), comes from Polish *Czerwona Ruś*. The origin of the name may be in the former ancient Russian town of *Cherven*, on a site now in eastern Poland. This and other towns around the upper reaches of the Western Bug are known to have been important in medieval times. The precise sense of "red" here is uncertain. The word is popularly said to relate to the red clothes worn by the Ukrainians, as distinct from the white garments of the White Russians (see **Belarus**).

Regar See **Tursunzade**.

Repino (Ре́пино) *Town, western Russia*. The town, on the Gulf of

Finland northwest of St. Petersburg, was originally known by the Finnish name of *Kuokkala*. In 1948 it was renamed as now for the Russian painter Ilya Yefimovich *Repin* (1844–1930), who lived here in what was then Finland from 1899 and who died and is buried here.

Revda (Ревдá) *Town, western Russia*. The town, west of Yekaterinburg, takes its name from the *Revda* River, on which it was built in the 1730s. The meaning of the river name is uncertain, and even its language of origin has not been decisively determined.

Revel See **Tallinn**.

Revolution Peak (Революции пик) *Mountain, east central Tajikistan*. The mountain, one of the highest in this section of the Pamirs, was named for the Russian *Revolution* following its first ascent by Russian climbers in 1954.

Rezh (Реж) *Town, western Russia*. The town, northwest of Yekaterinburg, takes its name from the *Rezh* River on which it arose around the ironworks founded here in 1773. The origin of the river name is uncertain. It may mean simply "stream," "tributary," referring to the larger Nitsa into which it flows.

Ridder See **Leninogorsk**[1].

Riga (Рúга) *Capital of Latvia*. The city is at the southern end of the Gulf of Riga on the Western Dvina. Its name probably refers to this location, and derives from a Baltic root word *ring* related to modern Latvian *ringe*, "river bend," "river pool."

Rikord Cape (Рикóрда мыс) *Cape, Kuril Islands, southeastern Russia*. The cape, at the southern end of Iturup island, was mapped in 1811 and named for the Russian naval commander and explorer Pyotr Ivanovich *Rikord* (1776–1855). A strait further north in the Kurils is also named for him.

Rioni (Риóни) *River, western Georgia*. The river rises in the Caucasus and flows southwest and then west to the Black Sea. Its name represents the Svan word *riyen*, meaning simply "river."

Rodniki (Роднúки) *Town, western Russia*. The town, northeast of Ivanovo, has a Russian name meaning "springs." Similar names are found elsewhere in this part of Russia (but rarely west of Moscow).

Rogachyov (Рогачёв) *Town, eastern Belarus*. The town, east of Bobruysk, appears to have a name deriving from the personal name *Rogach*, with the suffix *-yov* denoting possession. But the actual source may be in Russian *rog*, "headland" (literally, "horn"), referring to that on which the town stands, formed by the confluence of the small Drut River with the Dnieper.

Rogozhka (Рогóжка) *District, Moscow, western Russia*. The eastern district of Moscow takes its name from the former village here, itself so called since many of its inhabitants made their living by carting goods to the nearby village of *Rogozha* (now the town of **Noginsk**).

Roman Kosh (Романн-Кош) *Mountain, southeastern Crimea, southern Ukraine*. The mountain, the highest in the Crimean range, near the southeast coast, has a name that is said to derive from Turkic *orman*, "forest," and *kosh*, "shieling," the latter referring to a temporary shelter for shepherds, or to a place where sheep were kept at night. Recent authorities, however, see an ethnic origin for the name, with reference to the *Ramankul*, a Turkic people, who could have had an encampment here.

Romanov-Borisoglebsk See **Tutayev**.

Romanov-on-Murman See **Murmansk**.

Romanovsky Khutor See **Kropotkin**.

Romny (Ромны́) *Town, northeastern Ukraine*. The town, southwest of Sumy, has a name of Baltic origin, possibly from Lithuanian *romus*, "calm," "quiet," representing an earlier name of the Sula River on which the town stands.

Roshal (Роша́ль) *Town, western Russia*. The town, southwest of Vladimir, is named for the Russian revolutionary Semyon Grigoryevich *Roshal* (1896–1917), arrested and shot by counterrevolutionaries in the opening months of the Civil War.

Roslavl (Ро́славль) *Town, western Russia*. The town, southeast of Smolensk, is one of the many medieval Russian placenames ending in *-slavl*, formed from the personal names of princes. (Cf. **Mstislavl**, **Yaroslavl**.) In this case it is uncertain what the original placename was. It may have been *Rostislavl*, so that the prince was *Rostislav* ("growing in glory"). His identity, however, is uncertain. The town was founded in the first half of the 12th century.

Rossosh (Ро́ссошь) *Town, southwestern Russia*. The town, southeast of Liski, takes its name from the *Rossosh* River that forms a confluence with the Chyornaya Kalitva here. The river name derives from Russian *rassokha*, literally "fissure," referring to the point where a river in a ravine or gully divides into two.

Rostov (Росто́в) *Town, western Russia*. The historic town, southwest of Yaroslavl, is first mentioned in 862. Its name probably derives from a personal name *Rost*, a shortened form of *Rostislav*, with the final *-ov* either a possessive suffix or added on an analogy with other town names (such as **Saratov**). The town formerly had the alternate name of *Rostov-Yaroslavsky*, locating it near *Yaroslavl*, as distinct from the city that is now **Rostov-on-Don**. From the 12th through 17th centuries it was frequently known as *Rostov Velikij*, "Rostov the Great," since it was formerly the capital of the historic principality of the same name.

Rostov-on-Don (Росто́в-на-Дону́) *City, southwestern Russia*. The city, on the Don River a few miles above its estuary on the Sea of Azov, arose from a fortress built here in 1761. This was named the *Rostov* fortress for its church, which was dedicated to St. Dmitry of *Rostov* (1651–1709), metropolitan (bishop) of **Rostov**. The settlement that grew around the fortress became a town in 1796, and soon added its locational suffix to distinguish it from its historic eponym.

Rovno (Ро́вно) *City, western Ukraine*. The city, northeast of Lvov, dates from at least the 13th century. Its name remains of uncertain origin, however. It may be associated with Slavic *rov*, "channel," referring to the small Ustye River on which it stands, or with Russian *rovnyj*, "level," describing the flat terrain here.

Rovnoye (Ро́вное) *Village, south central Ukraine*. The village, southwest of Kirovograd, lies in the Lower Volga steppe plain. Hence its name, which means "level (place)."

Rubezhnoye (Рубе́жное) *Town, eastern Ukraine*. The town, northwest of Lisichansk, has a name that literally means "border (place)," perhaps because Russia's southern border reached this point at one stage. But the border could equally have been a local one, for example of a landowner's estate.

Rudnichny (Рудни́чный) *Town, western Russia*. The town, northeast of Vyatka, arose on the site of iron ore deposits here, west of the Middle Urals. Hence its name, from Russian *ruda*, "ore." There are several other places of the name. Cf. **Rudny**.

Rudny (Рудный) *Town, northern Kazakhstan*. The town, southwest of Kustanay, arose in 1957 when iron ore here was first mined. Hence its name, as the adjectival form of Russian *ruda*, "ore." There are other places of the name. Cf. **Rudnichny**.

Rudolf Island (Рудольфа остров) *Island, Franz Josef Land, northwestern Russia*. The northernmost island in the group was named by the Austrian explorer Julius von Payer for the Austrian crown prince *Rudolf* (1858-1889), only son of Emperor Franz Josef, who gave the name of **Franz Josef Land** as a whole. Cape Fligeli here is Russia's northernmost point.

Rugozero (Ругозеро) *Lake, northwestern Russia*. The lake, one of the many in Karelia, has a name (as do most of the others) based on Russian *ozero*, "lake." The first part of this name may represent Russian *ruga*, a word used in the 16th and 17th centuries for a tithe or land tax exacted by the state for the upkeep of churches and monasteries.

Rukhlovo See **Skovorodino**.

Rusanov Bay (Русанова залив) *Bay, Novaya Zemlya, northwestern Russia*. The bay, on the east coast of Severny (North) Island, is named for the Russian Arctic explorer Vladimir Aleksandrovich *Rusanov* (1875-1913), leader of expeditions here in 1910 and 1911. He and his team went missing in 1913 after setting off by sea to round the northern tip of Novaya Zemlya.

Russia (Россия) *Federal republic, Europe/Asia*. The Russia of today evolved historically from the Varangian (Scandinavian) territory of *Rus* (Русь) established in the 9th century, with Novgorod and Kiev as the respective northern and southern capitals. This is therefore the period when the name itself emerged. It is probably Scandinavian in origin, representing the Old Finnish name *Rus*, by which the Varangians themselves came to be known. Its basic meaning is probably "foreigners." Some toponymists, however, link the name with that of the *Ruotsi*, "rowers," the Swedish people who served as oarsmen on Viking ships. (This was also the source of *Ruotsi*, the Finnish name of Sweden.) After the decline of Kievan Rus in the 12th century, the empire of *Russia* emerged, with its name first recorded in the late 15th century as a Medieval Latin form of the ethnic name, "land of the *Russi*." (The Russian form of the name, with *o* where other languages have *u*, is probably due to Greek influence.) The name *Soviet Union* (Советский Союз), as the short form of the official title *Union of Soviet Socialist Republics* (Союз Советских Социалистических Республик), was first in use in 1922, when a *union* of socialist republics was set up with the *soviet* (Russian, "council") as the basic unit of local and national government. The name was unique in containing no geographical or ethnic element, allegedly so that the new socialist empire could expand to include other countries until (theoretically) it extended worldwide. With the collapse of the Soviet Union in 1991, the historic name *Russia* once again became official. It had never been abandoned, however, even in the USSR, where it was the short name of the Russian Soviet Federated Socialist Republic (RSFSR), the central and largest republic of the Soviet Union.

Russky Island (Русский остров) *Island, Kara Sea, northwestern Russia*. The island, the northernmost and largest in the Nordenskiöld Archipelago, has a name meaning simply "Russian island."

Rustavi (Руста́ви) *Town, southeastern Georgia.* The town, southeast of Tbilisi, arose in 1948 when an ironworks began operating here. The town was platted in 1944 on open land near the ruins of the ancient town of the same name, itself representing the Georgian words *ru*, "stream," "canal," and *tavi*, "beginning," "source." The reference is to the irrigation canal that leads from the Kura River here.

Ruzayevka (Руза́евка) *Town, western Russia.* The town, in Mordovia southwest of Saransk, is said to take its name from the Tatar prince *Uraz*, or *Urazay*, who obtained an estate here in 1631. The present town dates only from in 1893, when a workers' settlement arose during construction of the railroad from Moscow to Kazan.

Ryazan (Ряза́нь) *City, western Russia.* The city, on the Oka River southeast of Moscow, has its name mentioned in a late 11th-century document. However, the name is not that of the present city, but what is now the village of *Staraya Ryazan* ("Old Ryazan"), about 30 miles (48 km) further south on the Oka, which was formerly the capital of the principality of Ryazan. When this Ryazan was destroyed by the Mongol ruler Batu Khan in 1235, the capital was transferred to its present site at *Pereyaslavl-Ryazansky*, as it was then called (see **Pereyaslav-Zalessky**). In 1778 the town took its present name. Its origin is uncertain. One authority derives it from a local word *ryasa*, used for a marshy place. (Cf. **Ryazhsk**.) But it may be an ethnic name, from the *Erzya*, a Mordovian people.

Ryazhsk (Ря́жск) *Town, western Russia.* The town, southeast of Ryazan, probably takes its name from the *Ryasa* River, even though this is some distance away. The river name may derive from a local word *ryasa*, used for a marshy place. Cf. **Ryazan**.

Rybachye See **Issyk-Kul**².

Rybachy Peninsula (Рыба́чий полуо́стров) *Peninsula, northwestern Russia.* The peninsula, in the Barents Sea north of Murmansk, has a name meaning "fisherman's (settlement)." There are rich fishing grounds off the coast here.

Rybinsk (Ры́бинск) *City, western Russia.* The city, on the Volga northwest of Yaroslavl, was founded in the 11th century (or earlier) as a fishing village. Hence its name, from Russian *rybak*, "fisherman." It became a town in 1777 and subsequently underwent two changes of name. From 1946 to 1957 it was *Shcherbakov* (Щербако́в), for the government and Communist party official Aleksandr Sergeyevich *Shcherbakov* (1901–1945). When his name was discredited after the death of Stalin, the city reverted to its original name. In 1984 it was renamed *Andropov* (Андро́пов), on the death of the Soviet president Yury Vladimirovich *Andropov* (1914–1984), who had worked as a Volga boatman and been a student here. In 1989 it again reverted to its original name, following a reappraisal of Andropov's reputation.

Rybnitsa (Ры́бница) *Town, eastern Moldova.* The town, east of Beltsy, takes its name from the river that enters the Dniester here. Its own name means "fish (river)," from a word related to Russian *ryba*, "fish."

Rykovo See **Yenakiyevo**.

Rylsk (Рыльск) *Town, southwestern Russia.* The town, southwest of Kursk, takes its name from the *Rylo* River on which it stands. The river name is based on Russian *ryt'*, "to burrow."

Rzhev (Ржев) *City, western Russia.* The city, northwest of Moscow, dates from the 11th century or earlier and appears to take its name from that of some river, itself named for its rusty color, from Russian *rzha,* "rust." Rzhev is actually on the Volga.

Saaremaa (Сáарема) *Island, western Estonia.* The island, in the Baltic Sea northwest of the Gulf of Riga, has a name meaning "island land," from Estonian *saare,* "island," and *maa,* "land." The name is also spelled *Sarema,* and was formerly familiar in its German form of *Oesel.*

Sabirabad (Сабирабáд) *Town, eastern Azerbaijan.* The town, southwest of Baku, is named in commemoration of the Azerbaijani satirical poet *Sabir* (real name Mirza Alekper Tairzade) (1862–1911), whose work met with the approval of revolutionary circles. (His pseudonym means "patient," alluding to the repressive regime in which he wrote.) The final *-abad* is the familiar Iranian element meaning "town."

Sablino See **Ulyanovka**.

St. Petersburg (Санкт-Петербу́рг) *City, western Russia.* The well known city, at the mouth of the Neva River at the eastern end of the Gulf of Finland, arose from the fortress founded by Peter the Great on May 27, 1703. The fortress contained the church of St. *Peter* and St. Paul, and the town that grew up took its name from this as much as from *Peter* himself. Further, the city arose at a time when Christianity was envisioned as an ecumenical religion. The name thus mirrored that of Rome, where St. Peter's cathedral is named for the first pope. (St. Petersburg could well have been named for both saints, as were **Petropavlovsk** and **Petropavlovsk-Kamchatsky**. But "Peter's town" prevailed as a counterpart to the other "Peter's town" that was Rome.) The city was Peter's "window into Europe," and as such took a European form of the name, the Cyrillic characters representing German *Sankt-Peterburg.* This name lasted until World War I, when German names fell from favor. On August 18, 1914 it was thus modified to its Russian equivalent, *Petrograd* (Петрогрáд). On January 26, 1924, following the death of Lenin, it was further renamed *Leningrad* (Ленингрáд), and retained this name until 1991, when it reverted to the original. The colloquial name of the city is *Piter* (Пи́тер). A poetic name for it was (or is) *Petropol* (Петрóполь), as if Greek *Petropolis.* This appears in Pushkin's poem *The Bronze Horseman* (1837): *"I vsplyl Petropol', kak triton, po poyas v vodu pogruzhyon"* ("Petropolis as Triton rose, 'til water round his waist fast flows"). St. Petersburg (Petrograd) was capital of Russia from 1712 to 1918.

Sakhalin (Сахали́н) *Island, eastern Russia.* The island, north of Japan in the western part of the Sea of Okhotsk, has a name resulting from a misunderstanding. On a map made by French missionaries in the early 18th century, the lower reaches of the Amur River, which flows into the Tatar Strait opposite the northern end of Sakhalin, were named as *Saghalien anga hata.* This was a corrupt form of a Manchurian name meaning "course of the black river." The French geographer Jean-Baptiste d'Anville used this map for compiling an atlas of China and the East, published in 1737, and since the name extended from the Amur across to the island, he took it as applying to the latter, rather than the former. In the course of time the name became established for the island instead of the river, but was shortened to *Saghalien,* the first word noted by the missionaries. The indigenous Ainu name of the island, *Krafto,* was corrupted by the Japanese into *Karafuto.*

Saki (Са́ки) *Town, western Crimea, southern Ukraine.* The town, east of Yevpatoriya, is said to take its name from the *Saki* people who formerly inhabited this region. The source of their own name is uncertain.

Sakmara (Сакма́ра) *River, western Russia.* The river, a tributary of the Ural, has a name that is probably related to that of the *Samara*, on which **Samara** stands.

Salavat (Салава́т) *Town, western Russia.* The town, in Bashkortostan south of Sterlitamak, arose in 1954 from a settlement of oil workers and was named for the Bashkir national hero, *Salavat* Yulayev (1752–1800), who fought against Pugachyov in the Peasant War of 1773-75.

Salda See **Nizhnyaya Salda**.

Saldus (Са́лдус) *Town, western Latvia.* The town, west of Jelgava, is said to take its name from Lithuanian *saldus*, "sweet," "gentle," although the precise import of this is uncertain. It may somehow link up with the former German name of the town, *Frauenburg*, "women's town."

Salekhard (Салеха́рд) *Town, northern Russia.* The town, capital of the Yamalo-Nenets autonomous region, on the Ob River to the east of the Northern Urals, was founded in 1595 as a fortified post and was originally named *Obdorsk* (Обдо́рск), from the name of the **Ob** itself and Komi *dor*, "adjacent (place)." In 1933 it was renamed as now, from Nenets *salya*, "headland," and *khard*, "house," "settlement," referring to its location on a bend of the Ob.

Salmi (Са́лми) *Town, western Russia.* The town, in Karelia on the northeast coast of Lake Ladoga, derives its name from Finnish and Karelian *salmi*, "strait." The reference is to the strait between the town and the island that lies opposite it.

Salsk (Сальск) *Town, southwestern Russia.* The town, northeast of Krasnodar, was originally known as *Torgovaya* (Торго́вая), "trading place." In 1926 it was renamed as now for the *Sal* steppes here, themselves named for the *Sal* River, a tributary of the Don. The origin of the river name is uncertain.

Samara (Сама́ра) *City, western Russia.* The city, southeast of Kazan, takes its name from the *Samara* River on which it lies, at the point where it enters the Volga, which here flows in a large loop to the east. The river name is itself of uncertain origin. It may or may not be of the same origin as the *Samara* that is a tributary of the Dnieper in Ukraine. It is possible both names may link with that of the *Somme*, in northern France, which in Roman times was also known as the *Samara*. Samara was founded in 1586 and in 1935 was renamed *Kuybyshev* (Ку́йбышев), for the Soviet Communist party official Valerian Vladimirovich *Kuybyshev* (1888–1935), who organized an armed revolt in the city at the time of the Revolution and subsequent Civil War. The city reverted to its original name in 1991.

Samarkand (Самарка́нд) *City, eastern Uzbekistan.* The historic city was known as *Marakanda* from the 4th through 6th centuries AD, and the *-kand* of this is undoubtedly the Iranian word meaning "inhabited place," "town." The first part of the name is of uncertain origin. It is popularly derived from *Shamar*, the name of an Arab ruler who captured it. It is possible it may represent Iranian *asmara*, "stone." If so, the name of Samarkand has exactly the same sense as that of **Tashkent**.

Samoded (Самоде́д) *Town, western Russia.* The town, south of Arkhangelsk, arose in 1925 on the construction of a sawmill here. It was named in honor of G. I. *Samoded*, killed in 1919 during the Civil War.

Samotlor (Самотлóр) *Lake, central Russia*. The lake, just north of the Ob River in the West Siberian Plateau, has a Khanti name meaning "trap lake." It was so called by local people for its marshy location and difficulty of access.

Sannikov Land See **Sannikov Strait**.

Sannikov Strait (Сáнникова проли́в) *Strait, northern Russia*. The strait, in the New Siberian Islands, separates the Anzhu Islands from the Lyakhov Islands. It was discovered by the Yakut merchant and explorer Yakov *Sannikov* (?-?) in expeditions of 1808-11, and is named for him. An island reported by Sannikov in 1811 north of the New Siberian Islands was named *Sannikov Land* (Сáнникова Земля́) also for him. However, although it was subsequently charted by other navigators, it later disappeared, its icy terrain presumably broken up by the sea.

Sapozhnikov Glacier (Сапóжникова ледни́к) *Glacier, eastern Kazakhstan*. The glacier, in the Southern Altay range, is named for the Soviet botanist and geographer Vasily Vasilyevich *Sapozhnikov* (1861-1924), who made a special study of the region.

Sapozhok (Сапожóк) *Town, western Russia*. The town, southeast of Ryazan, takes its name from the old standard Russian word *sapozhok*, literally "little boot," used for a portion of land running into a forest, or for a wedge-shaped area of forest extending onto a stretch of land.

Saraktash (Сарактáш) *Town, southwestern Russia*. The town, east of Orenburg, has a name of Turkic origin meaning "sheep rock," from Tatar *saryk* or Bashkir *kharyk*, "sheep," and Tatar-Bashkir *tash*, "stone," "rock."

Saranpaul (Саранпáуль) *Village, western Russia*. The village, on the Lyapin River east of the Northern Urals, has a Mansi name meaning "Zyrian settlement." It was founded by a group of Komi-Izhma in the latter half of the 19th century. (The *Izhma* are a subgroup of the Komi people and originated from the river of this name, while *Zyrian* is a former name of the Komi generally.)

Saransk (Сарáнск) *Town, western Russia*. The town, the capital of Mordovia, was founded in 1641 as a defensive post on the southeastern border of the Russian empire. The town is on the *Insar* River and apparently takes its name from this. The river name itself means "big marsh." However, this explanation does not account for the *-an*.

Sarapul (Сарáпул) *Town, western Russia*. The town, in Udmurtia on the Kama River, has a name that has been explained as deriving from Turkic words *sara*, "yellow," and *pul*, "fish scale," supposedly referring to the sterlet (a type of small sturgeon) here.

Saratov (Сарáтов) *City, southwestern Russia*. The city, on the Volga northeast of Volgograd, was founded in 1590 as a fortified town to protect the Volga waterway from nomadic forays. Various explanations have been put forward for the name, the most popular being a derivation in Turkic *sari*, "yellow," and *tau*, "mountain." This could refer to the high land on the right bank of the Volga where the town arose. (In 1616, after a fire, it was transferred to the left bank, where it remained until 1674.) The reference could specifically be to the Sokolovaya ("falcon") mountain, which has yellowish slopes. According to local historians, this was known to Turkic people here in the 16th century as the *Sarytau*.

Saray-Komar See **Pyandzh**.

Sardarabad See **Oktemberyan**.

Sarepta See **Krasnoarmeysk³**.

Saryagach (Сарыага́ч) *Town, southern Kazakhstan*. The town, southwest of Chimkent, derives its name from the Turkic words *sary*, "yellow" (modern Turkish *sarı*), and *agach*, "tree" (modern Turkish *ağaç*). There must have been such a tree here at one time.

Sarychev, Mt. (Са́рычева вулка́н) *Volcano, Kuril Islands, southeastern Russia*. The active volcano, on Matua island, near the northern end of the Kuril chain, is named for the Russian navigator and hydrographer Gavriil Andreyevich *Sarychev* (1763–1831), who charted the coast of the Sea of Okhotsk and many of the Aleutian Islands.

Sarysu (Сарысу́) *River, central Kazakhstan*. The river derives its name from the Turkic words *sary*, "yellow" (modern Turkish *sarı*), and *su* (modern Turkish *su*), "water." In Kazakhstan the term *sarysu* is used for any river flowing across terrain that is predominantly yellow-colored clay or loess. The Sarysu here is formed from the confluence of the *Zhaksy* ("good") Sarysu and the *Zhaman* ("bad") Sarysu.

Sasyk (Сасы́к) *Lake, southwestern Crimea, southern Ukraine*. The lake, a saltwater lagoon, has a name of Turkic origin meaning "putrid," referring to its unpleasant smell. Cf. **Sasykkol**.

Sasykkol (Сасыкко́ль) *Lake, eastern Kazakhstan*. The lake, east of Lake Balkhash, has a Turkic name meaning "putrid lake," referring to the fetid odor of its waters. See also **Sasyk**.

Satka (Са́тка) *Town, western Russia*. The town, southwest of Zlatoust, arose around the metal- works that was founded here in 1757 at the confluence of the Bolshaya ("Big") and Malaya ("Little") *Satka* River. The name is thus that of the river, which may itself be based on Bashkir *sat*, "fork," "bifurcation," and so refer to the location of the town at the junction of the rivers mentioned. The final *-ka* would then be a Russian addition.

Saulkrasti (Са́улкрасты) *Town, central Latvia*. The town, northeast of Riga on the eastern shore of the Gulf of Riga, has a name meaning "sunny shore," from Latvian *saūle*, "sun," and *kraste*, "shore," "coast."

Schastye (Сча́стье) *Town, eastern Ukraine*. The town, northeast of Lugansk, has a Soviet ideological name meaning "happiness," "good fortune." The town is on the Donets River where one of the most powerful electric power stations in the former USSR came on stream in the early 1960s.

Schaulen See **Šiauliai**.

Schlüsselburg See **Petrokrepost**.

Sebastopol See **Sevastopol**.

Sebezh (Се́беж) *Town, western Russia*. The town, south of Pskov near the border with Latvia, dates from at least the 15th century, when it was a fortified post in the Pskov republic. Its name is of unknown origin, although river or lake names ending in *-ezh* are fairly common in this part of Russia, and the town is on a lake of the name. At one time it was known as *Ivangorod*, "Ivan's town," for *Ivan* the Terrible (1530–1584).

Sechenovo (Се́ченово) *Village, western Russia*. The village, southeast of Nizhny Novgorod, was originally known by the name of *Tyoply Stan* (Тёплый Стан), "warm district." This has been popularly explained as referring to the "warmth" with which

Ivan the Terrible was greeted by the inhabitants when passing through on one of his campaigns against the Tatar Khanate of Kazan. However, the name exists elsewhere, and was used for a frontier post where the guard could rest and warm themselves after duty in the open. The village was given its present name in 1945 in memory of the Russian scientist and physiologist Ivan Mikhaylovich *Sechenov* (1829–1905), who was born here.

Sedovo (Седо́во) *Town, southeastern Ukraine*. The town, on the coast east of Mariupol near the border with Russia, was originally the settlement of *Krivaya Kosa* (Крива́я Коса́), "crooked sandspit." In 1941 it was renamed as now for the Russian Arctic explorer Georgy Yakovlevich *Sedov* (1877–1914), who was born here. He died in the Arctic, and there are features on Novaya Zemlya also named for him.

Segezha (Сеге́жа) *Town, northwestern Russia*. The town, on Lake Vygozero, south of Belomorsk, takes its name from the *Segezha* River, which leaves the lake here. The name derives from Karelian *sees*, genitive *sekehen*, "clean," "bright," referring to its waters. The Karelian name of Lake *Segozero*, to the southwest, is thus *Seesjärvi*, "clean lake," with Finnish *järvi* and Russian *ozero* both meaning "lake."

Segozero, Lake See **Segezha**.

Selenga (Селенга́) *River, southern Russia*. The river rises in western Mongolia, flowing east then north across the Russian border into Buryaad to enter Lake Baykal. Its name is based on Evenki *sele*, "yellow," referring to the yellowish ore deposits found in its valley.

Seliger (Селиге́р) *Lake, western Russia*. The lake, northwest of Moscow, is said to have a Finnic name, with the second part the equivalent of modern Finnish *järvi*, "lake." The origin of the first part of the name is uncertain.

Semipalatinsk (Семипала́тинск) *City, northeastern Kazakhstan*. The city, on the Irtysh River near the Russian border, was founded as a fortress in 1718. Its name means "seven palaces," from Russian *sem'*, "seven," and *palata*, "palace," referring to the ruins nearby of a group of ancient buildings (in fact nine or ten in number). An alternate name for the ruins was *Kamennyye Mecheti*, "stone mosques."

Semirechye See **Dzhetysu**.

Sem Kolodezey See **Lenino**.

Semyonov Glacier (Семёнова ледни́к) *Glacier, eastern Kyrgyzstan*. The glacier, in the central Tien Shan, is named for its discoverer in 1857, the Russian geographer Pyotr Petrovich *Semyonov* (known from 1906 as Semyonov-Tyan-Shansky) (1827–1914). Mt. *Semyonov* (Семёнова пик) here is also named for him. (The addition to his name refers to the Tien Shan itself, which he explored that year.)

Semyonovka (Семёновка) *Town, northern Ukraine*. The town, northwest of Novgorod Seversky, was so named in the 17th century for its founder, *Semyon* Samoylovich, son of a famous hetman.

Senaki (Сена́ки) *Town, western Georgia*. The town, northwest of Samtredia, arose from a monastic settlement and is said to take its name from a Mingrelian word meaning "cells." In 1935 it was renamed *Mikha Tskhakaya* (Ми́ха Цхака́я), for the Georgian Communist politician Mikhail Grigoryevich *Tskhakaya* (1865–1950), with *Mikha* (from his first name) his party pseudonym when engaged in underground activities. In 1976 the town's name was shortened to *Tskhakaya*. It readopted its original name in 1991.

Senno (Сенно́) *Town, northeastern Belarus*. The town, in good pastureland northwest of Orsha, derives its name from Russian *seno*, "hay."

Serafimovich (Серафимо́вич) *Town, southwestern Russia*. The town, northwest of Volgograd, was originally a village by the name of *Ust-Medveditskaya* (Усть-Медве́дицкая), from its location at the mouth (Russian *ust'ye*) of the *Medveditskaya* River. In 1933 it received its present name, in honor of the Soviet writer Aleksandr Serafimovich *Serafimovich* (original surname Popov) (1863-1949), who was born near here.

Serdobsk (Сердо́бск) *Town, western Russia*. The town, southwest of Penza, takes its name from the *Serdoba* River on which it lies. The river name has been not very convincingly derived from a Mordovian word *syardo*, "deer," "elk."

Serebryany Bor (Сере́бряный бор) *District, Moscow, western Russia*. The western district of Moscow has a name that describes its main natural feature, a "silver wood." Many of the trees in the coniferous forest here are over 200 years old.

Sereda See **Furmanov**.

Sergey Kirov Islands (Серге́я Ки́рова острова́) *Island group, northwestern Russia*. The group of six small islands, in the Kara Sea, was discovered in 1934 and named for the Soviet politician *Sergey* Mironovich *Kirov* (1888-1934), a leading aide of Stalin. The largest in the group is **Isachenko Island**.

Sergiyev See **Sergiyev Posad**.

Sergiyev Posad (Се́ргиев Поса́д) *Town, western Russia*. The town, northeast of Moscow, is famous for its monastery of the Trinity and St. *Sergius*, founded in the mid-14th century by St. *Sergius* of Radonezh (1314-1392). A number of settlements grew up around it, which through the constant stream of pilgrims and worshippers developed into a thriving commercial town. Hence the name, meaning "Sergius's trading quarter." In 1919 the name was abbreviated to *Sergiyev*. In 1930 it was changed altogether to *Zagorsk* (Заго́рск), in memory of the Russian revolutionary Vladimir Mikhaylovich *Zagorsky* (original surname Lubotsky) (1883-1919), killed in the Civil War by a counterrevolutionary bomb in the Moscow headquarters of the regional Bolshevik committee, of which he was secretary. In 1991 the town reverted to its original name.

Sergo See **Stakhanov**.

Sernovodsk (Серново́дск) *Town, western Russia*. The town and health resort, northeast of Samara, is noted for its sulfurous springs. Hence its name, from Russian *sernyj*, "sulfurous," and *vody*, "waters."

Serov (Серо́в) *City, west central Russia*. The city, just east of the Middle Urals, arose in 1894 around an ironworks here manufacturing rails for the Transsiberian Railway. Its original name was *Nadezhdinsk* (Наде́ждинск), for *Nadezhda* Polovtseva, the ironworks owner. This name lasted until 1939, with the exception of the short period 1934-37, when the town was renamed *Kabakovsk* (Кабако́вск),for the Soviet Communist official Ivan Dmitriyevich *Kabakov* (1891-1937), a victim of the Great Purge. The present name was given in honor of the Soviet pilot Anatoly Konstantinovich *Serov* (1910-1939), who was born near here. He played an active part in the Spanish Civil War but was killed in an air crash.

Serpukhov (Се́рпухов) *City, western Russia*. The city, south of

Moscow, dates from at least the 14th century and is said to take its name from a dialect word *serpukh* meaning either "sickle" or used as the name of a species of herb (*Serratula tinctoria*). However, it may actually derive from a river name, although the city itself is on the Oka.

Sestra (Сестра́) *River, western Russia*. The river, north of Moscow, has a name that appears to represent the Russian word for "sister" but that probably derives from an Indoeuropean root element *ser-* meaning "flowing." The name is found elsewhere in Russia. Cf. **Sestroretsk**.

Sestroretsk (Сестроре́цк) *Town, western Russia*. The town, on the Gulf of Finland northwest of St. Petersburg, takes its name from the *Sestra* River here, with the second part of the name representing Russian *reka*, "river." Cf. **Sestra**.

Sevan (Сева́н) *Lake, northern Armenia*. The name is of uncertain origin. It has been popularly understood to mean "blue river," hence its Turkish name of *Gökcha*, from *gök*, "sky," and *çay*, "river." But the recent discovery of a lakeside stone with a hieroglyphic inscription dating from the first millennium BC suggests that the actual origin may be in a word *sunia*, "lake." The ancient Greek name of the lake was *Lychnitis*, identical to the old Greek name of Lake Ohrid on the border between Macedonia and Albania. The town of *Sevan* on the northwestern shore of the lake arose from a village called *Yelenovka*, presumably from the dedication of its church to St. **Helen**.

Sevastopol (Севасто́поль) *City, southwestern Crimea, southern Ukraine*. The city, on the Black Sea coast, was founded on the site of the Tatar port of Akhtiar ("white cliff") in 1783 when the Crimea became part of Russia. The following year it was given its present name, after the Greek style then in fashion. The meaning is "great city," from Greek *sebastos*, "august," and *polis*, "town," "city." There were some half-dozen ancient towns named *Sebastopolis* in honor of the emperor Caesar *Augustus*. One of them, also on the Black Sea but further east, was where modern **Sukhumi** now stands.

Severgin, Mt. (Северги́на́ вулка́н) *Volcano, Kuril Islands, southeastern Russia*. The active volcano, on Kharimkotan island at the northern end of the Kurils, was so named by the Russian navigator I. F. Kruzenshtern (cf. **Kruzenshtern Strait**) for the Russian mineralogist and chemist Vasily Mikhaylovich *Severgin* (1765–1826).

Severnaya Dvina See **Dvina**.

Severnaya Zemlya See **North Land**.

Severny (Се́верный) *Town, northern Russia*. The town, northeast of Vorkuta at the northern end of the Urals, has a name simply meaning "northern" (Russian *severnyj*). There are several places of the name, relating to their location in a particular region or with regard to some other place further south.

Severodonetsk (Северодоне́цк) *Town, eastern Ukraine*. The town, northeast of Lisichansk, was founded in 1934 in the Donbass on the site of a new chemical combine. For this reason it was at first known as *Leskhimstroy* (Лесхимстро́й), "timber chemical plant." In 1958 it was renamed as now, from its location on the *Seversky Donets* River (see **Donets**).

Severodvinsk (Северодви́нск) *Town and port, northwestern Russia*. The town, west of Arkhangelsk, takes its name from the *Severnaya Dvina* (Northern Dvina) River, at the mouth of which it lies. (See **Dvina**.) In 1938 it was renamed *Molotovsk*

(Мо́лотовск), for the Soviet prime minister Vyacheslav Mikhaylovich *Molotov* (1890–1986). It reverted to its original name in 1957 when he was stripped of party and state offices after joining the "antiparty" group that tried to depose Khrushchev.

Severo-Kurilsk (Се́веро-Кури́льск) *Town, Kuril Islands, southeastern Russia.* The town, on Paramushir island, at the northern end of the Kuril chain, has a name referring to its location, from Russian *sever*, "north," and the island group name. There is also an implied contrast with **Yuzhno-Kurilsk**, at the southern end of the chain.

Severomorsk (Северомо́рск) *Town, northwestern Russia.* The town, a port on the Kola Peninsula northeast of Murmansk, has a name meaning "northern sea," from Russian *sever*, "north," and a form of *more*, "sea." It was raised to town status in 1951 and before this was known as *Vayenga* (Ва́енга), for a river of this name.

Severouralsk (Североура́льск) *Town, western Russia.* The town, west of Krasnoturinsk at the northern end of the Middle Urals, arose in 1944 from the merging of two mining settlements: Petropavlovsky ("Peter and Paul") and *Severouralskiye Boksitovyye Rudniki* ("Northern Urals Bauxite Mines"). It thus took its name from the latter. The bauxite deposits were discovered only in 1931, however, near the Petropavlov ironworks that had been founded on the Vargan River here in 1758.

Seversky Donets See **Donets**.

Sevsk (Севск) *Town, western Russia.* The town, south of Bryansk, takes its name from the *Sev* River on which it lies. The river's own name is of uncertain origin.

Shabbaz See **Biruni**.

Shabrovsky (Шабро́вский) *Town, western Russia.* The town, in the Middle Urals south of Yekaterinburg, derives its name from Russian dialect *shaber*, "neighbor."

Shadrinsk (Ша́дринск) *Town, west central Russia.* The town, northwest of Kurgan to the east of the Middle Urals, has a name that could be of Tatar origin and represent the word *shedra*, "glade," "clearing." It may, however, have actually evolved from a personal name or nickname, itself based on Russian dialect *shadra*, "pockmarked."

Shakhrisabz (Шахриса́бз) *Town, southeastern Uzbekistan.* The town, south of Samarkand, has a name representing Tajik *shakhr-i-sabz*, "green town." The reference is to the oasis in which the town is located.

Shakhtinsk (Ша́хтинск) *Town, east central Kazakhstan.* The town, southwest of Karaganda, derives its name from its important coal-mining industry, from Russian *shakhta*, "mine," "pit." (The word itself comes from German *Schacht*, "mineshaft," itself related to *Schaft*, English *shaft*.)

Shakhty (Ша́хты) *City, southwestern Russia.* The city, northeast of Rostov-on-Don, is an important coal-mining center in the eastern part of the Donbass. Hence its name, from Russian *shakhty*, the plural of *shakhta*, "mine." Before 1920 the town was known as *Aleksandrovsk-Grushevsky* (Алекса́ндровск-Груше́вский), the first part of this being the placename proper, "Alexander's (place)," the second presumably for a local landowner or coalowner, *Grushevsky*, his name added to distinguish this *Aleksandrovsk* from the many others. See also **Kamensk-Shakhtinsky**.

Shakhty See **Gusinoozersk**.

Shakhtyorsk[1] (Шахтёрск) *Town, Sakhalin, eastern Russia.* The town, on the west coast of Sakhalin island north of Uglegorsk, arose by a coalmine and was named for its workers, from Russian *shakhtyor*, "miner."

Shakhtyorsk[2] (Шахтёрск) *Town, eastern Ukraine*. The town, in the Donbass east of Makeyevka, was originally known as the settlement of *Katyk* (Катык). It grew to be an important coal-mining center, so was accordingly given its present name in 1953, from Russian *shakhtyor*, "miner."

Shantar Islands (Шантáрские островá) *Island group, Sea of Okhotsk, eastern Russia*. The islands, in the western part of the Sea of Okhotsk, derive their name from the Nivkh word *shantar*, simply meaning "islands." Apart from Sakhalin, the islands are the only ones of any note in this sea.

Sharlyk (Шарлы́к) *Village, southwestern Russia*. The village, northwest of Orenburg, has a name deriving from Bashkir *shar*, "swamp," "marsh," with the suffix *-lyk* meaning similarly "marshy place."

Sharypovo (Шары́пово) *Town, southern Russia*. The town, southwest of Achinsk, arose as a village in 1922. The origin of its name is uncertain. In 1985 it was renamed *Chernenko* (Черне́нко), to commemorate the Soviet head of state Konstantin Ustinovich *Chernenko* (1911–1985), who was born near here. In 1988, following Gorbachev's perestroika and the reappraisal of political values, the city reverted to its original name.

Shatilov Forest (Шати́лов лес) *Forest, western Russia*. The forest, east of Oryol, was planted in the 19th century and is named for the agriculturist who advised on the project, I. N. *Shatilov* (1824–1889).

Shatlyk (Шатлы́к) *Town, southern Turkmenistan*. The town, west of Mary, has a name of Turkic origin, from *shat*, a term for a mountain spur or rocky height, and the adjectival suffix *-lyk*.

Shatsk (Шацк) *Town, western Russia*. The town, southeast of Ryazan, takes its name from the *Shacha* River on which it was founded as a defensive post in 1553. The origin of the river name is uncertain.

Shaturtorf (Шатуртóрф) *Town, western Russia*. The town, east of Moscow, takes the first part of its name from that of the nearby town of *Shatura* and the second from its main activity, the production of peat (Russian *torf*, related to English *turf*). The town arose from the peatworks set up to supply fuel for the Shatura hydroelectric power station here, which came on stream in 1925.

Shaumyani (Шаумя́ни) *Town, southern Georgia*. The town, south of Tbilisi, was originally known as *Shulaveri* (Шулавéри). In 1925 it was renamed as now for the Georgian revolutionary active in the Caucasus, Stepan Georgiyevich *Shaumyan* (1878–1918), who was born in Tbilisi Cf. **Shaumyanovsk**.

Shaumyanovsk (Шаумя́новск) *Town, western Azerbaijan*. The town, southeast of Gyandzha, was originally known as *Nizhny Agdzhakend* (Нижний Агджакéнд), "lower Agdzha's town." In 1938 it received its present name, in honor of the Georgian revolutionary active in the Caucasus, Stepan Georgiyevich *Shaumyan* (1878–1918). Cf. **Shaumyani**.

Shaytanka See **Pervouralsk**.

Shcheglovsk See **Kemerovo**.

Shcherbakov See **Rybinsk**.

Shcherbinovka See **Dzerzhinsk**[3].

Shchors (Щорс) *Town, northern Ukraine*. The town, northeast of

Chernigov, was originally known as *Snovsk* (Сновск), for its location on the *Snov* River. In 1935 it was renamed as now for the Ukrainian Civil War hero, Nikolay Aleksandrovich *Shchors* (1895–1919), who was born here. Cf. **Shchorsk**.

Shchorsk (Щорск) *Town, east central Ukraine.* The town, southwest of Dneprodzerzhinsk, was originally known as *Bozhedarovka* (Божедáровка), "God's gift." It was subsequently renamed for the Ukrainian Civil War hero, Nikolay Aleksandrovich *Shchors* (1895–1919).

Shchuchye Ozero (Щýчье Óзеро) *Town, western Russia.* The town, west of Krasnoufimsk, takes its name from the identically named lake here, its own name meaning "pike lake." These fish abound in its deep waters.

Shelekhov (Шéлехов) *Town, southern Russia.* The town, southwest of Irkutsk, arose in 1956 around an aluminum works, gaining urban status in 1962. It is named for Grigory Ivanovich *Shelekhov* (1747–1795), leader of an expedition to explore the coasts of Alaska at a time when the first Russian colonies were established there. (Shelekhov was one of the founders of the Russian-American Company that set up trading bases in Alaska and California. *Shelikof Strait* between Kodiak Island and mainland Alaska is also named for him.) Shelekhov died in Irkutsk.

Shemakha (Шемахá) *Town, eastern Azerbaijan.* The town, northwest of Baku, is located in the southeastern foothills of the Caucasus. Hence its name, from Arabic *shamaha*, "height."

Shemordan (Шемордáн) *Town, western Russia.* The town, in Tatarstan northeast of Kazan, derives its name from Tatar *shomort*, "cherry tree." The region has a profusion of such trees.

Shenkursk (Шéнкурск) *Town, northwestern Russia.* The town, northwest of Kotlas, is located near the point where the *Shenga* River, for which it is named, flows into the Vaga. Its name is a shortened form of *Shenga-kurya*, with *kurya* a local term for a river bend.

Sherkaly (Шеркáлы) *Village, north central Russia.* The village, on the Ob River northwest of Khanty-Mansiysk, has a name deriving from Komi *sher-kar*, "middle town," itself a translation of Mansi *yat-us*. The place was a "halfway house" where Russians traveling to the lower reaches of the Ob could engage local Komi as guides and interpreters.

Sherlovaya Gora (Шéрловая Горá) *Town, southern Russia.* The town, southeast of Chita near the border with Mongolia and China, is so called from the mountain here of this name, famous for its semiprecious minerals, such as topaz, amethyst, smoky quartz, and tourmaline. The first word of the name derives from Russian *sherl*, a borrowing of German *Schörl* (English *schorl*), a type of black tourmaline.

Shevchenko (Шевчéнко) *Town, southwestern Kazakhstan.* The town, on the south coast of the Mangyshlak Peninsula, arose in 1963 on the discovery of natural oil and gas here. It was at first named *Aktau* (Актáу), from Kazakh *ak*, "white," and *tau*, "mountain." The following year it was renamed in honor of the Ukrainian poet and revolutionary, Taras Grigoryevich *Shevchenko* (1814–1861), exiled here in the 1850s. Cf. **Fort Shevchenko**.

Shikotan (Шикотáн) *Island, Kuril Islands, southeastern Russia.* The island, one of the southernmost of the Kurils, has a name representing Ainu *shi*, "good," "large," and *kotan*, "place." The island is regarded as the most pleasant and picturesque in the chain, and has an approachable and well protected bay.

Shikuka See **Poronaysk**.

Shilka (Шилка) *River, southeastern Russia*. The river, one of two main headstreams of the Amur, which it joins on the Chinese border, derives its name from Evenki *shilki*, a term for a narrow valley. In its lower reaches, the river passes between steep rocky slopes.

Shiritoru See **Makarov**.

Shlisselburg See **Petrokrepost**.

Shmidt Island (Шмидта остров) *Island, North Land, northern Russia*. The northwesternmost island in the group is named for the Soviet scientist Otto Yulyevich *Shmidt* (1891–1956), leader of the expedition on board the *G. Sedov* that discovered it in 1930.

Shmidt Peninsula (Шмидта полуостров) *Peninsula, Sakhalin, eastern Russia*. The peninsula, at the northern end of Sakhalin island, was so named in 1908 for the Russian geologist F. B. *Shmidt*, who surveyed Sakhalin in 1860-61.

Shokalsky Island (Шокальского остров) *Island, northwestern Russia*. The island, in the Kara Sea at the northeastern end of the Gulf of Ob, is named for the Soviet oceanographer Yuly Mikhaylovich *Shokalsky* (1856–1940), who investigated a northern sea route. It was discovered in 1874 by the British explorer Joseph Wiggins, who named it *Black Island*. In 1922 the island was visited by a Russian government-sponsored exploration party who named it *Agnessa* (Агнесса) ("Agnes"), after their ship. This name obtained until 1926, when the island was officially renamed as now.

Shorsu (Шорсу́) *Town, eastern Uzbekistan*. The town, southwest of Kokand, has a name representing the Turkic words *shor* (Kazakh *sor*), "saltmarsh," and *su*, "water," "river." Cf. **Shurab**.

Shulaveri See **Shaumyani**.

Shuraabad (Шураабад) *Village, eastern Azerbaijan*. The village, northwest of Baku, has a modern name deriving from Azerbaijani *shura*, "Soviet," and Iranian *-abad*, "inhabited place," "settlement."

Shurab (Шураб) *Town, northern Tajikistan*. The town, southwest of Isfara near the border with Kyrgyzstan, takes its name from the river here. Its own name represents Turkic *shur*, "saltmarsh," and Iranian *ab*, "water," "river." Cf. **Shorsu**. There are several places of the same name in Iran.

Shuya[1] (Шу́я) *Town, western Russia*. The town, southeast of Ivanovo, takes its name from the river on which it lies. Its own name is probably of Finnic origin and may mean "thawed," "melted," referring to a river whose waters ran freely after a frozen winter. The town goes back to at least 1539, and was originally known as *Borisoglebskaya sloboda*, "Boris and Gleb's village," from the dedication of its church to these two Slavic saints. (Cf. **Borisoglebsk**.)

Shuya[2] (Шу́я) *Town, northwestern Russia*. The town, in Karelia north of Petrozavodsk, takes its name from the river on which it stands. The river's own name is generally regarded as deriving from Finnish *suo*, "marsh," "swamp." It rises in Lake **Suoyarvi** ("swamp lake") and flows into Lake Onega, and its earlier name was *Suoyoki*, "swamp river," from Finnish *suo* and *joki*, "river." It remains uncertain why the lake should have retained its original name while the river came to be known differently. It is difficult (although not impossible) to see

Shuya as a linguistic development of *Suoyoki*.

Šiauliai (Шяуляй) *Town, northern Lithuania*. The town, east of Klaipeda, dates from the 15th century, and has been known by various forms of the name, including *Saule* to 1795 and *Shavli* from then until 1917. The Germans knew it as *Schaulen*. The origin is probably in a personal name such as *Saul*.

Sibay (Сибай) *Town, southwestern Russia*. The town, in Bashkortostan southwest of Magnitogorsk, arose from the two settlements of *Starosibayevo* ("Old Sibay") and *Novosibayevo* ("New Sibay") that had themselves developed around the iron and copper deposits discovered here in the early 19th century. The name ultimately goes back to the Bashkir personal name *Sibay*.

Siberia (Сибирь) *Region, central and eastern Russia*. The broad region, extending west to east from the Urals to the Pacific, and north to south from the Arctic Ocean to central Kazakhstan and the borders of Mongolia and China, has a name of much disputed origin. Some authorities trace it back to the 5th century BC. It is most likely to be an ethnic name, deriving from that of a Finno-Ugrian people who inhabited the southern region of western Siberia. Under the influence of Tatar repression, the people were driven north while also being assimilated by the Tatars themselves. The name thus extended its range and came to apply to the Tatars in turn. It is first recorded as *Sebur* in a Persian map of 1375. Any attempts to link the name to a concrete word, such as Russian *sever*, "north," are purely speculative.

Siberian Sea See **Laptev Sea**.

Sibiryakov Island (Сибирякова остров) *Island, Kara Sea, northern Russia*. The island, in the southern part of the Kara Sea near the Yenisey estuary, was so named in 1878 by the Swedish explorer Nils Adolf Erik Nordenskiöld as a tribute to the Russian goldmine owner and authority on Siberia, Aleksandr Mikhaylovich *Sibiryakov* (1849–1893), who had financed his expedition.

Sim (Сим) *Town, southwestern Russia*. The town, in Bashkortostan west of Zlatoust, takes its name from the *Sim* River on which it arose from the ironworks founded here in the second half of the 18th century. The Bashkir name of the river is *Esem*, which possibly itself derives from a Turkic word meaning "silver" (modern Turkish *sim*). This would allude to the silvery color of the water.

Simbirsk (Симбирск) *City, western Russia*. The city, on the west bank of the Volga south of Kazan, was founded in 1648 as the fortress of *Sinbirsk*, believed to derive from a Tatar personal name. In 1780 this was modified to the present form. In 1924 it was renamed *Ulyanovsk* (Улвяновск), for V. I. *Ulyanov*, otherwise Lenin, who was born here. The city reverted to its original name in 1991.

Simferopol (Симферополь) *City, south central Crimea, southern Ukraine*. The city stands on the site of an ancient Scythian town and fortress that existed in the 4th century BC. The site was subsequently settled by the Tatars in the 15th century as *Ak-Mechet*, "white mosque." The present city was founded in 1784 and given a Greek-style name in the fashion of the day. It is usually explained as deriving from Greek *sumferō*, "I bring together," "I gather," and *polis*, "town," as if it "gathered" or united the various parts of Crimea by its central position. But it seems likely that the intended sense was another meaning of the Greek verb: "to be useful." This is illustrated by the city's historic coat of arms, which shows a beehive surrounded by bees. The town was thus effectively planned as a trading center. The name was a modern creation, and unlike most other Greek-style names had no classical prototype.

Simonovo (Си́моново) *District, Moscow, western Russia*. The southern district of Moscow takes its name from the medieval *Simonov* monastery here, itself so called as it was founded in 1379 on land owned by the boyar S. V. Khovrin, whose monastic name was *Simon*.

Sinelnikovo (Сине́льниково) *Town, eastern Ukraine*. The town, southeast of Dnepropetrovsk, takes its name from a Yekaterinoslav landowner of the 1780s, I. M. *Sinelnikov*, who fought in the Russo-Turkish wars.

Sintur (Си́нтур) *Lake, west central Russia*. The lake, east of the Central Urals, lies in the center of an extensive area of marshland, where it is surrounded by several smaller lakes. Hence its name, meaning "heart lake," from Mansi *sim*, "heart," and *tur*, "lake."

Sit (Сить) *River, western Russia*. The river, which flows into the Rybinsk Reservoir north of Moscow, derives its name from a basic Slavic word meaning "reed" (related to Polish *sitowie*, "bulrush").

Sivash (Сива́ш) *Inlet, Sea of Azov, northeastern Crimea, southern Ukraine*. The area of salt lagoons and marshes takes its name from a Turkic word for a shallow inlet, itself related to modern Turkish *sıvaşmak*, "to be dirty," "to become sticky." The local Russian name of the region is *Gniloe more*, "putrid sea," referring to its unpleasant smell. In summer the area is covered by a layer of mineral salts.

Sivomaskinsky (Сивома́скинский) *Town, northern Russia*. The town, southwest of Vorkuta, takes its name from the village of *Sivaya Maska*, itself named for its Komi founder, known as *Sivey Mazka*. (Komi *sivey* means "gray-haired," and *Mazka* is a pet form of the personal name *Mazay*.) Under Russian influence the name was popularly interpreted as *Sivaya Maska*, "gray mask."

Skadovsk (Скадо́вск) *Town, southern Ukraine*. The town, a resort on the Black Sea coast southeast of Kherson, takes its name from the local *Skadovsky* family who owned an estate here.

Skobelev See **Fergana**.

Skopin (Скопи́н) *Town, western Russia*. The town, south of Ryazan, probably takes its name from an old personal name *Skopa* rather than from Russian *skopa*, "osprey," or *skopit'sya*, "to gather," as has been proposed by some.

Skorodnoye (Скоро́дное) *Village, western Russia*. The village, southeast of Kursk, takes its name from a dialect word *skorodit'*, "to harrow." Other villages of the name exist elsewhere in southwestern Russia and Ukraine.

Skovorodino (Сковородино́) *Town, southeastern Russia*. The town, east of Yerofey-Pavlovich near the border with China, was originally known as *Rukhlovo* (Ру́хлово). In 1938 it was renamed to commemorate A. N. *Skovorodin*, a local Communist party official, who was executed by Japanese interventionists in 1920.

Skvira (Скви́ра) *Town, central Ukraine*. The town, southwest of Kiev, probably takes its name from that of a local river. If so, the river name may itself derive from a word related to Russian *skvernyj*, "bad," "foul," or to a local word *skvira*, "crevice."

Slantsy (Сла́нцы) *Town, western Russia*. The town, southwest of St.

Petersburg, arose from a slate-mining settlement established in the early 1930s. Hence its name, from Russian *slantsy*, "slates," "schist."

Slavgorod (Слáвгород) *Town, eastern Belarus.* The town, southeast of Mogilyov, was originally a village called *Propoysk* (Пропóйск), a development of a name recorded in 1150 as *Proposhesk* or *Prupoy*. The exact sense of this is uncertain, but it probably relates to the name of the *Pronya*, since the town stands at the point where this river enters the Sozh. In 1945 the town was renamed as now to mark the Soviet Army's victories in World War II, from Russian *slava*, "glory," and *gorod*, "town." Cf. **Slavsk**.

Slavsk (Слáвск) *Town, western Russia.* The town, northeast of Kaliningrad, was originally known by its German name of *Heinrichswalde*, "Heinrich's wood." It was renamed as now in 1946 to mark Soviet victory over the Germans in World War II, from Russian *slava*, "glory." Cf. **Slavgorod**.

Slavyansk (Славя́нск) *Town, eastern Ukraine.* The town, north of Kramatorsk, was founded in 1676 as the Cossack fortress of *Tor*, named for the river on which it lies. It was renamed *Slovensk* in 1784 by order of Catherine the Great when raised to town status. The name was based on (now obsolete) Russian *slovene*, "Slavs." In 1794 it assumed its present form, from Russian *slavyane*, with the same meaning. The name commemorates the liberation of the southern Slavs from Turkish domination.

Sloboda (Слободá) *Town, western Russia.* The town, southeast of Voronezh, has a name found elsewhere in western Russia. It derives from the historic word *sloboda* as a term for a settlement exempt from the usual state obligations, such as tolls and taxes. (The word is a form of Russian *svoboda*, "freedom.") Cf. **Slobodskoy**.

Slobodskoy (Слободскóй) *Town, western Russia.* The town, east of Kirov, was founded in 1546 and was originally known as *Sloboda*. Like other places of this name, it was so designated as it was exempt from the normal state obligations. Cf. **Sloboda**. It took the present (adjectival) form of the name in 1780, when it was raised to town status.

Slonim (Слóним) *Town, west central Belarus.* The town, west of Baranovichi, has a name meaning "protected," from a root *slon* related to Russian *zaslon*, "hiding place," "screen." The town is in a low-lying valley.

Sluch (Случь) *River, northwestern Ukraine.* The river has a name borne by others in the Dnieper basin. It probably derives from a Slavic root word related to modern Russian *luka*, "bend," referring to its winding course. See also **Slutsk**.

Slutsk (Слуцк) *Town, south central Belarus.* The town, south of Minsk, takes its name from the *Sluch* River on which it stands. See **Sluch**.

Slyudyanka (Слюдя́нка) *Town, southern Russia.* The town, at the western end of Lake Baykal, takes its name from the mica (Russian *slyuda*) that is its chief industrial product.

Smolensk (Смолéнск) *City, western Russia.* The city, on the Dnieper west of Moscow, is first recorded in the 9th century. The name was long believed to derive from that of the local people, who were known as the *smolyane*, "tar folk," from their custom of tarring their boats, from Russian *smola*, "tar," "pitch." But recent authorities derive the name from a topographic reference to the local soil, which is marshy and of a pitchlike color and consistency.

Snov (Снов) *River, western Russia.* The river, a tributary of the Desna, forms part of the boundary between Russia and Ukraine near the border with Belarus. Its name probably derives from an Indoeuropean root element meaning simply "flowing."

Snovsk See **Shchors**.

Snyatyn (Снятын) *Town, southwestern Ukraine.* The town, southeast of Ivano-Frankovsk, derives its name from *Kosnyata*, a local form of the personal name *Konstantin*, "Constantine," with the final -*yn* a possessive suffix.

Sochi (Со́чи) *Town and port, southwestern Russia.* The town, a popular resort on the Black Sea coast near the Georgian border, has a name of ethnic origin, from the *Shacha*, a Circassian people who at one time inhabited the region.

Sofrino (Со́фрино) *Town, western Russia*, The town, north of Moscow, was known in the 15th century as *Suponevo*, from the name of the estate owner here, *Suponev*. In the 16th century the village passed to Ivan *Safarin*, a Crimean merchant, and the name was altered accordingly to *Safarino*. The present name evolved from this.

Sokol (Со́кол) *Town, western Russia.* The town, northeast of Vologda, takes its name from the *Sokol* paper mill that was built here on the Sukhona River in the late 19th century. The name itself means "falcon."

Sokolniki (Соко́льники) *District, Moscow, western Russia.* The northeastern district of Moscow, now best known for its amusement park and sports stadium, stands on the site of a forest which in the 17th century was used for the czar's falconry. Hence its name, from Russian *sokol'nik*, "falconer" (from *sokol*, "falcon").

Soligalich (Солига́лич) *Town, western Russia.* The town, east of Vologda, was known in the 14th century as *Sol-Galitskaya*, from Russian *sol'*, "salt," and the name of the nearby town of *Galich*. This was subsequently modified to the present name. The region, in the Upper Volga basin, was long famous for its salt extraction.

Soligorsk (Солиго́рск) *Town, south central Belarus.* The town, south of Slutsk, arose in 1958 as a potassium-mining center and was originally called *Novo-Starobinsk* (Но́во-Старо́бинск), "New Starobin," for its proximity to the latter town. In 1959 it was renamed as now, from Russian *sol'*, "salt" (potassium is found in salt deposits), and either *gorod*, "town," or *gora*, "mining." Cf. **Solikamsk**.

Solikamsk (Солика́мск) *Town, western Russia.* The town, on the Kama River west of the Middle Urals, was founded in the second half of the 15th century by a saltmine, and subsequently became a major center of salt extraction. Hence its name, from Russian *sol'*, "salt," and the river name *Kama*. This form of the name was given to distinguish the place from the older salt-mining center of **Solvychegodsk**.

Sol-Iletsk (Соль-Иле́цк) *Town, southwestern Russia.* The town, south of Orenburg near the border with Kazakhstan, is a major salt-mining center. Hence its name, from Russian *sol'*, "salt," and the name of the *Ilek* River on which it lies. The town arose in the 17th century as a Cossack defensive post, and the fortress built in 1754 was known as *Iletskaya Zashchita*, "Ilek defense." The town that grew up came to be called simply *Iletsk*, and the first part of the name was added in 1945. The meaning of the river name is uncertain. It is not from Russian *il*, "silt."

Solnechnogorsk (Солнечногорск) *Town, western Russia.* The town, northwest of Moscow, arose in 1928 as the settlement of *Solnechnogorsky* (Солнечногорский), formed from the village of *Solnechnaya Gora,* "sunny hill," and the railroad settlement of *Podsolnechnoye,* "(place) by Solnechnaya Gora." The present form of the name came in 1938 when it was raised to town status.

Solnechnogorsky See **Solnechnogorsk.**

Solnechnoye (Со́лнечное) *Town, western Russia.* The town and resort, on the Gulf of Finland northwest of St. Petersburg, originally had the Finnish name of *Ollila.* It was given its present name in 1948. The ostensible meaning is "sunny," as appropriate for a seaside town. The specific reference, however, is to a performance of Maxim Gorky's play *Children of the Sun* (Russian *Deti solntsa*) staged in an open-air theater here in the summer of 1905.

Solomennoye (Соло́менное) *Town, western Russia.* The town, on Lake Onega northeast of Petrozavodsk, has a name that as it stands is the adjectival form of Russian *soloma,* "straw." The reference is presumably to the brickworks here, since bricks were originally made with straw as a binding agent. The biblical story about making bricks without straw (Exodus 5) is hardly likely to have been used here for ideological purposes.

Solovetsky Islands (Солове́цкие острова́) *Island group, northwestern Russia.* The islands, in the White Sea off the east coast of Karelia, take their name from a Saam (Lapp) word *suolov,* simply meaning "island." The colloquial Russian name for the islands, famous for their ancient monastery, is *Solovki.*

Solvychegodsk (Сольвычего́дск) *Town, western Russia.* The town, northeast of Kotlas, was founded in the 14th century and in the 15th century was known as *Soli Vychegodskiye,* "Vychegda salts," for the salt mines here by the **Vychegda** River (see this name). The name was subsequently modified to its present form. Cf. **Solikamsk.**

Soroka See **Belomorsk.**

Soroki (Соро́ки) *Town, northern Moldova.* The town, near the Ukrainian border, has a name representing Moldovan *saraki,* "poverty," a reminder of the town's difficult past. The name assumed its present form under the influence of Russian *soroka,* "magpie."

Sorokino See **Krasnodon.**

Sortavala (Со́ртавала) *Town, northwestern Russia.* The town, at the northern end of Lake Ladoga, north of St. Petersburg, has a name of disputed origin. Attempts have been made to derive it from Finnish *sortaa,* "to oppress," *sortua,* "to collapse," or *sorttava,* "cutting," this last allegedly relating to the town's location on a lengthy inlet. Until 1918 the town was known as *Serdobol,* generally regarded as a Russian form of the Finnish original name. The town is believed to have been founded in 1617.

Sosna (Сосна́) *River, western Russia.* The river, south of Moscow, is a tributary of the Don. Its name outwardly suggests Russian *sosna,* "pine," but this cannot be the meaning, since a river name derived from a tree would have an adjectival or other derivative form. The actual origin of the name is uncertain.

Sosnogorsk (Сосного́рск) *Town, northwestern Russia.* The town, east of Ukhta, has a name that blends Russian *sosna,* "pine," with *gorod,* "town," rather than *gora,* "hill." The town is in a low-lying region on the Izhma River. The latter gave its earlier name, to 1957, as *Izhma.*

Sosnovoborsk (Сосновобо́рск) *Town, western Russia*. The town, east of Penza, has a name descriptive of its location, from Russian *sosnovyj bor*, "pine forest." Until 1940 it was a village called *Litvino* (Литви́но). Cf. **Sosnovy Bor**.

Sosnovy Bor (Сосно́вый Бор) *Town, western Russia*. The town, on the Gulf of Finland west of St. Petersburg, has a name that is Russian for "pine forest," describing its natural surroundings.

Sovetabad (Советаба́д) *Town, eastern Uzbekistan*. The town, in the extreme east of the republic, near the border with Kyrgyzstan, was originally the village of *Karabagish* (Карабаги́ш), from Turkic words meaning "black gift" (modern Turkish *kara*, "black," and *bağış*, "gift"), referring to the fertility of the area in the Fergana Valley. In 1972 the town received its present name, found (or formerly found) elsewhere in Turkic-speaking regions, meaning "Soviet city." Cf. **Gafurov**.

Sovetabad See **Gafurov**.

Sovetsk[1] (Сове́тск) *Town, western Russia*. The town, northeast of Kaliningrad near the border with Lithuania, was originally known by the German name of *Tilsit*, from the *Tilsa* River that flows into the Neman here. Its own name derives from Lithuanian *tilszus*, "marshy." In 1946 it was renamed as now, from a shortened form of Russian *sovetskij*, "Soviet." (This adjective normally has no short form, but it was here used to accord with other placenames ending in *-sk*, such as *Bryansk* and *Kursk*.)

Sovetsk[2] (Сове́тск) *Town, western Russia*. The town, southwest of Kirov, was originally a village named *Kukarka* (Кука́рка). In 1937 it was given its present name, meaning "Soviet." (See **Sovetsk**[1].)

Sovetskaya Gavan (Сове́тская Га́вань) *Town and port, eastern Russia*. The town, a seaport on the Tatar Strait northeast of Khabarovsk, has a name meaning "Soviet harbor," from Russian *sovetskij*, feminine *sovetskaya*, "Soviet," and *gavan'*, "harbor." This is the name of the bay here that was discovered in 1853 by the Russian naval lieutenant Nikolay Konstantinovich Boshnyak (1830–1899), member of a local exploratory expedition, and named by him *Imperatorskaya gavan'* (Импера́торская га́вань), "Imperial Harbor," in honor of the reigning czar, Nicholas I (1796–1855). The bay was given its present name in 1923.

Sovetskoye See **Zelenokumsk**.

Soviet Union See **Russia**.

Spas-Demensk (Спас-Де́менск) *Town, western Russia*. The town, southeast of Smolensk, takes the first part of its name from the dedication of its church, from Russian *Spas*, "Savior," and the second part apparently from a personal name, *Demyan*, "Damian," also possibly a church dedication.

Spas-Klepiki (Спас-Кле́пики) *Town, western Russia*. The town, northeast of Ryazan, takes the first part of its name from the dedication of its church, from Russian *Spas*, "Savior," and the second part from the local word *klepik*, a term for a fish-cleaning knife, from a word related to modern Russian *klepat'*, "to rivet." The town was noted for fish gutting and cleaning here by the Pra River.

Spassk (Спасск) *Town, southern Russia*. The town, southeast of Novokuznetsk, takes its name from Russian *Spas*, "Savior," from the dedication of its church or monastery. There were many places of this name, and the larger ones added a second word for purposes of distinction. Cf. **Spassk-Dalny**, **Spassk-Ryazansky**.

Spassk See (1) **Bednodemyanovsk**, (2) **Kuybyshev**[2].

Spassk-Dalny (Спасск-Да́льний) *Town, southeastern Russia.* The town, northeast of Vladivostok, derives the first part of its name from the Russian word for "Savior" (see **Spassk**) and the second from *Dal'nij Vostok*, "Far East," denoting its location.

Spassk-Ryazansky (Спасск-Ряза́нский) *Town, western Russia.* The town, southeast of Ryazan, takes the first part of its name from the Russian word for "Savior" (see **Spassk**) and the second from **Ryazan**, denoting its location.

Spassk-Tatarsky See **Kuybyshev**[2].

Srednekolymsk (Среднеколы́мск) *Town, eastern Russia.* The town has a name meaning "middle Kolyma," denoting its location on the middle reaches of the *Kolyma* River, approximately midway between *Nizhnekolymsk* ("lower Kolyma") and *Verkhnekolymsk* ("upper Kolyma").

Sredneuralsk (Среднеура́льск) *Town, western Russia.* The town, northwest of Yekaterinburg, arose during construction in 1932 of the Sredneuralskaya ("Middle Urals") state regional electric power station. The station came on stream in 1936 and the power workers' settlement that developed around it gained town status in 1966.

Sredneye (Сре́днее) *Town, western Ukraine.* The town, southeast of Uzhgorod, has a name meaning "middle," presumably because it is midway between Uzhgorod and Mikachevo.

Sretensk (Сре́тенск) *Town, southern Russia.* The town, east of Chita, takes its name from the dedication of its church, from Russian *Sreteniye*, "Purification (of the Virgin Mary)." (The word literally means "meeting," referring to the meeting between Simeon and the infant Christ in the temple, as recounted in Luke 2:25-35.)

Stakhanov (Стаха́нов) *Town, eastern Ukraine.* The town, in the Donbass east of Kramatorsk, arose in the mid-19th century as the coal-mining settlement of *Kadiyevka* (Ка́диевка), presumably named for its initiator. It was at a mine on its outskirts that the face-worker Aleksey Grigoryevich *Stakhanov* (1906-1977) hewed a record amount of coal one August shift in 1935, thus inspiring the Stakhanovite system, whereby workers who met high production norms received special privileges and rewards. Kadiyevka became *Sergo* (Серго́) in 1937, but reverted to its original name in 1940. It eventually adopted Stakhanov's name in 1978.

Stalinabad See **Dushanbe**.

Stalingrad See **Volgograd**.

Stalino See **Donetsk**[1].

Stalinogorsk See **Novomoskovsk**.

Stalin Peak See **Communism Peak**.

Stalinsk See **Novokuznetsk**.

Stanislav See **Ivano-Frankovsk**.

Stanovoy Range (Станово́й хребе́т) *Mountain range, eastern Russia.* The range, between Yakutia and the Sea of Okhotsk, derives its name from the standard Russian word *stanovoy*, "main," "chief," distinguishing this range from other, smaller ones in the Russian Far East. The name does not derive from Russian *ostanovka*, "stop," as sometimes explained, supposedly because the range impeded Russian expansion eastward.

Stantsiya Regar See **Tursunzade**.

Staraya Russa (Ста́рая Ру́сса) *Town, western Russia.* The town, south of Novgorod, is recorded in documents dating from the 12th century. The name as it stands means "old Russa," with the first word representing Russian *staryj*, feminine *staraya*, "old," and the second perhaps related to *Rus*, the name of ancient Russia (which historically arose in this region).

Staritsa (Ста́рица) *Town, western Russia*. The town, southwest of Tver, was founded in 1297 on a slightly different site with the name *Gorodok*, "little town." In 1365 it was transferred to the banks of the Volga and was renamed *Novy Gorodok*, "new little town." It took its present name in the 15th century. It represents the standard Russian word *staritsa* used for an old river bed, here that of a river entering the Volga. The name is found elsewhere in this sense.

Starobelsk (Старобе́льск) *Town, eastern Ukraine*. The town, northeast of Lisichansk, arose from a settlement founded here in 1686 with the name *Staraya Belaya*, literally "old white." The second word may have referred to the color of the buildings, or else have symbolically referred to something favorable such as freedom from local tolls or taxes. The two words later blended to give the present name.

Starodub (Староду́б) *Town, western Russia*. The town, southwest of Bryansk near the Ukrainian border, is mentioned in a document dated 1096 and has a name meaning "old oak," from Russian *staryj*, "old," and *dub*, "oak." Oaks are noted for their longevity.

Starokadomsky Island (Старока́домского о́стров) *Island, northern Russia*. The island, south of North Land, was discovered by the crew of the icebreaker *Taymyr* in 1913 and the following year named for the ship's doctor, Leonid Mikhaylovich *Starokadomsky* (1875–1962).

Starosubkhangulovo (Старосубхангу́лово) *Village, southwestern Russia*. The village, in Bashkortostan southeast of Salavat, has a name meaning "Old Sobkhangol," with Russian *staryj*, "old," translating Bashkir *iske*. *Sobkhangol* is a common Turkic name.

Staroutkinsk See **Novoutkinsk**.

Stary Krym (Ста́рый Крым) *Town, eastern Crimea, southern Ukraine*. The town, west of Feodosiya, has a name meaning "old Crimea," as a Russian part-translation of its original Turkish name, *Eski-Kerim*. (See **Crimea**.) The present name was adopted in 1784 when the Crimea became part of Russia.

Stary Oskol (Ста́рый Оско́л) *Town, western Russia*. The town, southeast of Kursk, was founded in 1593 as a fortress on the southern frontier of the Russian empire and was at first simply named *Oskol*, for the river on which it stands. In 1655 the town of *Tsarev Alekseyev*, "Czar Alexis's (town)," further south on the same river, was renamed *Novy Oskol*, "new Oskol." The original *Oskol* then became *Stary Oskol*, "old Oskol," for purposes of distinction. See also **Oskol**.

Stavropol (Ста́врополь) *City, southwestern Russia*. The town, east of Armavir north of the Caucasus, was founded in 1777 as a fortified post to defend the southern frontier of the Russian empire. It was given a Greek-style name, in the fashion of the day, to mean "town of the cross," from Greek *stauros*, "cross," and *polis*, "town." The reference would have been to the Christian cross, and the name may have been adopted from the existing *Stavropol*, now **Tolyattigrad** (which see). From 1935 to 1943 the city was renamed *Voroshilovsk* (Вороши́ловск), for the

Soviet military leader and president, Kliment Yefremovich *Voroshilov* (1881-1969). It reverted to its original name following his disgrace in World War II.

Stavropol See **Tolyattigrad**.

Stekolny (Стекóльный) *Town, eastern Russia*. The town, north of Magadan, has a name that is the adjectival form of Russian *steklo*, "glass," referring to its glassworks.

Stepanakert See **Khankendy**.

Stepanavan (Степанавáн) *Town, northwestern Armenia*. The town, northeast of Leninakan, was originally named *Dzhalal-ogly*, for a local landholder. In 1924 it was given its present name, in honor of Stepan Georgiyevich Shaumyan (1878-1918), a Georgian revolutionary active in Transcaucasia, who was executed by the British in the Civil War. The final *-van* means "settlement," "land." Cf. **Shaumyani**, **Shaumyanovsk**.

Stepan Razin (Степáн Рáзин) *Town, eastern Azerbaijan*. The town, immediately east of Baku, derives its name from that of Stepan Razin (1630-1671), Cossack leader of a peasant rebellion on Russia's southeastern frontier.

Stepantsminda See **Kazbegi**.

Stepnoy See **Elista**.

Sterlitamak (Стерлитамáк) *Town, western Russia*. The town, in Bashkortostan south of Ufa, was founded in 1766 at the confluence of the Belaya and Sterlya rivers. Hence the name, from *Sterlya* and Bashkir *tamak*, "mouth." Any meaningful interpretation of the river name has so far proved elusive.

Stolby (Столбы́) *Nature reserve, southern Russia*. The nature reserve, south of Krasnoyarsk, was set up in 1925 to protect and study the animal and plant life of this mountain region. Its name means "Columns," referring to a tourist section containing around 80 groups of unusual rock formations. Many rocks have individual names, such as *Ded* ("The Grandfather"), *Krepost* ("The Fortress"), *Berkut* ("The Golden Eagle"), *Baba* ("The Old Woman"), etc.

Stoletiya Cape (Столéтия мыс) *Cape, northeastern Russia*. The cape, on the south coast of the Chukot Peninsula, has a name meaning "centennial cape," from Russian *stoletiye*, "centenary." It was so named in 1828 by the Russian navigator F. P. Litke (see **Litke Strait**), since exactly 100 years previously Vitus Bering had sailed through the **Bering Strait** to the east.

Stroitel (Строи́тель) *Town, southwestern Russia*. The town, northwest of Belgorod, has a name translating as "builder," referring to the construction materials manufactured here.

Stry (Стрый) *Town, western Ukraine*. The town, south of Lvov, takes its name from the river on which it lies. The river name means simply "current," and is related to words in various European languages such as Russian *struit'*, "to pour," German *Strom*, "river," and English *stream*.

Stuchka (Сту́чка) *Town, central Latvia*. The town, southeast of Riga, arose in the 1960s during construction of a hydroelectric power station. It is named for Pyotr Ivanovich *Stuchka* (1865-1932), a founder of the Latvian Communist Party, who was born near here.

Suchan See **Partizansk**.

Sudak (Судáк) *Town, southeastern Crimea, southern Ukraine*. The present name of the ancient town, southwest of Feodosiya, is a Turkic alteration of the historic Greek name *Sugdaia*. This itself is Iranian in origin, and possibly means "holy." More likely, however, it is related to the name of *Sogdiana*, the ancient country of Central Asia centered on modern Uzbekistan. In medieval times Sudak was recorded in Russian annals as *Surozh* (Сурож). Cf. **Surazh**.

Sufikishlak See **Akhunbabayev**.

Sukhoy Log (Сухой Лог) *Town, west central Russia.* The town, east of Yekaterinburg, arose in the 17th century and took the name of the site here, meaning "dry valley." (Russian *log*, related to *lezhat'*, "to lie," is a word for a long, broad gully.) The name is found elsewhere as a descriptive term for a specific natural feature.

Sukhumi (Сухуми) *City and port, northwestern Georgia.* The city that is now the capital of Abkhazia, on the Black Sea coast, arose on the site of the ancient Greek colony of *Dioscurias*, so named for the *Dioscuri*, the mythological twins Castor and Pollux. This then became the (Greek-named) Roman fortified town of *Sebastopolis*, "great town." (Cf. **Sevastopol**.) In medieval times the town was known as *Tskhumi*, from the Georgian word meaning "hot." When the town was under Turkish control from the 17th through 19th centuries, its name was *Sukhum-Kale*, which although still basically a Georgian name was understood to represent Turkish *su*, "water," "river," *kum*, "sand," and *kale*, "fortress," so that it was the "fortified place on the sandy river." Its Russian name of *Sukhum* was modified to the Georgian form *Sukhumi* in 1939.

Sulimov See **Cherkessk**.

Sumgait (Сумгаит) *Town, eastern Azerbaijan.* The town, on the Apsheron Peninsula northwest of Baku, has a name that is possibly of ethnic origin, from the *Sukait*, a Turkic people who settled here in medieval times when the country was overrun by Turks. The meaning of their name is unknown.

Sumy (Сумы) *Town, northern Ukraine.* The town, northwest of Kharkov, was founded in 1652 as a fortress by the *Sumka* River and takes its name from it. The origin of the river name is uncertain. A popular legend tells how three bags (Russian *suma*, "bag") were found when the foundations for the fortress were being dug. This accounts for the three moneybags that appear on the town's coat of arms even today.

Suoyarvi (Суоярви) *Town, northwestern Russia.* The town, in southern Karelia, west of Petrozavodsk, takes its name from the lake on which it stands. It means "swamp lake," from Finnish *suo*, "swamp," "marsh," and *järvi*, "lake." The lake must originally have been surrounded by marshland, with the town being built on its drier, southern side.

Superfosfatny (Суперфосфатный) *Town, eastern Uzbekistan.* The town, west of Samarkand, is named for its manufacture of *superphosphates*.

Surakhany (Сураханы) *Town, eastern Azerbaijan.* The town, on the Apsheron Peninsula northeast of Baku, has a name that may be of Iranian origin. A source in a word such as Tajik *surkh*, "red," has been proposed, referring to the reddish hue of the sandy soil here.

Surazh (Сураж) *Town, northeastern Belarus.* The town, northeast of Vitebsk, has a name that is possibly a transference of the name *Surozh*, the medieval name of modern **Sudak**, in Ukraine.

Surkhandarya (Сурхандарья) *River, southeastern Uzbekistan.* The river, a tributary of the Amudarya, derives its name from Iranian *darya*, "river" (as for the **Amudarya** itself), and Tajik *surkh*, "red." The reference is to the color of its waters.

Surkhob (Сурхоб) *River, northern Tajikistan*. The river has a name meaning "red water," from Tajik *surkh*, "red," and *ob*, "water." Further north, over the border in Kyrgyzstan, the river is identically known as the *Kyzylsu*, from Kirgiz *kyzyl*, "red," and *su*, "water."

Surozh See **Sudak**.

Sursk (Сурск) *Town, western Russia*. The town, east of Penza, takes its name from the *Sura* River on which it stands. Before 1953 it was known as *Nikolsky Khutor* (Никольский Хутор), "Nicholas's village," presumably from the dedication of its church.

Susanino (Сусанино) *Town, western Russia*. The town, northeast of Kostroma, was originally known as *Molvitino*, presumably for a local landowner. In 1938 it was renamed as now for the peasant hero Ivan *Susanin* (died 1613), who came from this region. (He was the subject of Glinka's opera *A Life for the Czar*, retitled *Ivan Susanin* after the Revolution.)

Suuksu (Сууксу) *Resort, southern Crimea, southern Ukraine*. The Black Sea resort, just south of Gurzuf, has a Tatar name meaning "cold water," from words related to modern Turkish *soğuk*, "cold," and *su*, "water."

Suvorovo (Суворово) *Town, southeastern Moldova*. The town, southeast of Bendery, was originally the village of *Kyzyl* (Кызыл), from the Turkish word for "cornel" (cf. **Lazovsk**). In 1949 it was renamed *Biruintsa* (Бируйнца), from the Moldovan word for "victory" (that of socialism). In 1964 it received its present name, for the Russian field marshal who fought successfully against the Turks, Aleksandr Vasilyevich *Suvorov* (1729–1800).

Suzdal (Суздаль) *Town, western Russia*. The town, north of Vladimir, is one of the oldest in Russia, dating from at least the 11th century, when its name is recorded as *Suzhdal'*. Its precise origin is unclear. It is almost certainly Slavic, and may be related to modern Russian *sozdat'*, "to create," which originally had the specific sense "to make out of clay" (from Old Russian *z'd*, "clay"). If so, the meaning could be "(place) made out of clay," otherwise "brick-built (place)." But the actual origin may be in a personal name translating something like "Potter." The place would thus have been named for a person so called.

Svanetia (Сванетия) *Historic region, western Georgia*. The name derives from that of the region's inhabitants, the *Svan*, with the Georgian suffix *-eti*, "place," combining with the Russian (and international) suffix of the same meaning, *-ia*. The ethnic name is said to derive from a root word meaning "refuge." The historic name is preserved in that of the *Svanetsky* Range in the western Caucasus.

Sverdlovsk See **Yekaterinburg**.

Svetlogorsk (Светлогорск) *Town, southeastern Belarus*. The town, west of Gomel, was originally known as *Shatilki*, from the family name of the landowners here, *Shatilo*. The present name was gained in 1961 and was intended to symbolize the rosy future of this region of the republic, from Russian *svetlyj*, "light," "bright," and *gorod*, "town." A more successful version of the name would have been *Svetlograd* (like *Leningrad*, *Volgograd*, and so on). Cf. **Svetlograd**. There are similar "bright" names elsewhere.

Svetlograd (Светроград) *Town, southwestern Russia*. The town, northeast of Stavropol, has a name meaning "bright town," from Russian *svetlyj*, "light," "bright," and the common *-grad*, "town." The name is a propitious one, designed to evoke a favorable social and economic future in Soviet terms. Cf. **Svetlogorsk**. Until 1965 the settlement here was known as *Petrovskoye* (Петро́вское).

Svetlovodsk (Светлово́дск) *Town, east central Ukraine*. The town, south of Kremenchug, has a name translating as "bright water," from Russian *svetlyj*, "light," "bright," and *voda*, "water." The name is partly ideological, but also factually refers to the hydroelectric power station constructed on the Kremenchug Reservoir here in 1954-60.

Svetogorsk (Светого́рск) *Town, northwestern Russia*. The town, northwest of St. Petersburg near the border with Finland, originally had the Finnish name of *Enso*. In 1948 it acquired its present name, literally meaning "town of light," from Russian *svet*, "light," and *gorod*, "town." The reference is said to be to a hydroelectric power station here. (Electricity brings light, and light symbolizes ideological enlightenment.)

Sviblovo (Сви́блово) *District, Moscow, western Russia*. The northern district of Moscow takes its name from the former village here, which arose on an estate owned in the 14th century by the voivode (army commander) F. A. *Sviblo*, a comrade-in-arms of Dmitry Donskoy.

Svir (Свирь) *River, western Russia*. The river, flowing from Lake Onega to Lake Ladoga, has a name of Finnic origin meaning "deep."

Svoboda See **Liski**.

Svobodny (Свобо́дный) *Town, southeastern Russia*. The town, a port on the Zeya River northwest of Belogorsk, has an ideological name meaning "free," perhaps intentionally evoking the concept of a "free port," i.e. one open to all on equal terms. Freight is off-loaded from rail to river transport here. Until 1924 the settlement was known as *Alekseyevsk* (Алексе́евск).

Svyatoy Nos (Свято́й Нос) *Cape, northern Russia*. There are various capes of this name in northern and northwestern Russia, with one opposite the New Siberian Islands, another opposite Kolguyev Island, and a third on the Kola Peninsula. There is also a peninsula of the name on Lake Baykal. The name means "holy cape," from Russian *svyatoy*, "holy," and *nos*, "cape" (literally "nose"). The name probably commemorates a cross erected as both a religious symbol and a landmark.

Syana See **Kurilsk**.

Syktyvkar (Сыктывка́р) *Town, western Russia*. The Komi capital, northeast of Kotlas, was founded as the fortified post of *Ust-Sysolsk* (Усть-Сысо́льск) in 1586. This name means "mouth of the *Sysola*," from the location of the place at the point where this river joins the Vychegda. The town that grew up kept this name until 1930, when it received its present name. *Syktyv* is the Komi name of the Sysola, and *kar* is the Komi word for "town." The name thus means "town on the Syktyv."

Synzhereya See **Lazovsk**.

Syrdarya (Сырдарья́) *River, Kazakhstan*. The river is formed by two headstreams in southern Kazakhstan, then flows generally west and northwest to enter the Aral Sea at its northeastern corner. The meaning of its name has not been conclusively established, although *darya* is the Iranian word for "river," as for the **Amudarya**, to the south. The initial *Syr-* may mean something like "great," "good," referring to its importance in the fertile Fergana Valley. It is unlikely to represent Turkic *sary*, "yellow," as has been suggested by some.

Sysert (Сысéрть) *Town, west central Russia.* The town, southeast of Yekaterinburg, arose in the early 18th century on the *Sysert* River and is named for it. The origin of the river name is uncertain. It is recorded in a document of 1662 as *Siser*.

Syzran (Сы́зрань) *City, western Russia.* The city, on the west bank of the Volga west of Samara, was founded in 1683 and takes its name from the *Syzran* River that enters the Volga here. The river name may be of Turkic origin, although its precise meaning is uncertain.

Taganrog (Таганрóг) *City, southwestern Russia.* The city, a port on an inlet of the Sea of Azov west of Rostov-on-Don, was founded in 1698 on the cape of the same name as a fortress and naval base. The name of the cape derives from Russian *tagan*, "trivet," and *rog*, "cape" (literally "horn"). The reference is probably to a signal fire or beacon set up on a large iron trivet here at some time. The official name of the fortress was *Troitskaya*, "Trinity," and the settlement that grew up around it became the town of *Troitsky* in 1775. In 1784 it was officially renamed as now, although the name had been popularly in use from the first.

Tagil See **Nizhny Tagil**.

Tajikistan (Таджикистáн) *Republic, Central Asia.* The republic, bordered to the north by Russia and Kyrgyzstan, to the east by China, to the south by Afghanistan, and to the west by Uzbekistan, takes its name from its indigenous people, the *Tajiks*, with *-stan* the Iranian word for "land," "country." The ethnic name is of uncertain origin but has been traced back to an Arab tribe named *Tau*.

Takhta-Bazar (Тахтá-Базáр) *Town, southern Turkmenistan.* The town, on the Murgab River near the Afghan border, has a name that appears to represent Turkic *takhta*, "bridge," and Iranian *bazar*, "market," so that the overall sense is "(place with a) market by the bridge."

Taldy-Kurgan (Талды́-Кургáн) *Town, southeastern Kazakhstan.* The town, northeast of Alma-Ata, arose in the 19th century as the village of *Gavrilovka* (Гаври́ловка), presumably so called from a personal name. In 1920 it was renamed as now. The name is descriptive of the topography: Kazakh *taldy* is a term for a region of willow trees (cf. **Talnoye**); *kurgan* means "hill."

Tallinn (Тáллин) *Capital of Estonia.* The seaport city, in the northwest of the republic on the Gulf of Finland, has a name that represents Old Estonian *tan linn* (modern Estonian *taani linn*), "Danish castle." This name arose in the 13th century, when the town was captured by the Danes, who built their own castle in place of the original Estonian one. From the 14th century to the 17th, the city was controlled successively by the Teutonic Knights, the Livonian Knights, and Sweden. Over this period it was known as *Revel* (Рéвель). The origin of this is disputed. Some authorities see its source in *Ryavala*, a name for the northern coastal district of Estonia. Others derive it more specifically from an Old Danish word that gave modern Danish *rev*, "sandbank," a word in turn related to English *reef*. Russian archives covering the period from 1223 to the 18th century mention the city by the alternate name of *Kolyvan'*, supposedly from one *Kalev*, said to be buried beneath the castle. (See also **Kolyvan**.)

The present name was officially established in 1917.

Talnoye (Тально́е) *Town, central Ukraine*. The town, southwest of Cherkassy, derives its name from *tal*, a word of Turkic origin meaning "willow." Cf. **Taldy-Kurgan**.

Taman (Тама́нь) *Peninsula, southwestern Russia*. The peninsula and cape, between the Sea of Azov and the Black Sea, has a name of uncertain origin. It probably evolved from the name of the medieval town of **Tmutarakan** that formerly existed here.

Tambov (Тамбо́в) *City, western Russia*. The city, east of Lipetsk, was founded in 1636 as a defensive post to guard against attacks from the Crimean Tatars. It was planned to build the original fortress on the Tsna River at the point where the *Tambov* flows into it. However, it was actually built some 13 miles (21 km) downstream, but kept the name of the original river. The origin of the river name itself is uncertain.

Tannu-Tuva See **Tuva**.

Tapiau See **Gvardeysk**.

Tarbagatay (Тарбагата́й) *Mountain range, eastern Kazakhstan*. The range, near the border with China, is said to take its name from a Turkic word *tarbaga*, "marmot," from the abundance of these animals here. However, another theory derives the name from a different creature, from Buryat *tarbazha*, "forest eagle." The final *-tay* of the name does not necessarily represent Turkic *tau*, "mountain."

Tarkhankut, Cape (Тарханку́тский полуо́стров) *Cape, western Crimea, southern Ukraine*. The extreme western point of the Crimea has a name based on Tatar *tarkhan*, a historic term for land and property whose holder enjoyed special privileges. The final *-kut*, found elsewhere in Ukrainian placenames, means simply "place."

Tarkhany See **Lermontovo**.

Tarnopol See **Ternopol**.

Tartu (Та́рту) *City, eastern Estonia*. A settlement of some kind has been on the site of the present city, west of Lake Chudskoye, since the 5th century. In 1030 the Kievan prince Yaroslav the Wise founded a fort here which he called *Yuryev* (Ю́рьев), after his Christian name, *Yury* (the equivalent of George). The Romans knew the site as *Torpatum*, however, as a latinized form of the indigenous Estonian name of the place, which was *Tarbata* or *Darpeten*. The Roman name then produced the form *Derpt* (Дерпт), which was officially adopted until 1893. (The German form of this also became familiar, as *Dorpat*.) In 1893 the old Slavic name *Yuryev* was reinstated, but in 1919 the Estonian name was established in its present form. Its meaning is unknown.

Tarutino (Тару́тино) *Town, southern Ukraine*. The town, southwest of Odessa near the border with Moldova, was founded in 1814 and named for the Russian victory over Napoleon in 1812 at the Battle of *Tarushino*, southwest of Moscow.

Tashauz (Ташау́з) *Town, northern Turkmenistan*. The town, near the border with Uzbekistan, was founded in the early 19th century as a fortress. Its name is said to have evolved from a Turkmen original form *Dash-khauz*, in which *dash* means "stone" and *khauz*, "reservoir." The overall sense is thus "stone reservoir." Tashauz is in an oasis not far from the Amudarya River.

Tashino See **Pervomaysk**[1].

Tashkent (Ташке́нт) *Capital of Uzbekistan*. The city, in the northeast of the republic on the border with Kazakhstan, has a long history which archaeologists trace back to the third or fourth millennium BC. Written records of the name date from the 4th and 5th centuries AD, and include the forms *Dzhadzh*, *Chachkent*, *Shashkent*, and *Binkent*. The present form of the name first occurs only in the 11th century. The early form *Dzhadzh* is probably related to *Tadzhik*, an ethnic name that at one time generally applied to all Muslims. *Tashkent* is usually explained as meaning "stone town," from Turkic *tash*, "stone," and *kent*, "town." The early forms *Chachkent* and *Shashkent* would thus have been corruptions of this, while *Binkent* occurs in the works of Arab geographers.

Tashkepri (Ташкепри) *Town, southern Turkmenistan*. The town, on the Murgab River (here flowing through a reservoir) northwest of Takhta-Bazar, has a Turkic name meaning "stone bridge," from *tash*, "stone," and *kepri* (modern Turkish *köprü*), "bridge."

Tashtagol (Таштагол) *Town, southern Russia*. The town, southeast of Temirtau, stands on the Kondoma River and has a name probably meaning "stony river," from Turkic *tash*, "stone," and Mongolian *gol*, "river."

Tashtyp (Таштып) *Village, southern Russia*. The village, southeast of Novokuznetsk, has a name of Turkic origin meaning "stony valley." The region here is mountainous, in the Western Sayan.

Tatarbunary (Татарбунары) *Town, southern Ukraine*. The town, southwest of Odessa, derives the first part of its name from the *Tatars* (see **Tatarstan**) and the second part from Bulgarian or Romanian *bunar*, "well," "spring."

Tatar Sea See **Laptev Sea**.

Tatarsk (Татарск) *Town, southern Russia*. The town, east of Omsk, arose in 1911 on the construction of a railroad link here. It is named for the local people, who are Siberian *Tatars*.

Tatarstan (Татарстан) *Republic, western Russia*. The republic, west of the Urals at the bend of the Middle Volga, takes its name from its indigenous people, the *Tatars*, with *-stan* the Iranian term for "land," "country." The ethnic name is of uncertain origin, despite various attempts to explain it. It may well simply mean "people." The etymology is further complicated by the fact that the name came to designate not just one ethnic group but, loosely, a whole number of Asian peoples, inhabiting a very wide territory. (Cf. **Tatar Strait**.) Further, the reputation of the Tatars as a fearsome or formidable people meant that their name became popularly associated with *Tartarus*, the hell or underworld of Greek mythology. Hence the spelling *Tartar* commonly found in the West.

Tatar Strait (Татарский пролив) *Strait, eastern Russia*. The wide strait, between Sakhalin island and the Russian mainland, has a name that is nothing to do with the *Tatars* proper, as the Turkic people who are the indigenous inhabitants of what is now **Tatarstan**. The name arose at a time when *Tatars* (or *Tartars*) was loosely used for any Turkic, Mongolian, or other Asian people, who collectively inhabited *Tatary* (or *Tartary*), a vast territory that extended east as far as the Pacific. The strait was discovered by the French navigator Jean François La Pérouse in 1787. He originally named it *Manche de Tartarie*, "Tartary sleeve." The present name arose when Sakhalin was found to be an island.

Taurage (Таураге) *Town, western Lithuania*. The town, northwest of

Kaunas, is said to have a name deriving from Old Lithuanian *tauras*, "bison" (related to Latin *taurus*, "bull"). The town was known to the Germans as *Tauroggen*.

Taurida See **Crimea**.

Tavda (Тавда́) *Town, west central Russia*. The town, north of Tyumen, takes its name from the river on which it lies. The river name derives from Mansi *tovt*, the term for a forest cleared by burning.

Tavolzhan (Таволжа́н) *Town, northeastern Kazakhstan*. The town, northeast of Pavlodar, takes its name from Lake *Tavolzhan*, by which it lies. The lake derives its name from Russian *tavolga*, "meadowsweet" (*Filipendia ulmaria*), a plant that grows here.

Tayga (Тайга́) *Town, southern Russia*. The town, southeast of Tomsk, arose during construction of the Transsiberian Railway, on which it now stands. Its name represents the Siberian dialect word *tajga*, "taiga," a term for a rocky, mountainous area and a general name for the coniferous forests that border the subarctic regions. (The word itself is of Turkic origin, and is related to Turkish *dağ*, "mountain.")

Taymyr (Таймы́р) *Peninsula, northern Russia*. The peninsula, between the Yenisey and Khatanga rivers, opposite North Land, takes its name from the *Taymyra* River that flows north through it (and through Lake Taymyr) into the Kara Sea. The river's own name is believed to be of Evenki origin and to mean "copious," "rich," referring to its abundance of fish rather than its waters. The island of *Taymyr* to the north of the peninsula was discovered and named for it in 1878 by Nordenskiöld (see **Nordenskiöld Archipelago**) when making the North East Passage on board the *Vega*.

Tayozhny (Таёжный) *Town, southern Russia*. The town, northeast of Krasnoyarsk, has a name that is an adjectival form of Russian *tajga*, "taiga," the geographical term for the coniferous forest region here. Cf. **Tayga**.

Tayshet (Тайше́т) *Town, southern Russia*. The town, east of Kansk, takes its name from the river here. The river name derives from an extinct Ket language and represents *tay*, "cold," and *shet*, "river." The town arose during construction of the Transsiberian Railway, on which it now stands.

Tba (Тба) *Resort, south central Georgia*. The mountain resort, southeast of Borzhomi, has a name representing Georgian *tba*, "lake."

Tbilisi (Тбили́си) *Capital of Georgia*. Archaeological evidence has shown that the city, in the east central part of the republic, dates back to the 3rd or 4th millennium BC. Its name represents Georgian *tbili*, "warm," referring to its many warm sulfur springs. The Greeks knew the city as *Tiphlis* or *Tiphilis*, and this gave the form *Tiflis* (Тифли́с), which was in general use until 1936, when the present, corrected spelling was adopted.

Teguldet (Тегульде́т) *Village, southern Russia*. The village, northeast of Tomsk, takes its name from the river here. Its own name is of Ket origin, from *tegul'*, "salty," and *det*, "river."

Teletsky, Lake (Теле́цкое о́зеро) *Lake, southern Russia*. The lake, in the northern Altay mountains, takes its name from the *Teles*, a local people who once lived on its shores. The local name for the lake is *Altyn-Kol*, from Altaic *altyn*, "gold," and *kol'*, "lake." The name is explained by a number of local legends. One links it to the nearby mountain of *Altyn-Tu*, "golden mountain," itself traditionally explained as meaning "rich in sable."

Telmanovo (Тéльманово) *Town, southeastern Ukraine.* The town, south of Makeyevka, was named for the East German Communist leader Ernst *Telman* (1886–1944). Cf. **Telmansk**.

Telmansk (Тéльманск) *Town, northern Turkmenistan.* The town, north of Tashauz on the border with Uzbekistan, takes its name from the East German Communist leader Ernst *Telman* (1886–1944). Until 1938 it was known as *Taza-Kala*.

Telposiz (Тéльпосиз) *Mountain, west central Russia.* The mountain, the highest in the Middle Urals, has a Komi name meaning "rock of the lair of winds," from *tel*, "wind," *poz*, "lair," and *iz*, "rock." The region is notorious for its adverse weather, and especially for the fierce winds that blow down from the summit, bringing cloud, rain, or snow.

Temir-Khan-Shura See **Buynaksk**.

Temirtau[1] (Темиртáу) *Town, east central Kazakhstan.* The town, northwest of Karaganda, has a Kazakh name meaning "iron mountain," from *temir*, "iron," and *tau*, "mountain." The reference is to the abundance of iron ore here. Until 1945 the former settlement was known as *Samarkandsky*, for the *Samarkand* reservoir here.

Temirtau[2] (Темиртáу) *Town, southern Russia.* The town, southeast of Novokuznetsk, has a Kazakh name meaning "iron mountain," from *temir*, "iron," and *tau*, "mountain." The reference is to the abundance of iron ore locally.

Temnikov (Тéмников) *Town, western Russia.* The town, in Mordovia northwest of Saransk, arose from a fortress built in 1536. Its name derives from Russian *temnik*, a historic term for a military commander and later for a tax collector and administrator in conquered Mordovian and Russian territory. (The word itself comes from Russian *t'ma*, "ten thousand," so that the nearest English equivalent would be *chiliarch*.)

Temryuk (Темрю́к) *Town, southwestern Russia.* The town, on the Kuban River west of Krasnodar, arose from the fortress built here in 1570 by the Kabardian prince *Temryuk* Aydarovich (died 1570s), and is named for him.

Tengiz (Тенгúз) *Lake, north central Kazakhstan.* The lake has a Turkic name meaning simply "sea," "lake" (modern Turkish *deniz*).

Teofipol (Теофúполь) *Town, western Ukraine.* The town, northwest of Khmelnitsky, was originally known as *Cholkhan*. In 1740 it was renamed for the wife of the landowner. Her first name must have been *Feofila* (a feminine form of the equivalent of *Theophilus*).

Terebovlya (Теребóвля) *Town, western Ukraine.* The town, southwest of Khmelnitsky, has a name based on Old Russian *terebit'*, "to clear (a wood of its trees)." Until 1944 the official form of the name was *Trembovlya* (Трембóвля).

Terek (Тéрек) *River, southwestern Russia.* The river rises in Georgia, then flows north through the Caucasus into Russia, where it turns east to enter the Caspian Sea. Its name has been given various meanings, including "river of Turks" (!), but the most likely origin is in a variant of Balkar *cherek*, "rapid one."

Terijoki See **Zelenogorsk**.

Ternopol (Тернóполь) *City, western Ukraine.* The city, southeast of Lvov, has what at first sight seems to be a Greek-style name (like **Stavropol** or **Sevastopol**) but that is actually of Slavic origin. It is a combination of Russian *tyorn*, "blackthorn," and *pole*, "field," referring to a tract of land overrun by blackthorn. The name was formerly familiar in the form *Tarnopol*.

Terpeniya Bay (Терпéния залѝв) *Bay, Sahkhalin, eastern Russia.* Sakhalin's main bay, on the southeastern side of the island, has a name representing Russian *terpeniye*, "patience." It was so named by the Dutch navigator M. G. de Vries, who in the summer of 1643 was delayed here by a persistent dense fog. The headland to the east of the bay has the same name.

Tezebazar (Тэзэбазáр) *Town, northern Turkmenistan.* The town, east of Tashauz near the border with Uzbekistan, has a Turkmen name meaning "new market."

Tien Shan (Тянь-Шань) *Mountain chain, eastern Kyrgyzstan/northwestern China.* The lofty mountain chain has a name of Chinese origin meaning "heavenly mountains," from *tiān*, "heaven," and *shān*, "mountain."

Tiflis See **Tbilisi**.

Tikhaya Bay (Тѝхая бýхта) *Bay, Franz Josef Land, northwestern Russia.* The bay, on the west coast of Hooker Island, has a name meaning "quiet bay." When Sedov's expedition (see **Sedovo**) wintered here in 1913–14 on board the *St. Phocas* their ship was not impeded by the surrounding ice. Hence the name. (Phocas was the patron saint of sailors. The suggestion of Greek *phōkē*, "seal," in the name makes it additionally suitable for a ship exploring the Arctic.)

Tikhoretsk (Тихорéцк) *Town, southwestern Russia.* The town, northeast of Krasnodar, has a name representing a blended form of Russian *tikhaya reka*, "quiet river," although there is no river here. There was a fashion for names of this type north of the Caucasus in the late 18th and early 19th centuries, when such places were founded. Other examples are *Prokhladny*, "cool," *Otradnaya*, "pleasing," *Spokoynaya*, "calm," *Udobnaya*, "convenient," *Ispravnaya*, "well-ordered," and *Besskorbnaya*, "sorrow-free."

Tikhvin (Тѝхвин) *Town, western Russia.* The town, southeast of St. Petersburg, is first recorded in 1383 as a *pogost* (religious settlement) named *Predtechensky*, from the church here dedicated to John the Baptist (Russian *Ioann predtecha*). It received its present name in 1724. It may be from the *Tikhvinka* River on which it stands, its own name possibly deriving from Finnish *tihkua*, "to ooze," or *tiheääk*, "thickly." But the river name could equally come from that of the town, with its slightly different form influenced by Finnish *joki*, "river."

Tiksi (Тѝкси) *Town and port, northern Russia.* The town, near the mouth of the Lena, arose in the 1930s when the northern sea route was opened. It is named for the bay here, with the bay's own name the Yakut word for "haven."

Tilsit See **Sovetsk**[1].

Tiraspol (Тирáсполь) *City, eastern Moldova.* The city, on the Dniester opposite Bendery, was founded in 1792 as a Russian fortified post on the site of a Moldavian fortress burned down by the Turks in 1787. In 1795 the settlement that had grown up here was given its Greek-style name, in the manner of the day. It derives from *Tyras*, the ancient Greek name of the Dniester, and Greek *polis*, "town."

Tmutarakan (Тмутаракáнь) *Historic town, southwestern Russia.* The former town, on the Taman Peninsula south of the Sea of Azov, arose in the 10th century on the site of the earlier settlement of *Tamatarkha*, and this forms the basis of the later name and that of modern **Taman**. The origin lies in Turkic *tamantarkan*, "title of rank." Only ruins now remain of the medieval original. It is possible this town also gave the name of *Tutrakan* in northeastern Bulgaria, near the border with Romania.

Tobolsk (Тобо́льск) *City, west central Russia.* The city, northeast of Tyumen, takes its name from the *Tobol* River on which it was founded in 1587. The river name is of uncertain origin. Some have linked it to Russian *tavolga*, "meadowsweet." Cf. **Tavolzhan**.

Toktogul (Токтогу́л) *Village, northwestern Kyrgyzstan.* The village, southwest of Bishkek, was originally known as *Muztor*. It was renamed in honor of the Kirgiz *akyn* (folk musician and poet) *Toktogul* Satylganov (1864–1933), who was born near here.

Toll Bay (То́лля зали́в) *Bay, northern Russia.* The bay, on the west coast of the Taymyr Peninsula, is named for the Russian geologist and Arctic explorer, Eduard Vasilyevich *Toll* (1858–1902). He and three companions went missing in November 1902 while making their way south on foot from Bennett Island over treacherous sea ice.

Tolmachyovo (Толмачёво) *Town, western Russia.* The town, south of St. Petersburg, was originally the village of *Preobrazhenskaya*, so named for the dedication of its church to the Transfiguration (Russian *Preobrazheniye*). In received its present name in 1919 in honor of the Russian revolutionary Nikolay Guryevich *Tolmachyov* (1895–1919), who when wounded near here during the Civil War while combatting the counterrevolutionary forces of Yudenich, shot himself to escape being taken prisoner.

Tolyatti See **Tolyattigrad**.

Tolyattigrad (Тольяттигра́д) *Town, western Russia.* The town, on the Volga (here forming the Kuybyshev Reservoir) northwest of Samara, was founded in 1738 as a fortified post designed for a Kalmyk prince who together with some companions had been converted to the Christian faith. (The prince died before the place was built, and it was thus occupied by his widow.) In 1739 the new settlement was given the Greek name of *Stavropol* (Ста́врополь), "town of the cross," from *stauros*, "cross," and *polis*, "town." The name was appropriate for a settlement of newly converted Christians. The place was raised to town status in 1780, and the town kept this name until 1964, when it was renamed *Tolyatti* (Толья́тти), for the Italian Communist leader Palmiro *Togliatti* (1893–1964), who had visited the Soviet Union several times and who actually died at Yalta in the Crimea. In 1991 this name was suffixed by Russian *-grad*, "town," rather than reverting to *Stavropol*. Cf. **Stavropol**.

Tomari (Томари́) *Town, Sakhalin, eastern Russia.* The town, on the southwest coast of the island, has an Ainu name meaning "haven."

Tomsk (Томск) *City, southern Russia.* The city, northeast of Novosibirsk, was founded in 1604 on the *Tom* River and takes its name from it. The river name is traditionally explained as deriving from the Ket word *toom*, "river." However, this same word can also mean "dark," so this could be a more exact descriptive sense.

Topki (То́пки) *Town, southern Russia.* The town, west of Kemerovo, derives its name from the plural form of Russian *topka*, "marshy place."

Torez (Торéз) *Town, eastern Ukraine*. The town, in the Donbass east of Makeyevka, was originally known as *Chistyakovo* (Чистякóво), presumably from a person named *Chistyakov*. In 1964 it was renamed as now for the French Communist leader Maurice *Thorez* (1900-1964), who took refuge in the Soviet Union in World War II when the Communist Party was banned by the Vichy government and who died on board a ship bound for the USSR.

Torgovaya See **Salsk**.

Toropets (Торóпец) *Town, western Russia*. The town, northeast of Velikiye Luki, takes its name from the *Toropa* River on which it lies. The river name has been related to Russian *toropit'*, "to hurry," with reference to its rapid current.

Torzhok (Торжóк) *Town, western Russia*. The town, northwest of Tver, is known to have existed in 1139. Its name means "trading place," from Russian *torg*, "market." Torzhok is on the main Moscow to St. Petersburg road at a crossing of the Tvertsa River.

Toyohara See **Yuzhno-Sakhalinsk**.

Transcarpathia (Закарпáтье) *Region, western Ukraine*. The region is so named as it is *beyond* (Latin *trans-*) or west of the *Carpathians* from the point of view of everywhere else in Ukraine.

Transcaucasia (Закавкáзье) *Region, Central Asia*. The region comprises what are now the three republics of Armenia, Azerbaijan, and Georgia. It is so named as it is *beyond* (Latin *trans-*) or south of the *Caucasus* from the point of view of Russia.

Trembovlya See **Terebovlya**.

Troitse-Lykovo (Трóице-Лы́ково) *District, Moscow, western Russia*. The western district of Moscow takes the second part of its name from the boyar B. M. *Lykov*, owner of an estate here in the 17th century. The first part refers to the church of the Trinity (Russian *Troitsa*), built here in the closing years of that century.

Troitsk (Трóицк) *Town, southwestern Russia*. The town, south of Chelyabinsk near the border with Kazakhstan, was founded in 1743 as a defensive post against nomadic raids and takes its name from the day on which the original encampment was set up, Pentecost or *Trinity* Sunday (Russian *Troitsa*, "Trinity").

Troparyovo (Тропарёво) *District, Moscow, western Russia*. The southwestern district of Moscow takes its name from a former village here. This arose from an estate held in the late 14th century by the boyar I. M. *Tropar'*. Hence the present name.

Trotsk See (1) **Chapayevsk**, (2) **Gatchina**.

Troyekurovo (Троекýрово) *District, Moscow, western Russia*. The district of western Moscow stands on the site of an estate known in the 16th century as *Khoroshovo*. In the 18th century it passed to the *Troyekurov* family of boyars. Hence the present name.

Trudovoy See **Kuybyshevsky**.

Tsaritsyn See **Volgograd**.

Tsaritsyno (Царúцыно) *District, Moscow, western Russia*. The southeastern district of Moscow lies on the site of an estate owned in the 16th century by Czarina Irina, sister of Boris Godunov, when it was known as *Bogorodskoye*, for the church here, dedicated to the Virgin Mary (Russian *Bogoroditsa*, literally "God-bearer"). In the 17th century it passed to the Streshnev family of boyars, then to the princely Golitsyn family. In 1712 it became known by the much less elevated name of *Chyornaya Gryaz'*, "Black Mud," and was presented by Peter the Great to the Moldavian prince Dmitry Konstantinovich Kantemir. (See **Kantemirovka**). In 1775 the village that had arisen passed to Catherine the Great and was duly named *Tsaritsyno*, from Russian *tsaritsa*, "czarina" (the title of a Russian empress). In the 19th century the place became a rural suburb of Moscow with several dachas (holiday cottages), and in 1939 amalgamated territorially with the newly formed **Lenino-Dachnoye**, although retaining its name as a distinct locality. It became part of Moscow proper in 1960.

Tsarskoye Selo See **Pushkin**.

Tsaryovokokshaysk See **Yoshkar Ola**.

Tselinograd See **Akmola**.

Tsementny (Цеме́нтный) *Town, west central Russia*. The town, in the Middle Urals northwest of Yekaterinburg, is named for its cement works, from the adjectival form of Russian *tsement*, "cement."

Tsesarevich See **Myortvy Kultuk**.

Tsimlyansk (Цимля́нск) *Town, southwestern Russia*. The town, southwest of Rostov-on-Don at the western end of the Tsimlyansky Reservoir, takes its name from the *Tsimla* River, which here enters the Don. The river name may be of Turkish origin, and a source in either Old Turkish *sin*, "grave," "monument," or modern *çim*, "turf," has been tentatively proposed.

Tskhakaya See **Senaki**.

Tskhenis Tskali (Цхенисцка́ли) *River, western Georgia*. The river, a tributary of the Rioni, has a name meaning "horse river," from Georgian *tskhenis*, "horse," "steed," and *tskali*, "river." Local legend tells that 6,000 horses of an invading Arab army perished by drowning here in 683 AD. The true origin may be much more prosaic.

Tsukulidze See **Khoni**.

Tsurukhaytuy See **Priargunsk**.

Tsyurupinsk (Цюру́пинск) *Town, southern Ukraine*. The town, southeast of Kherson across the Dnieper, was originally the ancient Greek settlement of *Elissa*. In medieval chronicles this name was russified to *Olesh'ye*, as if deriving from *ol'shanik*, "alder grove." Under the influence of southern Russian speech, this then became *Alyoshki* (Алёшки), as if related to the first name *Alyosha*, a familiar form of Aleksey. Following an abortive attempt in 1802 to rename it *Dneprovsk*, for the Dnieper, the town was given its present name in 1928 on the death of the Soviet Communist leader Aleksandr Dmitriyevich *Tsyurupa* (1870–1928), who was born here.

Tuapse (Туапсе́) *Town and port, southwestern Russia*. The town, on the Black Sea coast northwest of Sochi, was founded in 1838 as the fortress of *Velyaminskoye ukrepleniye* (Вельями́нское укрепле́ние), "Velyaminov's fortification," for the Russian general A. A. *Velyaminov*, a local army commander. The fortress and the settlement that grew up around it were made a town in 1896 with the present name of *Tuapse*, from the river so called here. The river's name is usually explained as meaning "two rivers," from Adygey *tua*, "two," and *psy* "water," "river." The river is formed by the confluence of two others.

Tubinsky (Туби́нский) *Town, southwestern Russia*. The town, in Bashkortostan southwest of Magnitogorsk, derives its name from Bashkir *tube*, "hill."

Tugulym (Тугулы́м) *Town, west central Russia*. The town, west of

Tyumen, takes its name from the small *Tugulymka* River on which it lies. The river name is of Tatar origin but uncertain meaning. Tatar *tugylma*, "mixed," "mingled," has been proposed.

Tukums (Тýкумс) *Town, western Latvia*. The town, west of Riga, has a Latvian name meaning "hilly," from *tukt*, "to swell."

Tula (Týла) *City, western Russia*. The city, south of Moscow, dates from at least 1146. Its name is said to derive from a Baltic word *tula*, meaning "new settlement," "colony." Support for a Baltic origin is given by the name of the river on which the town stands. This is the *Upa*, from Baltic *upe*, "river."

Tumanyan (Туманя́н) *Town, northern Armenia*. The town, south of Alaverdi, is named for the Armenian writer and folklorist Ovanes Tadevosovich *Tumanyan* (1869–1923), who was born near here. Prior to 1951 the town was named *Dzagidzor*.

Tunguska (Тунгýска) *River, central Russia*. The name is that of three tributaries of the Yenisey, flowing into it from east to west. From north to south they are: the *Lower Tunguska* (Ни́жняя Тунгýска), *Stony Tunguska* (Подка́менная Тунгýска), and *Upper Tunguska* (Ве́рхняя Тунгýска), now known as the **Angara**. The basic name is of ethnic origin, referring to the *Tungus*, whose own name means "far people." This was the Khanty name for the Evenki, who served as guides to Russians traveling through Siberia.

Tura (Турá) *Town, central Russia*. The town, on the Lower Tunguska River northeast of Yeniseysk, has a name that has been derived from *tura*, "settlement," "town," a word found in various Turkic and Mongolic languages, and that occurs elsewhere in southern Siberia.

Tura (river) See **Turinsk**.

Turinsk (Тури́нск) *Town, west central Russia*. The town, northwest of Tyumen, was founded in 1600 as a fortress and coachmen's settlement on the *Tura* River, and is named for the latter. The origin of the river name is uncertain, and it is unlikely to have evolved from Turkic (Tatar) *tura*, "town," as for **Tura**. It may well be of pre-Turkic origin. Also on the river and named for it are **Nizhnyaya Tura**, **Verkhnyaya Tura**, and **Verkhoturye**, among the most important places.

Turinskiye Rudniki See **Krasnoturinsk**.

Turkestan[1] (Туркеста́н) *Historic region, Central Asia*. The region, also known as *Turkistan*, occupies what are today the republics of Kyrgyzstan, Tajikistan, Turkmenistan, Uzbekistan, the northern part of Afghanistan, the southern part of Kazakhstan, and the western part of China. The name was intended to indicate the territory inhabited by *Turkic* peoples. It is not strictly accurate, however, since it includes Tajikistan, where the people are not Turkic, and it does not include Turkey, where they are. The name has the Iranian *-stan*, "land," "country," that most of its constituent countries also have. It is preserved today in the Kazakh town of **Turkestan**[2].

Turkestan[2] (Туркеста́н) *Town, southern Kazakhstan*. The town, northwest of Chimkent, is one of the oldest in Kazakhstan. It was known in the 10th century as *Shavgar*, then as *Yasy*, before the present name, meaning "land of the Turks," appeared in the 15th century. Cf. **Turkestan**[1].

Turkmenistan (Туркмениста́н) *Republic, Central Asia*. The republic, bordered by the Caspian Sea to the west, by Kazakhstan and Uzkekistan to the north and east, and by Iran and Afghanistan to the south, derives its name from its indigenous inhabitants, the *Turkmens* (also known as *Turkomans*), with the final Iranian *-stan* meaning "land," "country." The Turkmens have a name meaning "Turklike": they are a nomadic people, unlike the "settled" Turks of other countries.

Turov (Туров) *Town, southern Belarus.* The town, east of Pinsk, dates from at least the 10th century and is said to derive its name from a personal name. The meaning is thus "Tur's town." The personal name itself has been linked by some to Greek *tauros*, "bull," but by others to the name of *Thor*, the Scandinavian god of thunder.

Tursunzade (Турсунзаде) *Town, western Tajikistan.* The town, west of Dushanbe, was originally the settlement of *Stantsiya Regar* (Станция Регар), "Regar Station." In 1952 it was raised to town status and the name was shortened to simply *Regar* (Регар). In 1978 it was renamed as now for the Tajik poet Mirzo *Tursun-Zade* (1911-1977), who was born near here.

Turtkul (Турткуль) *Town, southwestern Uzbekistan.* The town, east of Urgench, was founded in 1873 and until 1920 was known as *Petro-Aleksandrovsk* (Петро-Александровск). Its present Turkic name means "quadrangle" (modern Turkish *dörtgen*), referring to the ruins of a rectangular fort here.

Tushino (Тушино) *District, Moscow, western Russia.* The northwestern district of Moscow, from 1939 to 1960 an independent town, takes its name from a former village. This arose from an estate held here in the late 14th century by the boyar Vasily Ivanovich. He went by the Russian nickname *Tusha* ("Hulk"), and this gave the present name.

Tutayev (Тутаев) *Town, western Russia.* The town, northwest of Yaroslavl, was formed in 1822 by the union of two distinct towns here either side of the Volga. The left-bank town was *Romanov*, founded in about 1370 by *Roman* Vasilyevich, Prince of Yaroslavl. The right-bank town was *Borisoglebsk*, founded in the 15th century and named for its church dedication to St. *Boris* and St. *Gleb*. The new unified town was at first known simply as *Romanov-Borisoglebsk* (Романов-Борисоглебск), but in 1918 received its present name, commemorating the young Red Army soldier I. P. *Tutayev* (1899-1918), killed in the Civil War during the counterrevolutionary Yaroslavl uprising of 1918.

Tuva (Тува) *Republic, southern Russia.* The republic, in the Yenisey basin along the border with Mongolia, takes its name from its indigenous population, the *Tuvans* or *Tuvinians*. The origin of their own name is uncertain. (Their own form of it is *Tyva*, now also in use for the republic.) The republic was formerly known as *Tannu-Tuva* (Танну-Тува), the first part of this representing the *Tannu*-Ola mountain range. Before 1921 the region was in Outer Mongolia and was known as *Uriankhai*, from a Mongolian name for the people meaning "previous ones," i.e. those who were there before the Mongols. (This name has also been popularly rendered as "ragamuffins," an interpretation now disavowed.)

Tuymazy (Туймазы) *Town, western Russia.* The town, in Bashkortostan west of Ufa, arose as a settlement for oil workers in 1937. The name is said to derive from Bashkir *tuymas*, "insatiable," "voracious," referring to local potholes or rock cavities that rapidly drain off any surface water. The cavities surround a cave known locally for the same reason as *Kerez-Tishik*, "Honeycomb Hole." However, the name may actually derive from that of a stream or river here.

Tver (Тверь) *City, western Russia.* The city, on the Volga northwest of Moscow, was founded in the 12th century, and takes its name from the river, now the *Tvertsa*, that enters the Volga here. The meaning of its own name is uncertain. In 1931 the city was renamed *Kalinin* (Калинин), for the Soviet statesman and titular head of state, Mikhail Ivanovich *Kalinin* (1875–1946), who was born near here. It reverted to its original name in 1990.

Tyatya, Mt. (Тятя) *Volcano, Kuril Islands, southeastern Russia.* The active volcano, on Kunashir island at the southern end of the chain, has a name representing Ainu *Chacha-Nupuri*, "father mountain."

Tynda (Тында) *Town, eastern Russia.* The town, northeast of Skovorodino, takes its name from the *Tynda* River, on which it stands. The original settlement of *Tyndinsky* (Тындинский) grew with the coming of the Baykal-Amur railroad, and received its present name when it was raised to town status in 1975. The river is said to derive its name from Evenki *tendy*, "coastal," suggesting that it was so called by 19th-century travelers who were used to following a coastal route, and who regarded the course of the river as an inland "coast" similarly.

Tyndinsky See **Tynda**.

Tyoplaya Gora (Тёплая Горá) *Town, western Russia.* The town, in the Central Urals northwest of Verkhnyaya Tura, has a name deriving from its elevated location. The site here is known as "warm mountain," probably because the snow melts earlier on the sheltered southern and eastern slopes than elsewhere in the area. Local folk explain the name differently, claiming that the allusion is to the days of horse-drawn transport, when carters and horses would sweat profusely in the effort of toiling up the incline, even in the coldest weather. This may have been so, but the name is found elsewhere for similar sites.

Tyoply Stan (Тёплый Стан) *District, Moscow, western Russia.* The southwestern district of Moscow arose from an amalgamation of earlier villages, two of which in the 17th century were respectively *Verkhny* ("Upper") and *Nizhny* ("Lower") *Tyoply Stan.* The basic Russian name means literally "warm camp," and is said to refer to the heated tents pitched here in winter by one of the Tatar khans when marching on Moscow in medieval times. But this may well be a folk fiction.

Tyoply Stan See **Sechenovo**.

Tyumen (Тюмéнь) *City, west central Russia.* The city, east of Yekaterinburg, was the first Russian town in Siberia, and was founded in 1586 on the site of the Tatar settlement of *Chingi-Tura*. This had arisen in the 14th century and had a name meaning "Chingis's town," allegedly referring to the Mongol ruler *Genghis Khan*, though he lived at least a century earlier. It took its present name from the existing Tatar name of the territory here. The origin is in *tyumen* or *tyumyan*, a word that in Turkic and Mongolic languages means "ten thousand." (Cf. modern Turkish *tümen*, Russian *t'ma*, "great number.") The word originally applied to an army of 10,000 men, then to the people whose members made up such an army, then to the territory of the people itself. The Russians probably regarded the name as appropriate for their newly fortified post.

Tyva See **Tuva**.

Uchaly (Учалы́) *Town, western Russia*. The town, in Bashkortostan northeast of Beloretsk, was formed in 1963 from the amalgamation of the settlements *Novyye Uchaly* ("New Uchaly") and *Malyye Uchaly* ("Little Uchaly"). These took their names respectively from the lakes of *Bolshiye Uchaly* ("Big Uchaly") and *Malyye Uchaly*. The basic name *Uchaly* is said to have evolved as a form of Bashkir *asyuly*, "angry," referring to the inhospitable waters of the lakes. The present form of the name evolved through Russian influence.

Udachny (Уда́чный) *Town, north central Russia*. The town, northwest of Yakutsk, arose in 1968 when a diamond mine was opened here. The name is properly that of the mine, and means "successful," implying that prospecting here had produced the hoped-for results.

Udmurtia (Удму́ртия) *Republic, western Russia*. The republic, west of the Middle Urals, takes its name from the *Udmurts* who are its indigenous inhabitants. Their own name is based on *murt*, a word of Iranian origin, meaning "person," that is indirectly linked with English *mortal*. The Udmurts were formerly known as the *Votyaks*, and this name now represents the initial *Ud-* of *Udmurt*. Its precise meaning is unclear.

Ufa (Уфа́) *City, western Russia*. The city, southwest of Chernikovsk, is the capital of Bashkortostan. It is named for the river on which it was founded in 1574 as a Russian fort on the site of the Bashkir defensive post of *Turatau*. The river name is probably related to the Indo-European root word *ab* or *ap* meaning simply "water."

Uglegorsk (Углего́рск) *Town, Sakhalin, eastern Russia*. The town, on the island's west coast, originally had the Japanese name of *Esutoru*. In 1946 it received its present name, meaning "coal town," from Russian *ugol'*, "coal," and *gorod*, "town." Coal is mined near the town.

Uglekamensk (Углека́менск) *Town, southeastern Russia*. The town, east of Vladivostok, is named for its coalmining industry, from Russian *kamennyj ugol'*, "coal." (Although *ugol'* alone can mean "coal," *kamennyj ugol'*, literally "rock coal," is used when distinction is needed from *buryj ugol'*, "lignite," literally "brown coal," or *drevesinyj ugol'*, "charcoal," literally "wood coal.")

Ugleuralsk (Углеура́льск) *Town, west central Russia*. The town, north of Gubakha to the west of the Middle Urals, arose in 1831 as a settlement of charcoal burners. In 1904 a coalmine opened here. Hence its name, which denotes its principal product and its location, from Russian *ugol'*, "coal," and *Ural*, "Urals."

Uglich (У́глич) *Town, western Russia*. The town, west of Yaroslavl, dates from at least the 10th century. In a document of 1148 the name is recorded as *Ugleche pole*, which suggests that the first word is based on a personal name, that of the owner of the *pole*, "field." Folk etymology derives the name from the Russian phrase *tut zhgli ugli*, "here they burned coals" (!).

Ugolny See **Beringovsky**.

Ukhta (Ухта́) *Town, western Russia*. The town, in the Komi republic northeast of Syktyvkar, arose in 1931 as the village of *Chibyu* (Чи́бью), so named for the river that is a tributary of the *Ukhta* here. In 1939 the village was renamed for the latter river. Its own name is probably of Finno-Ugrian origin meaning simply "river."

Ukhta See **Kalevala**.

Ukraine (Украйна) *Republic, southern Europe*. The republic, bordered on the west by Moldova, Romania, Slovakia, and Poland, on the north by Belarus, on the east by Russia, and on the south by the Black Sea, has a name meaning "borderland," from Russian *kraj*, "edge," in this case meaning land bordering the steppes. The name is first recorded in 1187, when it denoted the southwestern lands of ancient Russia. From the 14th century the Ukraine also became known as *Little Russia* (Ма́лая Русь, later Малоро́ссия), since it lay on the periphery of what was the main body of European Russia, *Great Russia* (Вели́кая Русь).

Ulala See **Gorno-Altaysk**.

Ulan-Ude (Ула́н-Удэ́) *City, southern Russia*. The city, capital of the Buryaad republic, to the south of Lake Baykal, was founded in 1666 as the Cossack winter settlement of *Udinskoye*, from the *Uda* River on which it lies. In 1689 it became the fortified post of *Verkhneudinskaya*, and in 1783 the town of *Verkhneudinsk* (Верхнеу́динск). In these names, the initial *Verkhne-* means "upper," referring not to the location of the place on the upper reaches of the Uda (it is actually at its mouth, at the point where it enters the Selenga), but so as to be distinguished from *Nizhneudinsk*, "lower Uda," another town altogether, on a river of the same name (and on its lower reaches), in the basin of the Angara. To travel by water from Nizhneudinsk ("Lower Uda") to Verkhneudinsk ("Upper Uda") it is thus necessary to ascend the Angara, cross Lake Baykal, and then ascend the Selenga. In 1934 Verkhneudinsk was renamed as now, with *Ulan* the Buryat word for "red" (in the revolutionary sense), and *Ude* the Buryat form of *Uda*.

Ulkan (Улька́н) *Town, southern Russia*. The town, northeast of Ust-Kut, takes its name from the river on which it lies. The river's own name is Evenki in origin, and means "little river."

Ulyanovka (Улья́новка) *Town, western Russia*. The town, southeast of St. Petersburg, was originally known as *Sablino* (Са́блино). It was renamed as now in 1922 for Lenin, whose original name was *Ulyanov*. In 1905-6 he visited his sister and mother here.

Ulyanovo (Улья́ново) *Town, eastern Uzbekistan*. The town, southwest of Khodzhent, was originally known as the settlement of *Obruchevo* (О́бручево), presumably so called for a landowner named *Obruchev*. In 1974 this was raised to town status and given its present name in honor of Lenin, whose original surname was *Ulyanov*.

Ulyanovsk See **Simbirsk**

Ungeny (Унге́ны) *Town, western Moldova*. The town, on the Prut River, which here forms the border with Romania, has a name deriving from Moldovan *unger*, "angle," "corner," indicating its location by a bend in the river. The suffix *-eny* denotes the inhabitants of a place, so that the people here were the "corner folk." (The name is thus identical linguistically, if not topographically, to that of the *Angles*, from *Angel*, who gave the name of *England*.)

Ungvar See **Uzhgorod**.

Union of Soviet Socialist Republics See **Russia**.

Ural (Ура́л) *River, western Kazakhstan*. The river rises in southwestern Russia in the Southern *Urals*. Hence its name. It then flows west, crossing into Kazakhstan, and at **Uralsk** turns south to continue its course to the Caspian Sea. Until 1775 it was known as the *Yaik*, but because it flowed through places associated with the Pugachyov Rebellion, Catherine the Great (whom Pugachyov had planned to depose) ordered it to be renamed *Ural*, so that it lost its "rebel" associations. *Yaik* is probably a Turkic name meaning "broad river."

Uralmedstroy See **Krasnouralsk**.

Urals (Урáл) *Mountain range, west central Russia*. The mountains, extending from the Kara Sea in the north to Kazakhstan in the south, traditionally mark the divide between Europe and Asia. Their name is usually derived from *Uraltau*, "Ural mountain," one of the range's highest peaks. This mountain's own name probably simply means "mountain," and is related to such words as Mansi *ur* and Evenki *ure*, both of which have this meaning. See also **Ural**.

Uralsk (Урáльск) *Town, western Kazakhstan*. The town, near the Russian border, takes its name from the **Ural** River on which it was founded as a Cossack fortress in 1613. It was originally named *Yaitsky gorodok*, "Yaik town," since the Ural was then known as the *Yaik*. When the river was renamed in 1775, the town was given its present name.

Urechye (Урéчье) *Town, south central Belarus*. The town, southeast of Slutsk, takes its name from its riverside location, from Russian *u rechki*, "by the little river."

Urman (Урмáн) *Town, western Russia*. The town, in Bashkortostan east of Chernikovsk, has a Bashkir name meaning "forest."

Urup (Урýп) *Island, Kuril Islands, southeastern Russia*. The island, north of Iturup, is one of the largest in the chain. Its name derives from Ainu *urup*, "salmon."

Ushachi (Ушáчи) *Town, north central Belarus*. The town, southwest of Polotsk, is located on the *Shat'* River, and takes its name from this, or more precisely from the original form of the name as *Ust'-Shat'*, "mouth of the Shat'."

Ushakov Island (Ушакóва óстров) *Island, northern Russia*. The island, in the Kara Sea east of Franz Josef Land, was discovered in 1935 by an expedition led by the Soviet polar explorer Georgy Alekseyevich *Ushakov* (1901–1963), and was named for him.

Ushkovo (Ушкóво) *Town, western Russia*. The town, northwest of St. Petersburg, is named for the Soviet hero Dmitry Konstantinovich *Ushkov* (1922–1944), killed in combat on the Karelian Isthmus.

Ushtobe (Уштобé) *Town, southeastern Kazakhstan*. The town, northwest of Taldy-Kurgan, has a Kazakh name meaning "three hills," from *ush*, "three," and *tobe*, "hill."

Usman (Усмáнь) *Town, western Russia*. The town, southeast of Lipetsk, takes its name from the river on which it was founded as a fortress in 1646. The identical river name may be of Iranian origin and mean "stony." Folk etymology, as usual, explains it as the name of a beautiful Tatar maiden who drowned in its waters.

Usolye (Усóлье) *Town, western Russia*. The town, on the Kama River opposite Berezniki, arose in 1606 as a center of salt production. Hence its name, from Russian *u soli*, "by the salt." Cf. **Usolye-Sibirskoye**.

Usolye-Sibirskoye (Усóлье-Сибúрское) *Town, southern Russia*. The town, northwest of Angarsk, arose in the late 17th century as a salt production center on the Angara River. Hence its name, from Russian *u soli*, "by the salt." It was known simply as *Usolye* until 1940, when *Sibirskoye*, "Siberian," was added to distinguish it from the identically named town west of the Urals. Cf. **Usolye**.

USSR See **Russia**.

Ussuri (Уссу́ри) *River, southeastern Russia*. The river, a tributary of the Amur, forms the border between Russia and China for much of its course. It takes its name from a Nanay people who once inhabited its banks. The meaning of their own name is unknown. Cf. **Ussuriysk**.

Ussuriysk (Уссури́йск) *City, southeastern Russia*. The city, north of Vladivostok, takes its name from the **Ussuri** River. It is actually some 93 miles (150 km) from this river, but is in a region generally named for its main river (just as some American states and British counties officially are). It was founded in 1898 from the union of two villages, Nikolsky and Ketritsevo. As such, it was at first called *Nikolsk-Ussuriysky* (Нико́льск-Уссури́йский). It kept this name until 1935, when it was renamed *Voroshilov* (Вороши́лов), for the Soviet military and political leader, Kliment Yefremovich *Voroshilov* (1881–1969). In 1957, on his fall from grace, it adopted its present name, as a more concise version of the original.

Ust-Abakanskoye See **Abakan**.

Ustinov See **Izhevsk**.

Ust-Kamenogorsk (Усть-Каменого́рск) *Town, eastern Kazakhstan*. The town, southeast of Semipalatinsk, was founded as a fortress in 1720 and named for its location at the mouth (Russian *ust'ye*) of the *Kamennaya* River, that is, at the point where it enters the Irtysh. The final *-gorsk* represents Russian *gorod*, "town." The river's own name means "stony," "rocky."

Ust-Katav (Усть-Ката́в) *Town, western Russia*. The town, just west of the northern end of the Southern Urals, arose around an ironworks here at the mouth (Russian *ust'ye*) of the *Katav* River, at the point where it flows into the Yuryuzan. Hence its name.

Ust-Kut (Усть-Ку́т) *Town, southern Russia*. The town, northeast of Bratsk, is located at the point where the *Kut* River flows into the Lena. Hence the name, with *Ust* meaning "mouth." The river name derives from Evenki *kuta*, "swamp," "quagmire," describing the nature of its valley.

Ust-Medveditskaya See **Serafimovich**.

Ust-Ordynsky (Усть-Орды́нский) *Town, southern Russia*. Until 1937 the town, northeast of Irkutsk, was a Buryat village known as *Khuzhir* (Хужи́р), from the Buryat word meaning "saltmarsh." At the same time, the local post office was known as *Ust-Ordynsky*, from its location at the mouth (Russian *ust'ye*) of the *Ordynka* River. In 1937 this name passed to the village in the form *Ust-Orda*, and the present name was adopted in 1941 when the place became an urban settlement.

Ust-Sysolsk See **Syktyvkar**.

Ust-Urt See **Ustyurt**.

Ustye (У́стье) *Town, western Russia*. The town, northwest of Vologda, takes its name from its location at the mouth (Russian *ust'ye*) of the Kubena River, at the point where it enters Lake Kubenskoye.

Ustyug See **Veliky Ustyug**.

Ustyurt (Устю́рт) *Plateau, southwestern Kazakhstan.* The plateau, between the Caspian Sea and Aral Sea, derives its name from Kazakh *ystyurt*, "level height," "plateau." A former name of the area was *Ust-Urt*, under the influence of names beginning *Ust-* (from the Russian word for a river mouth).

Ustyuzhna (У́стюжна) *Town, western Russia.* The town, southwest of Cherepovets, has a name that is usually explained as representing *Ust-Izhina*, meaning "mouth of the Izhina" (cf. similar *Ust-* names above). However, the town stands on the Mologa River, not the Izhina. Moreover, the earliest record of the town, in 1252, gives its name as *Zhelezny Ustyug*. The first word of this means "iron," and indicates that the town arose on the site of iron ore deposits. It was later noted for its ironworks, and in the 16th century was known by the name of *Ustyuzhna-Zheleznopolskaya*, the latter word representing *zheleznoye pole*, "iron field." The early name suggests that the small river which flows into the Mologa here was originally known as the *Yug*. If so, its name could be of Finno-Ugrian origin and mean simply "river." (Cf. **Veliky Ustyug**.)

Uuras See **Vysotsk**.

Uyedineniya Island (Уединéния óстров) *Island, Kara Sea, northwestern Russia.* The island, in the central Kara Sea west of the Sergey Kirov group, has a name describing its isolated location, from Russian *uyedineniye*, "solitude." It was discovered and named in 1878 by the Norwegian trader Edvard Johannesen.

Uzbekistan (Узбекистáн) *Republic, Central Asia.* The republic, between Turkmenistan and Afghanistan to the south, Kazakhstan to the north and west, and Kyrgyzstan and Tajikistan to the east, takes its name from its indigenous people, the *Uzbeks*. Their own name is traditionally linked with that of *Uzbek*, a 14th-century khan who was a descendant of Timur (Tamerlane). However, his own name could well have represented that of the people to which he belonged. The final *-stan* is the Iranian element meaning "land," "country."

Uzhgorod (У́жгород) *Town, western Ukraine.* The town, by the border with Slovakia, takes its name from the *Uzh* River on which it stands, with Russian *gorod*, "town," added. The earlier name of the town when in Austria-Hungary was *Ungvar*, where *Ung* is the river name, and *var* is the Hungarian word for "fortress." The name was apparently altered to its present form after the collapse of Austria-Hungary and the formation of Czechoslovakia in 1918, under the influence of neighboring names such as *Uzhok*, to the northeast.

Uzlovaya (Узловáя) *Town, western Russia.* The town, southeast of Tula, arose by a major railroad junction, where the line from Moscow to the Donbass intersects that from the Volga to the Baltic. Hence its name, from Russian *uzel*, "junction."

Vagarshapat See **Echmiadzin**.

Vakhrushev (Вáхрушев) *Town, Sakhalin, eastern Russia.* The coal-mining town, southwest of Poronaysk on the east coast of Sakhalin island, is named for the Russian Communist party official and coal industry minister Vasily Vasilyevich *Vakhrushev* (1902–1947).

Vakhrushevo (Вáхрушево) *Town, eastern Ukraine.* The town, in the Donbass northwest of Krasny Luch, is named for the Communist party official and coal industry minister Vasily Vasilyevich *Vakhrushev* (1902–1947). Cf. **Vakhrushev**.

Vakhsh (Вахш) *River, southwestern Tajikistan*. The river, a tributary of the Amudarya, is known in its upper reaches (in Kyrgyzstan) as *Kyzylsu*, "red river," and at the point where it crosses into Tajikistan as the *Surkhob*, with the same meaning. It becomes the *Vakhsh* when joined by the Obikhingou. Its name is of uncertain origin. It may derive from *Oxus*, the ancient name of the Amudarya itself.

Valaam (Валаа́м) *Island group, Lake Ladoga, northwestern Russia*. The island group, in the north of Lake Ladoga, formerly belonged to Finland, with the name *Valamo*. The origin of the name is uncertain, though it has become popularly associated with the biblical soothsayer Balaam (Russian *Valaam*).

Valday (Валда́й) *Town, western Russia*. The town, southeast of St. Petersburg, takes its name from the *Valday Hills* (Валда́йская возвы́шенность) here. The name was recorded in the 15th century as *Varovalday* or *Varyevalda*, and this is probably of Finno-Ugrian origin, from the element *vara-* or *varye-*, "hills," and *valda*, "region," so that the overall sense is "hilly district."

Valuyki (Валу́йки) *Town, western Russia*. The town, southeast of Belgorod, has a name that has been linked both with Russian *valuj*, a type of mushroom, and an identical local dialect word meaning "sluggard." It is possible the name may derive from a personal name or nickname in the latter sense.

Vapnyarka (Вапня́рка) *Town, southwestern Ukraine*. The town, east of Mogilyov-Podolsky, takes its name from Ukrainian *vapnyarka*, "lime-kiln," itself from *vapno*, "lime." There are other places of the name elsewhere in Ukraine and in northern Romania.

Varna (Ва́рна) *Village, southwestern Russia*. The village, east of Magnitogorsk, has a name commemorating the Russian capture of the Turkish fortress at *Varna*, eastern Bulgaria, in 1828 during the war for the liberation of Greece. The Russian Varna is only some 80 miles (128 km) north of **Bredy**, which commemorates *Breda*, and this region of Russia has several other places named for Russian historical victories. They include: *Balkany* (the Balkans), *Berlin* (Berlin, Germany), *Borodinovka* (Borodino, near Mozhaysk), **Chesma** (which see), **Fershampenuaz** (which see), *Izmaylovsky* (Izmail, on the border with Romania, southern Ukraine), *Kasselsky* (Kassel, Germany), *Kulikovsky* (Kulikovo, near Moscow), *Leyptsig* (Leipzig, Germany), *Parizh* (Paris, France), *Poltavka* (Poltava, eastern Ukraine), and *Rymniksky* (Rîmnicu-Sărat, eastern Romania). Their concentration here is explained by the fact that Cossacks from this region took part in many Russian campaigns, and in particular the Napoleonic Wars. In the mid-19th century it was thus decided to commemorate these campaigns and battles by bestowing their names on Cossack settlements. See also **Borodino**[2].

Varnavino (Варна́вино) *Town, western Russia*. The town, northeast of Nizhny Novgorod, is so called from a monk named *Varnava*, "Barnabas," who lived in the forests here in the 15th century. Other monks joined him, a monastery was built, and a settlement grew up around it.

Varnek (Ва́рнек) *Town, northern Russia*. The town, on the south coast of Vaygach island, takes its name from the bay here. The bay was discovered in 1902 by the Russian explorer Aleksandr Ivanovich *Varnek* (1858-1930), and is named for him.

Vasilkov (Васильков́) *Town, north central Ukraine*. The town, southwest of Kiev, was founded in the 10th century and is said to derive its name from the personal name *Vasilko*, borne by many Kievan and Galician princes. According to some authorities, the name specifically represents *Vasiliy* (English "Basil"), the second name of Grand Prince Vladimir Svyatoslavich, given on his acceptance of Christianity. Either way the final *-ov* is possessive, so that the meaning is "Vasilko's (town)" or "Vasiliy's (town)."

Vasilsursk (Васильсу́рск) *Town, western Russia*. The town, east of Nizhny Novgorod, was founded in 1523 in the reign of the Muscovy prince *Vasily* III as a defensive post against the Kazan khanate. It was thus named for him, originally as *Vasilgorod*, "Vasily's town." The second part of the present name is that of the *Sura* River, which enters the Volga here.

Vasilyevsky Island (Васи́льевский о́стров) *Island, St. Petersburg, western Russia*. St. Petersburg's largest island, at the mouth of the Neva River, bears a name that predates the founding of the city in 1703. It is recorded in an archive of 1500, although the identity of the particular *Vasily* (Basil) who gave it is uncertain. He was presumably the owner of the island. The Finnish name of the island was *Hirvisaari*, "Elk Island."

Vasilyovo See **Chkalovsk**.

Vasyugan (Васюга́н) *River, southern Russia*. The river, a tributary of the Ob, was originally known as the *Vasses* or *Vassis*, a name based on *ses* or *sis*, the Ket word for "river." This name gradually became contracted to *Vass* or *Vas*, and subsequently added *yugan*, the Khanty word for "river," when the original meaning of the name had been forgotten.

Vatutino (Вату́тино) *Town, central Ukraine*. The town, southwest of Cherkassy, was founded in 1949 and named for the Soviet general Nikolay Fyodorovich *Vatutin* (1901-1944), who commanded the 1st Ukrainian front here in World War II and who died of wounds sustained in combat.

Vayenga See **Severomorsk**.

Vaygach (Вайга́ч) *Island, northern Russia*. The island, between Novaya Zemlya and the Siberian mainland, derives its name from the North Russian term for an alluvial sandbank.

Velikaya (Вели́кая) *River, western Russia*. The river, flowing north into Lake Pskov (the southern arm of Lake Chudskoye), has a name meaning "big." It is was so named by contrast with some other, smaller river. The name is found elsewhere.

Velikiye Luki (Вели́кие Лу́ки) *Town, western Russia*. The town, southeast of Pskov, is first mentioned in a record of 1166. Old Russian *luka* meant "bow," "river bend," and *veliky* meant "big" (it now means "great"). The name overall thus means "big bend," referring to the location of the town in a wide bend of the Lovat River. (The name is grammatically plural, but does not have a plural sense.)

Velikoknyazheskaya See **Proletarsk**.

Veliky Ustyug (Вели́кий У́стюг) *Town, western Russia*. The town, southwest of Kotlas, is first mentioned in a chronicle of 1207. It is located on the Sukhona River at the point where the *Yug* enters. The second word of the name thus represents

Russian *ust'ye Yuga (reki)*, "mouth of the Yug (river)." Cf. **Ustyuzhna**. The first word means "big," so the name implies a comparison with a "little" place of the same name. It is uncertain where this is or was.

Velsk (Вельск) *Town, western Russia*. The town, northeast of Vologda, takes its name from the *Vel* River on which it lies. The river name is said to derive from Komi *vel'*, "upper," by contrast with the *Uftyuga* to the east, with a name based on Komi *ult*, "lower."

Velyaminskoye ukrepleniye See **Tuapse**.

Venera (Венéра) *Village, western Russia*. The Village, in Mordovia west of Saransk, has a name meaning "Venus." It is one of a number of planet names adopted after the 1917 Revolution to signify a place with a prophetically bright future. The name was originally that of a collective farm set up here in the late 1920s by settlers from the nearby village of Staryye Verkhisy.

Ventspils (Вéнтспилс) *City and port, western Latvia*. The city, on the Baltic coast northwest of Riga, was founded in 1242 and takes its name from the *Venta* River that enters the sea here, with Latvian *pils* meaning "town." Its prerevolutionary Russian name was *Vindava* (Виндáва), from the German name, *Windau*. This also represents the river name, itself of unknown origin.

Vereshchagino (Верещáгино) *Town, western Russia*. The town, west of Perm, was founded in 1898 as the railroad station of *Ocherskaya* (see **Ochyor**). The village that grew up here was then renamed *Voznesenskaya* (Вознесéнская) ("Ascension"), for the dedication of its church, and finally in 1915 as now. The name commemorates the Russian painter of battle scenes Vasily Vasilyevich *Vereshchagin* (1842–1904), who stopped here in 1904 on his way east to depict scenes of the Russo-Japanese War. That same year, however, he was killed when the battleship *Petropavlovsk* exploded at Port Arthur during the War.

Vereya (Верея́) *Village, western Russia*. The village, east of Orekhovo-Zuyevo, derives its name from the identical Russian dialect word meaning "gatepost." There is another village of the same name southeast of Mozhaysk.

Verkhnedneprovsk (Верхнеднепрóвск) *Town, eastern Ukraine*. The town, on the Dnieper west of Dnepropetrovsk, was founded in 1780 and has a name meaning "upper Dnieper," from *verkhne-*, "upper" and *Dnepr*, "Dnieper." Before construction of the hydroelectric station on the Upper Dnieper, there were rapids here that divided the river into two channels. Verkhnedneprovsk was located above the rapids. Hence its name, although it is actually nearer the mouth of Dnieper than its source and so in that respect is really "lower Dnieper."

Verkhnedvinsk (Верхнедви́нск) *Town, northern Belarus*. The town, northwest of Polotsk, was originally known as *Drissa* (Дри́сса), from its location on the river of this name. This unpleasant-sounding name (at least in Belorussian) was changed to the present one in 1962. The new name derives from Russian *verkhne-*, "upper," and *Dvina*, the latter being the Western Dvina River, of which the Drissa is a tributary. The town is only a short distance from the upper reaches of the Dvina.

Verkhneudinsk See **Ulan-Ude**.

Verkhneuralsk (Верхнеура́льск) *Town, southwestern Russia*. The town, northeast of Magnitogorsk, was founded in 1734 as a fortified post on the upper reaches of the *Ural* River. Hence its present name, with *Verkhne-* meaning "upper." However, it was founded at a time when the Ural was known as the *Yaik* (see **Ural**), so that its original name was *Verkhneyaitsk*. It was renamed as now in 1775, when the river was. The defensive post gained town status in 1781.

Verkhniye Sergi See **Nizhniye Sergi**.

Verkhnyaya Pyshma (Вéрхняя Пышмá) *Town, western Russia.* The town, just north of Yekaterinburg, was formed in 1946 from the two settlements of *Staropyshminsk* ("Old Pyshma") and *Pyshma*, and takes its name from the *Pyshma* River on which it stands, *Verkhnyaya* meaning "Upper." The river name is of uncertain origin, although there have been attempts to derive it from Tatar *poshmas*, "slow," referring to the current. It is almost certainly pre-Tatar, however.

Verkhnyaya Salda See **Nizhnyaya Salda**.

Verkhnyaya Tunguska See **Tunguska**.

Verkhnyaya Tura (Вéрхняя Турá) *Town, west central Russia.* The town, north of Nizhny Tagil, takes its name from the *Tura* River on which it lies. The first word of the name means "upper," referring to its location upstream from its namesake, *Nizhnyaya Tura*, "lower Tura." Both places began their existence as ironworks, founded respectively in 1737 and 1766, with the settlements that arose around each raised to town status in 1941 and 1949. They are approximately 18 miles (29 km) apart. For the origin of the river name, see **Turinsk**.

Verkhny Ufaley (Вéрхний Уфалéй) *Town, southwestern Russia.* The town, southwest of Yekaterinburg, takes the second word of its name from the **Ufa** River on which it lies, with the final *-ley* a Russian alteration of the Turkic possessive suffix *-le*, giving the overall sense "belonging to the Ufa." The first word means "upper," and relates to the ironworks that were built on the upper reaches of the Ufa in 1761. In 1813 a similar plant was built further down the river and developed into *Nizhny Ufaley*, "lower Ufaley." The two places are about 12 miles (19 km) apart. Verkhny Ufaley was raised to town status in 1940 while Nizhny Ufaley remained a "settlement of town type."

Verkhoturye (Верхотýрье) *Town, west central Russia.* The town, northeast of Verkhnyaya Tura, is located on the *Tura* River. It was founded in 1598 as a fortified settlement on the higher bank of the river at a time when a new, shorter route to Siberia down the Tura was opened. Although the name begins with *Verkho-*, "upper," the town is actually lower down the Tura than *Nizhnyaya Tura* ("lower Tura"). This came about because the names evolved at different periods and for different reasons. Verkhoturye is "upper" with regard to **Turinsk**, which lies below it, while *Nizhnyaya Tura* is so named because it is downstream from **Verkhnyaya Tura** ("upper Tura"). For the origin of the river name itself, see **Turinsk**.

Verkhoyansk (Верхоя́нск) *Town, northeastern Russia.* The town, in Yakutia northeast of Yakutsk, was founded in 1638 as a Cossack wintering station. It is located at the confluence of the Dulgalakh and Sartang rivers, which here form the *Yana*. Hence its name, with *Verkho-* meaning "upper." (It could hardly be further up the Yana than this.) The *Verkhoyansk Mountains* (Верхоя́нский хребéт), which extend in a broad arc to the east of the Lena and lower

Aldan rivers, are not named for the town. They are so called because the Dulgalakh and Sartang, which form the Yana, rise on their slopes.

Vetluga (Ветлу́га) *River, western Russia*. The river, a tributary of the Volga, and joining that river east of Nizhny Novgorod, is known to the local Mari people here as the *Vytla*. This name is based on a Finno-Ugrian root word *vete*, "water," the Mari form of which is *vyt* or *vyd*. The suffix *-la* denotes multiplicity, so that the name as a whole means "of many waters." The final *-uga* of the Russian name was added under the influence of other river names such as *Yezhuga*, *Pechuga*, and *Verduga*.

Vidnoye (Ви́дное) *Town, western Russia*. The town, just south of Moscow, has a name meaning "visible," "prominent," doubtless with reference to its elevated location, so that it can be seen from all sides.

Viipuri See **Vyborg**.

Vilgort (Ви́льгорт) *Village, western Russia*. The village, northwest of Krasnovishersk to the west of the Middle Urals, is recorded in the 16th century. Its name means "new settlement," from Komi-Permyak *vil'*, "new," and *gort*, "residence," "settlement."

Vilkitsky Island (Вильки́цкого о́стров) *Island, northwestern Russia*. The island, in the Kara Sea west of Dikson, was discovered by the British explorer Joseph Wiggins in 1874. In 1895 it was charted by the Russian hydrographer and polar explorer Andrey Ippolitovich *Vilkitsky* (1858–1913), and named for him. An identically named island, east of the New Siberian Islands, was discovered in 1913 by A. N. Zhokhov (see **Zhokhov Island**), and was named commemoratively for Vilkitsky just after his death. Cf. *Vilkitsky Strait*.

Vilkitsky Strait (Вильки́цкого проли́в) *Strait, northern Russia*. The strait, between North Land and the Russian mainland (at the Taymyr Peninsula), was discovered in 1914 and named in honor of the Russian hydrographer who discovered North Land in 1913, Boris Andreyevich *Vilkitsky* (1885–1961), son of A. I. Vilkitsky (see **Vilkitsky Island**).

Vilnius (Ви́льнюс) *Capital of Lithuania*. The city, in the east of the republic southeast of Kaunas, was founded in the 10th century on the *Viliya* River, at the point where the *Vilnya* flows into it. It is thus named for both rivers. The *Viliya* has a name meaning "big," from a Slavic root word to which Russian *velikij*, "great," is related. The Lithuanian name of the Viliya is *Nyaris*, of disputed origin. Until 1939 the official name of the city was *Vilno* (Ви́льно).

Vilno See **Vilnius**.

Vilyuy (Вилю́й) *River, eastern Russia*. The river, the longest tributary of the Lena, mainly in Yakutia, derives its name from the local root word *vil*, used for a place where fishermen traded and bartered with hunters.

Vindava See **Ventspils**.

Vinnitsa (Ви́нница) *City, west central Ukraine*. The city, south of Berdichev, is first mentioned in a chronicle of 1363 as a Lithuanian fortress. Its name is said to derive from Old Slavonic *veno* or *vino*, "gift of land." The reference would be to the Lithuanian princes who seized Vinnitsa and its lands in the 14th century and gave them as gifts to their nephews. However, some authorities derive the name from Ukrainian *vinnitsa*, "distillery."

Vinogradovo (Виногра́дово) *Village, western Russia*. The village, southeast of Moscow, is named for the Russian revolutionary S. I. *Vinogradov*, who was stationmaster here when the place was known as

Ashitkovo and who in 1905 was shot by czarist troops for his subversive activities.

Vishnevogorsk (Вишневогóрск) *Town, west central Russia.* The town, south of Yekaterinburg, takes its name from the *Vishnyovyye gory* (Vishnya Mountains), whose own name is said to derive from Russian *vishnya*, "cherry tree." The reference would be to the wild cherry.

Visim (Висúм) *Town, west central Russia.* The town, southwest of Nizhny Tagil, takes its name from the river on which it lies. It arose from an ironworks founded here by Akinfy Demidov in the 1740s, at the point where the Visim joins the larger Mezhevaya Utka River. The river name is of uncertain origin but probably simply means "river."

Visimo-Utkinsk (Висúмо-Ýткинск) *Town, west central Russia.* The town, southwest of Nizhny Tagil, takes its name from the *Visim* and *Utka* rivers, at the confluence of which it lies. It arose from an ironworks founded in 1771. For the origins of the river names, see **Visim** and **Novoutkinsk**.

Vistula Lagoon (Вúслинский залúв) *Lagoon, western Russia.* The lagoon, on the Gulf of Gdańsk in the Baltic Sea, is now divided between Russia and Poland. Its name refers to the *Vistula* (Вúсла), which flows into it east of Gdańsk. It is actually separated from the Gulf of Gdańsk by a long, narrow spit called in Russian *Baltiyskaya Kosa*, "Baltic spit," in Polish *Mierzeja Wiślana*, "Vistula spit," and in German *Frische Nehrung*, "cool spit." (The lagoon's former German name was *Frisches Haff*, "cool lagoon.")

Vitebsk (Вúтебск) *City, northeastern Belarus.* The city, southeast of Polotsk, takes its name from the *Vitba* River which enters the Western Dvina here. The river name itself has been derived from the local word *vit'*, "swamp," with the *-ba* suffix associating it with a particular place, as here.

Vize (Вúзе) *Island, northern Russia.* The island, in the Kara Sea between Franz Josef Land and North Land, was "predicted" in 1924 on the basis of calculations regarding the drift rate of ice here made by the Soviet geographer and explorer Vladimir Yulyevich *Vize* (1886–1954). When it was actually discovered in 1930, it was thus named for him.

Vladikavkaz (Владикавкáз) *City, southwestern Russia.* The city, southwest of Grozny, was founded in 1784 as a fortress to guard the Georgian Military Road through the Caucasus. It was given a name meaning "possessing the Caucasus," from Russian *vladet'*, "to possess," and *Kavkaz*, "Caucasus." The name was modeled on those of Russian princes of old, such as **Vladimir** ("possessing the world") and *Vladislav* ("possessing glory"). (The model would be used again for **Vladivostok**.) It kept this name until 1931 when it was renamed *Ordzhonikidze* (Орджоникúдзе), for the Georgian party leader Grigory Konstantinovich *Ordzhonikidze* (1886–1937), who had been a revolutionary in the Caucasus and who in the Civil War was instrumental in bringing Georgia under Soviet rule. In 1944 the city was renamed again as *Dzaudzhikau* (Дзауджикáу), from the name of the village near which the town had been originally founded. This name is based on a personal name, with *kau* meaning "village." In 1954 the name reverted to *Ordzhonikidze*, but finally returned to *Vladikavkaz* in 1990.

Vladimir (Владúмир) *City, western Russia.* The city, east of Moscow, is named for its founder, Grand Prince *Vladimir* Vsevolodovich Monomachus (1053–1125), who in

1108 built a fortress here to defend the Rostov-Suzdal principality from the southeast.

Vladimirovka See **Yuzhno-Sakhalinsk**.

Vladimir-Volynsky (Влади́мир-Волы́нский) *City, northwestern Ukraine*. The city, near the Polish border, is known to have existed in the 10th century. It is in **Volynia** (hence the second part of the name), and was founded in the reign of the Kievan prince *Vladimir* Svyatoslavich (died 1015) (hence the first part).

Vladislavov See **Kudirkos-Naumiestis**.

Vladivostok (Владивосто́к) *City and port, southeastern Russia*. The well known Far East port was founded in 1860 as a military post. Its name thus has a military significance, and means "possessing the east," from Russian *vladet'*, "to possess," and *vostok*, "east." This type of name had a precedent in **Vladikavkaz** (which see).

Vladychino (Влады́чино) *District, Moscow, western Russia*. The eastern district of Moscow arose on the site of land owned until the 18th century by the Moscow patriarchs. Hence the name, from Russian *vladyka*, "master," the title of the higher orders of Orthodox clergy. Cf. **Vladykino**.

Vladykino (Влады́кино) *District, Moscow, western Russia*. The northern district of Moscow stands on the site of lands owned in the 14th century by the boyar P. F. Velyaminov. This gave the original name of the village, *Velyaminovo*. In 1653 the territory passed to the Moscow patriarchate, and this gave its present name, from Russian *vladyka*, "master," the title of the higher orders of Orthodox clergy. Cf. **Vladychino**.

Volchansk[1] (Волча́нск) *Town, northeastern Ukraine*. The town, near the Russian border northeast of Kharkov, was founded in 1674 and takes its name from the *Volchya* River on which it lies. The river's name represents the feminine of *volchij*, the adjectival form of *volk*, "wolf." The town was at first known as *Volchi vody*, literally "wolf waters."

Volchansk[2] (Волча́нск) *Town, west central Russia*. The town, north of Karpinsk, arose around a coalfield discovered in the second half of the 19th century. The settlement that developed was at first named *Lesnaya Volchanka*, "Volchanka of the woods," from the *Volchanka* River here. The river's own name appears to be based on Russian *volk*, "wolf," but this could be a folk etymology, arising to explain a non-Russian (possibly Mansi) name of unknown meaning.

Volga (Во́лга) *River, western Russia*. Russia's best known river rises south of St. Petersburg and flows generally southeast then southwest before again turning southeast to enter the Caspian Sea. Like many other lengthy rivers, it has had different names at different times for its different sections. The Greek geographer Ptolemy knew the lower reaches of the river as the *Rha* in the 2nd century AD. This name is probably of Iranian origin and means simply "river." Until about the 9th century, the lower and middle reaches of the river were known by the Turkic name of *Itil*, related to Tatar *idel*, "big river." The upper reaches of the river have long been known as the *Volga*. The origin of this name is uncertain. It may well be of ethnic origin, and be that of a people who lived on its banks. However, the uppermost part of the river is in a region that was long inhabited by Baltic folk. It is therefore possible that the name relates to the Baltic word *valka*, "stream," "source." At the same time, there are those who point to a possible association with Russian *vlaga*, "moisture." But if this is the case, what was the river called before the Slavs came to it in the 8th or 9th century? See also **Volkhov**.

Volgodonsk (Волгодо́нск) *Town, southwestern Russia*. The town, on the Don River at the western end of the Tsimlyansky Reservoir, southwest of Volgograd, arose during construction of the *Volgo-Don* Canal (1948–52), and takes its name from it. The original settlement was raised to town status in 1956.

Volgograd (Волгогра́д) *City, southwestern Russia*. The city, northeast of Rostov-on-Don, was founded in the 16th century on an island in the *Volga* at a point where the *Tsarytsyn* enters it. The objective was to guard the waterway at the portage here between the Don and the Volga. The settlement was thus originally known as *Tsaritsyn* (Цари́цын), for the more distinctive river. (In the early 17th century the community was destroyed by fire, and was rebuilt on the right bank of the Volga.) This early name came to be popularly associated with *tsaritsa*, "czarina," so was deemed to have royal associations. In fact the river name is of Turkic origin, evolving from *sary-su*, "yellow water." In 1925 the city that had grown up was renamed *Stalingrad* (Сталингра́д), for the Soviet leader Iosif Vissarionovich Stalin (1879–1953), who had masterminded the defense of Tsaritsyn against counterrevolutionaries in the Civil War. It was thus now "Stalin's town," and as such was famous for the Siege of Stalingrad in World War II, in which the city at bitter cost held out against the Germans. In 1961, following destalinization, it was again renamed, so that it is now the "Volga city."

Volgo-Kaspiysky (Во́лго-Каспи́йский) *Town, southwestern Russia*. The town lies southwest of Astrakhan in the delta of the *Volga* which here enters the *Caspian* Sea. Hence its name.

Volgorechensk (Волгоре́ченск) *Town, western Russia*. The town, on the Volga southwest of Kostroma, takes its name from its location, from *Volga* and an adjectival form of Russian *reka*, "river." The town arose in 1964 during construction of the Kostroma state regional electric power station here.

Volhynia See **Volynia**.

Volkhov (Во́лхов) *Town, western Russia*. The town, east of St. Petersburg, takes its name from the *Volkhov* River on which it stands. The origin of the river name is uncertain, but it may be related to that of the **Volga**. The town developed at the time of the construction of the hydroelectric station here in the 1920s. For that reason it was known for a while as *Volkhovstroy*, "Volkhov construction site." The original name of the village and railroad station here was *Zvanka* (Зва́нка).

Volochayevka (Волоча́евка) *Town, eastern Russia*. The town, west of Khabarovsk, is said to take its name from M. S. *Volochayev*, the leader of the Kuban Cossacks who came to settle here in 1908 when conditions were unfavorable further west. (The story goes that the czarist authorities wanted to name the new settlement for the governor general, but a Cossack council decided the matter and the popular choice won.) A second settlement arose on the site in the late 1930s when the railroad was extended to Komsomolsk-on-Amur. This was officially known as *Volochayevka Vtoraya*, "Second Volochayevka," but the basic name is the one now normally used.

Vologda (Вологда) *City, western Russia*. The city, north of Yaroslavl, arose in the 12th century on a portage between the Sukhona and Sheksna rivers. It takes its name from the *Vologda* River, which here is some 20 miles (32 km) from its point of entry into the Sukhona. The river name is said to be of Finnic origin, deriving from *valgada*, "white." However, it is more likely to be pre-Finnic, and its precise meaning is uncertain.

Volokolamsk (Волоколамск) *Town, western Russia*. The town, northwest of Moscow, has a name meaning "Lama portage," from the *Lama* River on which it lies and Russian *volok*, "portage," a portage being a location where cargo and boats are transported overland from one river to another. The town arose in the 12th century and was originally on the portage between the Lama and the Ruza (a tributary of the Moskva). It was subsequently transferred from its initial swampy site to the present one, some 12 miles (20 km) away.

Volsk (Вольск) *Town, western Russia*. The town takes its name from the *Volga*, on which it lies northeast of Saratov. It arose in the 17th century, and at first was a village called *Malykovka*. It was raised to town status in 1780 and was then renamed *Volgsk*. The g of this was later dropped for ease of pronunciation.

Volynia (Волынь) *Region, northwestern Ukraine*. The present region, also known as *Volhynia*, is the modern survival of a much larger historic territory, extending over an area of east central Europe. It was divided in 1921 between Poland and Russia, but the Polish section was taken in the partition of 1939 and forms the present administrative region of Ukraine. The name is said to derive from some similar placename, although which is uncertain.

There may be a link with the town of *Wolin*, northwestern Poland. The name appears elsewhere in eastern Europe, for example as the village of *Volyně* in the southwestern Czech Republic.

Volzhsk (Волжск) *Town, western Russia*. The town, west of Kazan, lies on the *Volga* river at the northern end of the Kuybyshev Reservoir. Hence its name. Until 1940 it was known as *Lopatino* (Лопатино), presumably for an early landowner here.

Volzhsky (Волжский) *Town, southwestern Russia*. The town, on the left bank of the *Volga*, opposite Volgograd, arose in 1951 during construction of the vast Volga hydroelectric station here. Its original name was *Derevyanny gorodok*, "wooden settlement." It then progressed to *Kamenny gorodok*, "stone settlement," before gaining its present name in 1954, when the community was raised to town status. The name is the adjectival form of *Volga*.

Vorkuta (Воркута) *Town, northwestern Russia*. The town, just west of the northern end of the Northern Urals, arose in 1931 when coal was discovered here. It takes its name from the river on which it stands. The river name is said to represent Nenets *varkuta*, "abounding in bears," from *vark*, "bear." Old-timers here tell how at one time bears ventured some distance into the tundra when foraging for cloudberries.

Voronezh (Воронеж) *City, western Russia*. The city, east of Kursk, is first mentioned in a monastic chronicle of 1177. It takes its name from the *Voronezh* River on which it stands, near the point where it enters the Don. The origin of the river name is disputed. According to some recent authorities, it was "imported" here from the *Voronezh* that is now a small town in northern Ukraine. That name is said to derive from the Slavic personal name *Voroneg*, itself based on *voron*, "raven." On the other hand, the river name may have evolved as a prime name, from Mordovian *vor*, "forest," and *nezhe*, "defense," so that the river is a "forest defense" at the edge of ancient Mordovian territory. But this second account does not explain the link, if any, between the Ukrainian placename and that of the Russian city.

Voronin Island (Воро́нина о́стров) *Island, northern Russia*. The small island, in the Kara Sea between North Land and the Siberian mainland (here the Taymyr Peninsula), was discovered in 1930 by the icebreaker *G. Sedov* and was named for the ship's captain, Vladimir Ivanovich *Voronin* (1890–1952).

Vorontsovo (Воронцо́во) *District, Moscow, western Russia*. The southwestern district of Moscow takes its name from the village formerly here. This was owned in the 14th century by the boyar F. *Voronets*. Hence the name. An earlier alternate name was *Troitskoye*, for the dedication of the church here to the Trinity (Russian *Troitsa*).

Vorontsovo-Aleksandrovskoye See **Zelenokumsk**.

Voroshilov See **Ussuriysk**.

Voroshilovgrad See **Lugansk**.

Voroshilovsk See (1) **Kommunarsk**, (2) **Stavropol**.

Vorskla (Во́рскла) *River, central Ukraine*. The river, a tributary of the Dnieper, has a name of uncertain meaning. It may be of Iranian origin and relate to Ossetic *vors*, "white." As usual, folk etymology has devised a colorful story to explain it. After his victory over the Swedes at Poltava (1709), Peter the Great dropped his monocle in the water here and exclaimed: "This river should be called 'Lens Thief' (*vor stkla*)" (!).

Vose (Босе́) *Town, southwestern Tajikistan*. The town, southwest of Kulyab, is named for *Vose*, the leader of a peasant uprising in Bukhara in 1885.

Voskresensk (Воскресе́нск) *Town, western Russia*. The town, southeast of Moscow, arose in 1862 by a railroad station and took its name from the dedication of its church to the *Resurrection* (Russian *Voskreseniye*).

Voskresensk See **Istra**.

Vostok See **Neftegorsk**[2].

Vozdvizhenskoye (Воздви́женское) *Village, western Russia*. The village, southwest of Sergiyev Posad, takes its name from the dedication of the church originally here, which was to the Exaltation of the Cross (*Vozdvizheniye*).

Vozhd Proletariata (Вождь Пролетариа́та) *Town, western Russia*. The town, with its turf extraction industry east of Moscow, was founded in 1934 and given a name translating as "Leader of the Proletariat," a title of Lenin.

Vozhe (Во́же) *Lake, western Russia*. The lake, southeast of Lake Ladoga, is said to have a name of Komi origin, from *vozh*, "spring," "source." The *Vozhega* River that flows into it has a name based on the same word.

Voznesenskaya See **Vereshchagino**.

Vrangel Island See **Wrangel Island**.

Vsekhsvyatskoye (Всехсвя́тское) *District, Moscow, western Russia*. The northwestern district of Moscow takes its name from the former village here. Its original name in the 15th century was *Svyatyye Ottsy*,

"Holy Fathers." From the late 17th century it was known by the present name, for the church built here in 1683 and dedicated to All Saints (Russian *Vsexh Svyatykh*).

Vsevolodo-Blagodatsky (Всéволодо-Благодáцкий) *Town, west central Russia*. The town, southwest of Ivdel, takes its name from the first of a family of factory owners in this part of the Urals, *Vsevolod* Andreyevich Vsevolozhsky, active here in the late 18th and early 19th centuries. The second part of the name means "abundance," and relates to the rich veins of iron ore in the Middle Urals. Cf. **Aleksandrovsk**.

Vsevolozhsk (Всéволожск) *Town, western Russia*. The town, east of St. Petersburg, derives its name from the local grandee V.A. *Vsevolozhsky*, owner of the large estate of Ryabovo here in the 19th century. The name was originally *Vsevolozhskaya*, that of a railroad station set up in 1890 when the line was extended to Ryabovo. The settlement of *Vsevolozhskoye* that grew up around it received its present name when it was raised to town status in 1963.

Vulkaneshty (Вулканéшты) *Town, southern Moldova*. The town, southeast of Kagul, derives its name from the Moldovan family name *Vulkan*, itself from a word meaning "wolf" (Russian *volk*), with *-eshty* the possessive suffix, meaning "belonging to."

Vyatka (Вя́тка) *City, western Russia*. The city, north of Kazan, was in existence as a Novgorodian settlement in the 14th century. It was originally known as *Khlynov*, for the *Khlynovitse* River, which enters the *Vyatka* here. In 1781 it was renamed *Vyatka* for the latter river. Its own name is probably of ethnic origin, and related to that of the *Votyaks*, the earlier name of the Udmurts (see

Udmurtia). In 1934 the city was renamed *Kirov* (Ки́ров), commemorating the Soviet politician Sergey Mironovich *Kirov* (1888–1934), who was born at Urzhum, a few miles to the south. In 1991 the city reverted to its earlier name.

Vyazma (Вя́зьма) *Town, western Russia*. The town, northeast of Smolensk, arose in the 9th or 10th century and takes its name from the *Vyazma* River on which it lies. The river name is of disputed origin. It may not necessarily derive from a word related to Russian *vyazkij*, "sticky," "boggy," as has been explained, and the final *-ma* suggests that that the ultimate origin may not be Slavic but Finno-Ugrian.

Vyazniki (Вя́зники) *Town, western Russia*. The town, west of Dzerzhinsk, has a name that appears to mean "(place) surrounded by elms," from Russian *vyaz*, "elm." Cf. **Berezniki**.

Vyborg (Вы́борг) *Town, western Russia*. The town, near the border with Finland northwest of St. Petersburg, arose as a Swedish fortress in 1293 on the site of an earlier Novgorodian settlement. The name is usually explained as meaning "holy castle," from Swedish *vi*, "holy," "sacred," and *borg*, "castle," "town." If so, the name has the same origin as that of the Danish city of *Viborg*. On the other hand, the Swedish name may have evolved from *Viipuri*, the Finnish name of the place, itself of uncertain origin, although this is usually explained as a rendering of the Swedish name.

Vychegda (Вы́чегда) *River, northwestern Russia*. The river, the longest tributary of the Northern Dvina, has a name that is said to derive from the Old Mansi words *vich*, "damp meadow," and *yegda*, "river." The river indeed flows through low-lying, marshy terrain.

Its Komi name is *Ezhva*, "meadow river," which is similar in meaning.

Vyshgorod (Вышгород) *Town, northern Ukraine*. The town, on the Dnieper north of Kiev, is recorded in the 10th century as being the town of Princess Olga, wife of Prince Igor of Kiev. The name itself means literally "high town," from a Slavic word related to Russian *vyshe*, "higher." This could apply to an elevated site or, as probably here, to an important place. Its prime origin was undoubtedly as a Russian rendering of Greek *akropolis*, "high town," the term for the central and highest part of a Greek city, where its citadel stood. (Hence the *Acropolis* in Athens, on which the Parthenon stands.) Vyshgorod was the place of residence of Kievan princes in the 11th and 12th centuries.

Vyshny Volochyok (Вышний Волочёк) *Town, western Russia*. The town, northwest of Tver, was founded on a portage between the Msta and Tvertsa rivers. Hence its name, meaning "upper portage," from Old Russian *vyshnij*, "upper," and *volok*, "portage" (a location where cargo was carried overland between two rivers). This portage must have been "upper" in relation to one further down.

Vysokovsk (Высоковск) *Town, western Russia*. The town, northwest of Moscow, has a name based on Russian *vysokij*, "high," referring to its elevated site.

Vysokoye (Высокое) *Town, western Belarus*. The town, northwest of Brest near the Polish border, was recorded in the 14th century as *Vysokiy Gorod*, "high town," and the present name evolved from this. The terrain here is relatively elevated.

Vysotsk (Высоцк) *Town, western Russia*. The town, on Vysotsky Island southwest of Vyborg, takes its name from the Russian machine gunner K. D. *Vysotsky*, killed here in 1940 in the Winter War against Finland. The Finnish name of the town before 1948 was *Uuras*.

Vzmorye (Взморье) *Town, Sakhalin, eastern Russia*. The town, on the east coast of Sakhalin island south of Makarov, has a name that is the standard Russian word for "sea coast." The town is on the Sea of Okhotsk.

Wilczek Land (Вильчека Земля) *Island, Franz Josef Land, northwestern Russia*. The island, one of the largest in the group, lies to the west of Graham Bell Island. It is named for Count Hans *Wilczek* (1837–1922), the Austrian naturalist and explorer who financed the expedition of Payer and Weyprecht that discovered it in 1873.

Windau See **Ventspils**.

Wrangel Island (Врангеля остров) *Island, northeastern Russia*. The island, in the Chukchi Sea off the northeastern Siberian coast, was charted (but not discovered) in 1823 by the Russian Arctic explorer Ferdinand Petrovich *Wrangel* (1796–1870), working on information from local people and his own observations. (The island's existence had been proposed in 1787 by the Russian Arctic traveler G. A. Sarychev.) In 1867 the island was actually discovered by the American whaler Thomas Long, captain of the *Nile*, who named it for *Wrangel*. This was not final, however. In 1881 Captain Hooper of the American ship *Thomas Corwin* named the island *New Columbia*, and in 1924–25 there were Soviet plans to name it *Krasny Oktyabr* ("Red October") or *Davydov*, the latter for the Russian explorer Boris Vladimirovich *Davydov* (1883–1925), who arrived at the island on board the *Krasny Oktyabr* in 1924 and planted the Red Flag on it by way of claiming Soviet possession. However, a government committee decreed in 1926 that the name *Wrangel* should be the official one.

Yablonovy Mountains (Яблоновый хребе́т) *Mountain range, southern Russia.* The mountains, between Lake Baykal and the border with Mongolia and China, have a name that appears to represent the adjective form of Russian *yablonya*, "apple tree." However, it actually derives from the Buryat name of one of the passes here, *Yabalgani-Daban*, "traversable pass."

Yadrin (Я́дрин) *Town, western Russia.* The town, in Chuvashia southwest of Cheboksary, takes its name from the factory here that made cannon balls during the war with the Kazan khanate (captured by Ivan the Terrible in 1552). The origin is thus in Russian *yadro*, "(cannon) ball," "shot."

Yakhroma (Я́хрома) *Town, western Russia.* The town, north of Moscow, takes its name from the river here. The river name is of uncertain origin, but has been accounted for by folk etymologists who tell the following story: The wife of Prince Yury Dolgoruky, founder of Moscow, was out hunting with her husband when she stumbled crossing the river and cried "I am lame!" (*Ya khroma*).

Yakovlevskoye See **Privolzhsk**.

Yakunchikov See **Krasny Mayak**.

Yakutia See **Yakut-Sakha**.

Yakut-Sakha (Яку́т-Са́ха) *Republic, east central Russia.* The republic, formerly known as *Yakutia*, takes its name from the *Yakuts*, its indigenous people. Their own name is usually explained as meaning "border folk," from a Turkic word related to modern Turkish *yaka*, "side." More precisely, it is probably of Evenki origin, from the word *yeko*, with plural form *yekot*. This was applied to any non-Evenki, that is, to someone who was an "outsider." (The Yakuts are ultimately of southern Turkic origin, and their language is a Turkic one.) The second part of the name represents the Yakuts' own name for themselves. *Sakha* simply means "person."

Yakutsk (Яку́тск) *Town, east central Russia.* The Siberian town, on the Lena River northwest of Okhotsk, was founded in 1632 as a fortified Cossack post. It was originally known as *Lensky ostrog*, "Lena stockade," or *Yakutsky ostrog*, "Yakut stockade." The latter name prevailed and gave the present name. It derives from that of the indigenous people, the *Yakuts*. (See **Yakut-Sakha**.)

Yalta (Я́лта) *Town, southern Crimea, southern Ukraine.* The town, on the Black Sea coast south of Simferopol, was known in the 12th century as *Dzhalita*. This itself evolved from ancient Greek *aigialos*, "coast," "shore." The Greeks, driven out of the Crimea by the Turks, took the name north with them to what is now the coastal village of *Yalta*, southwest of Mariupol on the Sea of Azov.

Yalutorovsk (Ялу́торовск) *Town, west central Russia.* The town, southeast of Tyumen, arose in 1639 as the fortified post of *Yalutorovsky*, taking this name from the ruins of a former Tatar fortress here known as *Yavlu-tura*, "warrior town."

Yamal (Яма́л) *Peninsula, northern Russia.* The lengthy peninsula, between the Kara Sea and the Gulf of Ob, has a Nenets name meaning "end of the land," from *ya*, "land," and *mal*, "end." The name thus equates to *Finistère* in France, *Finisterre* in Spain, *Land's End* in England, and *Pembroke* in Wales.

Yamantau (Яманта́у) *Mountain, southwestern Russia.* The mountain, the highest peak in the Southern Urals, southeast of Ufa, has a Bashkir name meaning "bad mountain." Its slopes are covered in forests and swamps, making it unsuitable for pastureland. Local herdsmen must therefore travel far to find good grazing grounds for their animals.

Yamburg See **Kingisepp**.

Yampol (Ямполь) *Town, eastern Ukraine*. There are four towns of this name in Ukraine. This one is northeast of Slavyansk. The others are respectively in the west, northeast of Ternopol, in the north, east of Novgorod Seversky, and in the southwest, on the Moldovan border, southeast of Mogilyov-Podolsky. As it stands, the name appears to combine Russian *yam*, "mail staging-post," or *yama*, "pit," with Greek *polis*, "town," or Russian *pole*, "field." All the towns are in a region where other *-pol* names exist, and the "town" (rather than the "field") interpretation is probably to be preferred, at least by comparison with *Yamburg* (see **Kingisepp**).

Yanaul (Янаул) *Town, western Russia*. The town, in Bashkiria east of Neftekamsk, has a Bashkir name meaning "new village," from *yany*, "new," and *aul*, "village."

Yangi-Aryk (Янги-Арык) *Village, southwestern Uzbekistan*. The village, south of Urgench, has a name meaning "new canal" or "new channel," from Uzbek *yangi*, "new," and *aryk*, "canal," "channel." The name is common where there are irrigation canals, as here by the Amudarya.

Yangibazar (Янгибазар) *Town, northwestern Kyrgyzstan*. The town, west of Kara Kul, has an Uzbek name meaning "new market," from *yangi*, "new," and *bazar*, "market." The name is found elsewhere in both Uzbekistan and parts of Tajikistan. Cf. **Ordzhonikidzeabad**.

Yangibazar See **Ordzhonikidzeabad**.

Yangiyer (Янгиер) *Town, eastern Uzbekistan*. The town, south of Gulistan, has an Uzbek name meaning "new land," from *yangi*, "new," and *yer*, "land." The town's prerevolutionary name was *Chernyayevo* (Черняево), for the Russian general Mikhail Grigoryevich *Chernyayev* (1828-1898), army commander in Central Asia in the 1860s and later governor general of Turkestan.

Yantarny (Янтарный) *Town, western Russia*. The town, on the Baltic Sea northwest of Kaliningrad, is noted for its manufacture of amber goods. Hence its name, from Russian *yantar'*, "amber." The former German name of the town was *Palmnicken*.

Yaroslavl (Ярославль) *City, western Russia*. The city, northeast of Moscow, was founded in about 1010 by the Kievan grand prince *Yaroslav* the Wise (c. 978-1054), and is named for him. The final *-l* of the name is a possessive suffix, so that the place-name means "Yaroslav's (town)."

Yar Sale (Яр-Сале) *Village, northwestern Russia*. The village, northeast of Salekhard, has a Nenets name meaning "sandy cape." Cf. **Salekhard** itself.

Yasinovataya (Ясиноватая) *Town, eastern Ukraine*. The town, just north of Donetsk, is so named for the river here. Its own name is based on Russian *yasen'*, "ash tree."

Yasnaya Polyana (Ясная Поляна) *Village, western Russia*. The village, south of Tula, is noted as the birthplace and residence of Leo Tolstoy. Its name, meaning "bright glade," is or was found elsewhere for country seats in Russia and Ukraine, and Tolstoy's great fame undoubtedly prompted further adoption of the name. In many cases the name was extended to the villages that grew up around such residences.

Yefremov (Ефрéмов) *Town, western Russia*. The town, southeast of Tula, arose in 1672 as a defensive post. It is said to take its name from the Cossack leader *Yefrem*, active here in the 17th century. But this origin lacks documentary support.

Yegorlyk (Егорлы́к) *River, southwestern Russia*. The river, which enters the Proletarsk Reservoir on the Western Manych River, has a Turkic name meaning "crooked," from its winding course.

Yegoryevsk (Егóрьевск) *Town, western Russia*. The town, southeast of Moscow, dates from at least the 15th century and was at first known as *Vysokaya*, "high," "elevated." When a church was built and dedicated to St. *George* this name was modified to *Yegorye Vysokoye*. The present name was given in 1778 when the village was raised to town status.

Yekaterinburg (Екатеринбу́рг) *City, west central Russia*. The city, in the Middle Urals, was founded in 1723 and was given a German-style name meaning "Catherine's town," in honor of *Catherine* I (1684–1727), wife of Peter the Great. Peter was "westward-looking." Hence the German name for this Russian town, founded at the point where Asia meets Europe. (Cf. **St. Petersburg** for a prototype German name in the czar's own honor.) In 1924 the city was renamed *Sverdlovsk* (Свердлóвск), in honor of the Soviet titular chief of state, Yakov Mikhaylovich *Sverdlov* (1885–1919), who had been a revolutionary leader here in 1905-06 and 1917. In 1991 it reverted to its original name. The czarist name was sullied when Nicholas II, the last czar, was executed here together with his family in 1918.

Yekaterinenshtadt See **Marks**.

Yekaterinodar See **Krasnodar**.

Yekaterinopol (Екатеринóполь) *Town, south central Ukraine*. The town, southwest of Cherkassy, was originally the village of *Kal'niboloto*, apparently from a personal name and Russian *boloto*, "swamp." It was renamed as now in 1795 by order of Catherine the Great. One might assume that it was renamed for her, as "Catherine's town," with the Greek-style *-pol* suffix found elsewhere. However, it is hardly likely that she would have chosen such an insignificant place to bear her name, especially as she already had the greater and worthier *Yekaterinoslav* (now **Dnepropetrovsk**). It thus seems likely that the name was given for another Catherine. A suitable candidate would have been Princess *Yekaterina* Pavlovna, one of Catherine's granddaughters. Cf. **Balta, Olgopol**.

Yekaterinoslav See **Dnepropetrovsk**.

Yelabuga (Елáбуга) *Town, western Russia*. The town, in Tatarstan northeast of Nizhnekamsk, arose as a village in the second half of the 16th century. It probably derives its name from the Tatar personal name *Alabuga*, "tiger" (literally "spotted bull," from words related to Turkish *ala*, "speckled," and *boğa*, "bull").

Yelensk See **Balta**.

Yelets (Елéц) *City, western Russia*. The city, west of Lipetsk, was founded in the 12th century by the Ryazan principality as a defensive post against the Polovtsians. It takes its name from the dialect word *elets*, "forest verdure," a term usually implying an oak wood.

Yeletsky (Елéцкий) *Town, northwestern Russia*. The town, at the northern end of the Urals south of Vorkuta, takes its name from the *Yelets* River on which it lies. The river's own name is of uncertain origin.

Yelgava See **Jelgava**.

Yelizavet (Елизаве́т) *District, Yekaterinburg, west central Russia.* The city's southern district evolved from the settlement that arose around an ironworks founded here in 1722 and named for *Yelizaveta* Petrovna (1709-1762), younger daughter of Peter the Great and Catherine I (for whom **Yekaterinburg** itself is named), the future Empress of Russia (from 1741). The name originated as the German form of the forename, not the Russian, i.e. from *Elisabeth*.

Yelizavetgrad See **Kirovograd**.

Yelizavetpol See **Gyandzha**.

Yelizovo (Е́лизово) *Town, eastern Russia.* The town, on the Kamchatka peninsula northwest of Petropavlovsk-Kamchatsky, was originally known by the name of *Zavoyko* (Заво́йко), for the Russian admiral Vasily Stepanovich *Zavoyko* (1810-1898), who led the defense of Petropavlovsk (now Petropavlovsk-Kamchatsky) against French and English forces in 1854. In 1924 it was renamed as now for G. *Yelizov*, leader of a partisan detachment who in 1922 was killed on Kamchatka by counterrevolutionaries.

Yelnya (Е́льня) *Town, western Russia.* The town, southeast of Smolensk, has a name based on Russian *yel'*, "fir tree." The *-nya* element is characteristic of this part of Russia and of Belarus to the west.

Yemanzhelinsk (Еманжели́нск) *Town, southwestern Russia.* The town, south of Chelyabinsk, arose around a fortress of the same name built in 1747 and itself named for the small *Yemanzhelinka* River here. Its name derives from Tatar or Bashkir *yaman*, "bad," and a dialect form of Tatar *yelga* or Bashkir *yylga*, "river." The overall sense is thus "bad river." The river's water has a high mineral content, which makes it unsuitable for drinking.

Yenakiyevo (Ена́киево) *Town, eastern Ukraine.* The industrial town, in the Donbass northeast of Donetsk, arose as a mining settlement in 1883, its name presumably from an original owner or employer. From about 1928 until 1935 it was renamed *Rykovo* (Ры́ково), for the Soviet Communist official Aleksey Ivanovich *Rykov* (1881-1938), a victim of the Great Purge. (He was expelled from the party in 1937.) A new name was thus needed, and it was given in 1935 as *Ordzhonikidze* (Орджоники́дзе), for the Georgian Communist Grigory Konstantinovich *Ordzhonikidze* (1886-1937). But he also fell from favor following a suspected suicide, and in 1943 the town readopted its original name.

Yenisey (Енисе́й) *River, central Russia.* The great Siberian river rises in the south of the country and flows generally north to enter the Kara Sea. Its name is based on Evenki *yene*, "big river," as applied to the river below the point where the Angara enters it. The Kets, who later settled in this region, adopted the Evenki name and added their own name to it. This was *Ses*, "river," so that the overall name was something like *Yeneses*, which gave the present Russian form *Yenisey*. Above the Angara, the river had the local name *Kem*. This also means "river," and is related to the name of the **Kama**, west of the Urals.

Yenotayevka (Енота́евка) *Village, southwestern Russia.* The village, on the Volga northwest of Astrakhan, is in Kalmykia, and its Kalmyk name is *Shine-balgazyn*, "new town." This has prompted some to propose a source for the first part of the Russian name in Turkish *yeni*, "new." But this leaves the rest of the name unexplained. The true origin is probably in a personal name such as *Yenotay*.

Yerevan (Ереван) *Capital of Armenia*. The city, in the west of the republic, is one of the oldest in the world. According to a hieroglyphic inscription discovered in 1964 during archaeological excavations, Argishti I, king of Urartu, built a fortress here called *Erebuni* in about BC 782. The present name thus evolved from this. The name itself is probably that of a family clan or local people. Its meaning is speculative, and interpretations have ranged from "shining descendant of the eagle" to "first to appear after the flood." Until 1936 the name's official Russian spelling was *Erivan* (Эривань).

Yermak (Ермак) *Town, northeastern Kazakhstan*. The town, on the Irtysh River south of Pavlodar, takes its name from the Cossack leader *Yermak* Timofeyevich (died 1585), one of the pioneers in Russia's acquisition of Siberia.

Yermolovsk See **Leselidze**.

Yerofey-Pavlovich (Ерофей Павлович) *Town, southeastern Russia*. The town, west of Skovorodino near the border with China, here marked by the Amur River, arose in 1909 when the railroad reached here. It takes its name from the Russian explorer *Yerofey Pavlovich* Khabarov (c. 1610-after 1667), who made several expeditions in the region of the Amur and who gave the name of **Khabarovsk**.

Yessentuki (Ессентуки) *Town, southwestern Russia*. The town, west of Pyatigorsk, arose in the 1830s on the site of a military fort built in 1798. It takes its name from the *Yessentuk* River here. The origin of the river's name is uncertain, although it has accrued diverse etymologies, including: (1) "habitual refuge," from Cherkess (Circassian) *yesen*, "to accustom," and *tukku*, "refuge," "corner"; (2) "living hair" (for the curative powers of its waters), from Karachay *yessen*, "living," and *tyuk*, "hair"; (3) "nine banners," from the Mongolian. None of these warrants serious consideration, however. The town is a noted health resort.

Yevpatoriya (Евпатория) *Town, southwestern Crimea, southern Ukraine*. The town, northwest of Simferopol, stands on the site of the ancient Greek colony of *Kerkinitida*, a name perhaps based on the same element as that of **Kerch**. The ancient Greeks gave the place the name *Eupatoria*, allegedly in honor of the king of Pontus, Mithridates *Eupator* (died 63 BC), his byname meaning "(born) of a noble father." The Turks captured the town in the 14th century and renamed it *Gezlëv*. When the Crimea became part of Russia in 1783 this name was "russified" as *Kozlov* (Козлов), which continued in parallel with the Greek name down to the 19th century until the latter prevailed. One of the poems in the *Sonety Krymskie* ("Crimean Sonnets") (1826) by the Polish poet Adam Mickiewicz is titled (in translation) "Mountain view from the plains of Kozlov."

Yeysk (Ейск) *Town and port, southwestern Russia*. The town, on the east coast of the Sea of Azov, takes its name from the *Yeya* River, which enters the sea here. The origin of the river name is problematical.

Yezhovo-Cherkessk See **Cherkessk**.

Yoshkar Ola (Йошкар-Ола) *Town, western Russia*. The town, northwest of Kazan on the Malaya Kokshaga River, a tributary of the Volga, was founded in 1584 by order of Czar Fyodor I Ivanovich after Russia's acquisition of Mari territory here. (The town is now the Mari-El capital.) Its original name was thus

Tsarev gorod na Kokshayke, "czar's town on the Kokshaga." This was later smoothed somewhat to *Tsaryovokokshaysk* (Царёвококшайск). In 1919, after the Revolution, it was renamed *Krasnokokshaysk* (Краснококшайск), with *Krasno-*, "red," replacing the czarist element. In 1927 it received its present name, from Mari *yoshkar* "red," and *ola*, "town."

Yug (Юг) *River, western Russia.* The river, a headstream of the Northern Dvina, has a name of Finno-Ugrian origin meaning simply "river," related to Finnish *joki* in the same sense. The form of the name has been influenced by Russian *yug*, "south," as if alluding to its location to the south of the Northern Dvina.

Yumaguzino (Юмагузино) *Village, southwestern Russia.* The village, in Bashkortostan southeast of Salavat, has a name derived from the Bashkir personal name *Yomaguzha*. This literally means "lord of Friday," referring to the holiest day of the Muslim week.

Yurmala See **Jurmala**.

Yuryev See **Tartu**.

Yuryevets (Юрьевец) *Town, western Russia.* The town, on the Volga northwest of Nizhny Novgorod, was founded in 1225. It is popularly said to take its name from Grand Prince *Yury* Dolgoruky, founder of Moscow. However, he died in 1157, so the name must derive from some other *Yury*, not necessarily a prince.

Yuryev-Polsky (Юрьев-Польский) *Town, western Russia.* The town, northeast of Sergiyev Posad, was founded in 1152 by Grand Prince *Yury* Dolgoruky (1090s–1157), founder of Moscow, and is named for him. The second part of the name distinguished this *Yuryev* from the one that is now **Tartu**. It derives from Russian *pole*, "field," since this region was noted for its farmland.

Yuryuzan (Юрюзань) *Town, southwestern Russia.* The town, southwest of Zlatoust, takes its name from the river on which it stands. The river's own name is Bashkir in origin and means "big valley (river)," from *yur*, "big," and *uzen*, "valley."

Yuzhno-Kurilsk (Южно-Курильск) *Town, Kuril Islands, southeastern Russia.* The town, on Kunashir island, the southernmost of the Kurils, was so named in 1946 with regard to this location, from Russian *yuzhno-*, "southern," and *Kuril*. Its earlier Japanese name was *Furukamappu*. Cf. **Severo-Kurilsk**.

Yuzhno-Sakhalinsk (Южно-Сахалинск) *Town, Sakhalin, eastern Russia.* The town, in the southeastern part of Sakhalin island, has a name relating to its location, from Russian *yuzhno-*, "southern," and *Sakhalin*. It was founded in 1882 and was originally known as *Vladimirovka* (Владимировка). From 1905 to 1946, when under Japanese control, it was known as *Toyohara*, "eastern plain."

Yuzhno-Uralsk (Юужноуральск) *Town, western Russia.* The town, on the eastern slopes of the Southern Urals northwest of Troitsk, has a name meaning "Southern Urals," from Russian *yuzhno-*, "southern," and *Ural*. The town developed from the state regional thermal electric power station constructed here in 1948 on the Udelka River.

Yuzovka See **Donetsk**[1].

Zadonsk (Задонск) *Town, western Russia.* The town, southeast of Tula, is first recorded in the 14th century with the name of *Teshev*, for the *Teshevka* River that enters the Don here. In 1779 it adopted its present name, meaning "beyond the Don," from Russian *za*, "over," "beyond," and *Don*. The town arose on the east bank of the Don, which here formed the boundary of the territory of old Russia.

Zagorsk See **Sergiyev Posad**.

Zakarpatye See **Transcarpathia**.

Zakavkazye See **Transcaucasia**.

Zaleshchiki (Залéщики) *Town, southwestern Ukraine*. The town, on the Dniester north of Chernovtsy, is presumably so named for the original inhabitants of the region, who lived "beyond the forest," from Russian *za*, "beyond," and *les*, "forest." In classical terms they were thus "Transylvanians."

Zangezur Range (Зангезýрский хребéт) *Mountain range, southern Armenia*. The range is said to be so called from an old name for this region, *Tsakeridzor*, meaning "ravine of caves."

Zapolyarny (Заполя́рный) *Town, northwestern Russia*. The town, northwest of Murmansk, arose in 1956 when copper and nickel deposits were first mined here. Its name relates to its location, inside the Arctic Circle, from Russian *za*, "beyond," and *polyarnyj*, "polar." (Russians know the Arctic Circle as *Severnyj polyarnyj krug*, "Northern Polar Circle.")

Zaporozhye (Запорóжье) *City, southeastern Ukraine*. The city, on the Dnieper south of Dnepropetrovsk, was founded in 1770 as the fortress of *Aleksandrovskaya*, so named for Field Marshal *Aleksandr* Mikhaylovich Golitsyn (1718–1783), who commanded the army in Ukraine in the war against Turkey in 1768-69. The town that grew up around it was named *Aleksandrovsk* (Александрóвск) in 1806. In 1921 this royalist name was abandoned in favor of the present one, which means "beyond the rapids," from Russian *za*, "beyond," and *porogi*, "rapids." There are no rapids here now, but before the hydroelectric station was built in 1932 across the southern part of the river's middle reaches, its many rapids seriously obstructed river traffic.

Zaraysk (Зарáйск) *Town, western Russia*. The town, northwest of Ryazan, has a name that may either represent the local word *zarazy*, a term for a steep cliff or (by extension) defensive post, or else derive from *za*, "beyond," and *Ray*, a local river name. The town itself is on the Osyotr, a tributary of the Oka.

Zaslavl (Заслáвль) *Town, west central Belarus*. The town, west of Minsk, was formerly known as *Izyaslavl*, taking this from one of the princes named *Izyaslav*. Cf. **Izyaslav**.

Zatishye See **Elektrostal**.

Zavodoukovsk (Заводоукóвск) *Town, southwestern Russia*. The town, southeast of Tyumen, derives its name from the *Uk* River, a tributary of the Tobol, on which it stands. The name was first used in the form *Ukovsky zavod*, "Uk factory," for the winery that was recorded as operating here in the 18th century. The meaning of the river name is uncertain. Tatar or Bashkir *uk*, "arrow," has been suggested, perhaps referring to the river's sharply angled course as it enters the Tobol.

Zavodouspenskoye (Заводоуспéнское) *Town, southwestern Russia*. The town, southwest of Tyumen, takes its name from the *Uspensky zavod*, "Uspenka factory," a small papermill that was built in the village of *Uspenka* here in the late 19th century. The village, like others of the name, is so called from the dedication of its church to the Dormition (Assumption) (Russian *Uspeniye*) of the Virgin Mary.

Zavoyko See **Yelizovo**.

Zaysan (Зайсáн) *Lake, eastern Kazakhstan*. The lake has a name of uncertain origin. Folk etymology derives it from Kalmyk words meaning "blessed lake": in 1650 Kalmyks were supposed to have escaped starvation here by feeding off the fish in the lake.

Zelenodolsk (Зеленодóльск) *Town, western Russia*. The town, in Tatarstan on the Volga west of Kazan, arose in 1865 as the village of *Kabachishche* (Кабáчище), presumably from a form of *kabak*, "tavern." It was then known as *Zelyony dol*, "green valley," before taking the current form of its name in 1932.

Zelenogorsk (Зеленогóрск) *Town, western Russia*. The town, on the Gulf of Finland northwest of St. Petersburg, has a name simply meaning "green town," from Russian *zelyonyj*, "green," and *gorod*, "town." When part of Finland the town was known as *Terijoki*, from Finnish *töyry*, "little hill," and *joki*, "river."

Zelenograd (Зеленогрáд) *Town, western Russia*. The town, northwest of Moscow, arose as a satellite town for Moscow in 1960, and takes its name from the forestland where it was sited, from *zelyonyj*, "green," and *-grad*, "town."

Zelenokumsk (Зеленокýмск) *Town, southwestern Russia*. The town, northeast of Georgiyevsk, takes the first part of its name from Russian *zelyonyj*, "green," and the second part from the *Kuma* River on which it lies. To 1963 it was a village with the archetypal prerevolutionary name of *Vorontsovo-Aleksandrovskoye* (Воронцóво-Александрóвское), but from then to 1965, when it took its present name, it was renamed in sharp contrast as *Sovetskoye* (Совéтское), "Soviet."

Zelensk See **Leninsk**[2].

Zelyonaya Roshcha (Зелёная Рóща) *Town, southwestern Russia*. The town, southeast of Rostov-on-Don, has a name that is simply the Russian for "Green Grove."

Zemetchino (Земéтчино) *Village, western Russia*. The village, northwest of Penza, has a name that may be based on Old Russian dialect *zemets*, "beekeeper," or else derive from a person so nicknamed. Less likely is an origin in Russian *zemshchina*, a historic term for boyar domains, as distinct from *oprichnina*, lands under Ivan the Terrible.

Zemgale (Зéмгале) *Historic region, northern Latvia*. The region to the south of the Gulf of Riga was at one time known by this name, which means "lowland."

Zeravshan (Зерaвшáн) *River, Central Asia*. The river rises at the western end of the Altay Mountains and flows generally west through northwestern Tajikistan and southeastern Uzbekistan to disappear into the desert near Bukhara without reaching the Amudarya. Its name is said to derive from Tajik *zer*, "gold," and *rekhtan*, "to scatter," referring to its importance in irrigation. But there could be a real link with gold, which was at one time panned in its upper reaches. In its course past Samarkand the Zeravshan divides into two: a northern branch *Akdarya*, "white river," and a southern branch *Karadarya*, "black river." These then reunite, and in its lower reaches it is known as the *Karakuldarya*, "black lake river."

Zernograd (Зерногрáд) *Town, southwestern Russia*. The town, southeast of Rostov-on-Don, arose in 1933 around an experimental grain farm set up in 1929. Hence its name, from Russian *zerno*, "grain," "corn," and the familiar *-grad*, "town."

Zhamanakkol (Жаманакко́ль) *Lake, central Kazakhstan.* The lake, northeast of the Aral Sea, has a name comprising Kazakh *zhaman,* "bad," *ak,* "white," and *kol',* "lake." As elsewhere in the region, the lake is "bad" because its waters are bitterly salt. It is "white" through its appearance.

Zhamantuz (Жаманту́з) *Lake, northern Kazakhstan.* The lake, northwest of Kokchetav, has a name comprising Kazakh *zhaman,* "bad," and *tuz,* "salt." The lake is "bad" because its salt water makes it unfit for drinking. There are several lakes of this name in northern Kazakhstan. Another is in the northeast, north of Karaganda.

Zhanatas (Жаната́с) *Town, southern Kazakhstan.* The town, northwest of Dzhambul, arose in 1969 when phosphorite deposits were discovered here. The Kazakh name, alluding to this discovery, means literally "new stone." (Phosphorites are found as deposits in rocks.)

Zhdanov See **Mariupol.**

Zhdanovsk (Жда́новск) *Town, southern Azerbaijan.* The town, east of Stepanakert, is named for the Soviet politician and Communist Party secretary Andrey Aleksandrovich *Zhdanov* (1896–1948).

Zhelaniya, Cape (Жела́ния мыс) *Cape, North Land, northern Russia.* The northernmost cape in North Land has a name meaning "desire." It was so named by the Dutch navigator Willem Barents (see **Barents Sea**), who reached this point in 1596 and pronounced it to be at the "desired angle" of his course. The present name is thus to some extent ambiguous.

Zheleznodorozhny (Железнодоро́жный) *Town, western Russia.* The town, east of Moscow, arose with the coming of the railroad (Russian *zheleznaya doroga,* literally "iron way"). Its original name was *Obiralovka* (Обира́ловка). In 1939 this became *Zheleznodorozhnaya* (implying *stantsiya,* "station"), then as now when the settlement was raised to town status in 1952. (It is at Obiralovka that the tragic heroine of Tolstoy's *Anna Karenina* commits suicide by leaping under a train.)

Zheleznodorozhny See **Kungrad.**

Zheleznogorsk (Железного́рск) *Town, western Russia.* The town, southwest of Oryol, arose in 1957 when exploitation began of the iron ore in the Kursk Magnetic Anomaly. Hence its name, "iron town" or "iron mountain," from Russian *zheleznyj,* "iron," and either *gorod,* "town," or *gora,* "mountain" (the latter implying an iron mine).

Zheleznogorsk-Ilimsky (Железного́рск-Или́мский) *Town, southern Russia.* The town, midway between Bratsk and Ust-Kut, arose in 1948 when geologists discovered a rich deposit of iron ore here. They named a nearby mountain *Zheleznaya,* "iron," accordingly. An ore dressing and concentration plant was brought into operation here in 1965, and the resulting settlement was named *Zheleznogorsk,* for the mountain. However, to be distinguished from the **Zheleznogorsk** near Oryol, *Ilimsky* was added, referring to the *Ilim* River here.

Zheleznovodsk (Железново́дск) *Town and resort, southwestern Russia.* The town, a health resort and spa northwest of Pyatigorsk in the northern Caucasus, has a name meaning "iron waters," from Russian *zheleznyj,* "iron," and *voda,* "water." The reference is to nearby Mt. *Zheleznaya* ("iron mountain"), with its ferriferous mineral springs.

Zhety-Kol (Жетыко́ль) *Lake, southwestern Russia.* The lake, near the border with Kazakhstan east of Orsk, has a Kazakh name meaning "seven lakes." "Seven" in such cases often means "many," though here the map shows that there are indeed seven: two small lakes to the north of the largest, and four more to the southwest. There are lakes of the same name in Kazakhstan itself, and that country has other "seven" names, such as *Zhetikara*, "seven hills," *Zhetizhar*, "seven ravines," and *Zhetiaral*, "seven islands."

Zhigulyovsk (Жигулёвск) *Town, western Russia*. The town, on the Volga northwest of Samara, arose when oil was discovered here and construction of the huge Volga hydroelectric station began in 1951. The original name of the village was *Otvazhnoye* (Отва́жное), "courageous." The present name derives from the *Zhiguli* hills to the south. The meaning of their own name is uncertain.

Zhitomir (Жито́мир) *City, west central Ukraine*. The city, west of Kiev, was founded in the second half of the 9th century. Archive material suggests that the name is that of the original founder or landowner here. It is not known who this was. Legend has its own theory: he was *Zhitomir*, favorite of the Kievan princes Askold and Dir, who did not wish to serve Prince Oleg.

Zhizdra (Жи́здра) *River, western Russia*. The river, a tributary of the Oka southwest of Moscow, is believed to have a name of Baltic origin, representing Lithuanian *žigždras*, "coarse sand."

Zhokhov Island (Жо́хова о́стров) *Island, New Siberian Islands, northwestern Russia*. The island, in the De Long group, was discovered in 1914 by an expedition led by Lieutenant Aleksey Nikolayevich *Zhokhov* (1885-1915), who the previous year had also discovered **Vilkitsky Island**.

In 1916 it was named *Novopashenny Island* (Новопа́шенного о́стров), for the Russian Arctic explorer Pyotr Alekseyevich *Novopashenny* (1881-?), but in 1926 was officially renamed as now for Zhokhov.

Zholkva See **Nesterov**[2].

Zhovten (Жо́втень) *Town, western Ukraine*. The town, northeast of Ivano-Frankovsk, has a name that is the Ukrainian word for "October," alluding to the October Revolution of 1917. The name is (or was) found elsewhere in Ukraine, as is the adjectival form *Zhovtnevoye* (Жовтне́вое).

Zhukopa (Жу́копа) *River, western Russia*. The river, a tributary of the Volga northwest of Rzhev, is said to have a name meaning "fish river," from Baltic words *zukis*, "fish," and *ape*, "river."

Zhukovsky (Жуко́вский) *Town, western Russia*. The town, southeast of Moscow, arose on the site of the workers' settlement of *Otdykh* (О́тдых), "rest," for its location on the Moskva River. In the 1930s it was renamed *Stakhanovo* (Стаха́ново), for the record-setting Soviet coal miner A.G. *Stakhanov* (1906-1977). (Cf. **Stakhanov**.) In 1947 it was renamed as now to mark the centennial of the birth of the Russian physicist and "father of aviation," Nikolay Yegorovich *Zhukovsky* (1847-1921).

Zhyoltaya Reka See **Zhyoltyye Vody**.

Zhyoltyye Vody (Жёлтые Во́ды) *Town, east central Ukraine*. The town, southwest of Dneprodzherzhinsk, has a name translating as "Yellow Waters." The reference is to the color of the water of the small river here, caused by iron ore deposits, which were first mined in the late 19th century. The original settlement was called *Zhyoltaya Reka* (Жёлтая Река́), "Yellow River," and adopted its present name in 1957 when it was raised to town status.

Zilupe (Зилупе) *Town, eastern Latvia.* The town, near the Russian border, takes its name from the river on which it lies. The river name means "blue river," from Latvian *zils*, "blue," and *upe*, "river."

Zimny Bereg (Зимний Берег) *Coast, northwestern Russia.* The coast is that of the eastern shore of the White Sea, north of Arkhangelsk. Its name means "winter shore," and refers to the winter trades of the coast dwellers here. Its name contrasts with the more southerly **Letny Bereg.**

Zinovyevsk See **Kirovograd.**

Zlatoust (Златоуст) *City, western Russia.* The city, at the southern end of the Middle Urals, west of Chelyabinsk, was founded in 1754 as an ironworks on the site of a village that was itself named for the dedication of its church to St. John *Chrysostom* (Russian *Zlatoust*, literally "golden mouth"). The village was raised to urban status in 1865.

Zmeiny Island (Змейный остров) *Island, Black Sea, southern Ukraine.* The island, in the northwestern part of the Black Sea, belongs to Ukraine and has a name meaning "snake [island]," apparently for the snakes on it. In classical times it was known as *Leuce*, from Greek *leukos*, "white," supposedly for the color of its rocks. "According to the poets, the souls of the ancient heroes were placed there as in the Elysian fields... From that circumstance it has often been called the island of the blessed." (*Lemprière's Classical Dictionary*.)

Zmiyov (Змиёв) *Town, northeastern Ukraine.* The town, south of Kharkov, was founded in the 17th century and probably has a name of personal origin. In 1976 it was renamed commemoratively as *Gotwald* (Готвальд) for the Czech Communist leader and state president, Kliment Gottwald (1896-1953). The town reverted to its original name in 1991 on the breakup of the Czech Communist party and of Czechoslovakia itself.

Zolotoy Rog (Золотой Рог) *Inlet, southeastern Russia.* The inlet is that on which Vladivostok lies in Peter the Great Bay. Its name means "Golden Horn," and was given in 1859 for the inlet's similarity to the better known Golden Horn on which Istanbul stands. "Golden" in both cases implies rich fishing grounds.

Zugres (Зугрэс) *Town, eastern Ukraine.* The town, in the Donbass east of Donetsk, arose in the 1920s when an electric power station was built here. Its name represents a shortened form of Russian *Zuyevskaya GRES*, the acronym representing *gosudarstvennaya rajonnaya elektrostantsiya*, "state regional electric power station." The station is itself named for the nearby village of *Zuyevka*.

Zvanka See **Volkhov.**

Zvenigorod (Звенигород) *Town, western Russia.* The town, west of Moscow, is first mentioned in a document dated 1339 and is said to take its name from its bells, from Russian *zvenet'*, "to ring," and *gorod*, "town." It is not clear whether these were church bells or those of a watch tower (announcing the approach of an enemy). According to one school of thought, "ring" relates not to bells but to the rushing or "purling" of the Moskva River here.

Zvenigovo (Звенигово) *Town, western Russia.* The town, on the Volga northwest of Kazan, is said to take its name from the dialect plant name *zvenika* (perhaps a type of bear grass), or from a personal name based on this.

Zyryanovsk (Зыря́новск) *Town, eastern Kazakhstan.* The town, southeast of Ust-Kamennogorsk, arose following the discovery of metalliferous minerals here in 1791 by G. G. *Zyryanov*, an apprentice metalworker who had been exiled here. It is thus named for him.

Zyuzelsky (Зю́зельский) *Town, west central Russia.* The town, southwest of Yekaterinburg, takes its name from the small *Zyuzelka* River here. The name is found for rivers and streams elsewhere in the region. Its latter half is Turkic *yelga*, "river," "stream," which suggests that the first part is also Turkic. Its basic meaning, however, is unknown.

Appendix I: Common Placename Elements

The following is a listing of some of the commoner elements beginning and ending placenames in the former Soviet Union, together with an example of a name containing the element in question. The language or language family of origin is indicated in parentheses, with language names abbreviated as follows: Arm. = Armenian; Germ. = German; Iran. = Iranian; Lat. = Latvian; Russ. = Russian; Turk. = Turkic; Ukr. = Ukrainian. Other language names, such as Greek, are given in full.

A. To begin name

Ak-	white (Turk.)	Aksu
Ay-	saint (Turk.)	Ay-Petri
Bel-	white (Russ.)	Belgorod
Berez-	birch (Russ.)	Berezina
Bog-	God (Russ.)	Bogorodsk
Bolsh-	big (Russ.)	Bolshoye Boldino
Bor-	pine wood (Russ.)	Borovsk
Buk-	beech (Russ.)	Bukovina
Chern-	black (Russ.)	Chernomorskoye
Chervon-	red (Ukr.)	Chervonoarmeysk
Elektro-	electric (Russ.)	Elektrogorsk
Gorn-	mountain, mine (Russ.)	Gornozavodsk
Gorod-	town (Russ.)	Gorodok
Kamen-	rock, stone (Russ.)	Kamenka
Kara-	black (Turk.)	Karabash
Kivi-	rock (Estonian)	Kiviõli
Krasn-	red (Russ.)[1]	Krasnoarmeysk
Kyzyl-	red (Turk.)	Kyzyltash
Les-	forest (Russ.)	Lesogorsk
Mal-	little (Russ.)	Maloarkhangelsk
Medn-	copper (Russ.)	Mednegorsk

243

Nefte-	copper (Russ.)	Mednegorsk
Nizhn-	lower (Russ.)	Nizhny Novgorod
Nov-	new (Russ.)	Novgorod
Perv-	first (Russ.)	Pervomaysk
Petro-	Peter (Russ.)	Petrokrepost
Po-	along (Russ.)[2]	Podolia
Pod-	under, near (Russ.)[3]	Podkumok
Pri-	near, by, -"side" (Russ.)[4]	Privolzhsk
Ryb-	fish (Russ.	Rybinsk
Sever-	north (Russ.)	Severodvinsk
Shakhar-	town (Turk.)	Shakhrisabz
Shakht-	mine, pit (Russ.)	Shakhtinsk
Soli-	salt (Russ.)	Soligorsk
Solnechno-	sunny (Russ.)	Solnechnogorsk
Sosn-	pine (Russ.)	Sosnovoborsk
Sovet-	Soviet (Russ.)	Sovetsk
Spassk-	Savior (Russ.)	Spassk-Dalny
Sredn-	middle (Russ.)	Srednekolymsk
Star-	old (Russ.)	Starobelsk
Svet-	light, bright (Russ.)	Svetlograd
Svyat-	saint, holy (Russ.)	Svyatoy Nos
Tash-	rock, stone (Turk.)	Tashkent
Troits-	Trinity (Russ.)	Troitsk
Tropl-	hot, warm (Russ.)	Tyoply Stan
Ugle-	coal (Russ.)	Ugleuralsk
Ust-	river-mouth (Russ.)	Ust-Katav
Velik-	great (Russ.)	Velikiye Luki
Verkh-	upper (Russ.)	Verkhoyansk
Vyshn-	higher (Russ.)	Vyshny Volochyok
Vysok-	high (Russ.)	Vysokoye
Yuzhn-	southern (Russ.)	Yuzhnosakhalinsk
Za-	beyond, over, "trans"- (Russ.)[5]	Zadonsk
Zavod-	factor, works (Russ.)	Zavodoukovsk
Zelen-	green (Russ.)	Zelenograd
Zhelezn-	iron (Russ.)	Zheleznogorsk
Zhyolt-	yellow (Russ.)	Zhyoltyye Vody

B. To end name

-abad	town (Iran.)	Ashkhabad
-akan	town (Arm.)	Leninakan
-armeysk	army (Russ.)	Krasnoarmeysk
-bazar	market (Turk., Russ.)	Yangibazar

Appendix I

-burg	town, fort (Germ.)	Yekaterinburg
-dag	moutain (Turk.)	Karadag
-darya	river (Iran.)	Kashkadarya
-dolsk	valley (Russ.)	Zelenodolsk
-gorod	town (Russ.)	Novgorod
-gorsk	mountain, mine (Russ.)[6]	Belogorsk
-grad	town (Russ.)	Volgograd
-gvardeysk	guard (Russ.)	Krasnogvardeysk
-iz	mountain (Komi)	Telposiz
-kala	fort, town (Iran.)	Makhachkala
-kalns	hill (Lat.)	Gaizina Kalns
-kent	town (Iran.)	Tashkent
-kuduk	well (Turk.)	Uchkuduk
-kul	lake (Turk.)	Issyk-Kul
-kum	sand, desert (Turk.)	Karakum
-kurya	bay, inlet (Komi)	Shenkursk
-lahta	bay, inlet (Finnish)	Kandalaksha
-luka	river bend (Russ.)	Velikiye Luki
-morsk	sea (Russ.)	Chernomorsk
-nos	cape (Russ.)	Taygonos
-ozero	lake (Russ.)	Segozero
-pils	town (Lat.)	Daugavpils
-pol	town (Greek)	Sevastopol
-rechensk	river (Russ.)	Dalnerechensk
-retsk	river (Russ.)	Beloretsk
-sk	of, at, on (Russ.)[7]	Tomsk
-sor	saltmarsh (Kazakh)	Tenteksor
-stan	land, country (Iran.)	Tajikistan
-tash	rock, stone (Turk.)	Koktash
-tau	mountain (Turk.	Dzhamantau
-va	water, river (Komi-Permyak)	Sosva
-vodsk	water (Russ.)	Zheleznovodsk
-yar	steep bank (Turk.)	Krasnoyarsk
-yogi	river (Karelian)	Iokanga
-zavodsk	factory, works (Russ.)	Gornozavodsk

---

1. See Introduction, page 1.
2. See Appendix II.
3. See Appendix II.
4. See Appendix II.
5. See Appendix II.
6. See Introduction, page 1.
7. See Introduction, page 1.

Appendix II: Regional Names

The territory of the former Soviet Union is subdivided into political or geographical regions by means of a number of official or general names. The most obvious region is the republic, so that apart from Russia itself there are 14 sovereign states with mainly ethnic names, such as Estonia or Kazakhstan. (The complete list appears in the opening paragraph of the Introduction, p. 1.) Each state then has its own political or administrative units, corresponding to the states and counties of the United States or the counties and districts of Great Britain. As of 1995, the Russian Federation comprises 89 such divisions: 49 regions, six autonomous territories, 21 republics, ten autonomous areas, two autonomous cities (Moscow and St. Petersburg), and one autonomous Jewish region (Birobidzhan). The Russian terms for the different divisions sometimes appear in English atlases and gazetteers.

The term for a *region* is *oblast'* (область), a word formed historically from the prefix *ob-*, "around," and a main element related to the *volost* that was the smallest territorial unit in prerevolutionary Russia. (This itself comes from a root word related to modern Russian *vlast'*, "power.") The actual name of the region always appears in Russian in the adjectival form. Again, this is also sometimes used in English printed sources. One thus has *Amurskaya oblast'* for "Amur Region." (The noun *oblast'* is feminine, so that the adjective will always have the feminine ending, *-skaya*, in grammatical agreement.) Almost all region names are those of the towns and cities that are their capitals. (Amur is an exception, as a river name. This region's capital is Blagoveshchensk.)

The term for a *territory* is *kraj* (край), a word literally meaning "edge" and seen in the name *Ukraine* ("border territory"). (Historically the word is related to the verb *kryt'*, "to cover.") This noun is masculine, so has the masculine form of the adjective, *-sky*, as seen in one of the most familiar such names, *Primorsky kraj* ("Maritime Territory"), bordering the Sea of Japan in the Far East.

The term for a *republic* is *respublika* (республика), a word so close to English that it is usually translated rather than transliterated. The name of a republic can appear either in adjectival form, followed by the feminine noun *respublika*, or in one-word noun form. Thus one has either *Karel'skaya Respublika* or simply *Kareliya*. (The *-iya* ending in such cases is usually rendered *-ia* in English, so here Karelia.) In Soviet days these republics were officially designated "Autonomous Soviet Socialist," so that Karelia was the *Karel'skaya Avtonomnaya Sovetskaya Sotsialisticheskaya Respublika* or *Karel'skaya ASSR*.

The term for an *area* is *okrug* (óкруг), a word historically comprising the prefix *o-*, "around," and *krug*, "circle." (The related verb *okruzhit'* means "to surround.") This noun is masculine, so that the adjectival form of the name is used, e.g. *Chukotsky okrug*, "Chukot Area." Most area names are ethnic in origin, and are generally not used alone to denote the geographical entity. The exception is *Taymyr*, which

Appendix II

is not an ethnic name, and so can denote both the peninsula and the autonomous administrative area. Ukraine, somewhat similarly, has 24 regions and one autonomous republic (Crimea), while Belarus has six provinces.

Other states of the former Soviet Union have various terms for their administrative regions. The Asian republics have provinces, which like the Russian *oblast'* are usually based on the names of their capitals. In the Baltic republics, Estonia has counties, Latvia has rural districts, and Lithuania has regions, as well as cities of republic jurisdiction. Moldova also has rural districts. The Transcaucasian republics, Georgia, Armenia, and Azerbaijan, are currently in a state of political flux. Abkhazia, for example, was until recently an autonomous republic, but in 1994 declared itself an independent state. Georgia rejected its legality, however.

Aside from these official names, various general names are in use to describe particular geographical areas of the old USSR. They are chiefly found with the prefixes *po-*, *pod-*, *pred-*, *pri-*, and *za-* followed by a noun form of the appropriate geographical object, whether a name or a generic word. The regional name itself usually ends in *-ye*. (1) The prefix *po-*, as listed in Appendix I (above), means "along," and is related to the initial *po* in Latin *positus*, "placed," and so to *po-* in English *position*. As its meaning implies, it is used in the names of regions along extended natural objects such as rivers, valleys, or coasts. The following are well-known examples:

Pokutye (Покýтье), the region along the upper reaches of the Prut River and the right bank of the Dniester, historically the southeastern portion of Galicia. The name is based on Ukrainian *kut*, "corner," referring to the angle of land here. Cf. **Krasny Kut** in main text. The region belonged to Poland from 1387 to 1772, to Austria and Austria-Hungary from 1772 to 1918, and to Poland again from 1919 to 1939, when it passed to Ukraine.

Polesye (Полéсье), the region in the western part of the East European (Russian) Plain. See **Polesye** in main text.

Pomorye (Помóрье), the historic region along the White Sea coast between the towns of Kem and Onega. The name also sometimes applies to the more extensive region from Lake Onega to the Northern Urals. This territory belonged to the principality of Novgorod from the 12th through 15th centuries, after which it became part of Russia. The root of the name is Slavic *more*, "sea," and the name as a whole corresponds to *Pomerania* as a designation for the historic region along the Baltic.

Povolzhye (Повóлжье), the region along the middle and lower reaches of the Volga, regarded as economically associated with this river.

(2) The prefix *pod-* means "under," "near," and is used for a name designating the region around a particular town or city. The best known example is *Podmoskovye* (Подмоскóвье), meaning the region around Moscow. This name is also used colloquially for the officially defined Moscow Region (*oblast'*). The prefix itself equates to English *sub-*, although this is not used to form English regional names.

(3) The prefix *pred-*, meaning "before," "in front of," is rarely found in official names, so is not listed above in Appendix I. It is usually found with the names of mountain ranges or chains, and linguistically equates to English *pre-* or *cis-*. The following are well-known examples:

Predbaykalye (Предбайкáлье), the region to the west of Lake Baykal. Cf. *Zabaykalye* (below).

Predkarpatye (Предкарпáтье), the region to the northeast of the Carpathians, i.e. western Ukraine. Cf. *Zakarpatye* (below).

Predkavkazye (Предкавкáзье), the region to the north of the Caucasus, i.e. in southwestern Russia. English *Ciscaucasia* is sometimes used for this. Cf. *Zakavkazye* (below).

Preduralye (Предурáлье), the region to the west of the Urals. Cf. *Zauralye* (below).

(4) The prefix *pri-*, meaning "near," "by," is added to the name of a natural geographical feature to give the name of a region bordering that feature. In this respect it corresponds to the English *-side* in such names as Britain's Clydeside, Humberside, Merseyside, Tayside, Tyneside. (Generic "lakeside," "riverside," "seaside," "waterside" are also evoked.) Well known examples of Russian *pri-* names include the following:

Priamurye (Приамýрье), the region around the Amur River in the Far East, to the south of the Stanovoy Range and the estuary of the Uda River on the Sea of Okhotsk. It is greater than the territorial limits of the Amur Region.

Pribaltika (Прибáлтика), the region to the east of the Baltic coast, including the Baltic republics of Estonia, Latvia, and Lithuania, and the Kaliningrad Region of Russia.

Pribaykalye (Прибайкáлье), the region to the west and north of Lake Baykal. Cf. *Predbaykalye* (above) and *Zabaykalye* (below).

Primorye (Примóрье), the region of the Far East bordering the Sea of Japan, including (or equating to) the Primorsky Kray. The word *primor'ye* also exists generically in Russian for any seaside place.

Priuralye (Приурáлье), the region to the east and west of the Urals. The former, in eastern Europe, is separately known as the *Preduralye* (see above); the latter, in western Siberia, as the *Zauralye* (see below).

(5) The prefix *za-*, meaning "beyond," "over," equates to English *trans-*, and is usually found with river and mountain names. Well known examples are as follows:

Zabaykalye (Забайкáлье), the region to the east of Lake Baykal. English *Transbaikalia* is sometimes used for this. Cf. *Predbaykalye* (above).

Zakarpatye (Закарпáтье), the region to the southwest of the Carpathians, i.e. southwestern Ukraine, otherwise **Transcarpathia** (see this entry in main text). The name is also used for the Transcarpathian Region of Ukraine.

Zakavkazye (Закавкáзье), the region to the south of the Caucasus, otherwise **Transcaucasia** (see this entry in main text).

Zamoskvorechye (Замоскворéчье), a name used historically for the region of Moscow that lies within the loop of the Moskva River, to the south of the Kremlin.

Zanemanye (Занéманье), a historic region in Lithuania south of the Neman River, ruled by the Teutonic Knights in the 13th through 15th centuries and then passing to Poland, Prussia, and Russia before becoming part of Lithuania in 1918.

Zauralye (Заура́лье), the region to the east of the Urals. Cf. *Preduralye* (above).

Zavolzhye (Заво́лжье), the region to the east of the Volga, bounded by the Volga in the west, the northern uplands of the East European (Russian) Plain in the north, the Ural River in the east, and the Caspian Depression (the lowlands north of the Caspian Sea) in the south. There is no *Predvolzhye* to serve as a western counterpart.

Select Bibliography

The following selection of titles is oriented towards those that are actively useful or informative in the matter of Russian placenames and placenames of the republics of the former Soviet Union. They include books, dictionaries, atlases, gazetteers, guides, journals, and individual articles. They range in scope from the particular (geographically defined) to the general, and in style and content from the popular to the academic. Many of them were consulted in the preparation of the present book. Russian and non-English titles are translated in parentheses for ease of reference, and Russian titles, where not preceded by an author's name, are alphabetized as if transliterated into the Roman alphabet.

Ageyenko, F.L, and M.V. Zarva. Словарь ударений для работников радио и телевидения (Dictionary of stresses for radio and television staffs). Moscow: Russkij yazyk, 1984.

Ageyeva, R.A. Происхождение имён рек и озёр (The origin of the names of rivers and lakes). Moscow: Nauka, 1985.

Ageyeva, R.A. Страны и народы: происхождение названий (Countries and peoples: the origin of names). Moscow: Nauka, 1990.

Akhmanova, O.S. (ed.-in-chief). Микротопонимия (Microtoponymy). Moscow: Izdatel'stvo Moskovskogo universiteta, 1967.

Атлас Мира (Atlas of the World). Moscow: GUGK, 1984.

Atlas of Russia and the Post-Soviet Republics. Hastings: Arguments and Facts Media, in conjunction with Moscow: Argumenty i fakty/AKTAR-PKO "Kartografia," 1994.

Атлас СССР (Atlas of the USSR). 3d ed. Moscow: GUGK, 1983.

Baedeker, Karl. *Russia.* Leipzig: Karl Baedeker, 1914.

Barashkov, V.F. Знакомые с детства названия (Names familiar from childhood). Moscow: Prosveshcheniye, 1982.

Batowski, Henryk. *Słownik nazw miejscowych Europy środkowej i wschodniej XIX i XX wieku* (Dictionary of 19th- and 20th-century placenames of central and eastern Europe). Warsaw: Państwowe wydawnictwo naukowe, 1964. ·

Большая Советская Энциклопедия (Big Soviet encyclopedia). 3d ed., 30 vols. Moscow: Sovetskaya Entsiklopediya, 1970–78.

Bushmakin, S.K. (ed.) Словарь географических названий СССР (Dictionary of geographical names of the USSR). 2d rev. & enld. ed. Moscow: Nedra, 1983.

Chazov, Ye.I. (chief ed.) Курорты. Энциклопедический словарь (Health resorts. An encyclopedic dictionary). Moscow: Sovetskaya Entsiklopediya, 1983.

Cherpillod, André. *Dictionnaire étymologique des noms géographiques* (Etymoogical dictionary of geographical names). 2d ed. Paris: Masson, 1991.

Select Bibliography

Columbia-Lippincott Gazetteer of the World. New York: Columbia University Press, 1952 (with 1961 supplement).
Dal', Vladimir. Толковый Словарь живого великорусскаго языка (Explanatory dictionary of the living Great Russian language). 4 vols. 3d ed. St. Petersburg: M. O. Volf, 1912.
Dambe, Vallija. *Latvijas apdzīvoto vietu un to iedzīvotāju nosaukumi* (The names of populated places and inhabitants of Latvia). Riga: Zinātne, 1990.
Darinsky, A.V. География Ленинграда (The geography of Leningrad). Leningrad: Lenizdat, 1982.
Ежегодник Большой Советской Энциклопедии (Yearbook of the Big Soviet encyclopedia). Issues 16-34. Moscow: Sovetskaya Entsiklopediya, 1972-90.
Florinsky, Michael T. (ed.) *McGraw-Hill Encyclopedia of Russia and the Soviet Union.* New York: McGraw-Hill, 1962.
Fölkersam, Wolfgang. *Ortsnamenänderungen in der Sowjetunion* (Placename changes in the Soviet Union). *Osteuropa* No. 14, 1964.
Geybullayev, G.A. Топонимия Азербайджана: Историко-этнографическое исследование (The toponymy of Azerbaijan: Historico-ethnographical research). Baku: Elm, 1986.
Gilbert, Martin. *Imperial Russian History Atlas.* London: Routledge & Kegan Paul, 1978.
Gilbert, Martin. *Soviet History Atlas.* London: Routledge & Kegan Paul, 1979.
Gorbachevich, K. S., and Ye. P. Khablo. Почему так названы? (Why so called?). (The origins of the names of the streets, squares, islands, rivers and bridges of Leningrad.) Leningrad: Lenizdat, 1985.
Gorbanevsky, M.V. Новые названия в Подмосковье (New names in the Moscow region). *Russkaya rech'* No. 4 (July-August) 1978.
Gorbanevsky, M.V. Имена земли Московской (Names of the land of Moscow). Moscow: Moskovsky rabochy, 1985.
Gorbanevsky, M.V., and V.Yu. Dukelsky. По золотому кольцу России (Around the Golden Ring of Russia). *Russkaya rech'* No. 4 (July-August) 1980-No. 5 (September-October) 1982.
Grushevsky, A.V. Словарь родовых географических названий у народов и народностей СССР (A Dictionary of ancestral geographical names of the peoples and nationalities of the USSR). *Geografiya v shkole* No. 3, 1940.
Имена московских улиц (The names of Moscow streets). 3d rev. ed. Moscow: Moskovsky rabochy, 1979.
Имени Ленина (Named for Lenin). Tashkent: Uzbekistan, 1980.
Исторические названия — памятники культуры (Historic names are cultural memorials). *Russkaya rech'* No. 5 (September-October) 1989.
Kalesnik, S.V. (chief ed.) Энциклопедический словарь географических названий (Encyclopedic dictionary of geographical names). Moscow: Sovetskaya Entsiklopediya, 1973.
Kert, G., and N. Mamontova. Загадки карельской топонимики (Riddles of Karelian toponymy). 2d ed. Petrozavodsk: Kareliya, 1982.
Konkashpayev, G.K. Словарь казахских географических названий (Dictionary of Kazakh geographical names). Alma-Ata: Izdatel'stvo Akademii nauk Kazakhskoj SSR, 1963.
Konkobayev, K. Топонимия Южной Киргизии (The toponymy of Southern Kirgizia). Frunze: Ilim, 1980.
Koyshybayev, Ye. Краткий толковый словарь топонимов Казахстана (Concise explanatory dictionary of the toponyms of Kazakhstan). Alma-Ata: Nauka, 1974.

Kuskov, V.P. Краткий топонимический словарь Камчатской области (Concise toponymical dictionary of the Kamchatka Region). Petropavlovsk-Kamchatsky: Dal'nevostochnoye knizhnoye izdatel'stvo, 1967.

Losique, Serge. *Dictionnaire étymologique des noms de pays et de peuples* (Etymological dictionary of names of countries and peoples). Paris: Klincksieck, 1971.

Ludvikova, L., and L. Skokan. *The Soviet Union: A Guide and Information Handbook*. Translated from the Czech by E. Skelley. London: Collet's, 1976.

Maslennikov, B.G. Морская карта рассказывает (The sea chart tells a story). 2d ed. Moscow: Voyenizdat, 1986.

Matveyev, A.K. Географические названия Урала: Краткий топонимический словарь (Geographical names of the Urals: A concise toponymical dictionary). Sverdlovsk: Sredne-Ural'skoye knizhnoye izdatel'stvo, 1987.

Melkheyev, M.N. Географические имена (Geographical names). Moscow: Gosudarstvennoye uchebno-pedagogicheskoye izdatel'stvo Ministerstva prosveshcheniya RSFSR, 1961.

Melnikov, S.Ye. О чём говорят географические названия: Историко-лингвические и краеведческие заметки (What geographical names tell: Historico-linguistic and local study notes). Leningrad: Lenizdat, 1984.

Moiseyev, A.I. Севастополь, Чистополь (названия городов на - поль) [(Sevastopol, Chistopol (names of towns in *-pol*)] *Russkaya rech'* No. 1 (January-February) 1994.

Москва: энциклопедия (Moscow: An encyclopedia). Moscow: Sovetskaya Entsiklopediya, 1980.

Murzayev, E.M. Очерки топонимики (Studies in toponymy). Moscow: Mysl', 1974.

Murzayev, E.M. "Образ места" (The image of a place). *Russkaya rech'* No. 1 (January-February) 1993-No. 4 (July-August) 1993.

Murzayev, E.M. География в названиях (Geography in names). 2d ed. Moscow: Nauka, 1982.

Murzayev, E.M. Словарь народных географических терминов (Dictionary of folk geographical terms). Moscow: Mysl', 1984.

Murzayev, E.M., V.A. Nikonov, and V.V. Tsybulsky (eds.) Ономастика Востока (Onomastics of the East). Moscow: Nauka, 1980.

Настольный энциклопедический словарь-справочник (Encyclopedic handbook and reference dictionary). 2d ed. Moscow: Prometey, 1927.

Neroznak, V.P. Названия древнерусских городов (The names of ancient Russian towns). Moscow: Nauka, 1983.

The New Encyclopædia Britannica. 15th ed., 32 vols. Chicago: Encyclopædia Britannica, 1993.

Nikonov, V.A. Краткий топонимический словарь (Concise toponymical dictionary). Moscow: Mysl', 1966.

Official Standard Names Gazetteer no. 42: U.S.S.R. U.S., Interior Department, Board on Geographic Names. 2d ed. Washington: June 1970.

Peterson, Charles B. "The Nature of Soviet Place-Names." *Names* (Journal of the American Name Society). Vol. 25, No. 1, March 1977.

Pospelov, Ye.M. Важнейшие изменения названий географических объектов в связи с изменениями на политической карте мира (1900-1965 гг.) (The most important changes in the names of geographical objects as a result of changes on the political map of the world (1900-1965), in A.G. Shiger, Политическая карта мира (1900-1965) (The political map of the world (1900-1965). 2d ed. Moscow: Politizdat, 1966.

Pospelov, Ye.M. Топонимика в школьной географии (Toponymy in school geography). Moscow: Prosveshcheniye, 1981.

Pospelov, Ye.M. Туристу о географических названиях (Geographical names for the tourist). Moscow: Profizdat, 1988.
Pospelov, Ye.M. Школьный топонимический словарь (School toponymical dictionary). Moscow: Prosveshcheniye, 1988.
Room, Adrian (comp.) *Place-Name Changes 1900-1991*. Metuchen, NJ: Scarecrow Press, 1993.
Rubtsova, Z.V. Названия деревень — часть народной культуры (Names of villages are part of national culture). *Russkaya rech'* No. 6 (November-December) 1989.
Rut, M.E. (ed.-in-chief) Номинация в ономастике (Naming in onomastics). Sverdlovsk: Izdatel'stvo Ural'skogo universiteta, 1991. (Contains 19 articles by different authors, 10 of which are on placenames.)
Словарь географических названий Казахстана (Джезказганская область) (Dictionary of the geographical names of Kazakhstan (Dzhezkazgan Oblast)). Alma-Ata: Nauka, 1990.
Словарь географических названий СССР (Dictionary of geographical names of the USSR). 2d ed. Moscow: Nedra, 1983.
Smolitskaya, G.P. Топонимический словарь Центральной России (A toponymical dictionary of Central Russia). *Russkaya rech'* No. 4 (July-August) 1994-.
Smolitskaya, G.P., and M.V. Gorbanevsky. Топонимия Москвы (The toponymy of Moscow). Moscow: Nauka, 1982.
Solntseva, N.A. (ed.) Всё Подмосковье. Географический словарь Московской области (All around Moscow. A geographical dictionary of the Moscow Region). Moscow: Mysl', 1967.
Sturmfels, Wilhelm, and Heinz Bischof. *Unsere Ortsnamen* (Our placenames). Bonn: Dümmlers, 1961.
Superanskaya, A.V. (ed.-in-chief) Восточнославянская ономастика: материалы и исследования (East Slavonic onomastics: materials and papers). Moscow: Nauka, 1979.
Superanskaya, A.V. Что такое топонимика? (What is toponymy?). Moscow: Nauka, 1985.
Taylor, Isaac. *Names and Their Histories*. London: Rivington, Percival, 1896.
Telberg, Ina. *Russian-English Geographical Encyclopedia*. New York: Telberg Book Co., 1960.
The Times Atlas of the World. 9th ed. London: Times Books, 1992.
Tryoshnikov, A.F. (chief ed.) Географический энциклопедический словарь: Географические названия (Geographical encyclopedic dictionary: geographical names). 2d ed. Moscow: Sovetskaya Entsiklopediya, 1989.
Unbegaun, B.O. "Les noms des villes russes: la mode slavonne" (The names of Russian towns: the Slavonic fashion). *Selected Papers on Russian and Slavonic Philology*. Oxford: Clarendon Press, 1969.
Unbegaun, B.O. "Les noms des villes russes: la mode grecque" (The names of Russian towns: the Greek fashion). *Selected Papers on Russian and Slavonic Philology*. Oxford: Clarendon Press, 1969.
Uspensky, Lev. Загадки топонимики (Riddles of toponymy). Moscow: Molodaya gvardiya, 1969.
Utechin, S.V. *Everyman's Concise Encyclopaedia of Russia*. London: J. M. Dent, 1961.
Vartanyan, E.A. История с географией, или жизнь и приключения географических названий (History with geography, or the life and adventures of geographical names). Moscow: Detskaya literatura, 1986.

Vasmer, Max. *Russisches etymologisches Wörterbuch* (Russian etymological dictionary). Heidelberg: 1950–58, translated from German as Этимологический словарь русского языка (Etymological dictionary of the Russian language) with additions by O.N. Trubachyov. 2d ed., 4 vols. Moscow: Progress, 1986–87.
Volostnova, M.B. (comp.) Словарь русской транскрипции географических названий (Dictionary of Russian transcriptions of geographical names). Part I: USSR. Moscow: Gosudarstvennoye uchebno-pedagogicheskoye izdatel'stvo ministerstva prosveshcheniya RSFSR, 1955.
Volostnova, M. *Dictionary of Russian Geographical Names*. Transliterated and translated by T. Deruguine. New York: Telberg Book Co., 1958.
Volostnova, M.B. Словарь географических названий СССР (Dictionary of geographical names of the USSR). Moscow: Nedra, 1968.
Vorobyova, I.A. Топонимика Западной Сибири (The toponymy of Western Siberia). Tomsk: Izdatel'stvo Tomskogo universiteta, 1977.
Webster's New Geographical Dictionary. Springfield, MA: Merriam-Webster, 1988.
Where's Where: A Descriptive Gazetteer. London: Eyre Methuen, 1974.
Yanko, M.T. Топонимический словарь-справочник: Украинская ССР (Toponymical dictionary and handbook: Ukrainian SSR). Kiev: Radyanska shkola, 1973.
Yefremov, Yu.K. Курильское ожерелье (Kuril carcanet). Moscow: Geografgiz, 1962.
Yefremov, Yu.K. О географических названиях Южного Сахалина и Курильских островов (The geographical names of Southern Sakhalin and the Kuril Islands). *Geografiya v shkole*, No. 3, 1949.
Yeremiya, A.I. Географические названия рассказывают (Geographical names tell their story). Kishinyov: Shtiintsa, 1982.
Yerofeyev, I.A. Имя Ленина на карте Родины (The name of Lenin on the map of the Motherland). 2d ed. Moscow: Prosveshcheniye, 1985.
Yusupov, E.Yu. (ed.) Имени Ленина (Named for Lenin). Tashkent: Uzbekistan, 1980.
Zhuchkevich, V.A. Краткий топонимический словарь Белоруссии (Concise toponymical dictionary of Belorussia). Minsk: Isdatel'stvo BGU im. V.I. Lenina, 1974.
Zhuchkevich, V.A. Общая топонимика (General toponymy). 3d ed. Minsk: Vysheyshaya shkola, 1980.

Cyrillic-to-Roman Index

This index lists the Russian originals of all headwords in the book, together with their English equivalents (whether as translation or transliteration). It also lists all Russian cross-references that have their Cyrillic forms in the entries. These lead to their English headwords, not simply to their English equivalents. Thus Агнécca leads not to Agnessa but to *See* Shokalsky Island.

Identically named places are differentiated by a geographical or other indicator in Russian in parentheses. This even applies to cross-references (i.e. to historic names). For example, the three former places Ak-Mechet are distinguished respectively as having been in western Crimea, southern Crimea, and Kazakhstan, while each is cross-referred individually to Chernomorskoye, Simferopol, and Kzyl-Orda.

There are two general omissions from the Index: (1) early (pre–19th-century) Russian names whose Cyrillic forms are not given in the main entries; (2) previous non-Russian names. The latter means, for example, that earlier German or Japanese names do not appear in the Index. This is because the Index is specifically Cyrillic-oriented. However, where a non-Russian name was assimilated into an established Russian form, such as Finnish Кексгольм for modern Priozyorsk, or English Риддер for Leninogorsk, it is included.

As mentioned in the Introduction, most non-Russian countries of the former Soviet Union, such as the Baltic states and Asian republics, have many names that are not properly "Russian" at all. However, they had, and still have, Russian equivalents, and therefore appear in the Index as such.

Finally, all Russian names are stressed, as in the headwords of the main entries. This even applies for the cross-references, which as dummy entries in the main text are not followed by their Cyrillic equivalents, as the main headwords are.

Абáй Abay
Абастумáни Abastumani
Абазá Abaza
Абакáн Abakan
Абдýлино Abdulino
Абезь Abez
Абовян Abovyan
Абрáмцево Abramtsevo
Абхáзия Abkhazia
Агáповка Agapovka
Агинское Aginskoye

Агнécca *See* Shokalsky Island
Агро-Пýстынь Agro-Pustyn
Адайхóх Aday Khokh
Аджáрия Adzharia
Адзьва Adzva
Адлер Adler
Адыгéя Adygeia
Азáнка Azanka
Азербайджáн Azerbaijan
Азизбéков Azizbekov
Азóв Azov

Cyrillic-to-Roman Index

Азо́вское мо́ре Azov, Sea of
Ай Ay
Ай-Пе́три Ay Petri
Ай-Тодо́р Ay Todor
Академгородо́к Akademgorodok
Акаде́мии зали́в Academy Bay
Акаде́мии Нау́к хребе́т Academy of Sciences Range
Акбула́к Akbulak
Акдарья́ See Zeravshan
Ак-Довура́к Ak Dovurak
Аккерма́н See Belgorod-Dnestrovsky
Ак-Мече́ть (западный Крым) See Chernomorskoye
Ак-Мече́ть (южный Крым) See Simferopol
Ак-Мече́ть (Казахстан) See Kzyl-Orda
Акмола́ Akmola
Акмо́линск See Akmola
Акмолы́ See Akmola
Акса́ково Aksakovo
Акса́й Aksay
Аксу́ Aksu
Акта́у See Shevchenko
Актю́бинск Aktyubinsk
Акъя́р Akyar
Алаверди́ Alaverdi
Алаги́р Alagir
Алаза́ни Alazani
Алако́ль Alakol
Алапа́евск Alapayevsk
Алата́у Ala Tau
Ала́тырь Alatyr
Алда́н Aldan
Александри́я Aleksandriya
Алекса́ндров Aleksandrov
Алекса́ндровск (на Урале) Aleksandrovsk
Алекса́ндровск (близ Благовещенска) See Belogorsk[1]
Алекса́ндровск (Украина) See Zaporozhye
Алекса́ндровск-Груше́вский See Shakhty
Алекса́ндровский пост See Aleksandrovsk-Sakhalinsky
Алекса́ндровск-Сахали́нский Aleksandrovsk-Sakhalinsky
Александро́поль See Kumayri
Алекса́ндры Земля́ Alexandra Land
Алексе́евка Alekseyevka

Алексе́евск See Svobodny
Але́ксин Aleksin
Алёшки See Tsyurupinsk
Али́-Байрамлы́ Ali Bayramly
Алма́-Ата́ Alma Ata
Алма́зный Almazny
Алта́й Altay
Алтына́й Altynay
Алу́пка Alupka
Алче́вск See Kommunarsk
Альма́ Alma
Амангельды́ Amangeldy
Амба́рчик Ambarchik
Амдерма́ Amderma
Ами́ньево Aminyevo
Амударья́ Amudarya
Аму́р Amur
Анаба́р Anabar
Ана́дырь Anadyr
Ана́па Anapa
Ангара́ Angara
Анга́рск Angarsk
Анджие́вский Andzhiyevsky
Андреа́поль Andreapol
Андро́пов See Rybinsk
Анжу́ острова́ Anzhu Islands
Анипе́мза Anipemza
Антраци́т Antratsit
Ану́чина о́стров Anuchin Island
Апати́ты Apatity
Апре́левка Aprelevka
Апшеро́нский полуо́стров Apsheron
Араба́тская Стре́лка Arabat, Tongue of
Арага́ц Aragats
Ара́гви Aragvi
Ара́кс Araks
Аралсульфа́т Aralsulfat
Ара́льск Aralsk
Ара́льское мо́ре Aral Sea
Арами́ль Aramil
Арара́т Ararat
Аргая́ш Argayash
Аргу́нь Argun
Арда́тов Ardatov
Ардо́н Ardon
Арзама́с Arzamas
Аркти́ческого Институ́та острова́ Arctic Institute Islands
Армави́р Armavir
Арме́ния Armenia
Армя́нск Armyansk

Арпа́ Agra
Арсе́ньев Arsenyev
Арск Arsk
Арташа́т Artashat
Арте́к Artek
Артём Artyom
Артёма о́стров Artyom Island
Артёмовск Artyomovsk
Артёмовский Artyomovsky
Арти́ Arti
Арха́нгельск Arkhangelsk
Арха́нгельское Arkhangelskoye
Архи́по-О́сиповка Arkhipo Osipovka
Арци́з Artsiz
Асбе́ст Asbest
Аска́ния-Но́ва Askaniya-Nova
Аска́рово Askarovo
Аски́но Askino
Ассаке́ *See* Leninsk²
Аста́пово *See* Lev Tolstoy
Астраха́н-База́р *See* Dzhalilabad
Астраха́нь Astrakhan
Атбаса́р Atbasar
Атка́рск Atkarsk
Аулие́-Ата́ *See* Dzhambul
Ауэ́зов Auezov
Ахалкала́ки Akhalkalaki
Ахалци́хе Akhaltsikhe
Ахма́това зали́в Akhmatov Bay
Ахтуба́ Akhtuba
Ахты́рка Akhtyrka
Ахунбаба́ев Akhunbabayev
Ачи́нск Achinsk
Ачи́т Achit
Аша́ Asha
Ашхаба́д Ashkhabad
Аюда́г Ayu Dag
Ая́н Ayan

Бабада́г Babadag
Ба́бушкин Babushkin
Багда́ди Bagdadi
Багратио́новск Bagrationovsk
Бадахша́н Badakhshan
Бадхы́з Badkhyz
Байда́рские воро́та Baydarsky Pass
Байка́л Baykal, Lake
Байра́м-Али́ Bayram-Ali
Бака́л Bakal
Бакса́н Baksan
Баку́ Baku
Бакырчи́к *See* Auezov
Балаба́ново Balabanovo
Балакла́ва Balaklava
Балахна́ Balakhna
Балаши́ха Balashikha
Балашо́в Balashov
Балка́рия *See* Kabardino-Balkaria
Ба́лта Balta
Балти́йск Baltiysk
Балти́йский порт *See* Paldiski
Балти́йское мо́ре Baltic Sea
Балха́ш Balkhash, Lake
Ба́льцер *See* Krasnoarmeysk¹
Бам Bam
Бара́новичи Baranovichi
Ба́ренцево мо́ре Barents Sea
Барнау́л Barnaul
Баро́нск *See* Marks
Барсакельме́с Barsa-Kelmes
Баталпаши́нск *See* Cherkessk
Бату́ми Batumi
Бату́рин Baturin
Бауманаба́д *See* Pyandzh
Бахму́т *See* Artyomovsk
Бахчисара́й Bakhchisaray
Башанта́ *See* Gorodovikovsk
Башки́рия *See* Bashkortostan
Башкортоста́н Bashkortostan
Бегова́т *See* Bekabad
Бего́мль Begoml
Беднодемья́новск Bednodemyanovsk
Бе́жецк Bezhetsk
Бе́жица Bezhitsa
Бекаба́д Bekabad
Белару́сь Belarus
Бе́лая Belaya
Бе́лая Це́рковь Belaya Tserkov
Бе́лгород Belgorod
Бе́лгород-Днестро́вский Belgorod-Dnestrovsky
Белёв Belyov
Бели́нский Belinsky
Белого́рск (Россия) Belogorsk¹
Белого́рск (Украина) Belogorsk²
Бе́лое о́зеро Beloye Ozero
Белозёрск Belozyorsk
Беломо́рск Belomorsk
Белоозёрск Beloozyorsk
Белоре́цк Beloretsk
Белоре́ченск Belorechensk
Белору́ссия *See* Belarus

Белоца́рск See Kyzyl
Белоще́лье See Naryan-Mar
Белу́ха Belukha
Бе́лый Bely
Белько́вский о́стров Belkovsky Island
Бе́льцы Beltsy
Бенде́ры Bendery
Бе́ннетта о́стров Bennett Island
Берди́чев Berdichev
Бердя́нск Berdyansk
Береза́нь Berezan
Березина́ Berezina
Березники́ Berezniki
Берёзово Beryozovo
Бе́рингово мо́ре Bering Sea
Бе́ринговский Beringovsky
Бессара́бия Bessarabia
Бет-Пак-Дала́ Betpak-Dala
Бешта́у Beshtau
Бийск Biysk
Били́бино Bilibino
Би́ржи See Madona
Би́рзула See Kotovsk³
Биробиджа́н Birobidzhan
Бируи́нца See Suvorovo
Бируни́ Biruni
Битю́г Bityug
Бишке́к Bishkek
Благове́щенск Blagoveshchensk
Благода́ть Blagodat
Бо́брики See Novomoskovsk
Бобро́в Bobrov
Бобру́йск Bobruysk
Богдано́вич Bogdanovich
Боголю́бово Bogolyubovo
Богоро́дицк Bogoroditsk
Богоро́дск (близ Ни́жнего Но́вгорода) Bogorodsk
Богоро́дск (близ Москвы́) See Noginsk
Богоро́дское See Kamskoye Ustye
Богосло́вск See Karpinsk
Богусла́в Boguslav
Богуча́р Boguchar
Божеда́ровка See Shchorsk
Бозда́г Bozdag
Бо́ково-Антраци́т See Antratsit
Бокситого́рск Boksitogorsk
Болва́нский Нос Bolvansky Nos
Бо́лград Bolgrad
Бологое́ Bologoye

Бо́лохово Bolokhovo
Бо́лхов Bolkhov
Большеви́к Bolshevik
Больши́е Со́ли See Nekrasovskoye
Большо́е Бо́лдино Bolshoye Boldino
Большо́й Бе́гичев, о́стров Bolshoy Begichev
Большо́й Иреме́ль Bolshoy Iremel
Бондю́жский See Mendeleyevsk
Бор Bor
Борзна́ Borzna
Бори́сов Borisov
Бори́сово Borisovo
Борисогле́бск Borisoglebsk
Бори́споль Borispol
Борови́чи Borovichi
Борово́е Borovoye
Бо́ровск Borovsk
Бородино́ (Россия) Borodino¹
Бородино́ (Украина) Borodino²
Борщёв Borshchyov
Бошняко́во Boshnyakovo
Бра́гин Bragin
Бра́слав Braslav
Братск Bratsk
Бре́ды Bredy
Бре́жнев See Naberezhnyye Chelny
Брест Brest
Брест-Лито́вск See Brest
Брова́ры Brovary
Бродокалма́к Brodokalmak
Бро́ды Brody
Бро́нницы Bronnitsy
Брянск Bryansk
Буг Bug
Бугульма́ Bugulma
Бугурусла́н Buguruslan
Бу́да-Кошелёво Buda-Koshelyovo
Будённовск Budyonnovsk
Бузулу́к Buzuluk
Буи́нск Buinsk
Буй (го́род) Buy¹
Буй (река́) Buy²
Буйна́кск Buynaksk
Букача́ча Bukachacha
Букови́на Bukovina
Булу́н Bulun
Бу́нге Земля́ Bunge Land
Бу́рмантово Burmantovo
Бурсо́ль Bursol
Буря́ад Buryaad
Буря́тия See Buryaad

Cyrillic-to-Roman Index

Буссо́ль проли́в Bussol Strait
Бутурли́новка Buturlinovka
Бухара́ Bukhara
Бырра́нга Byrranga
Бы́стрица Bystritsa

Вагаршапа́т *See* Echmiadzin
Ва́енга *See* Severomorsk
Вайга́ч Vaygach
Валаа́м Valaam
Валда́й Valday
Валу́йки Valuyki
Вапня́рка Vapnyarka
Ва́рна Varna
Варна́вино Varnavino
Ва́рнек Varnek
Василёво *See* Chkalovsk
Васи́льевский о́стров Vasilyevsky Island
Василько́в Vasilkov
Васильсу́рск Vasilsursk
Васюга́н Vasyugan
Вату́тино Vatutino
Ва́хрушев Vakhrushev
Ва́хрушево Vakhrushevo
Вахш Vakhsh
Вели́кая Velikaya
Вели́кие Лу́ки Velikiye Luki
Вели́кий У́стюг Veliky Ustyug
Великокня́жеская *See* Proletarsk
Вельск Velsk
Вельями́нское укрепле́ние *See* Tuapse
Вене́ра Venera
Ве́нтспилс Ventspils
Вереща́гино Vereshchagino
Верея́ Vereya
Ве́рный *See* Alma-Ata
Верхнедви́нск Verkhnedvinsk
Верхнедне́провск Verkhnedneprovsk
Верхнеу́динск *See* Ulan-Ude
Верхнеура́льск Verkhneuralsk
Ве́рхние Серги́ *See* Nizhniye Sergi
Ве́рхний Уфале́й Verkhny Ufaley
Ве́рхняя Пышма́ Verkhnyaya Pyshma
Ве́рхняя Салда́ *See* Nizhnyaya Salda
Ве́рхняя Тунгу́ска *See* Tunguska
Ве́рхняя Тура́ Verkhnyaya Tura
Верхоту́рье Verkhoturye
Верхоя́нск Verkhoyansk

Ветлу́га Vetluga
Взмо́рье Vzmorye
Ви́дное Vidnoye
Ви́зе Vize
Ви́льгорт Vilgort
Вильки́цкого о́стров Vilkitsky Island
Вильки́цкого проли́в Vilkitsky Strait
Ви́льно *See* Vilnius
Ви́льнюс Vilnius
Ви́льчека Земля́ Wilczek land
Вилю́й Vilyuy
Винда́ва *See* Ventspils
Ви́нница Vinnitsa
Виногра́дово Vinogradovo
Виси́м Visim
Виси́мо-У́ткинск Visimo-Utkinsk
Ви́слинский зали́в Vistula Lagoon
Ви́тебск Vitebsk
Вишневого́рск Vishnevogorsk
Владивосто́к Vladivostok
Владикавка́з Vladikavkaz
Влади́мир Vladimir
Влади́мир-Волы́нский Vladimir-Volynsky
Влади́мировка *See* Yuzhno-Sakhalinsk
Влады́кино Vladykino
Влады́чино Vladychino
Вождь Пролетариа́та Vozhd Proletariata
Во́же Vozhe
Воздви́женское Vozdvizhenskoye
Вознесе́нская *See* Vereshchagino
Во́лга Volga
Волгогра́д Volgograd
Волгодо́нск Volgodonsk
Во́лго-Каспи́йский Volgo-Kaspiysky
Волгоре́ченск Volgorechensk
Волжск Volzhsk
Во́лжский Volzhsky
Во́логда Vologda
Волокола́мск Volokolamsk
Волоча́евка Volochayevka
Во́лхов Volkhov
Волча́нск (Украина) Volchansk[1]
Волча́нск (Россия) Volchansk[2]
Во́лынь Volynia
Вольск Volsk
Воркута́ Vorkuta
Воро́неж Voronezh
Воро́нина о́стров Voronin Island
Воронцо́во Vorontsovo

Воронцо́во-Алекса́ндровское *See* Zelenokumsk
Вороши́лов *See* Ussuriysk
Вороши́ловгра́д *See* Lugansk
Вороши́ловск (Россия) *See* Stavropol
Вороши́ловск (Украина) *See* Kommunarsk
Во́рскла Vorskla
Восе́ Vose
Воскресе́нск Voskresensk
Воскресе́нск *See* Istra
Восто́к *See* Neftegorsk[2]
Вра́нгеля о́стров Wrangel Island
Все́володо-Благода́цкий Vsevolodo-Blagodatsky
Всеволожск Vsevolozhsk
Всехсвя́тское Vsekhsvyatskoye
Вулкане́шты Vulkaneshty
Вы́борг Vyborg
Высоко́вск Vysokovsk
Высо́кое Vysokoye
Высо́цк Vysotsk
Вы́чегда Vychegda
Вышго́род Vyshgorod
Вы́шний Волочёк Vyshny Volochyok
Вя́зники Vyazniki
Вя́зьма Vyazma
Вя́тка Vyatka

Гаври́ловка *See* Taldy-Kurgan
Гаври́лов Поса́д Gavrilov Posad
Гаври́лов Ям Gavrilov Yam
Гага́рин Gagarin
Га́гра Gagra
Газ-Ача́к Gaz-Achak
Газли́ Gazli
Гали́ция Galicia
Га́лич Galich
Ганджа́ *See* Gyandzha
Ганчешты́ *See* Kotovsk[2]
Гарм Garm
Гастелло Gastello
Гастелло и́мени Gastello, imeni
Га́тчина Gatchina
Гаурда́к Gaurdak
Гафу́ров Gafurov
Гварде́йск Gvardeysk
Гво́здева острова́ *See* Diomede Islands
Гдов Gdov
Гегечко́ри Gegechkori
Гёйгёль Gyoygyol
Геленджи́к Gelendzhik
Генрие́тты о́стров Henrietta Island
Гео́рга Земля́ George Land
Гео́ргиевск Georgiyevsk
Гео́ргиу-Деж *See* Liski
Гера́льд о́стров Herald Island
Гжатск *See* Gagarin[1]
Гига́нт Gigant
Гисса́рский хребе́т Hissar Mountains
Глубо́кое о́зеро Gluboe, Lake
Гове́рла Goverla
Голови́но Golovino
Головнина́ вулка́н Golovnin, Mt.
Голо́дная степь *See* Betpak-Dala
Голу́твин Golutvin
Го́лый Карамы́ш *See* Krasnoarmeysk[1]
Го́мель Gomel
Горба́тов Gorbatov
Го́ри Gori
Го́рки Gorki
Го́рки Ле́нинские *See* Gorki
Го́рловка Gorlovka
Го́рно-Алта́йск Gorno-Altaysk
Горнозаво́дск (Украина) Gornozavodsk[1]
Горнозаво́дск (Россия) Gornozavodsk[2]
Го́рный Щит Gorny Shchit
Горня́к Gornyak
Городе́ц Gorodets
Городи́ще Gorodishche
Городовико́вск Gorodovikovsk
Городо́к (Беларусь) Gorodok[1]
Городо́к (Россия) Gorodok[2]
Горохове́ц Gorokhovets
Горше́чное Gorshechnoye
Го́рький *See* Nizhny Novgorod
Горячево́дский Goryachevodsky
Горя́чий Ключ Goryachy Klyuch
Го́твальд *See* Zmiyov
Гра́йворон Grayvoron
Гремя́чинск Gremyachinsk
Грэ́эм-Белл о́стров Graham Bell Island
Григорио́поль Grigoriopol
Гроде́ково *See* Pogranichny
Гро́дно Grodno
Гро́зный Grozny

Грузия Georgia
Грумм-Гржимайло ледник Grumm-Grzhimaylo Glacier
Грёсовский Gresovsky
Грязи Gryazi
Грязовец Gryazovets
Губкин Gubkin
Гузар Guzar
Гукера остров Hooker Island
Гулистан Gulistan
Гундоровка *See* Donetsk²
Гурьев Guryev
Гурьевск Guryevsk
Гусев Gusev
Гусиное озеро Gusinoye, Lake
Гусиноозёрск Gusinoozersk
Гусь-Железный Guz-Zhelezny
Гусь-Хрустальный Gus-Khrustalny
Гянджа Gyandzha

Давид-Городок David-Gorodok
Давлеканово Davlekanovo
Дагестан Dagestan
Далматово Dalmatovo
Дальнереченск Dalnerechensk
Дангауэровка Dangauerovka
Даниловка Danilovka
Данков Dankov
Дарвазский хребет Darvaz Range
Дарг-Кох Darg-Kokh
Дарьялское ущелье Daryal Pass
Даугавпилс Daugavpils
20 лет ВЛКСМ пик *See* Pobeda Peak
Двигательстрой *See* Kaspiysk
Двина Dvina
Двинск *See* Daugavpils
Дворянская Терешка *See* Radishchevo
Двуреченск Dvurechensk
Дегтярск Degtyarsk
Дежнёва мыс Dezhnyov Cape
Дейнау Deynau
Де-Кастри De Kastri
Де-Лонга острова De Long Islands
Демидов Demidov
Дербент Derbent
Дерпт *See* Tartu
Десна Desna
Детское Село *See* Pushkin
Джалал-Абад Dzhalal

Джалилабад Dzhalilabad
Джалиль Dzhalil
Джамантау Dzhamantau
Джамбул Dzhambul
Джанкой Dzhankoy
Джансугуров Dzhansugurov
Джаркент *See* Panfilov
Джезказган Dzhezkazgan
Джетысу Dzhetysu
Джульфа Dzhulfa
Джунгарский Алатау Dzungarian Ala Tau
Дзауджикау *See* Vladikavkaz
Дзержинск (Россия) Dzerzhinsk¹
Дзержинск (Беларусь) Dzerzhinsk²
Дзержинский *See* Naryan-Mar
Дианы пролив Diana Strait
Дидковского горá Didkovsky
Диксон Dikson
Димитров Dimitrov
Димитровград Dimitrovgrad
Диомида острова Diomede Islands
Дмитриевск *See* Makeyevka
Дмитрия Лаптева пролив Dmitry Laptev Strait
Дмитров Dmitrov
Днепр Dnieper
Днепродзержинск Dneprodzerzhinsk
Днепропетровск Dnepropetrovsk
Днестр Dniester
Добрянка Dobryanka
Докучаевск Dokuchayevsk
Докшицы Dokshitsy
Долгодеревёнское Dolgoderevenskoye
Домбай Dombay
Домбай-ульген *See* Dombay
Дон Don
Донбасс Donbass
Донец Donets
Донецк Donetsk
Дорогобуж Dorogobuzh
Дорогомилово Dorogomilovo
Дорохово Dorokhovo
Дрезна Drezna
Дрисса *See* Verkhnedvinsk
Дрогичин Drogichin
Дрогобыч Drogobych
Дружба Druzhba
Дубна Dubna
Дубно Dubno
Дубовка Dubovka

Дубосса́ры Dubossary
Дуди́нка Dudinka
Дуна́й Danube
Душанбе́ Dushanbe
Дыхта́у Dykh Tau
Дюртюли́ Dyurtyuli
Дятько́во Dyatkovo

Евпато́рия Yevpatoriya
Егорлы́к Yegorlyk
Его́рьевск Yegoryevsk
Ежо́во-Черке́сск See Cherkessk
Ейск Yeysk
Екатеринбу́рг Yekaterinburg
Екатериненшта́дт See Marks
Екатеринода́р See Krasnodar
Екатерино́поль Yekaterinopol
Екатериносла́в See Dnepropetrovsk
Ела́буга Yelabuga
Е́лгава Jelgava
Еле́новские Карье́ры See Dokucha-
 yevsk
Еле́нск See Balta
Еле́ц Yelets
Еле́цкий Yeletsky
Елизаве́т Yelizavet
Елизаветгра́д See Kirovograd
Елизаве́тполь See Gyandzha
Е́лизово Yelizovo
Е́льня Yelnya
Еманжели́нск Yemanzhelinsk
Ена́киево Yenakiyevo
Енисе́й Yenisey
Енота́евка Yenotayevka
Ерева́н Yerevan
Ерма́к Yermak
Ермоло́вск See Leselidze
Ерофе́й Па́влович Yerofey-Pavlovich
Ессентуки́ Yessentuki
Ефре́мов Yefremov

Жаманакко́ль Zhamanakkol
Жаманту́з Zhamantuz
Жаната́с Zhanatas
Жанне́тты о́стров Jeannette Island
Жда́нов See Mariupol
Жда́новск Zhdanovsk
Жела́ния мыс Zhelaniya, Cape
Железново́дск Zheleznovodsk
Железного́рск Zheleznogorsk

Железного́рск-Или́мский
 Zheleznogorsk-Ilimsky
Железнодоро́жный (Россия)
 Zheleznodorozhny
Железнодоро́жный (Узбекистан)
 See Kungrad
Жёлтая Река́ See Zhyoltyye Vody
Жёлтые Во́ды Zhyoltyye Vody
Жетыко́ль Zhety-Kol
Жигулёвск Zhigulyovsk
Жи́здра Zhizdra
Жито́мир Zhitomir
Жо́втень Zhovten
Жо́лква See Nesterov[2]
Жо́хова о́стров Zhokhov Island
Жуко́вский Zhukovsky
Жу́копа Zhukopa

Заводоуко́вск Zavodoukovsk
Заводоуспе́нское Zavodouspenskoye
Заво́йко See Yelizovo
Заго́рск See Sergiyev Posad
Задо́нск Zadonsk
Зайса́н Zaysan
Закавка́зье Transcaucasia
Закарпа́тье Transcarpathia
Зале́щики Zaleshchiki
Зангезу́рский хребе́т Zangezur
 Range
Заполя́рный Zapolyarny
Запоро́жье Zaporozhye
Зара́йск Zaraysk
Засла́вль Zaslavl
Зати́шье See Elektrostal
Зва́нка See Volkhov
Звени́гово Zvenigovo
Звени́город Zvenigorod
Зелёная Ро́ща Zelyonaya Roshcha
Зелёного́рск Zelenogorsk
Зеленогра́д Zelenograd
Зеленодо́льск Zelenodolsk
Зеленоку́мск Zelenokumsk
Зе́ленск See Leninsk[2]
Зе́мгале Zemgale
Земе́тчино Zemetchino
Зеравша́н Zeravshan
Зерногра́д Zernograd
Зи́лупе Zilupe
Зи́мний Бе́рег Zimny Bereg
Зино́вьевск See Kirovograd
Златоу́ст Zlatoust

Змеи́ный о́стров Zmeiny Island
Змиёв Zmiyov
Золото́е кольцо́ Росси́и Golden Ring of Russia
Золото́й Рог Zolotoy Rog
Зугрэ́с Zugres
Зыря́новск Zyryanovsk
Зю́зельский Zyuzelsky

Ива́на Гро́зного вулка́н Ivan Grozny, Mt.
Иванго́род Ivangorod
Ива́ново Ivanovo
Ива́ново-Вознесе́нск See Ivanovo
Ива́но-Фра́нковск Ivano-Frankovsk
Иваще́нково See Chapayevsk
ИвГРЭ́С See Komsomolsk
И́вдель Ivdel
И́вня Ivnya
Ига́рка Igarka
Игу́мен See Cherven
И́дрица Idritsa
Иже́вск Izhevsk
Ижо́ра Izhora
"Изве́стий" острова́ Izvestia Islands
Изма́йлово Izmaylovo
Изумру́д Izumrud
Изя́слав Izyaslav
Ик Ik
Или́ Ili
Илова́йск Ilovaysk
И́ловля Ilovlya
И́луксте Ilukste
Ильи́нский Ilinsky
Ильи́ч Ilich
Ильичёвск Ilichyovsk
И́льмень Ilmen
Ильме́нский хребе́т Ilmen Range
Има́н See Dalnerechensk
И́мандра Imandra
Имере́тия Imeretia
Импера́торская га́вань See Sovetskaya Gavan
Ингерманла́ндия See Izhora
Ингода́ Ingoda
И́нгрия See Izhora
Ингу́л Ingul
Ингуле́ц Ingulets
Ингуше́тия Ingushetia
Индиги́рка Indigirka
Инкерма́н Inkerman

Ио́ри Iori
Ирби́т Irbit
Ирги́з Irgiz
Иренды́к Irendyk
Ирку́тск Irkutsk
Ирты́ш Irtysh
Иса́ченко о́стров Isachenko Island
Иссы́к-Куль (о́зеро) Issyk-Kul[1]
Иссы́к-Куль (го́род) Issyk-Kul[2]
Исто́бное Istobnoye
И́стра Istra
И́ткуль Itkul
Итуру́п Iturup
Ишимба́й Ishimbay

Йошка́р-Ола́ Yoshkar-Ola

Кабако́вск See Serov
Кабарди́но-Балка́рия Kabardino-Balkaria
Каба́чище See Zelenodolsk
Кавка́з Caucasus
Кагу́л Kagul
Каджеро́м Kadzherom
Ка́диевка See Stakhanov
Ка́дом Kadom
Казали́нск Kazalinsk
Казанджи́к Kazandzhik
Каза́нь Kazan
Казахста́н Kazakhstan
Казбе́ги Kazbegi
Казбе́к Kazbek
Ка́инск See Kuybyshev[1]
Кала́ Kala
Калара́ш Kalarash
Калата́ See Kirovgrad
Кала́ч Kalach
Кала́ч-на-Дону́ Kalach-on-Don
Ка́левала Kalevala
Кали́нин See Tver
Калинингра́д (на Ба́лтике) Kaliningrad[1]
Калинингра́д (близ Москвы́) Kaliningrad[2]
Калмы́кия Kalmykia
Калу́га Kaluga
Каля́зин Kalyazin
Ка́ма Kama
Ка́менец Kamenets
Ка́менец-Подо́льский Kamenets-Podolsky

Ка́менка Kamenka
Ка́менское See Dneprodzerzhinsk
Ка́менск-Ура́льский Kamensk-Uralsky
Ка́менск-Ша́хтинский Kamensk-Shakhtinsky
Ка́мень-на-Оби́ Kamen-on-Ob
Камо́ Kamo
Ка́мское У́стье Kamskoye Ustye
Камча́тка Kamchatka
Камы́шин Kamyshin
Камышло́в Kamyshlov
Кананико́льское Kananikolskoye
Кана́ш Kanash
Кандага́ч See Oktyabrsk²
Кандала́кша Kandalaksha
Ка́нев Kanev
Канибада́м Kanibadam
Ка́нин полуо́стров Kanin Peninsula
Канск Kansk
Кантеми́ровка Kantemirovka
Капсу́кас See Marijampole
Ка́ра See Kara Sea
Карабаги́ш See Sovetabad
Караба́х See Nagorno-Karabakh
Караба́ш Karabash
Кара́-Бога́з-Гол Kara-Bogaz-Gol
Карага́й Karagay
Караганда́ Karaganda
Карада́г Karadag
Карадарья́ (Кыргызста́н) Karadarya
Карадарья́ (Узбекиста́н) See Zeravshan
Каракалпакста́н Karakalpakstan
Каракли́с Karaklis
Карако́л See Przhevalsk
Караку́ль Karakul
Караку́мы Kara Kum
Карасу́ Karasu
Карасубаза́р See Belogorsk²
Карата́у Karatau
Каратобе́ Karatobe
Карача́ево-Черке́сия Karachay-Cherkessia
Карача́евск Karachayevsk
Ка́ргополь Kargopol
Каре́лия Karelia
Каркини́тский зали́в Karkinit Bay
Ка́рла Ма́ркса пик Karl Marx Peak
Ка́рло-Ли́бкнехтовск Karlo-Libknekhtovsk
Карпа́ты Carpathians

Карпи́нск Karpinsk
Карсакпа́й Karsakpay
Ка́рские воро́та Kara Strait
Ка́рское мо́ре Kara Sea
Карталы́ Kartaly
Карши́ Karshi
Каря́гино See Fizuli
Каси́мов Kasimov
Касли́ Kasli
Каспи́йск Kaspiysk
Каспи́йское мо́ре Caspian Sea
Касто́рное Kastornoye
Касу́м-Исма́йлов Kasum-Ismailov
Ката́в-Ива́новск Katav-Ivanovsk
Ката́йск Kataysk
Каттакурга́н Kattakurgan
Кату́нь Katun
Каты́к See Shakhtyorsk²
Ка́унас Kaunas
Ка́уфмана пик See Lenin Peak
Кафирнига́н Kafirnigan
Кахо́вка Kakhovka
Ка́ча Kacha
Качкана́р Kachkanar
Каши́ра Kashira
Кашкадарья́ Kashkadarya
Ексго́льм See Priozyorsk
Ке́мерово Kemerovo
Кемь Kem
Кента́у Kentau
Керки́ Kerki
Ке́рчевский Kerchevsky
Керчь Kerch
Кеть Ket
Кзыл-Орда́ Kzyl-Orda
Кива́ч Kivach
Ки́виыли Kiviõli
Ки́ев Kiev
Ки́жи Kizhi
Ки́зел Kizel
Кизля́р Kizlyar
Киквидзе Kikvidze
Кили́я Kiliya
Ки́мовск Kimovsk
Ки́нгисепп (Россия) Kingisepp
Ки́нгисепп (Эстония) See Kuressaare
Ки́нешма Kineshma
Кирги́зия See Kyrgyzstan
Киржа́ч Kirzhach
Кири́ллов Kirillov
Ки́ров (близ Росла́вля) Kirov
Ки́ров (близ Каза́ни) See Vyatka

Кировабáд (Азербайджан) *See* Gyandzha
Кировабáд (Таджикистан) *See* Pyandzh
Ки́рова зали́в Kirov Bay
Кировакáн *See* Karaklis
Кировгрáд Kirovgrad
Кировогрáд Kirovograd
Ки́ровск Kirovsk
Ки́ровский Kirovsky
Кирсáнов Kirsanov
Кисловóдск Kislovodsk
Кишинёв Kishinyov
Клáйпеда Klaipeda
Клин Klin
Клинцы́ Klintsy
Клухóри *See* Karachayevsk
Ключевскáя Сóпка Klyuchevskaya Sopka
Ключи́ Klyuchi
Кля́зьма Klyazma
Княги́нино Knyaginino
Кóбрин Kobrin
Кóвда Kovda
Кóвель Kovel
Кóвно *See* Kaunas
Коврóв Kovrov
Кóжва Kozhva
Козéльск Kozelsk
Козлóв *See* Michurinsk
Козьмодемья́нск Kozmodemyansk
Кóйвисто *See* Primorsk¹
Кóйданово *See* Dzerzhinsk²
Кокáнд Kokand
Кóксовый Koksovy
Коктáш Koktash
Коктебéль *See* Planyorskoye
Кокчетáв Kokchetav
Кóла Kola
Колгу́ев Kolguyev
Когри́в Kologriv
Кóлокол Kolokol
Колóмна Kolomna
Коломы́я Kolomyya
Кóлпино Kolpino
Колхи́да Colchis
Колывáнь Kolyvan
Колымá Kolyma
Кóльский полуóстров Kola Peninsula
Кольчу́гино *See* Leninsk-Kuznetsky
Командóрские островá Commander Islands

Комáрно Komarno
Комáрово Komarovo
Кóми Komi
Коммунáрск Kommunarsk
Коммуни́зма пик Communism Peak
Комсомóлец (Россия) Komsomolets
Комсомóлец (Казахстан) *See* Myortvy Kultuk
Комсомóльск Komsomolsk
Комсомóльск-на-Амýре Komsomolsk-on-Amur
Конакóво Konakovo
Кóндопога Kondopoga
Конжакóвский Кáмень Konzhakovsky Kamen
Конотóп Konotop
Константи́новка Konstantinovka
Константи́нов Кáмень Konstantinov Kamen
Константиногрáд *See* Krasnograd
Копéйск Kopeysk
Копетдáг Kopet-Dag
Корженéвского ледни́к Korzhenevsky Glacier
Корженéвской пик Korzhenevskaya Peak
Кóркино Korkino
Кóростень Korosten
Коротоя́к Korotoyak
Корсáков Korsakov
Кóрсунь-Шевчéнковский Korsun-Shevchenkovsky
Кóрфа зали́в Korf Bay
Коря́к Koryak
Костромá Kostroma
Котéльнич Kotelnich
Котéльный óстров Kotelny Island
Кóтлас Kotlas
Кóтлин Kotlin
Котóвск (Россия) Kotovsk¹
Котóвск (Молдова) Kotovsk²
Котóвск (Украина) Kotovsk³
Коунрáдский Kounradsky
Кóхтла-Я́рве Kohtla-Järve
Коцюби́нское Kotsyubinskoye
Краматóрск Kramatorsk
Крáсная Поля́на Krasnaya Polyana
Крáсная Прéсня *See* Presnya
Красноармéйск (близ Сарáтова) Krasnoarmeysk¹
Красноармéйск (близ Москвы́) Krasnoarmeysk²

Красноармейск (близ Волгограда) Krasnoarmeysk³
Краснова гора Krasnov, Mt.
Красновидово Krasnovidovo
Красновишерск Krasnovishersk
Красноводск Krasnovodsk
Красногвардейск (Узбекистан) Krasnogvardeysk
Красногвардейск (Россия) See Gatchina
Красноград Krasnograd
Краснодар Krasnodar
Краснодон Krasnodon
Красное Село Krasnoye Selo
Краснознаменск Krasnoznamensk
Краснокамск Krasnokamsk
Краснококшайск See Yoshkar Ola
Краснооктябрьский Krasnooktyabrsky
Краснополье Krasnopolye
Красноселькуп Krasnoselkup
Краснослободск Krasnoslobodsk
Краснотурьинск Krasnoturinsk
Красноуральск Krasnouralsk
Красноусольский Krasnousolsky
Красноуфимск Krasnoufimsk
Краснощёково Krasnoshchyokovo
Красноярск Krasnoyarsk
Красный Ключ Krasny Klyuch
Красный Кут Krasny Kut
Красный Лиман Krasny Liman
Красный Луч Krasny Luch
Красный Маяк Krasny Mayak
Красный Октябрь Krasny Oktyabr
Красный Яр Krasny Yar
Кременец Kremenets
Кременчуг Kremenchug
Креницына вулкан Krenitsyn, Mt.
Крестовый перевал Krestovy Pereval
Крестцы Kresttsy
Кривая Коса See Sedovo
Кривой Рог Krivoy Rog
Криндачёвка See Krasny Luch
Кристинополь See Chervonograd
Кронштадт Kronshtadt
Кропачёво Kropachyovo
Кропоткин Kropotkin
Кропоткина хребет Kropotkin Range
Крубера хребет Kruber Range
Крузенштерна пролив Kruzenshtern Strait

Крыжина хребет Kryzhin Range
Крылатское Krylatskoye
Крым Crimea
Крюково Kryukovo
Кубань Kuban
Кувандык Kuvandyk
Куделька See Asbest
Кудиркос-Наумёстис Kudirkos-Naumiestis
Кудымкар Kudymkar
Кузбасс Kuzbass
Кузнецк (близ Пензы) Kuznetsk
Кузнецк (близ Новосибирска) See Novokuznetsk
Кузнецово See Konakovo
Кузнецовск Kuznetsovsk
Куйбышев (близ Новосибирска) Kuybyshev¹
Куйбышев (близ Ульяновска) Kuybyshev²
Куйбышев (близ Сызрани) See Samara
Куйбышевка-Восточная See Belogorsk¹
Куйбышевский Kuybyshevsky
Кукарка See Sovetsk²
Култук Kultuk
Куляб Kulyab
Кума Kuma
Кумайри Kumayri
Кумертау Kumertau
Кунашир Kunashir
Кунград Kungrad
Кунгур Kungur
Кунцево Kuntsevo
Кура Kura
Курган Kurgan
Курган-Тюбе Kurgan-Tyube
Курессааре Kuressaare
Курземе Kurzeme
Курильск Kurilsk
Курильские острова Kuril Islands
Курск Kursk
Курский залив Kursky Zaliv
Курчатов Kurchatov
Кустанай Kustanay
Кусье-Александровский Kusye-Aleksandrovsky
Кутаиси Kutaisi
Кушва Kushva
Кушка Kushka
Кушнарёнково Kushnarenkovo

Кызы́л (Россия) Kyzyl
Кызы́л (Молдова) See Suvorovo
Кызылага́ч See Kirov Bay
Кызы́л-Кия́ Kyzyl-Kiya
Кызылку́м Kyzyl Kum
Кызылта́ш Kyzyltash
Кыргызста́н Kyrgyzstan
Кышты́м Kyshtym

Лабытна́нги Labytnangi
Ла́дожское о́зеро Ladoga, Lake
Ла́душкин Ladushkin
Ла́зарев Lazarev
Ла́зарева о́стров Lazarev Island
Ла́заревское Lazarevskoye
Лазо́вск Lazovsk
Ла́кинск Lakinsk
Ла́ма Lama
Лаперу́за проли́в La Pérouse Strait
Ла́птевых мо́ре Laptev Sea
Ла́рга Larga
Ла́твия Latvia
Лахденпо́хья Lakhdenpokhya
Ла́ча Lacha
Лби́щенск See Chapayev
Лебеди́н Lebedin
Лебедя́нь Lebedyan
Лев Толсто́й Lev Tolstoy
Ле́на Lena
Ле́нин Lenin
Ленинаба́д (на реке Сырдарья) See Khodzhent
Ленинаба́д (к юго-востоку от Ходжента) See Gafurov
Ленинака́н See Kumayri
Ле́нина пик Lenin Peak
Ленингра́д See St. Petersburg
Ле́нино Lenino
Леногорск (Казахстан) Leninogorsk[1]
Леногорск (Россия) Leninogorsk[2]
Ле́нино-Да́чное Lenino-Dachnoye
Ле́нинск (Россия) Leninsk[1]
Ле́нинск (Узбекистан) Leninsk[2]
Ле́нинск-Кузне́цкий Leninsk-Kuznetsky
Ленкора́нь Lenkoran
Ле́нское мо́ре See Laptev Sea
Ле́пель Lepel
Ле́рмонтово Lermontovo
Леселидзе Leselidze
Лесны́е Поля́ны Lesnyye Polyany
Лесого́рск Lesogorsk
Лесозаво́дск Lesozavodsk
Лесопи́льное Lesopilnoye
Лесхимстро́й See Severodonetsk
Ле́тний бе́рег Letny Bereg
Лефо́ртово Lefortovo
Лива́дия Livadiya
Ливо́ния Livonia
Ли́да Lida
Ли́епая Liepāja
Ли́пецк Lipetsk
Ли́сий Нос Lisy Nos
Лисича́нск Lisichansk
Ли́ски Liski
Лися́нского полуо́стров Lisyansky Peninsula
Литва́ Lithuania
Литви́но See Sosnovoborsk
Ли́тке проли́в Litke Strait
Ли́хвин See Chekalin
Лихосла́вль Likhoslavl
Ло́бва Lobva
Лоде́йное по́ле Lodeynoye Pole
Лозова́я Lozovaya
Ломоно́сов Lomonosov
Ло́нга проли́в Long Strait
Лопа́сня See Chekhov[2]
Лопа́тино See Volzhsk
Лопа́тка Lopatka, Cape
Лосиноостро́вск See Babushkin[2]
Ло́хвица Lokhvitsa
Лубны́ Lubny
Лу́га Luga
Луга́нск Lugansk
Лугово́й Lugovoy
Лужники́ Luzhniki
Лукоя́нов Lukoyanov
Лусава́н See Charentsavan
Луту́гино Lutugino
Лухови́цы Lukhovitsky
Луцк Lutsk
Лы́сые Го́ры Lysyye Gory
Лы́сьва Lysva
Львов Lvov
Льгов Lgov
Люба́нь Lyuban
Лю́берцы Lyubertsy
Лю́беч Lyubech
Люди́ново Lyudinovo
Ля́ховские острова́ Lyakhov Islands

Магада́н Magadan
Магни́тка Magnitka
Магни́тная Magnitnaya
Магнитого́рск Magnitogorsk
Ма́дона Madona
Майко́п Maykop
Ма́йкор Maykor
Мака́ров Makarov
Мака́рьев Makaryev
Мака́рьево Makaryevo
Маке́евка Makeyevka
Мала́хов Malakhov
Ма́лая Ви́шера Malaya Vishera
Ма́лая Русь See Ukraine
Малоарха́нгельск Maloarkhangelsk
Малори́та Malorita
Малоро́ссия See Ukraine
Малоя́з Maloyaz
Малояросла́вец Maloyaroslavets
Малы́гина проли́в Malygin Strait
Мамады́ш Mamadysh
Мамо́ново Mamonovo
Мангли́си Manglisi
Мангышла́к Mangyshlak
Ма́ныч Manych
Ма́рганец Marganets
Маргила́н Margilan
Мари́ Mari
Мари́инск Mariinsk
Мари́инский Mariinsky
Мари́инский Поса́д Mariinsky Posad
Мариу́поль Mariupol
Мария́мполе Marijampole
Маркс Marks
Маркшта́дт See Marks
Марциа́льные Во́ды Martsialnyye Vody
Мары́ Mary
Ма́точкин Шар Matochkin Shar
Махара́дзе See Ozurgeti
Махачкала́ Makhachkala
Маце́ста Matsesta
Маяко́вский See Bagdadi
Мая́чный Mayachny
Мглин Mglin
Мегре́лия See Mingrelia
Ме́грера Megrera
Медве́дково Medvedkovo
Медвежьего́рск Medvezhyegorsk
Медве́жьи острова́ Bear Islands
Медного́рск Mednegorsk
Междуре́ченск Mezhdurechensk

Межева́я У́тка See Novoutkinsk
Мезе́нь Mezen
Мелеке́сс See Dimitrovgrad
Ме́ленки Melenki
Мелеу́з Meleuz
Мелито́поль Melitopol
Ме́лкое о́зеро Melkoye, Lake
Ме́мель See Klaipeda
Менгре́лия Mingrelia
Менделе́ева вулка́н Mendeleyev, Mt.
Менделе́ево Mendeleyevo
Менделе́евск Mendeleyevsk
Мерв See Mary
Мёртвый Култу́к Myortvy Kultuk
Мещёра Meshchyora
Мещо́вск Meshchovsk
Миа́сс Miass
Микоя́н-Шаха́р See Karachayevsk
Мингеча́ур Mingechaur
Минера́льные Во́ды Mineralnyye Vody
Минск Minsk
Минуси́нск Minusinsk
Минья́р Minyar
Мио́ры Miory
Мир-Баши́р Mir-Bashir
Мирзачу́ль See Gulistan
Мирзоя́н See Dzhambul
Ми́рный Mirny
Миха́йлов Mikhaylov
Миха́йловск Mikhaylovsk
Ми́ха-Цхака́я See Senaki
Мичу́ринск Michurinsk
Могилёв Mogilyov
Могилёв-Подо́льский Mogilyov-Podolsky
Можа́йск Mozhaysk
Мозжо́к Mozdok
Мо́зырь Mozyr
Молда́вия See Moldova
Молдо́ва Moldova
Молоде́чно Molodechno
Молодогварде́йск Molodogvardeysk
Мо́локово Molokovo
Мо́лотовск See Perm
Мо́лотовск (близ Вя́тки) See Nolinsk
Мо́лотовск (близ Арха́нгельска) See Severodvinsk
Моло́чная Molochnaya
Моне́тный Monetny
Мончего́рск Monchegorsk

Мордо́вия Mordovia
Моро́зова и́мени Morozova imeni
Москва́ Moscow
Моско́вия Muscovy
Мосты́ Mosty
Мра́морский Mramorsky
Мста Msta
Мстисла́вль Mstislavl
Мценск Mtsensk
Мцхе́та Mtskheta
Му́дъюга Mudyuga
Муе́зерский Muyezersky
Мука́чево Mukachevo
Мурзи́нка Murzinka
Му́рманск Murmansk
Му́ром Murom
Му́ствээ Mustvee
Му́стла Mustla
Му́ху Muhu
Мушке́това гора́ Mushketov, Mt.
Муюнку́м Muyunkum
Мы́совск *See* Babushkin¹
Мыт Myt
Мыти́щи Mytishchi

На́бережные Челны́ Naberezhnyye Chelny
На́вля Navlya
Навои́ Navoi
На́волоки Navoloki
Нага́ева бу́хта Nagayev Bay
Наго́рно-Караба́х Nagorno-Karabakh
Наде́ждинск *See* Serov
Наде́жды проли́в Nadezhda Strait
На́льчик Nalchik
На́рва Narva
Нарима́нов Narimanov
Наро́дная Narodnaya
Нары́м Narym
Нары́н Naryn
Нарья́н-Мар Naryan-Mar
Нафтала́н Naftalan
Нахичева́нь Nakhichevan
Нахо́дка Nakhodka
Небит-Даг Nebit-Dag
Нева́ Neva
Не́вельск Nevelsk
Неве́льского проли́в Nevelskoy Strait
Невья́нск Nevyansk

Не́жин Nezhin
Незаме́тный *See* Aldan
Некра́совское Nekrasovskoye
Не́ман Neman
Не́нец *See* Yamal-Nenets
Не́рехта Nerekhta
Не́рчинск Nerchinsk
Нерюнгри́ Neryungri
Не́свиж Nesvizh
Не́стеров (Россия) Nesterov¹
Не́стеров (Украина) Nesterov²
Нефтеаба́д Nefteabad
Нефтего́рск (близ Апшеронска) Neftegorsk¹
Нефтего́рск (на Сахалине) Neftegorsk²
Нефтека́мск Neftekamsk
Нефтеку́мск Neftekumsk
Нефтечала́ Neftechala
Нефтею́ганск Nefteyugansk
Нефтяны́е Ка́мни Neftyanyye Kamni
Нижнево́лжск *See* Narimanov
Ни́жние Серги́ Nizhniye Sergi
Ни́жний Агджаке́нд *See* Shaumyanovsk
Ни́жний Но́вгород Nizhny Novgorod
Ни́жний Таги́л Nizhny Tagil
Ни́жний Уфале́й *See* Verkhny Ufaley
Ни́жняя Салда́ Nizhnyaya Salda
Ни́жняя Тавда́ *See* Tavda
Ни́жняя Тунгу́ска *See* Tunguska
Ни́жняя Тура́ *See* Verkhnyaya Tura
Ни́кель Nikel
Ники́тинские про́мыслы *See* Kirovsky
Никола́ев Nikolayev
Никола́евск (Казахстан) *See* Kustanay
Никола́евск (Россия) *See* Pugachyov
Никола́евск-на-Аму́ре Nikolayevsk-on-Amur
Нико́льский Ху́тор *See* Sursk
Нико́льск-Уссури́йский *See* Ussuriysk
Нико́поль Nikopol
Новаба́д (центральный Таджикистан) Novabad¹
Новаба́д (западный Таджикистан) Novabad²

Нóвая Земля́ Novaya Zemlya
Нóвая Ла́дога Novaya Ladoga
Нóвая Ля́ля Novaya Lyalya
Нóвая Па́шня See Gornozavodsk[1]
Нóвая Письмя́нка See Leninogorsk[2]
Нóвая Сиби́рь Novaya Sibir
Нóвгород Novgorod
Нóвгород-Се́верский Novgorod-Seversky
Новоалта́йск Novoaltaysk
Новобелоката́й Novobelokatay
Новогра́д-Волы́нский Novograd-Volynsky
Новогру́док Novogrudok
Новодви́нск Novodvinsk
Новокузне́цк Novokuznetsk
Новокýйбышевск Novokuybyshevsk
Нóво-Марии́нск See Anadyr
Новомичу́ринск Novomichurinsk
Новомоскóвск Novomoskovsk
Новониколáевск See Novosibirsk
Новопáшенного óстров See Zhokhov Island
Новопаши́йский See Gornozavodsk[1]
Новопокрóвка See Liski
Новополóцк Novopolotsk
Новорже́в Novorzhev
Новоросси́йск (Россия) Novorossiysk
Новоросси́йск (Украина) See Dnepropetrovsk
Новорóссия See Novorossiysk
Новосиби́рск Novosibirsk
Новосиби́рские островá New Siberian Islands
Новоси́л Novosil
Новосинегла́зовский Novosineglazovsky
Нóво-Старóбинск See Soligorsk
Новотрóицк Novotroitsk
Новоузе́нск Novouzensk
Новоулья́новск Novoulyanovsk
Новоýткинск Novoutkinsk
Новочебокса́рск Novocheboksarsk
Новочерка́сск Novocherkassk
Новоша́хтинск Novoshakhtinsk
Новоэкономи́ческое See Dimitrov
Нóвые Черёмушки Novyye Cheryomushki
Нóвый Афóн Novy Afon
Нóвый Донбáсс See Dimitrov
Нóвый Маргела́н See Fergana
Нóвый Оскóл Novy Oskol

Ноги́нск Noginsk
Ноли́нск Nolinsk
Нор-Баязе́т See Kamo
Нóрдвик Nordvik
Норденше́льда архипела́г Nordenskiöld Archipelago
Норденше́льда мóре See Laptev Sea
Нори́льск Norilsk
Нукýс Nukus
Нуратáу Nuratau
Нуре́к Nurek
Нухá See Sheki
Ны́роб Nyrob
Нюхча Nyukhcha
Нязепетрóвск Nyazepetrovsk

Обдóрск See Salekhard
Обига́рм Obigarm
Обирáловка See Zheleznodorozhny
Обнинск Obninsk
Обручева горá Obruchev, Mt.
Обручево See Ulyanovo
Общий Сырт Obshchy Syrt
Обь Ob
Овидиóполь Ovidiopol
Ови́нище Ovinishche
Овруч Ovruch
Оде́сса Odessa
Одинцóво Odintsovo
Озёрск Ozyorsk
Озургéти Ozurgeti
Ойрóт-Турá See Gorno-Altaysk
Окá Oka
Октемберя́н Oktemberyan
Октя́брьск (Россия) Oktyabrsk[1]
Октя́брьск (Казахстан) Oktyabrsk[2]
Октя́брьский Oktyabrsky
Октя́брьской Револю́ции óстров October Revolution Island
Олóнец Olonets
Ольвиóполь See Pervomaysk[2]
Ольги зали́в Olga Bay
Ольгóполь Olgopol
Ольховáтка Olkhovatka
Ольхóн Olkhon
Омск Omsk
Онéга Onega
Онéжское óзеро Onega, Lake
Опóчка Opochka
Ораниенбáум See Lomonosov
Оргéев Orgeyev

Оргтру́д Orgtrud
Орджоники́дзе (Росси́я) *See* Vladikavkaz
Орджоники́дзе (Украи́на) *See* Yenakiyevo
Орджоникидзеаба́д Ordzhonikidzeabad
Орджоникидзегра́д *See* Bezhitsa
Ордуба́д Ordubad
Орёл Oryol
Оренбу́рг Orenburg
Оре́хово-Зу́ево Orekhovo-Zuyevo
Орло́в *See* Khalturin
Орск Orsk
О́рша Orsha
Оса́ Osa
Осе́тия Ossetia
Оси́нники Osinniki
Осинто́рф Osintorf
Осипе́нко *See* Berdyansk
Оско́л Oskol
Оста́нкино Ostankino
О́стров Ostrov
Остро́г Ostrog
Острого́жск Ostrogozhsk
Остя́ко-Вогу́льск *See* Khanty-Mansiysk
Отва́жное *See* Zhigulyovsk
О́тдых *See* Zhukovsky
Отра́дное Otradnoye
Оха́нск Okhansk
Охо́тское мо́ре Okhotsk, Sea of
Оча́ков Ochakov
Ош Osh
Ошмя́ны Oshmyany

Па́влово Pavlovo
Па́вловск (близ Санкт-Петербу́рга) Pavlovsk[1]
Па́вловск (близ Воро́нежа) Pavlovsk[2]
Павло́вский Поса́д Pavlovsky Posad
Павлогра́д Pavlograd
Павлода́р Pavlodar
Па́йде Paide
Па́йер Pay-Yer
Пай-Хо́й Pay-Khoy
Па́лдиски Paldiski
Па́лех Palekh
Пами́р Pamirs
Па́мяти 13 Борцо́в Pamyati 13 Bortsov

Па́мять Пари́жской Комму́ны Pamyat Parizhskoy Kommuny
Паневежи́с Panevėžis
Панфи́лов Panfilov
Папа́нина мыс Papanin, Cape
Парамуши́р Paramushir
Па́рма Parma
Партиза́нск Partizansk
Па́хтусова о́стров Pakhtusov Island
Паши́я Pashiya
Пе́йпус *See* Chudskoye, Lake
Пенджике́нт Pendzhikent
Пе́нза Penza
Первома́йск (Росси́я) Pervomaysk[1]
Первома́йск (Украи́на, близ Никола́ева) Pervomaysk[2]
Первома́йск (Украи́на, близ Стаха́нова) Pervomaysk[3]
Первома́йский *See* Novodvinsk
Первоура́льск Pervouralsk
Переко́п Perekop
Пересла́вль-Зале́сский Pereslavl-Zalessky
Переясла́в Pereyaslav
Переясла́в-Хмельни́цкий *See* Pereyaslav
Перло́вка Perlovka
Пе́рмское *See* Komsomolsk-on-Amur
Пермь Perm
Перо́вск *See* Kzyl-Orda
Першотра́венск Pershotravensk
Песо́чня (близ Бря́нска) Pesochnya
Песо́чня (близ Калу́ги) *See* Kirov
Петерго́ф *See* Petrodvorets
Петра́ Вели́кого зали́в Peter the Great Bay
Петра́ острова́ Peter Islands
Петра́ Пе́рвого хребе́т Peter the First Range
Пе́тро-Алекса́ндровск *See* Turtkul
Петро́ва ледни́к Petrov Glacier
Петро́в Вал Petrov Val
Петро́вск Petrovsk
Петро́вск-Забайка́льский Petrovsk-Zabaykalsky
Петро́вский заво́д *See* Petrovsk-Zabaykalsky
Петро́вское *See* Svetlograd
Петро́вск-Порт *See* Makhachkala
Петрогра́д *See* St. Petersburg
Петрогра́дский о́стров Petrograd Island

Петродворе́ц Petrodvorets
Петрозаво́дск Petrozavodsk
Петрока́менское Petrokamenskoye
Петрокре́пость Petrokrepost
Пе́тро-Ма́рьевка See Pervomaysk³
Петропа́вловск Petropavlovsk
Петропа́вловск-Камча́тский Petropavlovsk-Kamchatsky
Петушки́ Petushki
Пе́ченга Pechenga
Печо́ра Pechora
Печо́ры Pechory
Пи́нега Pinega
Пинск Pinsk
Пионе́р Pioneer
Пионе́рский Pionersky
Пиря́тин Piryatin
Пи́ткяранта Pitkyaranta
Пишпе́к See Bishkek
Планёрское Planyorskoye
Пласт Plast
Плёс Plyos
Плеще́ево о́зеро Pleshcheyevo, Lake
Побе́ды пик Pobeda Peak
Повене́ц Povenets
Пограни́чный Pogranichny
Подка́менная Тунгу́ска See Tunguska
Подку́мок Podkumok
Подли́пки See Kaliningrad²
Подо́лия Podolia
Подо́льск Podolsk
Поду́шкино Podushkino
Покро́в Pokrov
Покро́вск Pokrovsk
Покро́вское-Стре́шнево Pokrovskoye-Streshnevo
Поле́сск Polessk
Поле́сье Polesye
Поло́ги Pologi
Поло́нное Polonnoye
Полотня́ный Polotnyany
По́лоцк Polotsk
Полта́ва Poltava
Полтора́цк See Ashkhabad
Полу́ночное Polunochnoye
Поля́рный Polyarny
По́речье See Demidov
Поронайск Poronaysk
Порт-Ильи́ч Port-Ilich
Посёлок и́мени Хамзы́ Хакимзаде́ See Khamza

Посёлок строи́телей Ка́мской ГЭС See Chaykovsky
Посье́т Posyet
По́ти Poti
Почи́нок Pochinok
Пошехо́нье-Волода́рск Poshekhonye-Volodarsk
Поя́рково Poyarkovo
Пра́вда Pravda
Пра́вдинск (близ Калининграда) Pravdinsk¹
Пра́вдинск (близ Нижнего Новгорода) Pravdinsk²
Преображе́нская See Kikvidze
Преображе́нское Preobrazhenskoye
Пре́сня Presnya
Пржева́льск Przhevalsk
Приаргу́нск Priargunsk
Привокза́льный Privokzalny
Приво́лжск Privolzhsk
Прику́мск See Budyonnovsk
Прилу́ки Priluki
Примо́рск (близ Санкт-Петербурга) Primorsk¹
Примо́рск (близ Калининграда) Primorsk²
Примо́рский край Primorsky Kray
Примо́рье See Primorsky Kray
Приозёрск Priozyorsk
При́пять Pripyat
При́шиб See Leninsk¹
Провиде́ния Provideniya
Прогре́сс Progress
Пролета́рск Proletarsk
Промы́шленный Promyshlenny
Пронск Pronsk
Про́нчищева бе́рег Pronchishchev Coast
Про́нчищевой бу́хта Pronchishchev Bay
Пропо́йск See Slavgorod
Проску́ров See Khmelnitsky
Прут Prut
Псеку́пс See Goryachy Klyuch
Псков Pskov
Пугачёв Pugachyov
Пу́дож Pudozh
Пути́вль Putivl
Путя́тин Putyatin
Пу́чеж Puchezh
Пу́шкин Pushkin
Пу́шкино Pushkino

Пу́шкинские Го́ры Pushkinskiye Gory
Пышма́ See Verkhnyaya Pyshma
Пяндж Pyandzh
Пя́рну Pärnu
Пятиго́рск Pyatigorsk
Пятиха́тки Pyatikhatki

Раде́хов Radekhov
Радзиви́лов See Chervonoarmeysk
Ради́щево Radishchevo
Радови́цкий Radovitsky
Ра́домышль Radomyshl
Ра́донеж See Gorodok[2]
Раздо́льное Razdolnoye
Ра́менское Ramenskoye
Раненбу́рг See Chaplygin
Рассве́т Rassvet
Растя́пино See Dzerzhinsk[1]
Ратма́нова о́стров Ratmanov Island
Рахья́ Rakhya
Ревда́ Revda
Ре́вель See Tallinn
Револю́ции пик Revolution Peak
Рега́р See Tursunzade
Реж Rezh
Ре́пино Repino
Ре́чица Rechitsa
Ржев Rzhev
Ри́га Riga
Ри́ддер See Leninogorsk[1]
Рико́рда мыс Rikord Cape
Рио́ни Rioni
Ро́вно Rovno
Ро́вное Rovnoye
Рогачёв Rogachyov
Рого́жка Rogozhka
Родники́ Rodniki
Рома́н-Кош Roman Kosh
Рома́нов-Борисогле́бск See Tutayev
Рома́нов-на-Му́рмане See Murmansk
Рома́новский Ху́тор See Kropotkin
Ромны́ Romny
Ро́славль Roslavl
Росси́я Russia
Ро́ссошь Rossosh
Росто́в Rostov
Росто́в-на-Дону́ Rostov-on-Don
Роша́ль Roshal
Рубёжное Rubezhnoye
Руго́зеро Rugozero

Рудни́чный Rudnichny
Ру́дный Rudny
Рудо́льфа о́стров Rudolf Island
Руза́евка Ruzayevka
Руса́нова зали́в Rusanov Bay
Ру́сский о́стров Russky Island
Руста́ви Rustavi
Ру́хловол See Skovorodino
Рыба́чий полуо́стров Rybachy Peninsula
Рыба́чье See Issyk-Kul[2]
Ры́бинск Rybinsk
Ры́бница Rybnitsa
Ры́ково See Yenakiyevo
Рыльск Rylsk
Ряжск Ryazhsk
Ряза́нь Ryazan

Са́арема Saaremaa
Сабираба́д Sabirabad
Са́блино See Ulyanovka
Са́ки Saki
Сакма́ра Sakmara
Салава́т Salavat
Салда́ See Nizhnyaya Salda
Са́лдус Saldus
Салеха́рд Salekhard
Са́лми Salmi
Сальск Salsk
Сама́ра Samara
Самарка́нд Samarkand
Самоде́д Samoded
Самотло́р Samotlor
Санкт-Петербу́рг St. Petersburg
Са́нникова Земля́ See Sannikov Strait
Са́нникова проли́в Sannikov Strait
Сапо́жникова ледни́к Sapozhnikov Glacier
Сапожо́к Sapozhok
Сара́й-Кома́р See Pyandzh
Саракта́ш Saraktash
Саранпа́уль Saranpaul
Сара́нск Saransk
Сара́пул Sarapul
Сара́тов Saratov
Сардараба́д See Oktemberyan
Саре́пта See Krasnoarmeysk[2]
Сарыяга́ч Saryagach
Сарысу́ Sarysu
Са́рычева вулка́н Sarychev, Mt.

Сасы́к Sasyk
Сасыкко́ль Sasykkol
Са́тка Satka
Са́улкрасты Saulkrasti
Сахали́н Sakhalin
Сване́тия Svanetia
Свердло́вск *See* Yekaterinburg
Светлово́дск Svetlovodsk
Светлого́рск Svetlogorsk
Светлогра́д Svetlograd
Светого́рск Svetogorsk
Сви́блово Sviblovo
Свирь Svir
Свобо́да *See* Liski
Свобо́дный Svobodny
Свято́й Нос Svyatoy Nos
Се́беж Sebezh
Сева́н Sevan
Севасто́поль Sevastopol
Северги́на вулка́н Severgin, Mt.
Се́верная Двина́ *See* Dvina
Се́верная Земля́ North Land
Се́верный Severny
Се́верный Ледови́тый океа́н Arctic Ocean
Северодви́нск Severodvinsk
Северодоне́цк Severodonetsk
Северо-Кури́льск Severo-Kurilsk
Северомо́рск Severomorsk
Североура́льск Severouralsk
Се́верский Доне́ц *See* Donets
Севск Sevsk
Сеге́жа Segezha
Сего́зеро *See* Segezha
Седо́во Sedovo
Селенга́ Selenga
Селиге́р Seliger
Семёнова ледни́к Semyonov Glacier
Семёнова пик *See* Semyonov Glacier
Семёновка Semyonovka
Семипала́тинск Semipalatinsk
Семире́чье *See* Dzhetysu
Семь Коло́дезей *See* Lenino
Сена́ки Senaki
Сенно́ Senno
Серафимо́вич Serafimovich
Серге́я Ки́рова острова́ Sergey Kirov Islands
Се́ргиев *See* Sergiyev Posad
Се́ргиев Поса́д Sergiyev Posad
Серго́ *See* Stakhanov
Сердо́бск Serdobsk

Сере́бряный бор Serebryany Bor
Середа́ *See* Furmanov
Серново́дск Sernovodsk
Серо́в Serov
Се́рпухов Serpukhov
Сестра́ Sestra
Сестроре́цк Sestroretsk
Се́ченово Sechenovo
Сиба́й Sibay
Сиби́рское мо́ре *See* Laptev Sea
Сиби́рь Siberia
Сибиряко́ва о́стров Sibiryakov Island
Сива́ш Sivash
Сивома́скинский Sivomaskinsky
Сим Sim
Симби́рск Simbirsk
Си́моново Simonovo
Симферо́поль Simferopol
Сине́льниково Sinelnikovo
Си́нтур Sintur
Сить Sit
Скадо́вск Skadovsk
Скви́ра Skvira
Ско́белев *See* Fergana
Сковородино́ Skovorodino
Скопи́н Skopin
Скоро́дное Skorodnoye
Сла́вгород Slavgorod
Славск Slavsk
Славя́нск Slavyansk
Сла́нцы Slantsy
Слобода́ Sloboda
Слободско́й Slobodskoy
Сло́ним Slonim
Слуцк Slutsk
Случь Sluch
Слюдя́нка Slyudyanka
Смоле́нск Smolensk
Снов Snov
Сновск *See* Shchors
Сня́тын Snyatyn
Советаба́д (Узбекиста́н) Sovetabad
Советаба́д (Таджикиста́н) *See* Gafurov
Сове́тск (близ Калинингра́да) Sovetsk[1]
Сове́тск (близ Ки́рова) Sovetsk[2]
Сове́тская Га́вань Sovetskaya Gavan
Сове́тский Сою́з *See* Russia
Сове́тское *See* Zelenokumsk
Со́кол Sokol

Cyrillic-to-Roman Index

Сокóльники Sokolniki
Солигáлич Soligalich
Солигóрск Soligorsk
Соликáмск Solikamsk
Солнечногóрск Solnechnogorsk
Солнечногóрский *See* Solnechnogorsk
Сóлнечное Solnechnoye
Соловéцкие островá Solovetsky Islands
Солóменное Solomennoye
Сольвычегóдск Solvychegodsk
Соль-Илéцк Sol-Iletsk
Сорóка *See* Belomorsk
Сорóки Soroki
Сорóкино *See* Krasnodon
Сóртавала Sortavala
Соснá Sosna
Сосновобóрск Sosnovoborsk
Соснóвый Бор Sosnovy Bor
Сосногóрск Sosnogorsk
Сóфрино Sofrino
Сóчи Sochi
Союз Совéтских Социалистических Респýблик *See* Russia
Спас-Дéменск Spas-Demensk
Спас-Клéпики Spas-Klepiki
Спасск (близ Казани) *See* Kuybyshev[2]
Спасск (близ Новокузнецка) Spassk
Спасск (близ Пензы) *See* Bednodemyanovsk
Спасск-Дáльний Spassk-Dalny
Спасск-Рязáнский Spass-Ryazansky
Спасск-Татáрский *See* Kuybyshev[2]
Срéднее Sredneye
Среднеколы́мск Srednekolymsk
Среднеурáльск Sredneuralsk
Срéтенск Sretensk
СССР *See* Russia
Стáврополь (на Кавказе) Stavropol
Стáврополь (на Волге) *See* Tolyattigrad
Сталинабáд *See* Dushanbe
Стáлина пик *See* Communism Peak
Сталингрáд *See* Volgograd
Стáлино *See* Donetsk[1]
Сталиногóрск *See* Novomoskovsk
Стáлинск *See* Novokuznetsk
Станислáв *See* Ivano-Frankovsk

Становóй хребéт Stanovoy Range
Стáнция Регáр *See* Tursunzade
Стáрая Рýсса Staraya Russa
Стáрица Staritsa
Старобéльск Starobelsk
Стародýб Starodub
Старокáдомского óстров Starokadomsky Island
Старосубхангýлово Starosubkhangulovo
Староýткинск *See* Novoutkinsk
Стáрый Крым Stary Krym
Стáрый Оскóл Stary Oskol
Стахáнов Stakhanov
Стекóльный Stekolny
Степанавáн Stepanavan
Степанакéрт *See* Khankendy
Степáн Рáзин Stepan Razin
Степанцминда *See* Kazbegi
Степнóй *See* Elista
Стерлитамáк Sterlitamak
Столбы́ Stolby
Столéтия мыс Stoletiya Cape
Строи́тель Stroitel
Стрый Stry
Стýчка Stuchka
Сувóрово Suvorovo
Судáк Sudak
Сýздаль Suzdal
Сули́мов *See* Cherkessk
Сумгаи́т Sumgait
Сýмы Sumy
Суоя́рви Suoyarvi
Суперфосфáтный Superfosfatny
Сýраж Surazh
Сурахáны Surakhany
Сýрож *See* Sudak
Сурск Sursk
Сурхандарья́ Surkhandarya
Сурхóб Surkhob
Сусáнино Susanino
Сууксý Suuksu
Суфикишлáк *See* Akhunbabayev
Сухóй Лог Sukhoy Log
Сухýми Sukhumi
Сучáн *See* Partizansk
Счáстье Schastye
Сы́зрань Syzran
Сыктывкáр Syktyvkar
Сынжерéя *See* Lazovsk
Сырдарья́ Syrdarya
Сысéрть Sysert

Тавда́ Tavda
Таволжа́н Tavolzhan
Таври́да See Crimea
Таганро́г Taganrog
Таги́л See Nizhny Tagil
Таджикиста́н Tajikistan
Таёжный Tayozhny
Тайга́ Tayga
Таймы́р Taymyr
Тайше́т Tayshet
Талды́-Курга́н Taldy-Kurgan
Та́ллин Tallinn
Тально́е Talnoye
Тама́нь Taman
Тамбо́в Tambov
Та́нну-Тува́ See Tuva
Тарбагата́й Tarbagatay
Тарно́поль See Ternopol
Та́рту Tartu
Тару́тино Tarutino
Тарханку́тский полуо́стров Tarkhankut, Cape
Тарха́ны See Lermontovo
Татарбуна́ры Tatarbunary
Тата́рск Tatarsk
Тата́рский проли́в Tatar Strait
Тата́рское мо́ре See Laptev Sea
Татарста́н Tatarstan
Таураге́ Taurage
Тахта́-База́р Takhta-Bazar
Та́шино See Pervomaysk[1]
Ташке́нт Tashkent
Ташкепри́ Tashkepri
Таштаго́л Tashtagol
Ташты́п Tashtyp
Тба Tba
Тбили́си Tbilisi
Тверь Tver
Тегульде́т Teguldet
Теле́цкое о́зеро Teletsky, Lake
Те́льманово Telmanovo
Те́льманск Telmansk
Те́льпосиз Telposiz
Темирта́у (Казахста́н) Temirtau[1]
Темирта́у (Россия) Temirtau[2]
Темир-Хан-Шура́ See Buynaksk
Тёмников Temnikov
Темрю́к Temryuk
Тенги́з Tengiz
Теофи́поль Teofipol
Тёплая Гора́ Tyoplaya Gora
Тёплый Стан (район Москвы́) Tyoply Stan
Тёплый Стан (близ Арза́маса) See Sechenovo
Теребо́вля Terebovlya
Те́рек Terek
Терно́поль Ternopol
Терпе́ния зали́в Terpeniya Bay
Ти́кси Tiksi
Тильзи́т See Sovetsk
Тира́споль Tiraspol
Тифли́с See Tbilisi
Ти́хая бу́хта Tikhaya Bay
Ти́хвин Tikhvin
Тихоре́цк Tikhoretsk
Тмутарака́нь Tmutarakan
Тобо́льск Tobolsk
Токтогу́л Toktogul
То́лля зали́в Toll Bay
Толмачёво Tolmachyovo
Толья́тти See Tolyattigrad
Тольяттигра́д Tolyattigrad
Томари́ Tomari
Томск Tomsk
То́пки Topki
Торго́вая See Salsk
Торе́з Torez
Торжо́к Torzhok
Торо́пец Toropets
Трембо́вля See Terebovlya
Троеку́рово Troyekurovo
Тро́ице-Лы́ково Troitse-Lykovo
Тро́ицк Troitsk
Тропарёво Troparyovo
Троцк (близ Сама́ры) See Chapayevsk
Троцк (близ Санкт-Петербу́рга) See Gatchina
Трудово́й See Kuybyshevsky
Туапсе́ Tuapse
Туби́нский Tubinsky
Тува́ Tuva
Тугулы́м Tugulym
Туймазы́ Tuymazy
Ту́кумс Tukums
Ту́ла Tula
Туманя́н Tumanyan
Тунгу́ска Tunguska
Тура́ (го́род) Tura
Тура́ (река́) See Turinsk
Тури́нск Turinsk
Туркеста́н (район) Turkestan[1]

Туркеста́н (город) Turkestan[2]
Туркмениста́н Turkmenistan
Ту́ров Turov
Турсунзаде́ Tursunzade
Турткýль Turtkul
Турьи́нские Рудники́ *See* Krasnoturinsk
Тута́ев Tutayev
Ту́шино Tushino
Ты́нда Tynda
Ты́ндинский *See* Tynda
Тзэзбаза́р Tezebazar
Тюме́нь Tyumen
Тянь-Шань Tien Shan
Тя́тя Tyatya, Mt.

Углего́рск Uglegorsk
Углека́менск Uglekamensk
Углеура́льск Ugleuralsk
У́глич Uglich
У́гольный *See* Beringovsky
Уда́чный Udachny
Удму́ртия Udmurtia
Уедине́ния о́стров Uyedineniya Island
У́жгород Uzhgorod
Узбекиста́н Uzbekistan
Узлова́я Uzlovaya
Украи́на Ukraine
Ула́ла *See* Gorno-Altaysk
Ула́н-Удэ́ Ulan-Ude
Улька́н Ulkan
Улья́новка Ulyanovka
Улья́ново Ulyanovo
Улья́новск Ulyanovsk
Унге́ны Ungeny
Ура́л (река) Ural
Ура́л (горы) Urals
Уралмедьстро́й *See* Krasnouralsk
Ура́льск Uralsk
Уре́чье Urechye
Урма́н Urman
Уру́п Urup
У́смань Usman
Усо́лье Usolye
Усо́лье-Сиби́рское Usolye-Sibirskoye
Уссу́ри Ussuri
Уссури́йск Ussuriysk
Усти́нов *See* Izhevsk
Усть-Абака́нское *See* Abakan
У́стье Ustye

Усть-Каменого́рск Ust-Kamenogorsk
Усть-Ката́в Ust-Katav
Усть-Кут Ust-Kut
Усть-Медве́дицкая *See* Serafimovich
Усть-Орды́нский Ust-Ordynsky
Усть-Сысо́льск *See* Syktyvkar
Усть-У́рт *See* Ustyurt
У́стюг *See* Veliky Ustyug
У́стюжна Ustyuzhna
Устю́рт Ustyurt
Уфа́ Ufa
Ухта́ (близ Сосногорска) Ukhta
Ухта́ (близ Кеми) *See* Kalevala
Учалы́ Uchaly
Ушако́ва о́стров Ushakov Island
Уша́чи Ushachi
Ушко́во Ushkovo
Уштобе́ Ushtobe

Фабри́чный Fabrichny
Фадде́евский Faddeyevsky
Фа́кел Fakel
Федче́нко ледни́к Fedchenko Glacier
Феодо́сия Feodosiya
Фергана́ Fergana
Фе́рсмана гора́ Fersman, Mt.
Фершампенуа́з Fershampenuaz
Физули́ Fizuli
Фили́ Fili
Флоре́шты Floreshty
Фо́кино Fokino
Форт-Алекса́ндровский *See* Fort Shevchenko
Форт-Шевче́нко Fort Shevchenko
Фосфори́тный Fosforitny
Фра́нца-Ио́сифа Земля́ Franz Josef Land
Фру́нзе *See* Bishkek
Фря́зино Fryazino
Фу́рманов Furmanov

Хаба́ровск Khabarovsk
Хайпуды́рская губа́ Khaypudyrskaya Inlet
Хака́сия Khakassia
Хали́лово Khalilovo
Халту́рин Khalturin
Хамза́ Khamza
Ханкенды́ Khankendy
Ханла́р Khanlar

Хан-Те́нгри Khan-Tengri
Ханты́-Манси́йск Khanty-Mansiysk
Харито́на Ла́птева бе́рег Khariton Laptev Coast
Ха́рьков Kharkov
Хвалы́нск Khvalynsk
Хем-Белды́р See Kyzyl
Херсо́н Kherson
Хибиного́рск See Kirovsk
Хива́ Khiva
Хмельни́цкий Khmelnitsky
Хо́врино Khovrino
Ходже́нт (на реке Сырдарья) Khodzhent
Ходже́нт (к юго-востоку от Ходжента) See Gafurov
Хо́йники Khoyniki
Холм Kholm
Хо́ни Khoni
Хоре́зм (1) Khorezm, (2) Khwarism
Хоро́г Khorog
Хужи́р See Ust-Ordynsky

Царёвококша́йск See Yoshkar Ola
Цари́цын See Volgograd
Цари́цыно Tsaritsyno
Ца́рское Село́ See Pushkin
Целиногра́д See Akmola
Цеме́нтный Tsementny
Цесаре́вич See Myortvy Kultuk
Цимля́нск Tsimlyansk
Цукули́дзе See Khoni
Цурухайту́й See Priargunsk
Цхака́я See Senaki
Цхениска́ли Tskhenis Tskali
Цюру́пинск Tsyurupinsk

Чады́р-Лу́нга Chadyr Lunga
Чайко́вский Chaykovsky
Ча́мзинка Chamzinka
Чапа́ев Chapayev
Чапа́евка Chapayevka
Чапа́евск Chapayevsk
Чаплы́гин Chaplygin
Чарджо́у Chardzhou
Чарджу́й See Chardzhou
Чаренцава́н Charentsavan
Чатырда́г Chatyr Dag
Ча́шники Chashniki
Чебарку́ль Chebarkul

Чебокса́ры Cheboksary
Чека́лин Chekalin
Чека́новского кряж Chekanovsky Ridge
Челеке́н Cheleken
Челка́р Chelkar
Челю́скин мыс Chelyuskin, Cape
Челя́бинск Chelyabinsk
Чемба́р See Belinsky
Че́рвень Cherven
Черво́нная Русь Red Russia
Червоноарме́йск Chervonoarmeysk
Червоногра́д Chervonograd
Червонопартиза́нск Chervonopartizansk
Че́рдынь Cherdyn
Черёмушки Cheryomushki
Черепове́ц Cherepovets
Черка́ссы Cherkassy
Черке́сск Cherkessk
Черне́нко See Sharypovo
Черни́гов Chernigov
Черно́быль Chernobyl
Черновцы́ Chernovtsy
Черного́рск Chernogorsk
Чёрное мо́ре Black Sea
Черноисто́чинск Chernoistochinsk
Черномо́рское Chernomorskoye
Чернышёва кряж Chernyshyov Ridge
Чернь Chern
Черня́ево See Yangiyer
Черняхо́вск Chernyakhovsk
Чёрский Chersky
Чёрского хребе́т Chersky Range
Чесма́ Chesma
Чесноко́вка See Novoaltaysk
Че́хов Chekhov
Чече́ния Chechenia
Чёшская губа́ Chyoshskaya Bay
Чи́бью See Ukhta
Чимба́й Chimbay
Чимишли́я Chimishliya
Чимке́нт Chimkent
Чирчи́к Chirchik
Чи́стополь Chistopol
Чистяко́во See Torez
Чита́ Chita
Чихачёва хребе́т Chikhachyov Range
Чишмы́ Chishmy
Чка́лов See Orenburg
Чу Chu

Чува́шия Chuvashia
Чудско́е о́зеро Chudskoye, Lake
Чуко́тский полуо́стров Chukot Peninsula
Чуко́тское мо́ре Chukchi Sea
Чулы́м Chulym
Чурубай-Нура́ *See* Abay
Чусова́я Chusovaya
Чусово́й Chusovoy
Чу́хлома Chukhloma
Чу́я Chuya

Шабба́з *See* Biruni
Шабро́вский Shabrovsk
Ша́дринск Shadrinsk
Шайта́нка *See* Pervouralsk
Шанта́рские острова́ Shantar Islands
Шарлы́к Sharlyk
Шары́пово Sharypovo
Шати́лов лес Shatilov Forest
Шатлы́к Shatlyk
Шатурто́рф Shaturtorf
Шауми́ни Shaumyani
Шауми́новск Shaumyanovsk
Шахриса́бз Shakhrisabz
Шахтёрск (Россия) Shakhtyorsk[1]
Шахтёрск (Украина) Shakhtyorsk[2]
Ша́хтинск Shakhtinsk
Ша́хты (близ Ростова-на-Дону) Shakhty
Ша́хты (близ Улан-Удэ) *See* Gusinoozersk
Шацк Shatsk
Шевче́нко Shevchenko
Шёлехов Shelekhov
Шемаха́ Shemakha
Шеморда́н Shemordan
Шёнкурск Shenkursk
Шерка́лы Sherkaly
Шёрловая Гора́ Sherlovaya Gora
Шикота́н Shikotan
Ши́лка Shilka
Шлиссельбу́рг *See* Petrokrepost
Шми́дта о́стров Shmidt Island
Шми́дта полуо́стров Shmidt Peninsula
Шока́льского о́стров Shokalsky Island
Шорсу́ Shorsu
Шталлупёнен *See* Nesterov[1]
Шулаве́ри *See* Shaumyani

Шурааба́д Shuraabad
Шура́б Shurab
Шу́я (близ Иванова) Shuya[1]
Шу́я (близ Петрозаводска) Shuya[2]
Шяуля́й Šiauliai

Щегло́вск *See* Kemerovo
Щербако́в *See* Rybinsk
Щерби́новка *See* Dzerzhinsk[3]
Щорс Shchors
Щорск Shchorsk
Щу́чье О́зеро Shchuchye Ozero

Экибасту́з Ekibastuz
Электрово́з *See* Stupino
Электрого́рск Elektrogorsk
Электропереда́ча *See* Elektrogorsk
Электроста́ль Elektrostal
Электроу́гли Elektrougli
Эли́ста Elista
Эльбру́с Elbrus
Эльто́н Elton, Lake
Эма Ema
Эмба Emba
Э́нгельс *See* Pokrovsk
Энерге́тик Energetik
Эрива́нь *See* Yerevan
Эрмана хребе́т Erman Range
Эсто́ния Estonia
Эчмиадзи́н Echmiadzin

Юг Yug
Ю́жно-Кури́льск Yuzhno-Kurilsk
Ю́жно-Сахали́нск Yuzhno-Sakhalinsk
Южноура́льск Yuzhno-Uralsk
Ю́зовка *See* Donetsk[1]
Юмагу́зино Yumaguzino
Ю́рмала Jurmala
Ю́рьев *See* Tartu
Ю́рьевец Yuryevets
Ю́рьев-По́льский Yuryev-Polsky
Юрюза́нь Yuryuzan

Я́блоновый хребе́т Yablonovy Mountains
Я́дрин Yadrin
Яковлевское *See* Privolzhsk
Яку́нчиков *See* Krasny Mayak

Яку́тия *See* Yakut-Sakha
Яку́т-Са́ха Yakut-Sakha
Яку́тск Yakutsk
Я́лта Yalta
Ялу́торовск Yalutorovsk
Яма́л Yamal
Яманта́у Yamantau
Я́мбург *See* Kingisepp
Я́мполь Yampol
Яна́ул Yanaul
Я́нги-Ары́к Yangi-Aryk
Янгибаза́р (Кыргызстан) Yangibazar
Янгибаза́р (Таджикистан) *See* Ordzhonikidzeabad
Янгие́р Yangiyer
Янта́рный Yantarny
Яросла́вль Yaroslavl
Яр-Сале́ Yar Sale
Ясинова́тая Yasinovataya
Я́сная Поля́на Yasnaya Polyana
Я́хрома Yakhroma